THE KENNEDYS IN THE WORLD

THE
KENNEDYS
IN THE WORLD

How Jack, Bobby, and Ted
Remade America's Empire

LAWRENCE J. HAAS

Potomac Books
An imprint of the University of Nebraska Press

© 2021 by Lawrence J. Haas

All rights reserved. Potomac Books is an imprint of the
University of Nebraska Press.
Manufactured in the United States of America.

Library of Congress Cataloging-in-Publication Data
Names: Haas, Lawrence J., author.
Title: The Kennedys in the world: how Jack, Bobby,
and Ted remade America's empire / Lawrence J. Haas.
Description: Lincoln: Potomac Books, an imprint of the
University of Nebraska Press, 2021. | Includes bibliographical
references and index.
Identifiers: LCCN 2020025022
ISBN 9781640123847 (hardback)
ISBN 9781640124455 (epub)
ISBN 9781640124462 (mobi)
ISBN 9781640124479 (pdf)
Subjects: LCSH: Kennedy, John F. (John Fitzgerald), 1917–1963. |
Kennedy, Robert F., 1925–1968. | Kennedy, Edward M. (Edward
Moore), 1932–2009. | Kennedy family. | United States—Politics
and government—1945–1989. | United States—Politics and
government—1989–
Classification: LCC E842 .H34 2021 | DDC 973.922092/2—dc23
LC record available at https://lccn.loc.gov/2020025022

Set in Garamond Premier by Mikala R. Kolander.

To Marjie, my heartbeat
To Samantha, my hero

CONTENTS

Part 3

ILLUSTRATIONS

ACKNOWLEDGMENTS

"No man is an island," wrote the poet John Donne, and the sentiment has special meaning for the man who wrote *The Kennedys in the World*. I could not have done it without the assistance and support of a wide range of family, friends, and colleagues over the course of more than three years.

At the American Foreign Policy Council, where I hold the title of senior fellow, President Herman Pirchner, Senior Vice President Ilan Berman, and Vice President Richard Harrison provided me with the time of many of their research interns, who tracked down tens of thousands of pages of primary and secondary material for me: Christina Armes, Christy Beauchemin, Gabriella Bettino, Liam Bobyak, Brian Carpowich, Ulas Cini, Cannon Counsellor, Hayden Gilmore, Alexandria Hickey, Evelyn Johns, Nicholas Labecki, Jacob Levitan, Garrett Lynch, Lucas Lyons, Matt Maldonado, Tilly Moross, Robin Naylor, Piper Quinn, Tyler Russell, Gabrielle Timm, and Hannah Wallace. I thank them for their assistance, and I thank Annie Swingen, AFPC's director of external relations, and my other AFPC colleagues for their support.

The Alexander Hamilton Society, where I hold no title whatsoever, nevertheless provided generous support as well. I thank Executive Director Gabriel Scheinmann and Marketing and Development Associate Sydney Scribner for suggesting that the bright and energetic student members of AHS's chapters on university campuses across the country might help with my research, and I thank the students who did: Joshua Chang, Layne Smith, Kathryn Selinger, and Cameron Vega.

My AFPC and AHS researchers received the assistance of knowledgeable, patient, and helpful librarians at the John F. Kennedy Presidential Library and Museum, which holds the papers of Jack, Bobby, and Ted Kennedy. It has an enormous stock of speeches, oral history interviews, letters, and other material available online, and it makes more material available on an ongoing basis. The librarians pointed me in the right direction on numerous occasions, and they digitized material for me that is not yet available online.

My photography researcher, Caroline Couig, worked tirelessly to find the photos that would bring this book further to life. She was a joyful, collaborative, and dedicated colleague and a true partner.

At the Edward M. Kennedy Institute for the United States Senate, Alumni Relations Coordinator Tara Rendon proved a great source of ideas and assistance. Most importantly, she connected me with a host of ex-staffers to Ted Kennedy and with others in the Kennedy orbit. I thank those ex-staffers who generously allowed me to interview them and provided fresh insights about their former boss.

Betty Koed, the U.S. Senate historian, and her staff opened their files on the Kennedy brothers, all of whom served in the Senate, and they provided open access to the copy machine right next to my workspace.

At the University of Virginia's Miller Center, where she is director of presidential studies, Barbara Perry enhanced my research by providing her insights and offering her thoughts about others to contact. In addition, her 2013 biography, *Rose Kennedy: The Life and Times of a Political Matriarch*, was an important source of information for me.

Through our collaboration on my book proposal, my agent, Peter Bernstein, greatly improved the book. He has a keen appreciation of history and a refined sense of narrative, and he forces me to think harder about the focus of my efforts and how best to tell a story.

I thank Richard Cohen, Mark Fife, Marjorie Segel Haas, Matt Maldonado, Tilly Moross, Herman Pirchner, Kathryn Selinger, and Elizabeth Wood for reading the manuscript, providing helpful comments, and catching errors. I also thank Peter Bernstein who, in reading multiple drafts of my book proposal, read sample chapters and provided useful insights. I take sole responsibility for any errors that remain.

I was delighted to publish a second book with Potomac Books, which transformed my manuscript for *The Kennedys in the World* into published form with the same care and professionalism that it brought to *Harry and Arthur: Truman, Vandenberg, and the Partnership That Created the Free World*, my book of 2016.

No one supports my work more than my beautiful wife, Marjie, and our wonderful daughter, Samantha, as I isolate myself in my office not just in the early hours of my workdays but large chunks of our weekends. They are endlessly patient and unceasingly supportive, which explains why I continue to dedicate my books to them. They make my books, and everything else in my life, all the more worthwhile.

PROLOGUE

September 1939

"You can't trust the German Navy!" the bruised, burned, and distressed American survivors of the *Athenia*, the British passenger liner that the Nazis had sunk with a torpedo, screamed at Jack Kennedy.[1]

At just twenty-two on this September evening of 1939, Jack was in a tough spot. Joe Kennedy, the U.S. ambassador in London, had sent his son—who was on leave from Harvard while working for his father—to Glasgow, Scotland, to talk to the nearly three hundred stranded American survivors. After setting off for a leisurely journey across the Atlantic to Montreal, they spent "a rainy, cold night in lifeboats," with some of them frantically bailing water out of their leaking boats with their shoes. It was more than two days after their frightening ordeal until someone from America's embassy came to see them and, as one nineteen-year-old survivor put it, the person who did "was this kid who looked younger than I was."[2]

Now, "this kid" was telling a gathering of nearly two hundred of them that they would sail to the United States, but President Roosevelt would not provide a military convoy to protect them. "You will be safe in a ship flying the American flag," Jack explained. "Under international law, a neutral ship is safe." The harried survivors weren't buying it, however. "A convoy is imperative," insisted Thomas McCubbin, a gray-haired man from Montclair, New Jersey. "Ninety destroyers have just been commissioned by the United States Navy and surely they can spare us a few. Six billion dollars of United States Navy, and they cannot do this for us!" Another survivor noted that, two years earlier, "the whole Pacific Fleet was sent" to find Amelia Earhart. "We definitely refuse to go until we have a convoy," added a college student. "You have seen what they will do to us."[3]

Upon hearing back from Jack, Joe Kennedy told Secretary of State Cordell Hull in a diplomatic dispatch that the survivors were "in a terrible state of nerves" and suggested that Washington send a convoy or prepare to face "publicity and criticism of the government [that] would be unbelievable."[4] As it turned out, the ambassador later arranged for them to return home safely on a U.S. merchant ship.

Why, however, did Joe send Jack to Glasgow in the first place?

. . .

To be sure, the young Kennedy acquitted himself quite well.

He visited the survivors in hotels and hospitals and—until he relayed the news to the large group that FDR wouldn't send a convoy—he charmed them with his warm smile and soft touch. Pictured at one meeting, he sat behind a table with an earnest look on his face. He was the "schoolboy diplomat," as the London newspapers labeled him, an "ambassador of mercy" who "displayed a wisdom and sympathy of a man twice his age." Returning to the embassy, he kept working for the survivors and clashed with bureaucrats who didn't seem to share his sense of urgency.[5]

Nevertheless, Jack wasn't the logical person for the role. He held no government position, so he could only listen to the survivors and promise to relay their views to his father. To them, his arrival was as much insulting as reassuring.

Perhaps, as Joe Kennedy considered the situation and weighed the possibilities, he wasn't all that interested in finding the best person to greet the survivors. Perhaps, instead, he saw an opportunity to continue grooming Jack, as he would Bobby and Ted, for prominent roles on the world stage.

That, after all, was a task to which Joe and Rose Kennedy had devoted themselves ever since the boys were young.

. . .

We know a lot about Jack, Bobby, and Ted Kennedy. From books, movies, and, if we're old enough, memories, we know about their ambitions and achievements, struggles and setbacks, scandals and peccadillos. We see their faces, hear their voices, recall their landmark moments. They spent most of their lives on the public stage, and they occupy a sizable place in our national consciousness.

Nevertheless, we continue to learn more about the brothers, just as we learn more about other iconic figures of our past, no matter how many historians have made them the subject of inquiry. The latest reflections of friends and colleagues and the opening of more records offer the raw material for new insights. The passage of time inspires fresh perspectives about the events of yesteryear.

The Kennedys in the World tells an untold story about Jack, Bobby, and Ted, about a fascinating and, over time, hugely consequential aspect of their lives: from an early age, the brothers developed a deep understanding of the different peoples, cultures, and ideologies around the world; a keen appreciation for the challenges they presented for the United States; and a strong desire to reshape America's response to them. Once the brothers assumed power, each put a distinct mark on the American empire.

In their more than six decades on the public stage, from Jack's election to the House in 1946 to Ted's death from brain cancer in 2009, America was what it remains today—the world's greatest power, with roles and responsibilities that stretch across the planet. So, as the brothers remade America's empire, they invariably changed the world.

Because they proved so influential in shaping the U.S. global role, their story provides a telling window into the evolution of America's post-war empire.

. . .

What drove the boys to focus on the world at large and, once they assumed power, to shape America's role in it?

From their childhoods in the first half of the twentieth century, Jack, Bobby, and Ted Kennedy were prodded by the ruthless, demanding, win-at-all-costs Joe and his cold, distant, schoolmarm-ish wife, Rose, to learn about the world, urged to care about it, and told they could shape America's role in it. (So, too, was Joe Jr., the oldest son who would die during World War II at just twenty-nine, before he could fulfill the sky-high expectations for him and leave his own mark on the world.)

Joe and Rose led discussions with the boys about global events over meals, and Joe invited prominent figures to dine with them and enrich the conversations. He wrote to the boys about global events when he or they were away, sent them to travel overseas when they were old enough, arranged meetings for them with the world's leading figures, and secured jobs for them as foreign correspondents so that they could position themselves as global thinkers and relay their thoughts to would-be constituents back home.

Joe focused on his sons because he assumed that, in the male-dominated world of the early twentieth century, they were the ones who would apply the insights they gleaned over dinner to shape the world. "My work is my boys," he told a friend on the golf course, and he behaved that way.[6] To be sure, the family chatter about events abroad influenced the Kennedy girls as well and, as norms changed and opportunities arose, they, too, made their mark on the world. Eunice Kennedy Shriver founded the Special Olympics and advocated for children with special needs at home and abroad, and Jean Kennedy Smith served as America's ambassador to Ireland in the 1990s and worked closely with Ted to help bring peace to Northern Ireland. Nevertheless, it was Jack, Bobby, and Ted who bore the burden of expectation most heavily, who attained the highest offices, and who wielded the greatest power.

As they grew from boys to men, all three brothers traveled widely, sometimes with one another but more often with mentors, friends, or colleagues. They met with kings and czars, prime ministers and diplomats; they visited war zones and discussed conflicts with military officials; they walked streets and observed everyday life; and they developed insights into peoples, lands, and cultures that they later put to good use. They became gifted writers, with a sharp turn of phase and an eye for telling detail. Their notes, foreign dispatches, and other writings were rich in insight about the history, culture, and problems of other countries and, in turn, about America's challenges in working with them.

The relationships among the brothers evolved, and that, too, influenced their work in remaking America's global role.

. . .

We remember the Kennedys as a tightly knit clan, but for the brothers the story is far more complicated.

They were raised in privilege, driven to win, and challenged to measure up to one another, all of which nurtured several core Kennedy-esque traits in each of them. They were ultra competitive in whatever they contested, tireless in whatever they pursued, demanding on those who served them, courageous to the point of recklessness, and presumptuous to the point of audacity. Through early adulthood, they battled deep-seated insecurities about winning the respect of their overbearing father, who had set high standards for them, chastised them when they fell short, and pitted one against the other.

They were hardly carbon copies of one another, however. Their places in a loud, rambunctious clan of nine kids—Jack, the second; Bobby, the seventh; and Ted, the last—and the distinct expectations placed upon each of them shaped their personalities. So, too, did their long periods alone as their parents shipped them off to different boarding schools. In their youth they didn't know each other all that well, and, when they were together for summers and holidays, their personalities didn't always mesh.

Jack, who was happy and outgoing, found Bobby, who was awkward, moody, and eight years his junior, tough to be around and sometimes avoided him. By contrast, Jack felt an immediate bond with Ted, who was fourteen years his junior, and assumed the role of mentor to him. Ted worshipped Jack but somewhat at a distance, for he didn't know him well in his youth because the two were often apart. Bobby and Ted were often apart as well, but they spent more time with one another as youngsters than either of them spent with Jack, and, at important moments, Bobby looked out for his younger brother.

As the boys became men, all three came to know, like, and respect one another far more. They also more fully embraced the dictum of their father—a man embittered by the anti-Irish-Catholic bigotry he had faced and wary of the wider world—to rely on one another more than anyone else. Jack and Bobby developed an unshakeable bond during seven weeks together as young men in the Middle East and Asia in 1951, a bond that proved crucial as they steered the nation through disaster at the Bay of Pigs and peril during the Cuban Missile Crisis. Bobby and Ted grew tighter after Jack's death and, as senators, schemed together as they broke with Lyndon Johnson over Vietnam and other global challenges.

Their views about America's global role evolved considerably, due both to their experiences and to the nation's evolving challenges.

. . .

Jack, a man of charm and wit, depth and insight, energy and action, was the Cold Warrior *par excellence*. He fully embraced the "Cold War consensus" of his time—that America's top global challenge must be to "contain" Soviet-led communism—and he rewrote America's foreign policy to fight the Cold War more effectively. As he overcame dire illness and acute pain to reach the pinnacle of power, he worried that his nation would lack the comparable toughness to contain the Soviets.

The most cerebral of the brothers, he was a man of uncommon intelligence. As a House member and senator, he built a national reputation as a creative thinker on foreign affairs, delivering speeches that were works of depth and poetry. As president he was forced to grow quickly, to overcome an odd mix of personality: overconfidence in mastering the job, but insecurity in acting decisively at key moments. After learning valuable lessons from such early missteps as the Bay of Pigs fiasco, he skillfully resolved the Cuban Missile Crisis, defended America's presence in Berlin, secured a limited test-ban treaty with the Soviets, and laid the groundwork for more arms control, which he had hoped to pursue. He came to doubt his early decision to "make a stand" against communism in Vietnam and sent strong signals that he would withdraw after he presumably won reelection in 1964. Shortly before his death, he was rethinking his hardline policies toward China and Cuba. Haunted by his harrowing experience in the Pacific during World War II and fearful that miscalculation in Washington or Moscow would trigger nuclear war, he struggled to avoid war with the Soviets while protecting America's interests.

Jack applied insights from his travels and his voracious reading during his many long illnesses to push America's foreign policy in a starkly new direction. He believed the Cold War would be won or lost not in Europe but in the developing world, where restive populations were deciding between democracy and loyalty to the United States or communism and loyalty to the Soviet Union. Rather than support right-wing dictators and Europe's colonial governments, he wanted to nourish U.S. ties to grassroots populations, for he thought that was a better way to compete with the Soviets and Chinese over the long term. As a senator, he ruffled feathers abroad by urging Europe to free its colonies. As president he created the Alliance for Progress for Latin America and the Peace Corps for the world, showered more foreign aid on new nations in Africa, and met with their leaders. Jack's desire to improve America's global image also drove his efforts to address its racial problems at home, which were making nations of color hesitant to develop strong ties to the United States.

Throughout Jack's life, Bobby and Ted were Cold Warriors as well. In the 1950s Bobby worked on foreign policy for Senator Joe McCarthy, a red-baiting Wisconsin Republican and close family friend. He traveled across far-flung Soviet republics with Supreme Court Justice William Douglas, another family friend, and returned to disparage Moscow in speeches, interviews, and writings over its human rights abuses and economic backwardness. As Jack's closest confidante, he helped steady JFK's foreign policy after the Bay of Pigs, spearheaded the administration's subsequent efforts to topple Cuba's Fidel Castro, and worked closely with Jack to resolve the Cuban Missile Crisis. To improve America's global image, he worked with Jack on civil rights and toured fourteen countries in Europe and Asia in early 1962 as a "good will" ambassador.

Also in the '50s, Ted toured Europe with a friend, traveled across Africa with one of his Harvard instructors, and capped off his Africa excursion by meeting Jack for a sail on the Mediterranean and sharing his observations about the continent. He sought an arms control position in JFK's administration, but Jack rejected the idea as a bad career move for Ted, who was thinking about running for office down the road. Instead, Ted returned to Africa at Jack's suggestion and then traveled across Latin America and Europe before running successfully for the Senate in 1962 as a Cold War hawk.

. . .

After Jack died, LBJ took over, and the world changed, Bobby and Ted changed with it. They evolved from Cold War hawks into leading liberal doves and drove America's foreign policy in starkly new directions.

Bobby, a dark, often tortured figure, emerged from months of trauma after Jack's death as very much a new man. No longer constrained by Jack's views or subservient to his ambitions, he could take a fresh look at America's role in a world of new challenges and chart his own course. While Jack became a more seasoned leader over the years, Bobby became more of a revolutionary in rolled-up sleeves and a loose tie as he traveled the world and witnessed the horrid conditions in which many lived and worked.

For Bobby the political was also the personal, for he loathed LBJ and deemed him a crude, uncouth, and altogether unworthy successor to his suave, dynamic, and intellectual brother. Although Vietnam was the issue over which the two fought most fiercely, it was over Latin America where the first break between them on foreign policy occurred. Bobby resented LBJ's decision to rewrite Jack's approach to the region and opposed his decision to send thousands of troops to the Dominican Republic to quell a grassroots uprising.

Bobby changed not just because Jack was gone and he could be himself, but because the world changed. The more that Vietnam, a Cold War venture for Jack, descended into horror and stalemate, the more Bobby questioned the venture, its relationship to the Cold War, and his previous support for it. Bobby wasn't the first leader to question LBJ's policies in Vietnam. But, as the presumptive heir to Jack's presidential throne with a broad national following, he was the most important. He was no less a critic of communism, but he now viewed Vietnam as a much bigger problem for America than the Cold War. While Jack had worried about his nation's toughness to confront the Soviets, Bobby worried about its moral character as it slaughtered innocents with bombs and bullets in Vietnam.

Bobby was now a far different person from the one who had crudely questioned the courage of JFK's foreign policy advisors and pushed them relentlessly to topple Castro after the Bay of Pigs. A former Cold Warrior, he played a larger role than anyone else in destroying the Cold War consensus, leaving the world more unsettled and the country more divided over America's global role.

. . .

Ted, too, discarded his Cold War–centric outlook and broke with LBJ over Vietnam—but more slowly than Bobby, owing to their differences in personality and in how they approached politics.

Though smart, Ted was far less a deep thinker than Jack, far less likely to quote history and sprinkle poetry through his speeches. Though passionate, he was far less a man swept by passion than Bobby, the former altar boy who saw foreign policy (and most everything else) in terms of black and white, good and evil.

Ted, however, was the family's best politician. Cheery, garrulous, and ruggedly handsome, he was a glad-handing, back-slapping "happy warrior" who inherited his skills from his maternal grandfather, John "Honey Fitz" Fitzgerald, a former Boston mayor with whom he spent much time as a youngster. Unlike the impatient Jack and Bobby, Ted approached the Senate not as a waystation to higher office but as an ideal place to do fulfilling work over the long term, and he deferred to his political elders and learned the Senate's byzantine rules so he could more easily turn high-minded ideas into legislative achievements.

To an uncommon degree, Ted could tap the levers of power, build coalitions, turn dreams into reality, and achieve results on foreign policy—even when opposed by the president, who is always the nation's most powerful figure on foreign policy. He spearheaded the successful drives to impose sanctions on South Africa over apartheid, end proxy wars with the Soviets in Latin America, and make peace in Northern Ireland. In his low-key efforts that haven't received nearly the attention they deserve, he was remarkably successful in convincing Moscow and Beijing to free scores of political dissidents.[7] He was a singularly influential voice on foreign affairs for four decades after Bobby's death as America searched in vain for a consistent global role around which the nation could rally.

With Ted, our untold story about the three brothers ends on a surprising note. Of the three he was the least likely to succeed, due to the wayward ways of his youth and his propensity for self-inflicted wounds in adulthood. In the end, with his long Senate tenure, extraordinary political skills, and distinct imprint on so many of America's leading foreign policy challenges, he probably exerted a greater long-term impact on remaking America's global role than either Jack or Bobby.

. . .

Proud of one another, the brothers often quoted one another when making a point. After Jack's death, Bobby regularly used Jack's words in his own speeches, while Ted echoed both Jack and Bobby.

Notwithstanding the differences that emerged among them, they shared certain views and pursued certain goals throughout their lives. As Washington began to lead the free world after World War II, all three discarded the isolationism that their father stubbornly retained. They believed that America must play a prominent global role, and that it could serve as a beacon for others to emulate.

The brothers feared war, favored diplomacy, and sought to control the world's deadliest weapons. Jack considered his limited nuclear test-ban treaty with the Soviets his proudest achievement, and Bobby and Ted sought to build on his legacy by pursuing arms control and a comprehensive test ban. They all were deeply interested in the developing world and worked hard to shape America's role in it. Throughout Jack's life, they thought the developing world was central to America's prospects in the Cold War. After Jack's death, Bobby and Ted worked to promote the human rights and improve the living standards of hundreds of millions of people across Asia, Africa, and Latin America.

Beyond the words they used, the brothers also sounded like one another, speaking in similar cadences and issuing similar calls to action. At times one could read a Kennedy speech and not know who had delivered it.

. . .

For more than six decades after World War II, Jack, Bobby, and Ted Kennedy shaped broad issues of war and peace as well as the U.S. response to almost every major global challenge of their times: the Soviet Union and China; the Cold War and Cuba; the Dominican Republic and Chile; Nicaragua and El Salvador; Korea and Vietnam; South Africa and Northern Ireland; and Iraq (twice).

Through their experiences we see the United States fight proxy wars with the Soviets, promote human rights, secure freedom for dissidents, win the Cold War, and bring peace to Northern Ireland. We see America face stalemate in Korea, failure at the Bay of Pigs, and disaster in Vietnam and Iraq. And we see the nation struggle over China, Latin America, South Africa, and other hotspots.

The Kennedy story provides a window into our time as well. That's because America remains what it was in their time—a superpower in search of its most appropriate global role and how best to perform it. Should America protect itself and do little else? Should it also ensure global peace? Promote freedom and democracy? Confront autocrats? Assist dissidents? What should it do when its goals collide?

We have no easy answers, but the experiences of Jack, Bobby, and Ted offer lessons for today and beyond.

THE KENNEDYS IN THE WORLD

PART 1

I

"Like Carbonated Water"

"The people here keep saying their chin is up and that they can't be beaten," Ambassador Joe Kennedy wrote to his twenty-three-year-old son, Jack, from London on the late afternoon of September 10, 1940, with air raid sirens blaring outside, "but the people who have had any experience with these bombings don't like it at all."

As Hitler's *Luftwaffe* strafed London, Joe sent separate letters to Jack, Bobby, and Ted, who were back in America with the family, over the course of two days to relay his thoughts about the war. He was keenly sensitive to their different ages, so he tailored his letters to what he thought each could absorb intellectually and handle emotionally. He was most blunt with Jack, a young man of unusual depth who had already written the best-selling *Why England Slept* about Britain's reluctance to rearm in the 1930s; more explanatory with Bobby, an awkward and insecure boy of fourteen who had long craved a deeper engagement with his father; and most nurturing with Ted, who was just eight and, as the youngest of nine children, the object of much family doting.

"I am feeling very well," Joe told Jack before defending his isolationist views, which had grown increasingly controversial in America as the Nazi threat grew more menacing:

The only thing I am afraid of is that I won't be able to live long enough to tell all that I see and feel about this crisis. When I hear these mental midgets [U.S.A.] talking about my desire for appeasement and being critical of it, my blood fairly boils. What is this war going to prove? And what is it going to do to civilization? The answer to the first question is nothing: and to the second I shudder even to think about it.

To Bobby, he expressed his bitterness that the iron-willed Winston Churchill, who had replaced Neville Chamberlain as prime minister in May, wouldn't negotiate with Hitler—and he mused hopefully that perhaps Churchill's reign wouldn't last long. "The Government here is still very popular," he wrote:

> and Churchill is, of course, the God of all. Now how long that will last when people, like those in the East End of London today, are homeless and jobless, it is difficult to say. My opinion is that the people who just see this bombing from afar and who aren't direct sufferers from it, are standing up very well, but those who have lost their homes, their friends and their jobs, are not much different from other poor unfortunates who have suffered this air attack. Therefore, what the future of the government here will be one can't say, at least for the time being.

To Ted, he was warmer and more reassuring. "I don't know whether you would have very much excitement during these raids," he wrote:

> I am sure, of course, you wouldn't be scared, but if you heard all these guns firing every night and the bombs bursting you might get a little fidgety. I am sure you would have liked to be with me and seen the fires the German bombers started in London. It is really terrible to think about, and all those poor women and children and homeless people down in the East [E]nd of London all seeing their places destroyed. I hope when you grow up you will dedicate your life to trying to work out plans to make people happy instead of making them miserable, as war does today.[1]

Joe wrote often to the boys about global affairs when they were apart. When they were home, he tutored them in far more dynamic ways.

. . .

"I can hardly remember a mealtime," Bobby Kennedy said of his childhood, "when the conversation was not dominated by what Franklin D. Roosevelt was doing or what was happening around the world."[2]

Dinner among the Kennedys, with its stimulating conversation and lively banter, is the stuff of legend, but the boys' daily tutelage about global affairs actually began as all the children assembled for breakfast. After Mass each morning, Rose Kennedy read the newspaper over coffee or tea, whether the Boston papers in the family's early years, the *New York Times* after they moved to Bronxville, or the *Cape Cod Standard-Times* when they vacationed in Hyannis Port. She cut out stories of interest and pinned them to her outfit, a habit that she picked up from her father, Honey Fitz, who pinned newspaper items to his lapel and, when he ran out of room, stuffed them in his pockets. As the children converged for cereal and toast, Rose read an item at a time and asked questions.

She also pinned newspaper and magazine stories to a bulletin board that the children passed on their way to the table. "The boys and girls who were at the age of reading and reasoning," she recalled in typically clinical fashion, "were supposed to read or at least scan these enough to say something about the topics of the day—opinions, comments, questions, or confessions of sheer confusion or bewilderment or disbelief, at least something about current events during the mealtime conversations."[3]

Rose broadened her children's worldly knowledge with tours of historical sites, as the history-loving Honey Fitz had done for her. "I may have overdone it a little," she later admitted, "since there can be too much even of a good thing. My daughter Eunice says it seemed to her I was always dragging them off to Bunker Hill or Concord Bridge and there were times when she thought of me as a schoolteacher." Nevertheless, she added, "they did learn, their interest developed with the years, and I suspect that this may be one reason why as adults they wanted to serve the country in public life.

Jack, especially, was fascinated by history; he read it, wrote it, and lived it, and I think his sense of history guided his whole career and gave his Presidency a quality of its own."[4]

While Rose tutored all the children during the day, Joe focused the spotlight more squarely on the boys at dinner.

. . .

"My abiding memory," Jean Kennedy Smith later wrote of Jack and Joe Jr., "is at the dinner table each night, where they fed off each other's energy, debating the critical issues of the day with Dad. Who would win the election? Would there be war in Europe? Should the United States intervene?"[5]

Over a dinner that started promptly at 7:15 p.m., the talk was spirited, the atmosphere highly charged, as the boys were challenged to reason, argue, and convince. "I was young, but I remember those dinners," Ted Kennedy said not long before he died. "My father was like a game-show host asking questions. I was lucky. I was the baby, so I was exempt. But boy, oh boy, were they entertaining."[6]

Leading the discussions, Joe at times would unfurl a map of the world that hung on the wall to amplify a point. If one of his sons asked a question, he answered with great patience and insight. If one of their friends at the table piped up, he responded curtly and shifted his focus back to his sons. "Mr. Kennedy stimulated the boys into thinking for themselves," recalled Lem Billings, Jack's closest friend. "He argued with them and he encouraged them to form their own ideas and opinions. He encouraged them to thoroughly discuss why they felt certain ways, and he encouraged them to disagree with him."[7] During these conversations of the early 1930s, Joe Jr. and Jack were on the spot, for they were in their teens and old enough to engage in discussion.

In fact, Joe forced the boys to know about certain global issues before they even sat down. He would "assign a subject—Algeria, for example—to one child and instruct him to find all he could on the subject," explained Evelyn Lincoln, Jack's personal secretary in the Senate and White House. "Then he would tell the other chil-

"Like Carbonated Water"

dren to do the same so they could question the first one when he made his report and see how much he really knew. Both father and mother tried to develop alert minds in their children by giving them mental exercise, just as they encouraged physical exercise. And the same competitive spirit prevailed at the table discussions that was apparent in the touch football games on the lawn."[8]

To further broaden his sons' horizons, Joe brought to dinner such worldly figures as Charles Lindbergh and Henry and Clare Booth Luce. "As a parent," he wrote to a friend years later, "I picked out some men of great character whom I had known and tried to teach my children to follow them."[9]

. . .

"We learned early," Ted Kennedy recalled, "that the way to be an active part of dinner conversation was to have read a book, to have learned something new in school, or, as we got older, to have traveled to new places."[10]

Indeed, travel abroad also drove the boys' growing interest in the world. They each traveled extensively in their youth and met with top foreign officials, witnessing the making of history from front row seats. While Joe encouraged and often initiated their trips, it was Rose who set an example in her youth. During the summer of 1908 when she turned eighteen, Honey Fitz and his wife, Josie, took Rose and her sister, Agnes, on a two-month trip across Ireland, England, Belgium, France, Switzerland, Germany, and Holland. They walked through Phoenix Park in Dublin and visited Stratford-on Avon in England, strolling Shakespeare's house, the surrounding gardens, and the village. When the trip ended, the girls continued their schooling in Europe for the next year at a convent boarding school in Holland and, over the Christmas holidays, traveled across Germany. When Honey Fitz returned to Europe to bring the girls home, the three of them first toured Holland, Belgium, France, and England. After Honey Fitz, who had previously served as Boston's mayor, won back the post in 1910, Rose went with him to see the new Panama Canal and sailed with him as he led a

Boston Chamber of Commerce delegation to Hamburg, Brussels, Munich, Berlin, and Paris. She was so captivated by what she saw, and so curious about what she hadn't, that as a young woman she founded a prominent club for other young Catholic women who had traveled overseas and wanted to learn more about the world. She served as its president, and Honey Fitz arranged for dignitaries to speak before it.

Years later, one of Jack's friends came to dinner in Hyannis Port and witnessed the "excitement that was generated in this house where one boy was going to Spain and another was taking a trip to South America. . . . This whole family was in turmoil and moving in every direction, and vitally involved and interested in what was going on. I had never seen anybody like that, or any family like that."[11] Nor had Jacqueline Lee Bouvier, who left her first visit with the family in Hyannis Port thinking they were "like carbonated water and other families might be flat . . . they had so much interest in life—it was so stimulating."[12]

As a young adult in the late 1930s, Jack traveled widely at a time of growing global tensions—to attend the London School of Economics in the summer of 1935; across Europe in the summer of 1937; to France and then England the following summer to work in America's embassy in London when Joe was ambassador; and across Europe for more than half of 1939, including London to watch Parliament debate war with Germany. He was no passive tourist, content to stroll city streets and lounge on sunny beaches. Fixated on big questions of foreign policy, he talked to the people of each country to learn how they viewed the world, recording his thoughts in diaries and letters. He analyzed the differences among cultures and political systems, which would inform his decision-making in later years. "Poles are not Czechs, & they will fight," he wrote to a friend in the summer of 1939, as Nazi officials mused openly about seizing parts of Poland.[13] Unlike the Austrians and Czechs in earlier months, the Poles did in fact fight bravely when Germany and the Soviet Union invaded Poland from different sides, in September of 1939, before succumbing in about a month.

"Like Carbonated Water"

Bobby and Ted also traveled abroad in the late 1930s, accompanying the family to London when Joe became ambassador and to southern France for vacation. When they were old enough to go on their own, they traveled just as widely as Jack, and they, too, talked to people on the street and drew their own conclusions about different cultures and political systems.

. . .

"It is about time you came," FDR told Bobby, who was eleven, Ted, who was four, and their five sisters when they visited him at the White House in the early afternoon of January 20, 1937, less than an hour after he was sworn in for a second term. "How is your father? How can I put my arm around any of you? Which is the oldest? You are all so big."[14]

Joe and Rose raised their children to assume a public profile and with it a rightful place on the world stage, arranging meetings for them with leading figures and putting them in the spotlight rather than protecting their privacy. From the early 1930s through World War II, the names of some combination of Kennedy children appeared scores of times in the pages of the *New York Times* or what was then the *Boston Daily Globe*. The coverage of their exploits ranged from the superficial to the serious—from their appearances at high-society parties to Jack's heroic exploits aboard the PT-109 in 1943. By the time they were young men, Jack, Bobby, and Ted were receiving opportunities to speak and write about the world to national audiences, which reflected their prominence far more than their credentials.

When he was chairing the Securities and Exchange Commission in the mid-1930s, Joe mentioned to FDR that Bobby had started collecting stamps. FDR, who often distracted himself from the pressures of office by working on his own stamp collection, wrote to Bobby in July of 1935 and sent stamps, an album, and an invitation to see his collection when he was in Washington. Bobby mailed back a note of thanks for the stamps and album, and when the kids visited FDR after his swearing in, Bobby brought his collection. The president and the young boy compared stamps, passing a magnifying glass between each other. On that trip to Washington, the children attended FDR's swearing in, watched the inaugural parade, enjoyed a buffet lunch at the White House with three thousand others, and attended a reception. They spoke with Treasury Secretary Henry Morgenthau, Postmaster General James Farley, FDR advisor Felix Frankfurter, the president's son, Jimmy, and other prominent figures.

Two years later, when Joe was the ambassador in London, FDR approved his request to serve as America's representative to the coronation of Pope Pius XII at the Vatican. Joe brought Rose and all his children except Joe Jr., who was in Spain to witness its civil war up close. The Kennedys enjoyed a private audience with the pope (who had visited the family in Bronxville when he was touring America in 1936 as Cardinal Eugenio Pacelli), and they went to tea at the pope's official summer residence in Castel Gandolfo on what Joe later wrote was "the most thrilling day of our lives."[15] Two days later, the Kennedys watched the new pope give seven-year-old Ted his first Holy Communion, which was also the first Holy Communion that Pius XII gave anyone as pope.

When, in August of 1939, Jack wanted to get to Berlin through Prague, which the State Department had deemed "off-limits to U.S. tourists," Joe directed the Foreign Service to push him through—angering diplomat George Kennan, who was working in America's embassy in Prague and considered Jack, at just twenty-two, "obviously an upstart and ignoramus."[16]

. . .

"Goddamn it!" Joe Kennedy roared after a Boston newspaper labeled him an Irishman. "I was born in this country! My children were born in this country! What the hell does someone have to do to become an American?"[17]

Though the incident occurred well into Joe's adulthood, his reaction reflected the resentment that burned within him throughout his life over the anti-Irish-Catholic bigotry that he had faced—a resentment that he passed on to his sons. Like Rose, he was the grandchild of Irish Catholics who fled the potato famine of the late 1840s and settled in a Brahmin Boston that didn't welcome the many poor, unskilled, desperate immigrants who—forced to live in squalor—brought crime, prostitution, drunkenness, and disease to the once-quaint city. The anti-Irish-Catholic animus that plagued America in the late nineteenth and early twentieth centuries was particularly virulent in Boston and the rest of Massachusetts, as mobs burned churches and voters elected state leaders with openly anti-Catholic agendas. Joe and Rose suffered far less than most Irish Catholics because when they were growing up, their fathers were influential political leaders and, when they were adults, they were far wealthier than most. Nevertheless, they were keenly aware of the bigotry and sometimes victimized by it.

Among many slights, Joe was particularly hurt when, even as a popular leader of his sophomore class at Harvard in 1909–10, he wasn't invited to join one of its exclusive "final clubs" because he was Catholic. As one of America's most successful young business leaders, he was twice turned down for the board of the Massachusetts Electric Company for the same reason, before his selection in 1917. When he rented a summer home in 1922 for his growing family on the shore in Cohasset, a Massachusetts town of snooty Protestantism, its golf club strung him along for many weeks before rejecting his membership application. When, while the ambassador in London in 1938, rumors swirled that he would receive an honorary degree from Harvard, he was deeply hurt when the nominating committee rejected the idea—so much so that he didn't attend that graduation even though Joe Jr. was receiving his degree.

A banker, speculator, liquor distributor, and Hollywood mogul, Joe Kennedy was driven, ambitious, competitive, forceful, and decisive. Tall and thin, blue-eyed and bespectacled, red-haired and freckle-faced, he had a presence, a charisma, and he dominated conversations both professional and personal. He worked with his sleeves rolled up, lunched on crackers and milk, dictated to an assistant, and juggled phone calls. Strategic, detail-oriented, and disciplined, he was always eyeing the next business opportunity, the next financial conquest, the next chance to enjoy the limelight. "Let's have no frivolity today," he told a friend in typical fashion as the two prepared to play golf with a business prospect.[18] He was a man of considerable charm and, when relaxed, he smiled broadly, joked easily, and laughed infectiously, which in part explains his successful extra-marital pursuits. But he was demanding of those who worked for him and, when impatient, he could be abrasive, dismissive, and brutally candid. Rather than waste words, he got to the point. Sensitive to slights, whether real or imagined, particularly when his integrity was challenged, he was quick to anger and explosive in temper. He wanted what he thought he had earned, whether a top government job or public adulation, and he moped when it eluded him. Scarred by the bigotry he faced, he never let the chip fall from his shoulder.

Deeply embittered, Joe nurtured an us-versus-them mentality in his sons and directed them to trust one another before anyone else. When, in 1935, Joe, Rose, Jack, and his sister Kathleen ("Kick") were sailing on the SS *Normandie* to Europe, Joe met Lawrence Fisher, one of six Ohio brothers who established Fisher Body Co., which would produce millions of car bodies for General Motors with the insignia "Body by Fisher." Joe and Rose called for Jack, who came to his father's chair with, as Rose recalled, his "hair tossed" and his "necktie askew from playing in a game of deck tennis." "Jack," Joe told him, "I sent for you because I want you to meet Mr. Lawrence Fisher, one of the famous Fisher Body family. I wanted you to see what success brothers have who stick together."[19]

They should stick together, Joe thought, even when he disagreed with them, When, in 1934, Joe Jr. returned from a trip to the Soviet Union with British socialist Harold Laski, with whom he had studied at the London School of Economics, he promoted socialism over capitalism at the dinner table with his father and Jack. Jack took his brother's side, perhaps because he agreed but, just as likely, to needle the old man. Joe was more bemused than aggravated, however. "If I were their age," he said later, "I probably would believe what they believe, but I am of a different background and must voice my beliefs.... The important thing is that they should stand together."[20]

...

"For the Kennedys," Joe told Arthur Krock, the *New York Times* columnist and family enabler, "it's the castle or the outhouse. Nothing in between."[21]

The father instilled in the sons a bold, audacious, Kennedy-centric outlook that drove their pursuits and nourished their self-confidence. He taught them to win on their own terms, even if that meant violating convention, which explains in large part why they ran for high office at young ages. Joe set the highest of expectations for them, ordaining, "In this family we want winners." Nor did he tolerate self-pity when victory didn't come. "We don't want any crying in this house," he said.[22] That prompted the children to invent a family motto: "Kennedys don't cry." The kids got the message, competing fiercely at baseball, football, swimming, and sailing as youngsters and at politics as adults. "It wouldn't make any difference who you were," recalled Eddie Gallagher, a family friend who played ball with them. "They were running over you even as kids."[23]

Nothing nourished the audacity of Joe's sons more than watching him operate as America's ambassador in London. Joe had good reason to expect a top appointment from FDR, whom he met during World War I when Roosevelt was assistant secretary of the navy and Joe was leading a shipbuilding effort for the government. Joe strongly backed FDR for president in 1932, contributed heavily to his campaign, raised much more from others, convinced influential publisher William Randolph Hearst to endorse him, traveled with him around the country, and celebrated with him afterward. Endorsing FDR's reelection in 1936, Joe wrote a book (*I'm For Roosevelt*) to explain why. For each of FDR's campaigns, he brought many Irish Catholics and business leaders to his side. But after, at his brash demand, Roosevelt tapped him in late 1937 to represent the United States in its most vital embassy of the time (following appointments to chair the Securities and Exchange Commission and

U.S. Maritime Commission), he confused his position with FDR's. Joe sought less to represent FDR's views about Europe's coming war than to promote his own. When a suspicious FDR bypassed him by establishing a direct communications channel to Churchill, Joe took great umbrage and complained about the president to anyone within earshot.

In the late 1930s Joe thought that America should steer clear of Europe's troubles and build its own defenses so that, after vanquishing Britain, Germany wouldn't be tempted to turn its guns on the United States. Associated with the "Cliveden" set of British figures who sought a negotiated peace with Hitler, he praised Britain's Neville Chamberlain for his relentless efforts to appease Hitler and disparaged Churchill for maneuvering to bring America into the war (and for the whiskey on which Churchill seemed so dependent). Joe was working for a president, however, who wanted to awaken Americans to the Nazi threat and sidestep the Neutrality Acts of the 1930s to help the British. Rather than echo FDR's views, Joe routinely offered his own in speeches and letters to influential figures, thus undermining FDR's policies. That he also seemed to be angling for the Democratic presidential nomination in 1940 if Roosevelt chose not to run again further fueled FDR's hostility.

The problems stretched across Joe's two years as ambassador. FDR directed him to tone down the isolationist sentiments of his draft speech to the Pilgrim's Society in London in March of 1938. At the Trafalgar Day dinner in October, he ignited a firestorm in London and Washington by declaring, "It is unproductive for both the democratic and dictator countries to widen the divisions now existing between them. . . . After all, we have to live in the same world."[24] After Britain and France entered the war in late 1939, he told a Boston audience (which included Joe Jr. and Jack), "There's no place in the fight for us." Asked about isolationist sentiments in America when he returned to London in early 1940 after a visit home, he told reporters, "If isolation means a desire to keep out of war, I should say it is definitely stronger."[25] After resigning as ambassador, he told reporters in what he assumed was an off-the-record chat in

"Like Carbonated Water"

December of 1940, "Democracy is finished in England. It may be here."[26] He relied on the judgment of isolationist aviator Charles Lindbergh, who thought that Britain couldn't possibly hold out against Germany's aerial bombing.

Upon attracting FDR's slights and the public's scorn when his views grew increasingly out of favor, he lashed out at his Jewish critics in the White House and media in ugly anti-Semitic terms.

. . .

Although Joe encouraged his sons to think for themselves, they couldn't help but be influenced by the views of their domineering father. In their youth, they mouthed a bit of his isolationism and even some of his anti-Semitism. They defended him when he grew ever-more controversial while serving in London, cast aspersions on his critics, and advised him on how best to answer them publicly.

As adults, Jack, Bobby, and Ted all retained Joe's audacity, but they acquired the self-confidence to discard his views. They traveled the world, learned about its dangers, compared notes with one another, and concluded that America should engage rather than retreat. The isolationist father had nurtured three sons who believed that America had a vital role to play on the world stage.

2

"My Experience Was the War"

"Mr. Speaker," Rep. Jack Kennedy, who was just thirty and looked even younger, declared in his first House speech on foreign policy, "I rise to speak on the need and wisdom of aiding Italy immediately."

It was November 20, 1947, and Congress was meeting in "special session" to consider President Truman's request for $597 million in emergency aid for France, Italy, and Austria to help them prevent communist takeovers. At the time, Western Europe was still suffering mightily from the devastation of World War II, with too few jobs and too little food and fuel. "As we talk here today," Jack said, "riots and strikes are now ravaging the Italian peninsula," with "violent outbreaks in 20 cities. If Italy is to be saved, we must act immediately. . . . Today I speak particularly of Italy, for I feel that Italy stands in the most perilous position of any country in Western Europe. Italy, along with France, has been chosen by the Russians as the initial battleground in the communist drive to capture Western Europe. . . . The outlook for Italy will be hopeful if we give her funds and goods now."

By then, Jack believed that America's future was inextricably linked to the world's. "The peace and prosperity of this country," he told the Crosscup-Pishon American Legion Post in Boston in late 1945 as he mulled a run for Congress, "are truly indivisible from the peace and prosperity of the world in this atomic age." As he ran a year later, his platform declared, "The people of the United States and the world stand at a crossroads. What we do now will shape the history of civilization for many years to come."[1]

After Truman enunciated the Truman Doctrine in March of 1947 to help "free peoples who are resisting attempted subjugation" and requested $400 million for Greece and Turkey, the new House member expressed his support. "We have only to look at the map," Jack told the Carolina Political Union, a University of North Carolina student organization, two weeks after Truman's pronouncement, "to see what might happen if Greece and Turkey fell into the Communist orbit." He noted that U.S. support for Greece dated back to President Monroe, warned that Soviet domination of Europe or Asia would imperil America's security, drew dark parallels to Hitler's European conquests, argued that aid to Greece and Turkey would reduce the chances that America would later have to send its young men to war, and asserted that America's failure to act would send a dangerous signal of weakness around the world and let the Soviets achieve their longtime goal of attaining "an opening to the Mediterranean, with all of its strategic implications." The "central theme" of America's foreign policy, he said, was "the prevention of Russian domination of Europe and Asia. This is the foreign policy that I support most vigorously. Upon it depends our security and I believe the best hope of peace."

When, in June of 1947, Secretary of State George C. Marshall outlined his Marshall Plan to revive Europe's economy in a luncheon speech at Harvard, Jack supported that as well. By November, Truman hadn't yet unveiled a detailed proposal to implement the plan and Congress would need months to debate it after he did. Truman proposed the $597 million in emergency aid for France, Italy, and Austria until the more comprehensive Marshall Plan could take effect. In backing the Truman Doctrine, Marshall Plan, and emergency aid, Jack reflected the hardening attitudes in Washington about how best to contain the Soviets.

Not everyone was convinced that America should assume such a grand global role, however—not even everyone in Jack's family.

. . .

Throughout 1947, Joe Kennedy was watching events unfold with a wary eye. He opposed the Truman Doctrine and Marshall Plan, preferring that Europe solve its own problems. "You can't keep out communism with dollars," he argued, adding that if the communists seized Western Europe due to the isolationist policies that he was advocating, Europeans would soon see that communism couldn't fulfill its promises and they would "return to the economic and political systems of the West."[2]

One night in the late summer of 1947, Joe was chatting with Arthur Krock, the *New York Times* columnist, at the family's home in Palm Beach, Florida, when he began to offer his views about America's foreign policy, which were very different than Jack's. Rather than avoid a public split with his son, he seemed to relish one. Joe asked Krock to air his views, which he dutifully did in a September 14 piece. Instead of a multi-year American grant of perhaps $20 billion under the Marshall Plan, he proposed a $5 billion loan for Europe to start, and perhaps a larger American commitment if Europe showed progress and met other conditions.

Joe had discussed his plan with Senator Henry Cabot Lodge Jr. and Rep. John McCormack, the state's senior Senate and House member. His isolationism, however, had made him somewhat of a pariah by then and, Krock wrote, "Mr. Kennedy got virtually no public support for his thesis."[3]

The public debate between father and son seems odd, for how many fathers and sons want to argue in front of the whole world? For the Kennedy family, it was a testament to Joe's continuing desire for influence in America's halls of power and also to Jack's growing self-confidence.

By college, Jack had begun to develop a much different view from his father. His belief that America must assume a robust global role emerged from, in large measure, the loneliness of his youth.

. . .

"I enjoy your round-robin letters," Jack wrote to his mother in early 1942 when he was twenty-four.

To make her letter writing to nine children more manageable, Rose had begun to write what she called "round-robin" letters that were essentially the same for each child. Of them, Jack wrote, "I'm saving them to publish—that style of yours will net us millions. With all this talk about inflation and where is our money going— when I think of your potential earning power ... its [*sic*] enough to make a man get down on his knees and thank God for the Dorchester High Latin School which gave you that very sound grammatical basis which shines through every slightly mixed metaphor and each somewhat split infinitive."[4]

In this letter from Washington, where he was stationed with the Office of Naval Intelligence, Ensign Kennedy displayed the trademark charm for which he later became so widely known. From his early teens, he was quick witted, fun loving, irreverent, and mischievous. With his restless mind and captivating personality, he was invariably the center of any discussion in which he was partaking. Because he was so inquisitive, because his interests ranged so widely, life with him was never boring. When not engaged in stimulating conversation, he invented brain-teasing games for fun. He was often bemused, mocking himself as much as others, and he had a sharp eye for irony. His sister Kick, with whom he was very close, called him "the funniest boy alive,"[5] while a friend said his "sparkling" personality made time with him seem like "you were at a fair or something."[6]

But as Jack teased his mother in that letter, he revealed a darker reality that he often hid: he was bitter about the way she had raised him. When, two decades later, Arthur Schlesinger Jr., the White House special assistant and historian, asked President Kennedy how he could explain the successes of Joe and Rose's children in light of the failures of the Churchill and Roosevelt offspring, he replied, "Well no one can say that it was due to my mother. It was due to my father. He wasn't around as much as some fathers; but, when he was around, he made his children feel that they were the most important things in the world to him. He seemed terribly interested in everything we were doing. He held up standards for us, and he was very tough when we failed to meet his standards."[7]

To be sure, Rose Kennedy exuded a certain coolness toward *all* her children. Joe was far warmer and more demonstrative; he swept the children up in his arms when they were young, cuddled with them in bed, and shared hidden candy with each on occasion. Rose, by contrast, approached motherhood as a profession, something to which to devote herself in place of the more intellectual life she envisioned before her father dashed her dreams of attending Wellesley and sent her to religious schools in Boston, New York, and Europe. Strict, orderly, and officious, Rose demanded that her children arrive at set times for meals, lined them up to inspect their clothes and nails before they left in the morning, made sure they had their prayer books and rosaries for church, recorded their doctor visits and medications on index cards, taught them etiquette, and corrected the grammar of their letters. As punishment, she banished them to dark closets from a very young age (ignoring the tears of the youngest) and hit them on their hands or backsides with a ruler or coat hanger.

But of her nine children, Rose seemed ambivalent about Jack in particular, as witnessed by others and reflected in her writings. And, among the brothers, he seemed the only one to resent her cold treatment.

. . .

"Gee, you're a great mother," Jack blurted, in the spring of 1923 when he was not quite six, as Rose prepared for another of her frequent trips, this one to the West Coast with her sister, "to go away and leave your children all alone."

That Rose volunteered that story in her memoirs is revealing, as is her description of what followed. She often rationalized her shortcomings as a mother, and this time was no exception. After portraying Jack as "a rather frail little boy," with a "rather narrow face" and ears that "stuck out a little bit," she wrote that she was not

"My Experience Was the War"

just "taken aback" by his remark but also "enchanted and amused." "He was a funny little boy," she recalled, "and he said things in such an original, vivid way that I thought they were worth recording." Although Jack's remark made her feel "a little hard-hearted" and she was teary eyed upon leaving the next day, her guilt didn't last long. When, after leaving, she quickly returned to retrieve something she had forgotten, she found the children "all playing quite contentedly on the porch and apparently not missing me much at all. I resumed my journey with an easy conscience."[8]

Jack, however, didn't fully recover from this incident or similar others. Born on May 29, 1917, in an upstairs bedroom of his parents' wood-framed, seven-room house in Brookline, Massachusetts, John Fitzgerald Kennedy cried as a child when his mother left until he realized that his tears pushed her further away. As his friend Charles Spalding recalled years later, Rose was "so cold, so distant from the whole thing . . . I doubt if she ever rumpled the kid's hair in his whole life. . . . It just didn't exist: the business of letting your son know you're close, that she's there. She wasn't."[9] Nor did the years fully heal Jack's pain for, as an adult, he confided to a friend, "My mother never hugged me, never, never!"[10] Though Rose sometimes praised him for, say, his improved grades, more often she expressed exasperation over his sloppiness, tardiness, or irresponsibility. His spelling, she wrote, "never progressed beyond the point of being unreliable," and his penmanship "never evolved into more than a semi-legible scrawl."[11] Because he was often late for meals, she tried to teach him a lesson by leaving without him from their family's beach club when it was time for them to eat lunch, forcing him later to charm the kitchen staff into giving him what he had missed. Joe Kennedy also expressed exasperation at Jack on occasion, but he encouraged him as well, frequently assuring him that he was gifted and prodding him to fully exploit his sharp mind.

Most striking was how Rose reacted when Jack fell ill. Admittedly, she couldn't be much help when, at age two, he contracted scarlet fever, because she had just given birth to her second daughter, Kick, and couldn't risk infecting her. Joe took over, finding Jack a hospital bed in Boston and spending long afternoons at his side. While her absence during Jack's scarlet fever is understandable, Rose never visited him during his five teen years at Choate, the private boarding school that was sixty-five miles away in Wallingford, Connecticut, even when he spent weeks in its infirmary for one of his many illnesses. Far more than Rose, Joe provided the support, counsel, encouragement, and discipline that transformed Jack from a wayward, irresponsible, underachieving youth into an adult of uncommon purpose and commitment. He spoke with many of Jack's doctors about his maladies, prodded him to get his act together, took a deep interest in his schoolwork, and counseled him as he mulled his political future. He wrote disapprovingly to Choate's headmaster that his sixteen-year-old son "seems to lack entirely a sense of responsibility" but, in a letter to Jack a year later, told him encouragingly, "I definitely know you have the goods and you can go a long way. Now aren't you foolish not to get all there is out of what God has given you and what you can do with it yourself."[12]

Rose later expressed guilt that the time she felt forced to spend with Rosemary, the first daughter who was born a year after Jack and suffered from cognitive shortcomings, crowded out her time with Jack. Though Jackie Kennedy later assured Rose that Jack never said he felt neglected, Rose wrote, "The thought still bothers me a bit that he may have felt neglected when he was a little boy."[13]

While lonely for his mother, a young Jack Kennedy also was dodging body blows from his older brother.

. . .

Jack was "a very able boy, but definitely in a trap psychologically," a Columbia University psychiatrist concluded after meeting with him at Choate. "I am the boy who doesn't get things done," Jack told him. "If my brother [Joe Jr.] were not so efficient, it would be easier for me to be efficient." Jack knew that on his current path of mediocrity and mischief, he'd "never amount to anything."[14]

To Joe, Rose, and everyone else in the Kennedy orbit, Joe Jr. was the anointed one, the shining star with handsome looks, a muscular build, a magnetic smile, and a sure-footed way that would undoubt-edly take him to the greatest of places. "Well . . . , of course he *is* going to be President of the United States," Honey Fitz declared upon Joe Jr.'s birth in 1915—that is, after he played football and base-ball at Harvard and won all its "scholastic honors," became a "cap-tain of industry," and maybe served as mayor and governor.[15] Jack was thinner than Joe Jr., less healthy, less athletically gifted, and less sure of himself.

Though the boys were constant companions at home, at Choate, and at Harvard, tensions between them heightened Jack's loneli-ness. Joe and Rose stoked the competition between them, touting the accomplishments of one to motivate the other. Each reacted by belittling the accomplishments and savoring the suffering of the other. After Joe Jr. bragged to the thirteen-year-old Jack how tough he was, Jack wrote to his father, "The first thing he did . . . was to get sick so that he could not have any thanksgiving dinner. Manly Youth." After Joe Jr. showed him how to "Indian wrestle," Jack wrote, "I then through [*sic*] him over his neck."[16] When, years later, Jack finished the Harvard thesis that would later become his best-selling *Why England Slept*, Joe Jr. told his father after he read it that "it seemed to represent a lot of work but did not prove anything."[17]

Their competition was physical as well and, as such, far more dan-gerous for Jack. For all the lavish praise and high expectations that came his way, Joe Jr. felt threatened by his younger brother; perhaps he saw hints of the drive, charm, and brilliance that would later serve Jack so well and, if so, perhaps he feared that Jack would pass him in accomplishment. When the time came to choose sides for touch football on the Kennedy lawn, Joe Jr. and Jack always played on opposite sides, each determined to best the other. But the com-petition had a darker side, for Joe Jr. confronted his demons by abus-ing Jack. He smashed footballs into his stomach, crashed his bicycle into Jack's (once sending him to a doctor for twenty-eight stitches), and exchanged blows with him at night, leaving the other children to tremble as they heard the boys slam one another into walls. "He had a pugnacious personality," Jack recalled. "Later on it smoothed out but it was a problem in my boyhood."[18] Complaining to his parents was out of the question, for they had taught their children to fight their own battles, so Jack was left to endure the abuse alone. Whether their father, who was often away, knew about the fighting isn't clear. But Rose knew and, just as she had assured herself years earlier that her children would be fine when she left for her trip, she downplayed the fisticuffs between the brothers. "Thankfully," Rose later wrote, "they probably fought no more than other brothers so close in age do and, in fact, possibly less."[19]

The fighting stopped when the boys became men, but the competition continued—until it ended on a tragic note. In August of 1943, twenty-six-year-old Jack Kennedy earned national acclaim as commander of the PT-109 in the Pacific for rescuing his men after a Japanese destroyer sliced their boat in half. It was, Rose later noted, the first time Jack had bested his older brother, and it "must have rankled Joe Jr."[20] Indeed, it helped convince the older brother, who seethed with envy and was slow to compliment Jack, to accept a dangerous bombing mission over Germany a year later that he hoped would top Jack's feat but that killed him when his plane exploded. Joe Jr.'s death not only devastated his father, but it also left Jack with unresolved issues, further fueling his loneliness. With Joe Jr. gone and now idealized in everyone's minds, Jack told a friend that he was now "shadow boxing in a match the shadow is always going to win."[21]

While confronting the psychological burden of unresolved competition with a "shadow," Jack faced the more tangible burden of advancing his career with a body that made life a painful chore.

. . .

"President Kennedy would have been forty-seven in May of 1964," Bobby wrote shortly after Jack's murder. "At least one half of the days that he spent on this earth were days of intense physical pain. He had scarlet fever when he was very young, and serious back trouble when he was older. In between he had almost every other conceivable ailment. . . . But during all this time, I never heard him com-

"My Experience Was the War"

plain. I never heard him say anything that would indicate that he felt God had dealt with him unjustly."[22]

Bobby's glowing testament to Jack's stoicism in the face of intense pain was not hyperbolic, for others attested to it. For Jack, life was a daily struggle, a relentless chore. Rather than complain, he joked about his mysterious ailments in letters to friends from his bed at home or in hospitals, and he rarely mentioned them after he launched his political career. As a House member, senator, and president, he hid the crutches that he sometimes used from the public, just as he hid the searing pain that he often felt in his back or stomach. In the House, he leaned on colleagues and staff as he struggled to walk from his office to the House chamber. In the Senate—before a back operation of late 1954 that almost killed him—he often spent his full day at his seat in the chamber rather than walk back and forth to his office between votes, forcing his staff to cancel appointments, bring paperwork to him, and excuse his irritability. In Congress and the White House, he tried to ease his back pain by standing, leaning over his desk, planting his palms flat, and lifting the weight of his body off his back and onto his shoulders. "He would read and work that way," *New York Times* photographer George Tames recalled, "which was something I had seen him do many times."[23]

Illness shapes a person, and Jack was no exception. The constant pain, serious ailments, and multiple near-death experiences made him fateful about his future. "Took a peak [*sic*] at my chart yesterday," Jack wrote to his best friend, Lem Billings, in 1936 from a hospital bed in Boston, after cutting short his freshman year at Princeton due to illness. "Eat drink and make [out], as tomorrow or next week we attend my funeral."[24] He predicted that illness would prevent him from living beyond middle age, which explains why he was in such a hurry, so determined to make his days matter, so willing to live with reckless abandon. As president, he mused on occasion that if someone were determined to kill him, neither his private detail nor anyone else could prevent it. He even noted his vulnerability at the outset of his trip to Dallas in November of 1963, when his forebodings proved prophetic.

His life was a test of perseverance, tenacity, doggedness, and grit. Was he tough enough to overcome his pain? Could he find the strength, with a rickety back and aching stomach, to walk streets, climb stairs, shake hands, and deliver speeches, starting early in the morning and concluding late at night? He asked similar questions of the United States; perhaps he was projecting his own struggles onto his country. Could America find the strength, the will, and the fortitude to ensure its security, to confront its aggressive adversaries? Could democracy prevail against authoritarianism? Such questions dominated his thinking as he became an author and dabbled in journalism after returning from war. And they drove his foreign policy as he climbed the ladder of power.

Consumed with fear over America's capacity to prevail, he spoke in apocalyptic terms—not just at key moments but continuously. To Jack, whether the year was 1947 or 1963, the challenge was in Europe or Asia, or the issue was military or diplomatic, the nation was always at a "moment of maximum peril," facing "great danger," confronting "our most critical challenge." He warned that "time is running out," that we were confronting "a peril more deadly than any wartime danger we have ever known." He fretted over the "tide of events" that were always moving toward the Soviets, the coming communist "onslaught," the "major disaster" that was just around the corner, the "seemingly hopeless predicament," the "sense of paralysis . . . waning of hope . . . sense of drift . . . [and] gnawing dissatisfaction" that was afflicting us, and the threats to "the peace and security of the world" if not the "very continued existence of mankind."

"Trouble and danger are our constant companions," he told the Senate in typical fashion in 1954; "our enemies are powerful and implacable."

. . .

"We must be prepared to recognize democracy's weaknesses and capitalism's weaknesses in competition with a totalitarian form of government," Jack wrote in *Why England Slept*, explaining why Britain was slow to rearm in the 1930s as the Nazi threat mounted. "We

"My Experience Was the War"

must realize that one is a system geared for peace, the other for war. We must recognize that while one may have greater endurance, it is not immune to swift destruction by the other."[25]

Why England Slept was the culmination not only of Jack's studies at Harvard but of his many hours of rumination alone. "It was under his covers recovering that Jack developed his voracious and lifelong love of reading," his sister Jean wrote later. "As he became older, [he] became enthralled with history and legend: *King Arthur and his Knights, Lays of Ancient Rome, Treasure Island, The Arabian Nights, The Writings and Speeches of Daniel Webster*."[26] At home, Jack often curled up with a book on the porch or in the living room. As a teen at Choate, he was the only one of his friends to subscribe to the *New York Times* and read it thoroughly every day. His love of history, and his focus on big events and leading figures, never tired. As president in early 1961, he told *TIME*'s Hugh Sidey that his ten favorite books included David Cecil's *Melbourne*, Winston Churchill's *Marlborough*, Samuel Flagg Bemis's *John Quincy Adams*, Allan Nevins's *The Emergence of Lincoln*, Herbert Agar's *The Price of Union*, and Margaret Coit's *John C. Calhoun*.[27]

Why England Slept also represented Jack's declaration of intellectual independence from his father. Up to then, he had defended and largely echoed his father's isolationist views. After Joe Kennedy caused a firestorm in London in late 1938 when he downplayed the differences between democracies and dictatorships, Jack wrote him from Harvard that "while [the speech] seemed to be unpopular with the Jews, etc.," it "was considered to be very good by everyone who wasn't bitterly anti-Fascist."[28] Then, in an unsigned column, "Peace in Our Time," for the *Harvard Crimson* in October of 1939—a month after Germany invaded Poland, and Britain and France declared war on Germany—Jack disparaged what he called "militant democratic sympathy" that "brands immediately as heresy any concessions to the ogre Hitler" and "rejects as insulting the vaguest mention of a peace concluded over the body of a prostrate Poland." In other words, the West should hold its collective nose, sacrifice Poland if necessary, and cut a peace deal with Hitler. He urged FDR to serve as an intermediary between Germany and Britain, and he suggested that the British make "considerable concessions to Hitlerdom" that included "a puppet Poland" and a "free economic hand for the Nazis in eastern Europe" in exchange for Hitler's agreement to "disarm."[29] With that proposal, Jack seemed like a carbon copy of his appeasing-loving father.

By the time Jack turned twenty-three, in 1940, however, he was self-confident enough to chart his own path. He had traveled across Europe more than once and witnessed fascism's rise up close. Stirred by what he saw, he abandoned isolationism and sought an effective strategy of engagement. In *Why England Slept*, he addressed what he considered the central challenge: how could democracies—with peace-loving and slow-moving populations that might refuse to recognize mounting danger—compete with authoritarian regimes that could quickly launch war, regardless of public sentiment? Jack's book was a history of British failure, but he wrote it with a larger purpose: to prod his own country to avoid the same fate. In 1940 Britain was at war with a better-armed, more powerful foe, but it was not too late for America to fortify its own defenses. Though Jack didn't "believe necessarily" that, after defeating Britain, Germany would turn its guns on America, he thought that the United States should take no chances.[30] "In studying the reasons why England slept," he wrote, "let us try to profit by them and save ourselves her anguish."[31]

British leaders, Jack argued, were constrained by a public that was far more interested in balanced budgets and low taxes than the greater armaments that could threaten both; that feared financial ruin from rearmament far more than foreign aggression; that was largely pacifist; that considered British armaments less a prudent step than a hostile one that could trigger Germany's ire and undermine the League of Nations' efforts to keep the peace; and that questioned whether more armaments would protect Britain from aerial bombing in the first place. "The responsibility of the [British] leaders in not realizing and explaining the potentialities of Germany is heavy," Jack wrote. "But the English people must bear their share of the responsibility as well. They had been warned. Chur-

"My Experience Was the War"

chill and others had pointed out to them the dangers that menaced the country."[32]

However much they now disagreed over foreign policy, however, Jack's book reflected the pretensions that he and his father shared. Jack chose the title as a play on Churchill's 1938 classic, *While England Slept*, and, with astonishing presumption, asked his father to see whether the British leader would mind the public echo. At Joe's prodding, Jack secured Arthur Krock's help to transform a student paper into a published book and sent the manuscript to such British leaders as Neville Chamberlain and Stanley Baldwin.

. . .

When, as Jack was running for president, a magazine writer asked him what he remembered about the Great Depression, he explained that it wasn't economic hardship that shaped him. "My experience was the war," he said. "I can tell you about that."[33]

Like others who have served in war, Jack experienced its horrors and returned with a fervor to do what he could to prevent another one. His brush with death aboard the PT-109 as well as the bloody battles he witnessed nurtured his fears that America's future leaders would choose war without fully weighing the consequences in soldiers lost, families destroyed. This, too, was a theme to which he returned often in his years of public service. That Joe Jr. died at war further nourished his forebodings.

In a sense, he was haunted by war—or, as Jackie Kennedy put it, by "the poignancy of men dying young."[34] To be sure, he could relay the savagery that he witnessed in graphic detail. Describing a gun battle with a Japanese pilot who had parachuted into the water, he wrote to his parents in the spring of 1943, "We let go of everything but he didn't seem to get hit until finally an old soldier aimed with his rifle and took the top of his head off."[35] But like many war veterans who struggle with the memories of what they've endured, Jack was reluctant to articulate the details of his *own* harrowing experience on the PT-109—two crew members lost immediately in the explosion; hours in the water with the rest of his crew, clinging to the hull of his destroyed boat; hours more swimming between nearby islands in search of food and water; and days of hunger, thirst, and exhaustion before their rescue. He told a TV interviewer that his brush with death was merely an "interesting experience," and he tried in vain to dissuade a writer from penning a book about it.[36] He was uncomfortable with the accolades that came his way after saving his men. Asked about his heroic action, he once replied, "It was involuntary. They sank my boat."[37]

While at war, Jack disparaged those who blithely assumed that America's soldiers and seamen were eager to fight however long the war lasted. "When I read that we will fight Japs for years if necessary," he wrote his parents, "and will sacrifice hundreds of thousands if we must—I always check from where he's talking—it's seldom from out here."[38] "No one out here," he wrote to them on another occasion, "has the slightest interest in politics—they just want to get home—morning—noon—night." He mocked the "old American energy" of his colleagues, quoting Honey Fitz's line that "they give the impression of their brains being in their tails." Of Joe Jr.'s desire to contribute to the fight, he wrote, "I know it is futile to say so—but if I were he—I would take as much time about it as I could. He is coming out eventually—and will be here for a sufficiency— and he will want to be back the day after he arrives—if he runs true to the form of every one [*sic*] else."[39]

As Jack sought public office soon after the war, his wartime adventures shaped his attitudes. Running for the House in 1946, he described global conditions in typically dire terms and pledged to work for peace. "The people of the United States and the world stand at a crossroads," his platform statement declared.

> What we do now will shape the history of civilization for many years to come. We have a weary world trying to bind up the wounds of a fierce struggle. That is dire enough. What is infinitely far worse is that we now have a world which has unleashed the terrible powers of atomic energy. We have a world capable of atomic warfare. We have a world capable of destroying itself. The days which lie ahead

are most difficult ones. . . . Above all, day and night, with every ounce of ingenuity and industry we possess, we must work for peace. We must not have another war.[40]

He was haunted as well by the aftermath of war, which he surveyed on his return to Europe in 1945.

. . .

"The devastation is complete," Jack wrote from Berlin in July:

There is not a single building which is not gutted. On some of the streets the stench—sweet and sickish from dead bodies—is overwhelming. The people all have completely colorless faces—a yellow tinge with pale tan lips. They are all carrying bundles. Where they are going, no one seems to know. I wonder whether they do. They sleep in cellars. The women will do anything for food. One or two of the women wore lipstick, but most seem to be trying to make themselves as unobtrusive as possible to escape the notice of the Russians.[41]

Hitler was dead, World War II was over in Europe, and the United States, Britain, France, and the Soviet Union were occupying separate zones of Germany. But the allies had no long-term plan for Germany, and Washington was worried that Moscow might try to push the United States out and move itself in. "The question, therefore," Jack wrote in his trip diary, "is whether the other three occupying forces can afford to leave their zones. . . . If we don't withdraw and allow [the Germans] to administer their own affairs, we will be confronted with an extremely difficult administrative problem. Yet, if we pull out, we may leave a political vacuum that the Russians will be only too glad to fill."[42]

Earlier that year, Jack wrote about the United Nations organizing conference in San Francisco and Britain's parliamentary elections for Hearst newspapers—all of it arranged by his father, who was close to publisher William Randolph Hearst. The newspaper chain then sent him to the Potsdam conference of U.S., Soviet, and British leaders, which opened on July 17. He had left San Francisco disappointed, doubting the United Nations would accomplish much, although he thought that "the one ray of shining bright light" was "the realization, felt by all the delegates, that humanity cannot afford another war." On a hopeful note, he suggested that by providing a "bridge between Russia and the Western world," the United Nations "makes possible discussion and a personal relationship which can do much to ease mutual suspicion."[43] In San Francisco and Potsdam, he mingled with Truman and Eisenhower, Britain's Churchill and Anthony Eden, and other world leaders, further nurturing his interest in global affairs.

On his way to Potsdam, to which he traveled with Navy Secretary James Forrestal, he rode through Germany to survey the ruin. Berlin's carnage must have evoked mixed emotions in him. He had traveled across Europe in 1937 with Lem Billings and, as Billings later recalled, they both found the Germans "insufferable . . . so haughty and so sure of themselves." Jack and Lem would answer their "Heil Hitler" salutes with a raised hand and a mocking "Hiya, Hitler."[44] Jack returned to Germany two years later with another friend, but they fled Berlin when a mob pelted their car with rocks and bricks when they stopped to see a monument, perhaps because it carried British license plates.

In 1945, however, he was shaken by the suffering he witnessed. Of one twenty-two-year-old woman, he wrote, "When the Russians came, she and her two sisters were taken down to the cellar. Her clothes were 'taken out'—she gave them all her rings, cried, waved a bottle of wine. Her 'face was blue.' She demonstrated by swinging a bottle at me."[45]

. . .

Jack's diary, like his other writings during his formative years, reveals a young man wrestling with big questions of global affairs: How do democracies build support for war? How much longer can Western nations rule their colonial empires? Most of all, how can America prevail in its postwar struggle with the Soviets?

3

"He Was Like a Seventeenth-Century Jesuit Priest"

On a sunny day in the fall of 1951, Jack and Bobby Kennedy peered into the Taj Mahal, the ivory-white mausoleum in the Indian city of Agra. Jack wore a white shirt, light slacks, and a tie; Bobby sported a casual shirt and dress shorts; both men wore sunglasses. They looked relaxed and chummy.

If the truth be told, however, Jack hadn't wanted Bobby with him on his seven-week, twenty-five-thousand-mile excursion across the Middle East and Asia. At the time, Jack was serving his third term in the House, where he was a bored and restless backbencher with a limited public platform, and he dismissed himself as one of 435 "worms" in the unruly body. He yearned for a larger national role on foreign affairs and was mulling a Senate run for the following year. He went to Berlin in 1948 to see the Soviet blockade and U.S. airlift up close, and he traveled across Western Europe in early 1951 to assess the continent's strength and will to withstand Soviet aggression. Now, with a trip to the Middle East and Asia in October of that year, he hoped to enhance his foreign policy credentials. When his father asked him to take Bobby to broaden his brother's horizons, Jack objected, expressing concern that he would be a "pain in the ass" and relenting only at Joe's insistence.

The brothers, who were eight years apart, hadn't been especially close to that point. Though Jack walked the beach and tossed footballs with Bobby when they were boys, they didn't spend much time together. Jack was far more a mentor to the younger Ted, in whom he took a deep interest from the moment he asked his mother whether he could be "Godfather to the baby."[1] Nor did Jack and Bobby easily mesh because, in their early years, they were polar opposites in personality. While Jack was sunny and carefree, Bobby was brooding and anxious, and the former was often uncomfortable around the latter. After hearing that Bobby was coming to help with his first run for the House in 1946, Jack told a friend, "I can't see that sober, silent face breathing new vigor into the ranks" and suggested that he take Bobby "out to movies or whatever you two want to do."[2] Nor, in Bobby's formative years, did Joe and Rose do much to help him overcome his insecurities. They always assumed that Joe Jr. would do great things, and Joe came to assume the same about Jack. But they both worried that Bobby, who struggled in the shadow of his older brothers, wouldn't amount to much.

For all of Jack's trepidations about Bobby's presence, however, their trip would prove important to both of them. Jack came to see a depth in Bobby that he hadn't previously appreciated because, until then, he viewed Bobby as little more than his awkward kid brother. While overseas, meanwhile, the two came to agree on America's key challenge in competing with the Soviets across the developing world, which was rising nationalism: the desire of colonial populations to free themselves from outside domination. Further nourishing their bond, Bobby saved Jack's life by arranging to fly him to a military hospital in Okinawa when his Addison's disease sent his temperature soaring to 107, and Bobby sat at his bedside as he barely escaped death. A year later, Bobby would leave his job with the U.S. Justice Department in New York, where he was prosecuting fraud cases, to rescue Jack's floundering Senate campaign and propel his brother to an upset victory over Republican incumbent Henry Cabot Lodge Jr.

Before his momentous trip with Jack, however, Bobby had already traveled widely and written with notable sophistication about global events.

. . .

"Like a Seventeenth-Century Jesuit Priest"

"I was very pleased to get your note about Bobby," Joe Kennedy wrote to Lord Beaverbrook, the British press baron, in March of 1948. "He is just starting off and has the difficulty of trying to follow two brilliant brothers, Joe and Jack. That in itself is quite a handicap, and he is making a good battle against it."

Bobby had stopped to see Beaverbrook, who had served in Parliament and was a Churchill confidante, on his way to the Middle East, from where he would write for the *Boston Post* about the fighting between Jews and Arabs in Palestine. After meeting Bobby, Beaverbrook wrote to Joe Kennedy that he was "a remarkable boy. He is clever, has a good character, energy, a clear understanding, and fine philosophy. You are sure to hear a great deal of him if you live long enough."[3]

At twenty-two, Bobby was coming into his own, ready to relay his thoughts about America's role in the world. As with Jack, his views emerged from the struggles of his youth. Born on November 25, 1925, in Brookline, Massachusetts, Robert Francis Kennedy was a classic middle child, starved for attention as his father poured his hopes into Joe Jr. and Jack and the family doted on the younger Ted. He often seemed every bit the "runt" that his father cruelly labeled him, especially when standing beside his taller, smoother, more handsome older brothers.[4] In his youth, Jack dubbed him "black Robert" because, struggling with his demons, he often looked dour, sad, and fearful. Though warm, gentle, and generous, he was also shy and awkward, and he often stood with his hands in his pockets and his head buried in his neck. "I have a pretty good character on the whole," he wrote about himself at thirteen, "but my temper is not too good. I am not jelous [*sic*] of any one. I have a very loud voice, and talk alot [*sic*], but sometimes my talk is not very interesting."[5] Even as an adult, he never fully surmounted his insecurities. "Words came out of this mouth," one of Jack's friends said of Bobby when the latter was twenty, "as if each one spoken depleted an already severely limited supply."[6] Years later, when Bobby was an accomplished professional, his hands still trembled on occasion when he delivered an important speech, and he openly mocked his own efforts on the campaign trail. "Sometimes," he told a friend in adulthood, "I wish I never was born."[7]

His place in the family hierarchy fueled his thirst for notice. "I was the seventh of nine children," he noted later, "and when you come from that far down you have to struggle to survive."[8] Sensing that he was stuck among the sisters who surrounded him in age, with no room to shine, Rose showered him with extra affection. Bobby also sought a more personal engagement with his father, writing to him from Harvard in 1945: "I wish, Dad, that you would write me a letter as you used to Joe & Jack about what you think about the different political events and the war as I'd like to understand what's going on better than I do now." When his father obliged, Bobby replied, "Thanks very much for your letter, Dad, which is just what I wanted."[9]

To earn his siblings' notice, to prove he was every bit as brave as them, Bobby pursued reckless challenges—starting at age three when he jumped into Nantucket Sound while sailing with his siblings even though he didn't know how to swim, forcing Joe Jr. to rescue him. In a physical family, with brothers who all performed feats of courage as children and adults, Bobby was perhaps the bravest of all. At Harvard, he earned his way onto the football team, as a scrawny youth, through sheer will, and he played on a broken leg against Yale to earn a coveted school "letter." Through adulthood, he swam in swirling waters, skied steep slopes, and climbed dangerous mountains in a lifelong quest to prove himself. Overseas, he waded into hostile crowds against the advice of security details that couldn't guarantee his safety, and he was sometimes spat on and hit by eggs and tomatoes. He also inspected dangerous mines to survey working conditions. He lauded bravery, courage, and guts and openly disparaged others for their cowardice.

Not surprisingly, he brought passion to his early writings and, later, a swashbuckling approach to the global challenges of Jack's presidency.

. . .

"He was like a seventeenth-century Jesuit priest," Richard Nixon said of Bobby years after they shared the public stage, "passionate, one who brooked no opposition."[10]

While Jack found comfort in books, Bobby sought refuge in religion. Influenced by his deeply devout mother, he was a devoted altar boy, attended Mass often throughout his life, married the even more religious Ethel Skakel, and brought a strong sense of morality to foreign policy. More than the cool, cerebral, somewhat dispassionate Jack, who accepted the world's imperfections and crafted his policies accordingly, Bobby viewed foreign policy as he viewed all matters—in terms of black and white, good and evil—and he argued ferociously for his views. Though he changed his perspective about America's global role significantly after Jack's death, that didn't ease his passion. He expressed just as much certainty about his later views as he had about his earlier ones.

Through the early 1960s, the greatest evil in Bobby's eyes was communism, and it drove his decision to work for Senator Joe McCarthy in the 1950s, his obsession with toppling Cuba's Fidel Castro when Jack was president, and his desire to promote freedom over communism on his foreign travels. The passion of his young adulthood was well captured by a paper he wrote at the University of Virginia Law School, which he attended from 1948 to 1951, bemoaning FDR's concessions to Stalin at the Yalta Conference of early 1945 to coax the Soviet Union into the war against Japan.

As Yalta opened on February 4, Bobby wrote, "there was still a chance for peace in the post war world" if America's leaders understood the challenges before them and brought with them the "correct philosophy" to address them. Unfortunately, he wrote, the nation's leaders focused on the wrong problems and followed a "bankrupt philosophy" and, when the conference ended a week later, "we had taken the final step from which there was no salvation . . . President Roosevelt," he wrote, "felt that the way to beat the Common Enemy as well as to have future peace was to stay friendly toward Russia. This idea guided all his thoughts and actions and early in the war he decided how this could best be accomplished." FDR and his top aides, he concluded in dramatic fashion, made that philosophy "their guiding star throughout the entire war—a philosophy that reached its epitomy [*sic*] at Yalta, and ... spelled disaster and death for the world."[11]

In the coming years, Bobby would write just as harshly about the foreign policy failures of FDR's successors.

. . .

"I was in Palestine over Easter week," Bobby wrote in June of 1948 in the third of his four front-page pieces for the *Boston Post*, "and even then people knew there was absolutely no chance to preserve peace."

After Bobby graduated from Harvard in March, Joe sent him on a six-month trip abroad with a friend because he thought his son needed to know more about the world. He sailed on the *Queen Mary* to London and then traveled to Egypt, Palestine, Lebanon, Turkey, Greece, Italy, Belgium, the Netherlands, Germany, Austria, Czechoslovakia, Denmark, Sweden, and Ireland. As with Jack and Hearst newspapers three years earlier, Joe arranged for Bobby to write for the *Boston Post*. "Young Kennedy has been traveling through the Middle East," the newspaper announced in introducing his first piece, which appeared with a headshot of a smiling Bobby in jacket and tie, "and his first-hand observations, appearing exclusively in the *Post*, will be of considerable interest in view of the current crisis."

Though his articles appeared a month after the state of Israel was established in early May, Bobby had visited the area weeks before. As he arrived on the last weekend of March, global powers were debating the final status of what had been the British mandate, and Jews and Arabs were exchanging gunfire as they fought for the land that both thought was rightfully theirs. Bobby offered perspectives on America's global role that would later shape the advice he gave his brother as president and the positions he then advocated as a senator. Like Jack, he promoted a strong U.S. role in the world and argued that, on the world stage, America must promote freedom and democracy.

"Having been out of the United States for more than two months at this time of writing," he wrote, "I notice myself becoming more and more conscious of the great heritage and birthright to which we as United States citizens are heirs and which we have the duty to preserve. A force motivating my writing this paper is that I believe we have failed in this duty or are in great jeopardy of doing so. The failure is due chiefly to our inability to get the true facts of the policy in which we are partners in Palestine." Although, in 1917, Britain issued the "Balfour Declaration" that called for a "national home for the Jewish people in Palestine," Bobby wrote that, now, "The British government, in its attitude towards the Jewish population in Palestine, has given ample credence to the suspicion that they are firmly against the establishment of a Jewish state in Palestine."

Bobby was no longer his father's clone, willing to mouth Joe's ugly anti-Semitism to curry his favor. Now, he praised the courage, persistence, and grit of the Jews as they pursued their Zionist dreams amid the hostility of Arabs who greatly outnumbered them. "The Jewish people in Palestine who believe in and have been working toward this national state have become an immensely proud and determined people," he wrote. "It is already a truly great modern example of the birth of a nation with the primary ingredients of dignity and self-respect." Writing with a striking certainty about what he saw, he added, "The Jews who have been lucky enough to get to Palestine are hardy and tough.... They can go into the Mediterranean Sea and get drowned or they can stay and fight and perhaps get killed. They will fight and they will fight with unparalleled courage. This is their greatest and last chance. The eyes of the world are upon them and there can be no turning back."[12]

Bobby returned to Israel during his trip with Jack across the Middle East and Asia. That was months after Jack set out to assess the grit of West Europeans as they faced their Soviet adversary.

. . .

"You come from a very distinguished American family that exercises a great influence on American public opinion," Senator Walter George, the former isolationist who became an ardent internationalist after Pearl Harbor, told Jack in February of 1951 as the thirty-three-year-old House member testified at a joint hearing of the Senate's Foreign Relations and Armed Services committees. "I want to ask you very impersonally whether you remember the able speech of your father in December 1950. I think you know me well enough to know that I do not share his point of view."

Jack might have found George's warm-up amusing, for the senator was referring to a speech that Joe Kennedy delivered at the University of Virginia Law School—at the invitation of Bobby, who was president of the Student Legal Forum and, in that role, inviting prominent figures to speak on campus. In that "able speech," Joe again urged America's leaders to shift course by withdrawing from South Korea, where they had sent troops in June of 1950 to reverse the North's invasion, and by abandoning Europe. "Today it is idle to talk of being able to hold the line of the Elbe or the line of the Rhine," Joe told Bobby's classmates. "The truth is that our only real hope is to keep Russia, if she chooses to march, on the other side of the Atlantic, and make Communism much too costly for her to try and cross the seas. . . . Is it appeasement to withdraw from unwise commitments, to arm yourself to the teeth and to make clear just exactly how and for what you will fight?"[13]

When, a few years earlier, Joe had questioned the Truman Doctrine, Marshall Plan, and other key elements of Truman's foreign policy, a traditionally isolationist America was still coming to grips with its new global role. Though Truman pushed his bold "containment" policies through Congress, the debates were serious and more than a few lawmakers offered far less ambitious visions for America's global role. Skeptics questioned whether the nation could afford to finance Truman's vision and whether it would more readily provoke conflict with Moscow than contain it. By the time Joe Kennedy spoke at the University of Virginia Law School, however, the debate was essentially over. As he continued to question America's new role so stridently, Joe became an increasingly out-of-step, reviled figure.

Jack most certainly did not share his father's "point of view," as he told George. By then he had not only endorsed Truman's vision but also sought to inject more urgency into it. In January of 1949,

"Like a Seventeenth-Century Jesuit Priest"

as Mao's communists moved closer to ousting Chiang's U.S.-backed nationalists from mainland China, Jack lambasted Truman for what he considered a colossal U.S. setback—with language that was strikingly harsh for a young lawmaker to use against a president of his own party. "The responsibility for the failure of our foreign policy in the Far East," he told the House, "rests squarely with the White House and the Department of State. . . . So concerned were our diplomats and their advisors . . . with the imperfections of the democratic system in China after 20 years of war and the tales of corruption in high places that they lost sight of our tremendous stake in a noncommunist China." Blaming "vacillation, uncertainty, and confusion [that] has reaped the whirlwind," he declared, "This House must now assume the responsibility of preventing the onrushing tide of communism from engulfing all of Asia."

After America's "failure . . . in the Far East," Jack was now wondering whether the United States would do better in Europe.

. . .

For the first five weeks of 1951, Jack visited England, France, Italy, West Germany, Spain, and Yugoslavia. Upon his return, he offered his thoughts in a radio address that the Mutual Broadcasting Network carried across the country.

"My purpose in making this trip," he began in typically urgent terms when discussing the Soviet threat, "grew out of my realization that the most important task that would face this country and its government during the next few months would be the question of our relationship to Western Europe in the face of the growing threat of Soviet expansion. Upon the correct solution of that problem hangs the fate of millions of American lives. Indeed the very survival of the nation may hinge upon it."

Could Western Europe "be defended?" To Jack, the answer depended on "the existence in these countries of a will to resist—a determination to build up within them singly and collectively forces that, together with such aid as we may supply them, have a reasonable chance of dealing with the threatened aggression from the

East." It was the same issue that he raised in *Why England Slept*: Could democracies summon the will and make the sacrifices to ensure their survival?

Jack spoke of Europe's future in stark terms, questioning what its people were ready to do and willing to endure. "I talked," he told his radio audience,

> with men of every level—with French and German generals, with prime ministers and cabinet members, with our ambassadors, our High Commissioner in Germany, with political leaders, with [Yugo-slavia's Josip] Tito, and with the man in the street. The problem of European morale is, however, not merely what men say. It is also what men do. It is the capacity of their industry to devote signifi-cant portions to war purposes and still produce enough for basic and essential needs. It is their attitude toward manpower and its conscrip-tion, towards controls, towards taxes. It is their willingness to make sacrifices, to face deprivation, even to starve in defense of freedom.

After discussing the military resources and public morale of every country he visited, Jack closed on an ominous note. The "plain and simple fact," he said, was that Europe wasn't making the sacrifices needed to ensure its survival. That, in turn, raised big issues for America. "It is important that Western Europe be saved," he said, "but we cannot do so ourselves or pay a price that will endanger our own survival. We cannot link our whole fate to what is pres-ently a desperate gamble. We can and will survive despite Europe, but with her it will be that much easier. But Europe must know, as we are again learning to know, that freedom is born and held only by deep sacrifice."

By the time Jack testified at the Senate hearing two weeks later, he had developed an idea to coax more out of Europe.

. . .

From his earliest days, Jack Kennedy was a cold-blooded realist. Though his voice could soar and his words could inspire, he saw the world with clear eyes and sought practical ways to respond to it.

So it was no surprise when, in his Senate testimony, he acknowledged that the Soviet Union could conquer Europe if it wanted to over the coming two years. "It is obvious," he told the ten senators in attendance, "that there will not at the present rate be sufficient land forces in Europe to stop the Russians, if they should attack, until the beginning of 1953 at the earliest." Asked by Senator Alexander Wiley, a Wisconsin Republican, whether Western Europeans expected "Russia or her stooges" to "start something this year," he was just as clear minded in his response. No, he said, "everyone" thought the Soviets wouldn't attack because, among other reasons, America's nuclear weaponry remained a deterrent and the Soviets didn't want the challenge of feeding a conquered Europe. "In addition," Jack speculated about Moscow's seventy-two-year-old leader: "Stalin is an old man, and old men are traditionally cautious."

Jack sought to shorten Europe's two-year window of vulnerability by boosting Western troop levels. And while he wanted Washington to do its part by sending more men, he didn't want his country "caught," as he put it, "holding the bag." "Our aid," he said, "must be proportionate to the effort of the Europeans. This ratio should be at least six to one in mobile forces, considering that we are only one of twelve countries in the Atlantic Pact; that we are supplying large naval and air elements; that we have heavy commitments elsewhere; and that a substantial part of the equipment of the European forces will be American." With four U.S. divisions already in Europe, he recommended that Washington send two more—but not before the Western Europeans put thirty-six of their own divisions under the command of Dwight Eisenhower, NATO's supreme commander at the time. For each additional U.S. division, NATO's European members would have to contribute six. This "ratio system," Jack explained, would pressure America's allies to do their share because Washington would contribute more only if Europe did.

If the West was facing a test of its resolve, Jack suggested that America was meeting it more robustly than its allies. "In none of these other countries are they planning controls over their economies similar to ours," he said, "and in not any of these countries are they taking men as young or for as long a period as we will take them. My own conclusion was that while what they are going to do will require great sacrifices and while it is understandable that they are reluctant to do more, I think that they must do more if Europe is to be saved. The only way we are going to get them to do more is by giving American assistance on a ratio basis."

Rather than ease tensions by balancing East-West forces, Jack conceded that NATO's buildup could prove "provocative," prompting a Soviet attack. Nevertheless, he concluded that rejecting a buildup just to avoid that risk would be "the height of foolishness."

. . .

"Seven weeks is a short time to try and grasp these many problems," Jack told the nation in another radio address on the evening of November 14, 1951, after returning from his tour of the Middle East and Asia.

"But any Congressman, any Senator today, to be worthy of his salt," he said,

> must lift his vision from the immediate problems of his constituency to reach for an understanding of the role that America should play in the world. Foreign policy today, irrespective of what we might wish, in its impact on our daily lives, overshadows everything else. Expenditures, taxation, domestic prosperity, the extent of social sciences—all hinge on the basic issue of peace or war. . . . Just as Clemenceau once said, "War is too important to be left to the generals," I would remark that "Foreign policy is too important to all of us to leave it to the experts and diplomats."

Perhaps more than any words that he ever uttered, those words encapsulated Jack's philosophy of public policy, his fixation on foreign affairs, his fear of what might ensue if America did not act wisely on the world stage. It was a distinctly unusual way for a House member to approach his job. "All politics is local," the future House speaker, Tip O'Neill, who won Jack's House seat when Jack ran for the Senate, would famously say, and the vast majority of lawmakers approached their jobs that way. They focused overwhelmingly on the day-to-day domestic concerns of their constituents to ensure their reelections. Jack, who represented an overwhelmingly Democratic district, had the political luxury to focus abroad without having to worry much about losing his seat. His focus, however, also reflected his most heartfelt fears, for he believed, as he liked to say, that "domestic policy can only defeat us; foreign policy can kill us."

Throughout his seven weeks abroad with Bobby and their sister Pat, Jack immersed himself in conversation with top U.S. military and diplomatic officials as well as foreign leaders in Syria, Lebanon, Israel, Egypt, Iraq, Iran, Japan, India, Pakistan, Hong Kong, Korea, Vietnam, Thailand, Singapore, Malaya, Indonesia, and the Philippines. He first stopped in Europe to see Eisenhower, and he then spoke with generals Matthew Ridgway and James Lawton Collins in Asia. He and Bobby met with Pakistan's prime minister, Liaquat Ali Khan, lunched with India's prime minister, Jawaharlal Nehru, and dined at the home of Israel's prime minister, David Ben-Gurion. Jack explored the geographies and economies of the nations he visited; their racial, religious, and cultural make-up; and, most importantly, their likelihood of siding with Washington in its competition with Moscow. What was most striking, from his private notes as well as his speeches and interviews after his return, was his alarm about . . . well . . . everything. As he saw it, the United States was competing woefully against the Soviets. Washington was spending too little on defense, using foreign aid too clumsily, sending second-rate diplomats to represent America, and failing to adapt policy to on-the-ground reality.

"Certainly, I do not and one cannot blame America and her policies for all that has happened," he acknowledged over the radio, "for no matter what America might have done, nothing could have avoided nor will avoid the inevitable birth-pangs of Asia's rising nationalism. But amid this turmoil, I should have hoped that with our traditional concern for the independence of other peoples, our generosity, our desire to relieve poverty and inequality, we would— whatever else happened—have made friends throughout this world.

It is tragic to report that not only have we made no new friends, but we have lost old ones."

. . .

"Reason for spread of Communism," Jack jotted to himself after a stop in Malaya, "is failure of those who believe in democracy to explain this theory in terms intelligible to the ordinary man and to make its ameliorating effect on his life apparent. This especially true in Far East which does not have same experience and tradition in personal liberty, etc. that Westerners do—therefore, do not miss it."[14]

Jack returned from seven weeks abroad with two concerns: first, that U.S. officials didn't understand that hundreds of millions of people across the developing world were yearning for better lives and, second, that, as a result, America was creating a vacuum that communist forces were filling with promises of post-revolutionary bliss. Rather than build ties to the masses, Jack complained, Washington continued to work with ruthless anti-communist dictators and to support its British, French, and Dutch allies as they sought to maintain their colonies in the face of growing grassroots opposition.

"It is a troubled area of the world that I saw," Jack said over the radio, fleshing out what he had told the *New York Times* three days earlier.

It is an area in which poverty and sickness and disease are rampant, in which injustice and inequality are old and ingrained, and in which the fires of nationalism so long dormant have been rekindled and are now ablaze. It is an area of our world that for a hundred years and more has been the source of empire for Western Europe—for England and France and Holland. . . . This is also an area of revolution, which manifests itself at times in bloody riots and assassinations, in broad guerilla warfare as in Malaya and Burma where we did not dare even in daylight to move outside restricted city limits unless we were accompanied by heavily armed guards.

"Like a Seventeenth-Century Jesuit Priest"

Most importantly, Jack counseled, it was an area that was up for grabs in the Cold War. "Basically," he said, "this is an area of human conflict between civilizations striving to be born and those struggling desperately to retain what they have held so long. As such, it is obviously open to the inroads of communism but it also holds an enormous challenge to the penetration of American faiths and beliefs." The problem, he explained, was that America's traditional approaches to the area would not work. "If one thing was borne into me as a result of my experience in the Middle as well as the Far East," he said, "it is that communism cannot be met effectively by merely the force of arms. It is the peoples themselves that must be led to reject it, and it is to those people that our policies must be directed."

In speeches and interviews, Jack recommended that America not just shower nations with dollars but also provide "know-how," the "export of techniques" on a scale reminiscent of "the great missionary movement of the last century." He suggested that the way to nourish greater loyalty to America was not by making undeveloped nations more financially dependent on Washington but, instead, by giving them the skills to help themselves. He urged Washington to overhaul its public diplomacy so that the United States could reach the masses, not just elites with access to the Voice of America. He also urged Washington to send better diplomats to the Far East, severely chastising those who, with "some notable exceptions," remained "mainly in their own limited circles not knowing too much of the people to whom they are accredited, unconscious of the fact that their role is not tennis and cocktails but the interpretation to a foreign country of the meaning of American life and the interpretation to us of that country's aspirations and aims."

. . .

With his long trips to Europe and Asia, Jack developed a deeper, more sophisticated sense of America's global challenges. After defeating Henry Cabot Lodge Jr. and taking his new Senate seat in early 1953, he quickly grew dissatisfied with how the new president, one Dwight David Eisenhower, was meeting them.

4

"The Knife Itself Is Still in His Fist"

"This change in policy had momentous implications for all Americans and should be so understood," Senator Jack Kennedy declared at New York's Cathedral Club on January 21, 1954, a week after Secretary of State John Foster Dulles unveiled Eisenhower's "New Look" strategy.

Notwithstanding Ike's military *bona fides*, which Jack respected, the New Look was destined to trigger the young senator's derision. That's because it reflected none of the characteristics that Jack valued, whether in public policy or life. It lacked energy, depth, creativity, flexibility, and what he called "vigor," and it lacked nuance to respond to the complexity of an increasingly dynamic world.

The New Look called for maintaining a strong economy, launching covert activity, strengthening America's alliances, and, most of all, deterring aggression by threatening adversaries with nuclear annihilation. By exploiting America's nuclear superiority, the fiscally conservative Eisenhower believed that he wouldn't need a huge standing army or every new weapons system, so he could protect the nation and balance the budget at the same time. "The basic decision was to depend primarily upon a great capacity to retaliate, instantly, by means and at places of our choosing," Dulles explained. "Now the Department of Defense and the Joint Chiefs of Staff can shape our military establishment to fit what is our policy, instead of having to try to be ready to meet the enemy's many choices. . . . As a result, it is now possible to get, and share, more basic security at less cost."

Jack's dispute with Ike wasn't over goals because, as he noted, the Cold War consensus remained strong. Four months after Dulles unveiled the New Look, Jack told a Princeton University audience, "Republicans and Democrats alike agree on the need for strengthening and unifying the free world, ending communist aggression, building our national security, and seeking international disarmament and atomic control." To achieve those goals as threats proliferated, though, he thought America needed more than an all-or-nothing nuclear option. The Soviets were expanding their standing army and conventional weapons, increasing the dangers to Western Europe and other regions, while Washington and Moscow were competing for influence across the developing world. Jack bemoaned what he considered the failures of Ike's first fifteen months: communist advances in Indo-China, an uncertain truce in Korea, growing tensions with U.S. allies, inadequate investments in public diplomacy and global technical assistance, and unwarranted defense cuts. Rather than sacrifice defense at the altar of a balanced budget, he thought that Washington should strengthen America's defense capabilities and then write a budget to cover the costs. He called for more defense spending and a broader array of tools (which formed the basis of the "flexible response" strategy that he would later fashion as president).

As Jack was critiquing the New Look, Bobby was denouncing another perceived failure of Ike's foreign policy.

. . .

"Although Red China has been an open aggressor in Korea, many of our allies have been carrying on trade with and furnishing ocean transportation services to the Chinese Communists since the beginning of the war," Bobby wrote in July of 1953 in a report for the Senate Permanent Subcommittee on Investigations, which Joe McCarthy was chairing, after its hearings on trade between America's allies and China during the Korean War.

"This shocking policy of fighting the enemy on the one hand and trading with him on the other cannot be condoned," Bobby wrote in his typically passionate fashion. "In the opinion of this subcommittee and the Department of Defense, this indefensible trade policy has made our military operation in Korea a more difficult one and unquestionably has cost the lives of American and other Allied fighting men in Korea. While our allies who are engaging in this trade with Red China give many economic reasons why they should continue this profitable business, there is no logical or moral reason why any nation should trade with the enemy during a period of armed conflict."[1]

Bobby brought to the "Greek shipping crisis," as it was known, the relentless drive and unchecked judgmentalism that would mark his public career. McCarthy was an old friend of the Kennedys—a rowdy Irishman, tough anti-communist, and rollicking companion with whom they all seemed comfortable; he dated both Pat and Eunice Kennedy, and Bobby and Ethel asked him to be godfather to their first child, Kathleen. At Joe Kennedy's request, McCarthy hired Bobby as his subcommittee's assistant counsel in 1953 and McCarthy put him to work on Western trade with China. At the time, McCarthy was at the height of his powers, with Republicans controlling both the House and Senate and McCarthy chairing a subcommittee from which he could launch wide-ranging probes. After soaring to prominence in February of 1950 by alleging communist influence over Truman's foreign policy team, he was now a headache for Eisenhower. In the spring of 1953, he temporarily blocked Ike's appointment of highly regarded diplomat Charles Bohlen as ambassador to the Soviet Union because, he said, Bohlen had been "too important a part" of Truman's team to represent America in Moscow. He then criticized Eisenhower for his supposedly lackluster approach to Western trade with China. The shipping crisis put the twenty-seven-year-old Bobby in a brightly illuminated spotlight.

On the morning of March 28, 1953, Bobby accompanied McCarthy to a press conference at which the senator announced that, through the efforts of Bobby and other staffers, "the Greek owners of 242 merchant ships had agreed to stop trading with Red China, North Korea, and other communist countries." Bobby then

"The Knife Itself Is Still in His Fist"

sat directly behind McCarthy at his explosive hearings of March 30 and 31. Over two days, top Eisenhower officials suggested that McCarthy's agreement with the shipowners was "phony" because the administration had inked a deal with Greece's government six days earlier to restrict Greek ships from trading with China, and they complained that McCarthy was inappropriately infringing on the president's power to make foreign policy. Bobby testified at hearings on May 4 and 20 and walked the subcommittee through his findings: 193 "Western-flag vessels" traded with China in 1952 and voyaged there at least 445 times, 505,000 gross tons of shipping moved in and out of China on such vessels in December of 1952 alone, and so on.

The shipping crisis was a typical McCarthy affair, with lots of bluster and grandstanding. He took an old issue—two years earlier, a House member by the name of Jack Kennedy bemoaned Western trade with China in a House speech—and pretended it was new. McCarthy traded charges with administration officials, fraying relations and nourishing bitterness. At one hearing, he cut off the testimony of a State Department official and stormed out of the room. He made headlines and moved on, setting his sights on other alleged instances of American weakness against communism.

As he was when Joe Kennedy served as America's ambassador in London, Bobby was once again a witness to audacity, and he came to see the benefits of ignoring convention to achieve his goals.

. . .

Musing at one point about serving in a future Cabinet, Jack Kennedy said that "only Secretary of State or Defense" would interest him.[2]

By now, foreign policy was less a preference for Jack than an obsession, driven by what he considered America's wanting urgency, drive, commitment, and sacrifice. Through the Eisenhower years, in scores of speeches around the country, he sought to rally his nation to its global challenges. In Churchillian terms, he warned again and again that the hour was late while the peril was approaching. "These are difficult and dangerous days," he said at Boston College in February of 1953. "The structure of containment in many areas is cracking, and our horizons are lit by the lightning flash of distant conflict.... If the free world is to survive in this type of trial and trouble, if the line is to be held against the advancing hordes, then in the final analysis, and this we must know, it will depend on us." America, he said in Indianapolis that October, "was about to enter the most critical period in our long history." In Worcester, Massachusetts, in June of 1955, he cited the "brutal, physical side of that ominous war upon which we have bestowed the strong epithet 'cold.'" In Washington the following January, he said that Moscow had been "disappointingly successful" in turning "Germany, Yugoslavia, French North Africa, Egypt, India, and Japan" away from the West. In San Francisco that September, he denounced "Republican drift, inaction, and vacillation" that "have harmed our interests and principles of collective security in practically every corner of the world."

Particularly striking was how Jack denounced his Senate colleagues for their cowardice, for choosing "to appease political pressures at home and stay in office" rather than vote for the national interest. Perhaps he was already eyeing the presidency, was viewing the Senate as a temporary stop, and was unconcerned that his rhetoric would affect his relationships in the proud body. Or perhaps he simply believed that the times were too perilous, the dangers too clear, for narrowmindedness. "Damned neuters in the middle way of steering," Jack called his colleagues in public speeches, quoting from English playwright John Dryden's "the Duke of Guise."

"We cannot long afford the luxury of irresponsibility in national affairs," he declared at Northeastern University in December of 1953. "In 50 years the communists have moved outward with unparalleled swiftness so that now they control over one-third of the world's population and their shadow hangs heavy over the lives of many millions of men in the free world. Their economic system— rigidly controlled—devoted completely to the aggrandizement of the state, steadily is closing the gap in productive supremacy that once we enjoyed. The troubles and pressures of the 18th century when our country began pale in significance with those we now face, for basically challenged [are] all of the suppositions upon which our founders based our government."

At a Chamber of Commerce dinner in Albany, Georgia, in February of 1957, Jack issued his most dramatic warning of all. Irish poet John O'Reilly, he said, wrote,

> The world is large when its weary leagues
> Two loving hearts divide;
> But the world is small when your enemy is
> Loose on the other side.

"The world is small tonight," Jack then cautioned, "and our enemy is loose in it. It is the task of your nation in the years that lie ahead to meet this challenge with all the wisdom and all the understanding that have been bestowed upon us—as a nation."

In the mid-1950s, Jack and Bobby traveled to see the Soviet system up close, and what they witnessed did nothing to soften their views.

. . .

"Before we go overboard on all this business, and before we start cutting down on our armies and navies we should get something more than words from the Soviet Union," Bobby Kennedy told United Press in September of 1955 after a six-week tour of Soviet republics with Supreme Court Justice William Douglas. "We need something more than just a promise that everyone is in favor of peace."[3]

Two months earlier, Eisenhower had met with the Soviets' premier, Nikolai Bulganin, Britain's prime minister, Anthony Eden, and France's prime minister, Edgar Faure, in Geneva to advance global peace. Short on accomplishment, the summit nevertheless spurred talk of a new "spirit of Geneva," with hopes of less Cold War tension and more East-West cooperation. At the time, Soviet leader Nikita Khrushchev and Premier Bulganin were promoting a new Soviet openness in hopes of remaking Moscow's image and reducing Western hostility.

Not surprisingly, more than a few American lawmakers, newspaper correspondents, and others found the high hopes for a new day almost intoxicating. After all, it was just two years since the end of the Korean War, which had left 37,000 U.S. troops dead, 103,000 wounded, and the North and South merely in a cease-fire rather than permanent peace. Now, hopes for warmer U.S.-Soviet relations could not only justify lower defense spending, but they could also ease the anxieties of Americans who worried that they would die in a Cold War nuclear confrontation.

"There can be little doubt," the *New York Times*' Harry Schwartz wrote in August, "that the Soviet Iron Curtain has been partially lifted these past few months."[4] Moscow was letting more Westerners visit than at any time since the late 1930s, permitting more Soviet citizens to travel abroad to scientific conferences and other meetings, airing more Western views of global affairs through its state media, censoring fewer dispatches of foreign correspondents, and publishing a new magazine with foreign literature. The Kremlin reportedly was even rewriting its criminal code to better safeguard the rights of the accused.

In response, more people were flocking to the Soviet Union from around the world. While he was in Moscow, on the tail end of his Soviet excursion, Bobby crossed paths with a congressional delegation that included Senator Estes Kefauver, a leading Democratic presidential candidate for 1956. Other senators were expected in the coming weeks, including the influential Richard Russell, who chaired the Senate Armed Services Committee. Also in Moscow while Bobby was there were British parliamentarians, French tourists, and delegations from Asian nations—as well as Jean and Pat Kennedy and Pat's husband, actor Peter Lawford. Kefauver later said that while Khrushchev's government was firmly entrenched in Moscow, Western influences might alter the character of the communist state.

Bobby had just witnessed the horror of Soviet rule up close, however, and he was concerned that the West was now downplaying the Soviet threat.

. . .

"The Knife Itself Is Still in His Fist"

"The Soviet Central Asian Republics—," Bobby wrote in a four-page essay for the *New York Times* in April of 1956, "less known in the West, in proportion to their size and to the antiquity of their history, than any part of the civilized world—portray all the evils of colonialism in its crudest form."[5]

Joe Kennedy had asked Justice Douglas, a friend who had long sought a visa to visit the Soviet republics, to take Bobby with him so he could get an up-close look at communism in action. Douglas mentioned the idea to Bobby in 1951 when, at Bobby's invitation, Douglas spoke at the University of Virginia Law School. "Each time January came around, we applied" for visas, Bobby told the *Boston Daily Globe* on the eve of their trip. "I suppose if we wanted visas to Moscow or Leningrad, or a regular Cook's tour, we might have got them two or three years ago. Well, the visas just came through this year"—that is, amid Moscow's global charm offensive.[6] The two proceeded to travel over seven thousand miles, across lands that were populated by up to twenty million people. Though Bobby saw much to criticize—so much, in fact, that he later said he had "had enough" of the Soviet Union and didn't want to ever return—he also found himself on the defensive when, in conversations with Soviet citizens, he was asked repeatedly about America's treatment of its black citizens.[7] (America's racial problems were a vulnerability in its global competition with the Soviet Union that, when Jack was president, he and Bobby would work hard to address.)

Bobby grew convinced that Soviet rule over its republics left Moscow vulnerable in the court of global public opinion. When he took pen to paper about what he had seen—as he had for the *Boston Post* when writing about Palestine in 1948—Bobby mixed rich history with keen observation, painting a compelling portrait of Soviet hypocrisy. "The natives of this area, which was traveled by Marco Polo, conquered by Alexander the Great and Genghis Khan, and controlled by Tamerlane, are people of Turkish and Persian stock infused with a strong Mongolian strain," he wrote in his *New York Times* essay after visiting Baku, Bakhara, Samarkand, Stalinabad, Tashkent, Frunze, Barnaul, and Novosibirsk along with

Moscow and Leningrad. "They are as different from their European Russian masters as the Moroccan is from the Frenchman or the Malayan from the Englishman. They have the high cheekbones and general appearance of the Oriental; their dress is oriental; their customs are oriental, and their food—I particularly remember one meal of scrambled lamb's brains—is also oriental in style and content. And yet this area, larger than India and Pakistan, into which all of Western Europe could be easily fitted, and with a population exceeding that of Canada or Australia, is ruled with an iron hand by an alien race."

In writings, speeches, and interviews for months after his return, Bobby noted that Moscow controlled "all means of livelihood and all sources of income," with every worker a state employee, strikes prohibited, and job transfers requiring the government's permission. The typical person lived in "a mud hut, with a mud floor." The government allowed no free press, tolerated no criticism, and left no room for college students to debate politics. Moscow placed loudspeakers on streets and farms, in factories and stores, and aboard ships and trains to broadcast speeches by communist leaders. In once-thriving Muslim areas, the Kremlin replaced religion and family customs with its own rules, leaving parents "replaced by the state-operated nurseries and Youth Pioneer camps." Schools were segregated, with one set for European Russian children of light color and the other for local populations of darker color; state and collective farms were similarly segregated; and state repression included monitored conversations, purge trials, and slave labor.

"The evils of colonial policies of certain Western nations are now being widely publicized by the Soviets," Bobby concluded for the *Times*, highlighting what's at stake. "And yet at the same time, without protests from us, the Communists have wiped out the freedom of millions of people occupying an area larger than that of all Western Europe put together." It was, he wrote, "high time that we in the West understood and spotlighted" the matter, and that the leaders and people of the Middle East, Afghanistan, and Southeast Asia, where the Soviets sought to make inroads, "pondered . . . the

"The Knife Itself Is Still in His Fist"

fate of their brothers to the north in Turkmenistan, Uzbekistan, Tadzhikistan, Kirghizia, and Kazakhstan."

Soon after Bobby returned home in September of 1955, Jack set off for Poland, which he considered the most important of Moscow's Eastern European satellites, to assess the strength of Soviet control.

. . .

"People in the streets look reasonably well dressed," Jack wrote from Warsaw in October in a long essay that he sent to his state's newspapers, "but when a Westerner said this to a Polish woman, she replied in French: 'Mais vous ne savez pas quelle misere nous cachons.' (You do not know what misery we are hiding)."

After a stop in Rome to see the pope and another in Prague, Jack arrived in Warsaw for a look behind the Iron Curtain. In a four-page, single-spaced report that, like Bobby's about the Soviet republics, was rich and colorful, he mixed firsthand observation with historical context to speculate about Poland's prospects to free itself from Soviet control. A former journalist from his days writing for Hearst newspapers from San Francisco, London, and Potsdam as World War II was ending, he possessed a sharp turn of phrase and a flair for the dramatic—and he wrote less as a senator seeking legislative answers to a global challenge than a public intellectual educating the masses. "Unlike Prague Airport, which features pictures of the Czech President and [the Soviets'] Bulganin together and the Czech and Russian flags crossed," he wrote, "here because of traditional hatred of Russia by the Poles the Communists dare display only the historic Polish eagle. . . . Streets crowded with people but few cars . . . we passed the largest building in Eastern Europe: The Palace of Culture, an enormous skyscraper in Soviet style decorated with oriental minarets. It was a 'gift from the Russian people to their comrades in Poland' and is a constant reminder, were one needed, as it looms oppressively over the city of Warsaw, of the constant presence in the heartland of Poland of the Soviet Union."

Jack told of "crowded living conditions," with families doubling up and people refusing to leave their possessions alone for fear that someone will take them; of "fantastically high" prices for low-quality goods; of a store clerk who might earn 300 zlotys a week while "a small can of Maxwell House Coffee costs 200" and a pair of shoes might cost a month's salary; and of an old coat that a Scandinavian diplomat's wife gave to a Polish friend, who then traded it for a horse. Jack also described the government's "methods of forcing the Poles to conform" to communist rule. A family's housing, taxes, and children's education all depend on its "political reliability," and Catholics face severe discrimination, with their schools banned, their priests arrested, and their newspapers censored.

The police followed Jack wherever he drove and forced him to show his papers at checkpoints every fifty miles or so. As he walked the streets, police closed in whenever he spoke with Poles. "The people knew we were Westerners and were smiling and friendly," he reported. "Although there is a natural feeling of having been let down by the Western Powers, during and after the war, nevertheless there are few families in Poland who do not have a relative among the millions of Poles in the United States, and this represents a strong tie with our country. Then, too, the Polish people know that only through action by the free world can they ever hope to be free again."

Not surprisingly, Jack ended on an ominous note. Like Bobby, he expressed skepticism about "the spirit of Geneva" and warned that a U.S. rapprochement with the Soviets could dampen the spirits of the Poles, leaving their fight for freedom flagging. "Time works against them," he said of the Poles.

> It is upon the youth who have no recollection of a free Poland that the Communists concentrate their attention. Given control of the means of communications, given all the weapons of a modern police state, given control over education, given a limitation of the power and influence of the Church, given time to consolidate their gains, the Communists feel that they can remake Poland into an obedient instrument of Soviet policy. . . . If the Poles come to believe that we in the West have forgotten them, that we are willing to make an

"The Knife Itself Is Still in His Fist"

agreement with the Russians that does not provide for a Free Poland, then their courageous struggle to maintain their freedom may cease.

Of the "spirit of Geneva," he concluded, "The barbarian may have taken the knife out of his teeth to smile—but the knife itself is still in his fist."[8]

. . .

"Sometimes in the heat of a political convention," Jack Kennedy declared in nominating Adlai Stevenson for president at the 1956 Democratic National Convention in Chicago, speaking into four microphones and resting his hands on the podium, "we forget the grave responsibilities which we as delegates possess.

"We are selecting the head of the most powerful nation on earth, the man who literally will hold in his hands the powers of survival or destruction, of freedom or slavery, of success or failure for us all. We are selecting here today the man who for the next four years will be guiding, for good or evil, for better or worse, the destinies of our nation and, to a large extent, the destiny of the free world."

Jack argued that foreign policy was the predominant issue before the voters that November. "Of overwhelming importance," he said, "are the ever-mounting threats of our survival that confront us abroad, threats that require a prompt return to firm, decisive leadership. Each Republican year of indecision and hesitation has brought new communist advances—in Indo-China, in the Middle East, in North Africa, in all the tense and troubled areas of the world. The Grand Alliance of the West—that chain for freedom forged by Truman and Marshall and the rest—is cracking, its unity deteriorating, its strength dissipating."

Jack fell just short in a last-minute bid to seize the party's nomination for vice president after Stevenson left the choice to convention delegates, but the effort left him well-positioned for future glory. He schmoozed Democratic bigwigs from across the country, seeking their support. Meanwhile, the nation saw his telegenic face and heard his captivating voice numerous times during the televised convention—when he narrated a film about the party, nominated Stevenson for president, and conceded defeat over the vice-presidential nod to Senator Estes Kefauver. With his eye now squarely on a White House bid in 1960, he moved to further bolster his foreign policy credentials.

As Jack positioned himself for higher office in the summer of 1956, his youngest brother pursued his own global interests with a trip abroad.

5

"The Hour Is Late"

"Less than six months independent," Ted Kennedy wrote from Rabat, Morocco's capital, in September of 1956, "an infant Moroccan state gives more than the impression of an irrepressible collegian. It is feverishly trying to dismantle all the trappings of French rule by replacing them with distinctively Moroccan veneer."

Ted had followed his brothers to Harvard and, after graduating in the spring of 1956, wanted to see more of the world. It would not be his first trip abroad. Not only had he traveled to London with his family when his father was ambassador but, in the summer of 1950 when he was eighteen, Joe and Rose sent him to travel across Europe with his cousin, Joey Gargan, with whom he was very close. Though still a youngster, he displayed a keen appreciation for the geopolitical forces he witnessed. Writing his parents from Trieste, which was then a "free city" partly controlled by the United States and Britain and partly by Yugoslavian forces, Ted noted that in the U.S.-British sector, "everyone hates the British and likes the Americans." On the "outskirts of the city," however, "there are posters blaming the U.S. for intervention in Korea." In Venice, "the Communist Youth movement is ever increasing and they all march around at night in big mobs."[1]

His trip of 1956 was a more avowedly educational venture. At twenty-four, Ted was tall, muscular, dark haired, and ruggedly handsome. He had the look of a man on the move, but he had not yet settled on his future. When he decided to travel after graduation, he asked Jack where to go and Jack suggested Africa, where colonial populations were revolting against their Western rulers; independence movements created five new African countries in 1956 out of former colonies, another in 1957, and two more in 1958. Ted set off for Morocco and Tunisia (each created in 1956) as well as Algeria (which was then still a French colony) with Fred Holborn, one of his Harvard political science instructors. Once again, Joe Kennedy seized the opportunity to raise the public profile of one of his sons by arranging for Ted to write pieces for the International News Service (INS). Jack, meanwhile, used his contacts to arrange high-level meetings for him.

"After three weeks in Morocco," Ted wrote in one of his pieces—which, INS boasted, were "written expressly" for the news service—he was

> convinced that Moroccan nationalism has taken firm hold, that French influence is likely to wane even further, but that the outlines of the Moroccan nation a few years from now are almost impossible to foresee. Changes, long pent-up, are erupting everywhere and moving with incredible speed; an inchoate leadership is still trying to find its footing; and the perspectives of a future foreign policy for Morocco are still wavering and sensitive to foreign negotiations. Finally, the future of Morocco will be determined to a large degree by what happens in the next months in Algeria and what kind of policy the United States can offer Africa by the start of the new year.[2]

After his trip, Ted rendezvoused with an exhausted Jack, who had just come from the tumultuous Democratic National Convention in search of relaxation, for a sail on the Mediterranean. The conventional wisdom, which Ted nourished in his memoirs and interviews, holds that after Ted briefed Jack on what he witnessed in Africa, Jack used those insights to shape his landmark speech of July 1957 in which he urged France to negotiate Algeria's independence and Washington to put its weight behind the effort. In truth, Jack didn't need Ted's insights to shape his views about the developing world. He had witnessed the grassroots fervor sweeping the developing world on his own travels and, in his later years, he spoke passionately about the challenge that it posed for America. He undoubtedly expressed his views at the dinner table in those years when the Kennedys gathered for holidays and vacations. If anything, Ted left for Africa with Jack's views clear in his mind, and his observations echoed what Jack had previously enunciated.

Jack's perspective about the developing world helped shape Ted's views about not only Africa in the 1950s, but about America's struggles in Vietnam, Iraq, and elsewhere in the decades to come.

. . .

When Ted returned to Harvard in 1953 after a two-year exile due to a cheating scandal, he was, as one faculty member put it, "dismissed mostly . . . as a rock-jawed goof-off."[3] Jack later credited his father for pushing Ted to buckle down, transforming him from wayward playboy to legendary policymaker.

Born on February 22, 1932, in Boston, Edward Moore Kennedy was cute and chubby as a child. Though the youngest of nine, he, too, needed to earn his familial stripes. When he was six, Joe Jr. threw him into the waters of Nantucket Sound for failing to carry out a sailing command. At seven, his siblings pressured him into jumping off a rock on the Riviera that was at least twenty feet over the water. "I was pretty scared," he said later, "but they all seemed to be doing it."[4] As a twenty-eight-year-old surrogate for Jack on the presidential campaign trail out West, he ski-jumped from 180 feet even though he had never done anything like it before; suffered a deep bite from a bulldog that "just about took [his] arm off cleanly at the elbow"; rode a tough bronco named "Skyrocket" at a rodeo before the horse threw him to the ground; and was nearly shot by the owner of a 1956 Ford station wagon that he tried to hot-wire and drive to an event.[5]

He, too, was a lonely boy, shuffled among ten different schools in his youth. "That was hard to take," he admitted later, but he hid his loneliness because, as he put it, his brothers also were lonely at boarding school "so I shouldn't complain."[6] When he came home for a weekend, he often arrived to a largely empty house, with his father away for work, his mother traveling for pleasure, Joe Jr. and Jack at Harvard or war, and his other siblings at different boarding schools. His girth escaped neither notice nor comment by his parents and siblings, which must have proved painful. His siblings called him "Biscuits and Muffins" and "Fat Stuff," and in letters among family members in 1940, when he was eight, they routinely labeled him "fat," "fatter than ever," and so on.

Nevertheless, he must have received enough love from his parents to compensate for his loneliness because, unlike Jack, he seemed to harbor no resentments about his upbringing. Joe Kennedy pushed him just as he had pushed his older sons, expressing displeasure when Ted's grades and penmanship didn't measure up but also expressing his unconditional love, reassuring the boy. "You are my pal, aren't you?" Joe asked the eight-year-old in a letter from London, encouraging him to write more often.[7] Particularly striking was Ted's relationship with his mother, who admitted later that she was perhaps the warmest to her youngest child because she knew he would be her last. After Joe and Rose sent Ted, then nine, to join Bobby at Rhode Island's Portsmouth Abbey School in the spring of 1941, Ted recalled, "I got whooping cough and pneumonia, and I was very, very sick. I was in the hospital for about four or five weeks and missed a central part of the year." But unlike with Jack, whom Rose never visited when he was sick for long periods at Choate, Ted said that "Mother just canceled all of her plans, and just she and I went up to Cape Cod and spent the better part of three and a half months up there."[8] While he convalesced in bed, Rose cooked for him and read to him. As his strength returned, the two took walks together.

Rooted and self-confident, Ted found no need to recede into books like Jack or religion like Bobby to assuage his loneliness. Instead, he learned how to make friends quickly. "He ... scans the movie columns," Rose wrote to the other children about him when he was ten, "makes his dates, and goes confidently off without bothering anyone."[9]

The key to his later success, however, may lie less in the love of his parents than in his bond with a grandfather.

. . .

To be sure, Jack, Bobby, and Ted *all* inherited political ambitions, campaign skills, and global interests from *both* of their grandfathers, first-generation Americans who became prominent Democrats in late nineteenth-century Boston.

Joe's father, P. J. Kennedy, capitalized on the relationships he nourished as a saloon keeper to serve five straight one-year terms in the state House and then three straight two-year terms in the state Senate, but he wielded far more political influence as one of Boston's most powerful ward bosses—so powerful, in fact, that he delivered a seconding speech for Grover Cleveland at the 1888 Democratic National Convention in St. Louis. Rose's father, Honey Fitz, worked as an apprentice to a local political boss, delivered speeches on street corners to rally support for the party's favored candidates, and served on the city Common Council, in the U.S. House, and as Boston's mayor in a career in elective office that stretched from 1892 to 1919. Because P.J. died in 1929—when Jack was eleven, Bobby was three, and Ted was not yet born—it was Honey Fitz who shaped their futures far more.

Honey Fitz exuded energy, loved action, and hated idleness. As a boy, he exercised fiercely to strengthen his small frame, running throughout the day and doing sit-ups at night. In his drive to surmount his physical limitations, we see the roots of Jack's relentless efforts to overcome his painful maladies and his later calls for "vigor" to "get this country moving again." Honey Fitz was a man of broad interests, particularly of history and current events, both local and global. When Rose was a child, he took her on tours of historical sites in Boston and on trips across Europe. A voracious reader of books, magazines, and newspapers (as Jack became), he also was an avid collector of information. He'd sit in a chair, with reading material covering the floor in front of him and a pen knife in his hands, to clip news items of interest and pin them to his lapel or, when he ran out of room, elsewhere on his jacket with the straight pins that he carried for that purpose. He maintained the habit in retirement. (Ted, who was born the year Honey Fitz turned sixty-nine, recalled that, as a youngster, he would fetch newspapers for his grandfather and, before long, "his pockets would be bubbling with notes and papers and clippings."[10])

Vibrant, buoyant, and joyful, with blue eyes and a round face, Honey Fitz had a zest for life, for connecting with people, for infusing his stories with laughter and drama to charm and captivate his audiences. An unabashed showman, he found virtually any excuse to mount a chair, table, or stage to deliver a speech or sing a song. Nicknamed "Honey Fitz" for his sweet voice, he would often burst into his favorite song, "Sweet Adeline." He sang it so often on a trip to Central America, Rose later wrote, that one country came to believe it was America's national anthem and, as such, greeted President Franklin Roosevelt with it on his visit there years later, amusing FDR to no end.

But though Honey Fitz influenced all three brothers, it was Ted who spent the most time with him and became the most like him. While at school in West Newton, Massachusetts, he often visited the grandfather who, as he later put it, was "a second parent ... who would listen to my adolescent chatter, my hopes and dreams."[11] Whether they met in his office, lunched in the dining room of his hotel, or walked the streets of Boston, Ted watched as Honey Fitz shook hands, traded stories, dispensed advice, and offered condolences. When Ted entered the tradition-bound Senate at just thirty, he already knew how to stroke egos, slap backs, and trade favors—everything the impatient Jack and Bobby hated to do as senators—and it would prove vital to his legendary ability to turn ideas into policy. By that time, he also knew how to speak convincingly, for he had won a moot court competition as a senior at the University of Virginia Law School in 1959—a competition for which Ted, who was often inarticulate when speaking off the cuff, rehearsed alone in the woods around his house. Joe and Jack labeled Ted the family's best politician while Frank Morrissey, a family intimate, called him "the most naturally gifted political person I've ever met."[12]

Ted's legislative successes, however, were years away. While he was at law school, Jack continued to sound the alarm about America's global challenges.

. . .

"International events in recent months have accelerated in pace," Jack Kennedy wrote in a piece for *Foreign Affairs* in October of 1957, "and have been in a flux not yet comprehended by the leadership of our nation or taken account of in adjustments in the machinery of our foreign policy."

"To an observer in the opposition party," he wrote about Eisenhower's global stewardship, "there appear two central weaknesses in our current foreign policy: first, a failure to appreciate how the forces of nationalism are rewriting the geopolitical map of the world—especially in North Africa, southeastern Europe and the Middle East; and second, a lack of decision and conviction in our leadership, which has recoiled from clearly informing both the people and Congress, which seeks too often to substitute slogans for solutions, which at times has even taken pride in the timidity of its ideas."[13]

The year 1957 was a decisive one for both the nation and Jack. In October the Soviets launched Sputnik I, the world's first artificial satellite, the size of a beach ball and about 185 pounds, that orbited the earth in less than two hours. It ignited a coast-to-coast panic about Moscow's scientific advances and, with a head start in space, its threats to America's security. Leading newspapers and magazines ran breathless stories about Moscow's achievement, while leaders of both parties issued wake-up calls, urging Americans to discard their contented consumerism and support a serious national effort to invest in education, science, and other areas to strengthen America at home and abroad. In November came Sputnik II, which circled the earth with a dog named Laika. That month, the Gaither Report—the product of a committee that Ike appointed after Sputnik I—concluded that America could lose a war with the Soviets, called for massive defense increases, and proposed $30 billion to launch a nationwide program of nuclear fallout shelters.

That year Jack took some steps to raise his national profile on foreign policy. His article in *Foreign Affairs* was one of them, because by writing for America's most influential foreign policy journal, he showed that he was a serious thinker on global affairs. Also in 1957, and with the requisite approval of Senate Majority Leader Lyndon Johnson, he secured a seat on the Foreign Relations Committee, giving him a major new perch from which to influence the nation's foreign policy. Both Sputnik and the Gaither Report would shape his thinking in the months ahead.

Nothing that year, however, did more to raise Jack's profile on foreign affairs, signal his ambition, and highlight his audacity than his Senate speech about what France should do about Algeria.

. . .

"The most powerful single force in the world today," JFK declared on July 2, 1957, "is neither communism nor capitalism, neither the H-bomb nor the guided missile. It is man's eternal desire to be free and independent. The great enemy of that tremendous force of freedom is called, for want of a more precise term, imperialism— and today that means Soviet imperialism and, whether we like it or not, and though they are not to be equated, Western imperialism."

"Thus," he advised,

> the single most important test of American foreign policy today is how we meet the challenge of imperialism, what we do to further man's desire to be free. On this test more than any other, this nation shall be critically judged by the uncommitted millions in Asia and Africa, and anxiously watched by the still hopeful lovers of freedom behind the Iron Curtain. If we fail to meet the challenge of either Soviet or Western imperialism, then no amount of foreign aid, no aggrandizement of armaments, no new pacts or doctrines or high-level conferences can prevent further setbacks to our course and to our security. I am concerned today that we are failing to meet the

challenge of imperialism—on both counts—and thus failing in our responsibilities to the free world.

It was a breakthrough speech for Jack and reflected his years of thought about the developing world. As Ted had witnessed up close a year earlier, France was struggling to retain its grip on Algeria, one of its key African colonies. Nationalists launched a violent campaign in 1954 to oust the French, with "coordinated bombings, murder and sabotage" across the country.[14] Over time, the nationalists beefed up their forces, the French sent more troops to suppress them, and both sides employed brutal tactics that left many hundreds of thousands killed or injured. The nationalists disemboweled their victims, cut off their noses, sliced their faces, and left them to bleed to death. The French, with more than four hundred thousand troops by 1957 and aided by both airpower and Algerian vigilantes of French descent, tortured and killed their enemies in mass numbers. To Jack, France's struggle to retain control raised all the issues of Western colonialism, and its impact on Washington's effort to compete with Moscow across the developing world, with which he had grappled for years.

Dismissing the arguments of U.S. and French diplomats that Algeria was a matter solely for France to resolve, Jack said the war had "damaged" America's "leadership and prestige" at the United Nations; "undermined our relations with Tunisia and Morocco, who naturally have a sense of common cause with the aims of Algerian leaders; [and] affected our standing in the eyes of the free world . . . as well as our moral leadership in the fight against Soviet imperialism in the countries behind the Iron Curtain." In addition, it had "furnished powerful ammunition to anti-Western propagandists throughout Asia and the Middle East, [and] steadily drained the manpower, the resources, and the spirit of one of our oldest and most important allies." Though "reluctant to appear critical of our oldest and first ally," Jack judged the French harshly. France, he said, "seems welded to the same rigid formulas that have governed its actions in Algeria for so long," which was to fight rather than negotiate. Washington, meanwhile, provided Paris with military aid to continue the fight while supporting its dead-end approach to the conflict. "If," he said, "France and the West at large are to have continuing influence in North Africa—and I certainly favor a continuation of French influence in that area—then the essential first step is the independence of Algeria along the lines of Morocco and Tunisia . . . France cannot impose her will upon some 22 million Africans indefinitely. Sooner or later the French will have to recognize the existence of an Algerian state. The sooner, the cheaper in terms of men, money, and a chance to salvage something from the wreckage of the French Union."

Jack's speech, which garnered front-page coverage in the *New York Times* and *Washington Post*, caused no small stir in Paris and Washington. In Paris a motion in Parliament's upper house warned U.S. officials not to interfere in French affairs, while a right-wing group in the body expressed "indignation"; *Le Monde*, France's leading newspaper, termed Jack "badly informed" and "guilty of injustices and excesses"; and Defense Minister Andre Morice said that Jack's speech would just prolong the Algerian crisis and questioned whether he "passes peaceful nights without nightmares." In Washington, Secretary of State John Foster Dulles said that Algeria was mainly France's problem and he would be "very sorry to see it made ours."[15] The criticism only strengthened Jack's resolve. Six days after his speech, he returned to the Senate to dismiss his critics, call Algeria a "deadly time bomb," and restate his main point: "The worldwide struggle against imperialism, the sweep of nationalism, is the most potent factor in foreign affairs today. We can resist it or ignore it, but only for a little while; we can see it exploited by the Soviets, with grave consequences; or we in this country can give it hope and leadership, and thus improve immeasurably our standing and our security."

Jack was so adamant because he thought Western leaders were ignoring the lessons of another colonial conflict.

. . .

"It is an ironic and tragic fact," Jack told a Washington conference on Vietnam in June of 1956, that it was "being held at a time when the news about Vietnam has virtually disappeared from the front pages of the American press, and the American people have all but forgotten the tiny nation for which we are in large measure responsible."

As in Algeria, France was the colonial power in Indochina, which comprised the "Associated States" of Vietnam, Laos, and Cambodia. Japan seized Indochina from France during World War II and France sought to regain it after the war, but Paris never provided enough local autonomy to satisfy Ho Chi Minh and his Vietminh, and they launched a guerilla campaign for independence. By 1946 the French were bogged down in this mostly agricultural country of twenty-three million, and Washington was supporting them with military aid. Because Ho espoused communist thoughts, America's leaders—including Jack—viewed France's struggle as another Cold War fight against Soviet-led communism. By 1954 more than five hundred thousand French-led troops were fighting more than three hundred thousand Vietminh but, while out-numbered, the latter often held the upper hand by seizing the initiative. "Darkness is the unfailing ally of the Vietminh," a U.S. House delegation wrote early that year after visiting the area. "The Vietnamese farmer by day becomes a Vietminh soldier or collaborationist at night. Thus the enemy is nowhere and everywhere. Communist intelligence blankets the entire country."[16]

"The time has come," Jack told the Senate in April of 1954, "for the American people to be told the blunt truth about Indochina." Despite happy talk from Ike, other top U.S. officials, and military leaders, which Jack catalogued in great detail, France was not winning the war, raising serious questions about America's approach to it. As Jack noted, Secretary of State Dulles had hinted that Washington would send troops to prevent a communist takeover, and the French wouldn't likely continue their effort unless, at the very least, Washington provided greater sums of aid. While Jack favored joint U.S.-French action of some kind to defeat the communists, he said that "to pour money, materiel, and men into the jungles of Indochina without at least a remote prospect of victory would be dangerously futile and self-destructive." "It is time, therefore," he said, "for us to face the stark reality of the difficult situation before us without the false hopes which predictions of military victory and assurances of complete independence have given us in the past."

At the Washington conference two years later, however, Jack lauded what he considered a sharp turnaround. After the Vietminh routed the French at Dien Bien Phu in 1954, global powers split Vietnam into a communist-backed North and a West-backed South. Washington showered the South with economic, military, and other aid, and Jack considered its leader, Ngo Dinh Diem, a strong and committed democrat. After assuming the presidency in late 1955, one Vietnam expert later wrote, Diem "instituted a land reform program, improved agriculture, established an effective antimalaria program, and improved the educational system."[17] Now, to ensure that the South remained a strong anti-communist bulwark, Jack recommended that Washington expand its assistance by offering the South a "revolution—a political, economic, and social revolution far superior to anything the communists can offer—far more peaceful, far more democratic, and far more locally controlled."

By the late 1950s, Jack considered the South Vietnam of 1956 a lonely exception to America's incompetence in the developing world. Captivated by *The Ugly American*—the bestselling fictional account of 1958 about America's diplomats in Asia who hobnobbed with elites while ignoring local culture—he sent it to every senator and, with a few other public leaders, promoted it in a *New York Times* ad in January of 1959.

. . .

"The hour is late," Jack told the Senate in classically Churchillian terms in June of 1960, "but the agenda is long."

Five months after announcing that he was running for president, John F. Kennedy outlined a twelve-point plan to restore the nation's defenses and rethink its global strategies. The Cold War consensus remained intact; the two parties agreed that America's top foreign

"The Hour Is Late"

policy goal was still to contain the Soviets. Jack sought to broaden the discussion of how best to do it during a time of Soviet military and economic advances. "So let us abandon the useless discussion," he suggested, "of who can best 'stand up to Khrushchev,' or whether a 'hard' or 'soft' line is preferable. Our task is to rebuild our strength, and the strength of the free world—to prove to the Soviets that time and the course of history are not on their side, that the balance of world power is not shifting their way—and that therefore peaceful settlement is essential to mutual survival." America's leaders, he said, must "devise a national strategy . . . a comprehensive set of carefully prepared, long-term policies designed to increase the strength of the non-communist world." Without it, America would enter "the most critical period in our nation's history since that bleak winter at Valley Forge" and "our national security, our survival itself, will be in peril."

Jack called for creating a nuclear capacity that can survive "a surprise attack," restoring America's ability to fight a limited war effectively, rebuilding NATO, boosting capital to the developing world's undeveloped areas, making Latin American democracies full partners with the West, finding new ways to help Arab states and speed their acceptance of Israel, helping new African nations succeed economically so they won't turn toward Moscow, defending Berlin and addressing the broader challenges of a divided Germany and Europe, preparing new tools to loosen Moscow's grip on Eastern Europe, reassessing America's policy toward mainland China, developing new programs for peace and arms control, and strengthening America at home so it can more effectively defend the free world.

Jack's plan reflected proposals that he had unveiled all over America in the late 1950s. He had warned of two "gaps." Of a "missile gap" with Moscow that later proved more fiction than fact, he declared, "We . . . are about to lose the power foundation that has long stood behind our basic military and diplomatic strategy." Of an "economic gap" between the developed and developing world, he complained that, unlike the Soviet Union and China, "The United States of America, the richest nation on earth, has not given the poorer nations new hope." Rather than let fiscal and political concerns limit America's "foreign economic policy," he said, "It is time now for that effort to be based upon the requirements of the international economic situation—and our own national security." "The hard, tough question for the next decade," he declared, reviving the central issue of *Why England Slept*, "is whether any free society . . . can meet the single-minded advance of the communist system. . . . Have we the nerve and the will?" Foreign policy, he said, was the "one supreme, overriding issue confronting the American public today—one critical issue that affects, and is affected by, everything else we do as a nation and as individuals."

To a great extent, Jack's obsession with foreign affairs, particularly with the Soviets, reflected America's concerns. "The overwhelming majority of those interviewed," Gallup reported in July of 1960, "regard relations with Russia and the rest of the world as being the primary problem facing the nation today."[18]

6

"If It Wasn't for the Russians"

"It really is true," JFK told Richard Nixon in the Oval Office after a U.S.-backed effort to topple Fidel Castro collapsed at the Bay of Pigs in April of 1961, "that foreign policy is the only important issue for a President to handle, isn't it? I mean who gives a shit if the minimum wage is $1.15 or $1.25, in comparison to something like this?"[1]

As president, Jack governed in that spirit from the start. In his inaugural address of January 20, he included only two words on domestic policy—and only after an aide suggested that he at least acknowledge domestic affairs. In his State of the Union address ten days later, he told Congress, "No man entering upon this office, regardless of his party, regardless of his previous service in Washington, could fail to be staggered upon learning... the harsh enormity of the trials through which we must pass in the next four years. Each day the crises multiply. Each day their solution grows more difficult. Each day we draw nearer the hour of maximum danger, as weapons spread and hostile forces grow stronger ... the tide of events has been running out and time has not been our friend."

Jack did not expect a Cold War victory on his watch. He viewed the war in broad historical terms, as part of "a long twilight struggle ... against the common enemies of man: tyranny, poverty, disease, and war itself." He sought, however, to inject more urgency into America's effort and to make progress against the Soviets. In March he outlined his "flexible response" strategy of more defense dollars and more tools to address multiplying challenges.[2] That spring and summer, he spoke of a "relentless" and "bitter" struggle, a "deadly challenge," an "age-old battle for the survival of liberty itself," and "the need for courage and perseverance in the years to come."

He wanted to change the perception, which he sensed that people around the world shared, that the Soviets were on the move. That explains why he was so obsessed with Khrushchev's twenty-thousand-word speech of early January to communist party apparatchiks, in which he predicted communism's ultimate victory over capitalism and advocated national "wars of liberation" around the world to expand communist influence. Viewing the speech as an authoritative guide to Moscow's foreign policy, Jack read it many times, recited parts of it at Cabinet meetings and over dinner with friends, and sent it to every member of the National Security Council with instructions to "read, mark, learn and inwardly digest" and help him craft polices "tailored to meet these kinds of problems."[3]

Jack's desire to change global perceptions also explains why he broke with longstanding tradition: rather than deliver one State of the Union address in 1961, he delivered a second in May. He began where Khrushchev had ended. "The great battleground for the defense and expansion of freedom today," he declared, "is the whole southern half of the globe—Asia, Latin American, Africa and the Middle East—the lands of the rising people," the very places where Moscow sought victory in "wars of liberation." The Soviets, he explained, were trying to exploit the revolutions under way, sending arms and agitators to stoke guerilla war. He proposed steps to strengthen America's economy so that it could support a more robust foreign policy, more foreign aid and military assistance to help developing nations succeed in freedom rather than fall to communism, and a reorganized army with more dollars to "increase its non-nuclear firepower."

As he spoke in May of battles to come, he was still cleaning up a foreign policy disaster of a month earlier.

. . .

"If It Wasn't for the Russians"

Asked later how he had managed to ensnare himself in the Bay of Pigs fiasco, Jack acknowledged that he was unduly influenced by the outsized reputations of those who foisted the plan upon him.

"I believed the things I'd read in the magazines about all these people in government," he told the Associated Press' Jack Bell—people like Arleigh Burke, the stern, stately chief of naval operations who earned the nickname "Thirty-One Knot" during World War II for ordering U.S. destroyers under his command to travel at that speed; and Allen Dulles, the bespectacled, pipe-smoking CIA director. "I'd been reading a lot about them. I didn't really know them. I didn't know how good they were, but everything I read said they were tremendous. . . . What do you do in a case like that? I looked at all this," he said of the plan, "and it didn't look good. But look at the advice I had. . . . I couldn't judge the people I got the advice from."[4]

The CIA had cooked up the plan in the last months of Eisenhower's presidency. Some 1,200 to 1,500 Cuban exiles, trained by the CIA in Guatemala, would invade the island, supported from the air by B-26 bombers that other Cuban exiles would fly. Once the exiles had established a beachhead, many thousands of Castro opponents inside Cuba were expected to rise up and topple him. That way Washington would remove a troubling figure and potentially destabilizing regional force, presiding on an island just ninety miles from America's shore, without its fingerprints on the dirty work. If worse came to worse and Castro withstood the challenge, the guerillas would scamper into the mountains, establish an internal force, and harass the Cuban leader.

That Castro, in particular, was the target of a U.S.-backed coup under JFK, in particular, was more than a little ironic. After all, didn't Castro's rise confirm Jack's long-held views about the developing world? He seized power on January 1, 1959, promising to improve the lives of long-suffering Cubans, after a six-year guerilla effort against Fulgencio Batista, the U.S.-backed dictator. Wasn't this the very kind of revolutionary activity that Jack had predicted in the face of Western colonialism? Wasn't it especially predictable under Batista, a corrupt and ruthless leader who controlled Cuba's press, universities, and Congress and maintained power through rigged elections?

At first, neither America's leaders nor its people knew what to make of the bearded, thirty-two-year-old Castro, who preferred the khaki uniform of a revolutionary to formal attire. He toured the United States for eleven days in April of 1959 and was met by roaring crowds upon his arrival in Washington. On TV, in speeches, and in meetings that included a two-hour session with Vice President Nixon, he denied that he was a communist, expressed support for democracy, and said he would hold elections in Cuba. But he wouldn't set a firm date for elections, and he was evasive about whether his loyalties rested with Washington or Moscow. Back in Cuba, his regime continued to execute hundreds of former Batista officials and others by firing squad for their "war crimes."

When Castro nationalized all U.S.-owned oil refineries, factories, casinos, and other businesses in 1960, fueling fears that he was establishing a communist dictatorship, Eisenhower ended Washington's ties to the island and imposed a trade embargo. In launching the Bay of Pigs, JFK sought to topple Castro both to eliminate a communist regime and to ensure that it wouldn't stoke communist revolutions across Latin America—but not to derail the dreams that Castro had inspired among the Cuban people. In a sense, he wanted to put the revolution that Castro had launched on a democratic track.

. . .

The fiasco shook Jack to his core, for he was a man of reason and logic who, in this case, was swept up by emotion.

He was just weeks on the job when he received the plan. Some White House and State Department officials warned him that a U.S.-backed military operation of this kind would cause tensions with America's allies in Europe, Asia, Africa, and Latin America. While acknowledging the potential hit to America's image, Jack worried that he'd suffer politically if word got out, as it surely would, that he had rejected a plan to topple a communist foe. If nothing else, the Cuban exiles that the CIA was training would blast the new president for losing his nerve. Though he worried about prospects for success, he lacked the confidence to challenge the generals and spymasters of whom he had thought so highly, to ask tough questions, and to draw his own conclusions. As the plan collapsed not long after its launch on April 15, with Castro's forces killing more than a hundred of the exiles and imprisoning most of the others, he blamed himself for his stupidity and, for days, was inconsolable.

"How could I have done it?" he asked repeatedly aloud as he unburdened himself in front of aides and friends. "How could I have been so stupid?" He rubbed his eyes and mumbled to himself about the fiasco during meetings on other subjects. Though probably never serious, he told his closest friend, Lem Billings, and others in the days right after the fiasco that, with communist forces likely to make gains across the world in the years ahead, he wouldn't run for reelection. "Lyndon can have it in 1964," he said dismissively.[5] On the evening of April 18, as the magnitude of disaster grew apparent, he left an Oval Office meeting to wander around the Rose Garden by himself for nearly an hour. The next morning, after weeping in his bedroom, he came to a meeting with Senator Albert Gore "with messed hair and his tie askew" and seemed "extremely bitter."[6]

When, around that time, Jack summoned Senator Barry Goldwater, a likely Republican candidate to run against him in 1964, to the White House for a briefing on the disaster, he entered the room where Goldwater was sitting and, with a cigar in his mouth, blurted, "Do you want this . . . job?"[7]

. . .

Nothing about the plan, codenamed Operation Zapata, made sense—not the timing, not the content, not the rollout, and not the aftermath.

For starters, the invasion came just two weeks after Jack unveiled his Alliance for Progress, an economic development program for Latin America that was designed to raise living standards across the region and burnish America's image. It reflected his view that, to strengthen America's ties to the developing world, Washington must no longer resort to heavy-handed imperialism. With the Bay of Pigs, however, Washington was doing just that, toppling a hostile government in the region through military action. Not surprisingly, the plan lowered much of the hope that Jack had raised in the region with his talk of new ties and a more enlightened U.S. approach.

Had it worked, America's regional allies surely would have rallied to its side; they were no more enthralled with the bearded revolutionary in Havana than Washington was. Victory was a remote possibility from the start, however. When, in early April, JFK discussed the plan with Dean Acheson, the former secretary of state, while the two sat on a bench on the White House grounds, a surprised Acheson first expressed hope that Jack wasn't serious about approving it. "I don't know if I'm serious or not," he replied, "but this is the proposal and I've been thinking about it and it is serious in that sense." Horrified, Acheson observed that no one needed to "call in Price Waterhouse to discover that 1,500 Cubans weren't as good as [Castro's force of] 25,000 Cubans."[8] Besides, Washington could hardly keep its behind-the-scenes involvement a secret when, at that very time, America's leading newspapers were writing stories about the CIA training exiles to invade the island.

Moreover, the plan itself was a moving target. Jack had specified more than once that, if it failed and the exiles were stranded, he wouldn't send U.S. military forces to save them or take over the operation. Some top U.S. intelligence and military officials assumed that he'd have to change his mind if failure grew imminent, and some CIA officials who were training the exiles told them as much. Nor did Jack know that when CIA planners moved the landing site to the Bay of Pigs, about a hundred miles west of the original site in Trinidad, to make the plan look more like a guerilla operation, that left eighty miles of swamp between the beach and the mountains, making the exiles' escape impossible. Meanwhile, America's ambassador to the United Nations, Adlai Stevenson, publicly denied America's involvement as the plan unfolded because White House officials chose not to give him the details beforehand, leaving him publicly embarrassed and privately seething as the truth emerged.

That the Bay of Pigs subjected Jack to public mocking must have been especially cutting. When he was running for president, such Democratic icons as Harry Truman, Dean Acheson, and House Speaker Sam Rayburn wondered aloud whether he was seasoned enough for the job. After the fiasco, he was compared more than once to a child who had played with dangerous toys and lived to regret it. Acheson, who was in Europe when it unfolded, irritated Jack two months later in a speech to the Foreign Service when he said, "[The Europeans] began to have the sort of unbelieving attitude that somebody might have as he watched a gifted amateur practicing with a boomerang and suddenly knocking himself cold. They were amazed that so inexperienced a person should play with so lethal a weapon." Sir Howard Beale, Australia's ambassador to the United States at the time, recalled that "like the child who has put his hand on a hot stove—the President learned very quickly."[9]

Indeed, he *did* learn quickly, and he applied the lessons to the major global challenges that would come his way.

· · ·

"It was quite clear," a friend of Jack's said, that he was "a different person" after the Bay of Pigs, "more serious, more aware, deeper."[10] Gone was the airy confidence of late 1960, when he said of the presidency, "Sure, it's a big job. But I don't know anybody who can do it any better than I can."[11] Now, an aide recalled, "the exhilaration of the job was gone. He was no longer the young conquering hero . . . the young man smoking his cigar with his friends and telling them how much fun it was."[12] With the disaster just days old, he walked with diplomat Charles Bohlen in the Rose Garden and said "he had realized he would have to go much deeper into any operation of the nature of this kind with the consequences it could have than he had in regards to the Bay of Pigs."[13] Gone, too, was the airy confidence of some others, the sense, as Rayburn put it in the early days of his presidency, that JFK was "a man of destiny."[14] "There's a little pause because of Cuba," one top Democrat said. "We're taking a second look."[15]

While coming to grips with his role as commander in chief, with all the gravity that the title implied, Jack turned to Bobby. It was a lesson that Joe Kennedy had drilled into his sons: rely on one another before anyone else. Reflecting the doubts that lingered in his mind, Jack brought Bobby into the last few days of discussion about the plan. Based on what the CIA's deputy director, Richard Bissell, told him in a briefing, Bobby supported it. When it faltered almost immediately, Jack called Bobby in Williamsburg, Virginia, where he was preparing to speak at lunch to United Press International's managing editors. As soon as Bobby finished, he raced back to join the White House meetings that would continue for days. Before long, he came to share Jack's hostile feelings toward those who sold the plan based on false hopes and incomplete information.

"I made a mistake in putting Bobby in the Justice Department," JFK told Arthur Schlesinger Jr. while the disaster was unfolding. "He is wasted there. . . . Bobby should be in CIA."[16] Jack didn't move Bobby but, from then on, he leaned on him far more on all matters of foreign policy. For starters, he appointed Bobby, along with Allen Dulles and Arleigh Burke, to a Cuba Study Group, chaired by General Maxwell Taylor, to investigate the failure. After questioning some fifty witnesses, Bobby reached the same conclusion as Jack—that the president must weigh information and evaluate those providing it more carefully.

From there, Bobby's foreign policy portfolio grew exponentially. Though, as attorney general, he didn't sit on the National Security Council, Jack asked him to attend its meetings. He flew to the Ivory Coast as Jack's emissary in August of 1961 as it celebrated its independence, and he took a month-long "good will" tour across Europe and Asia in early 1962 to burnish America's global image. Later that year, he pushed, prodded, and challenged the president's top advisors during the Cuban Missile Crisis to find a way to remove the Soviet missiles without triggering a nuclear exchange, and he used back channels to send messages from JFK to Khrushchev at this and other tense moments. Typically, he spoke to Jack a few times a day by phone and often saw him at the White House. Working long days, evenings, and weekends helping Jack manage global crises and running the Justice Department, Bobby was focused, intense, direct, decisive, and demanding. He also was often brash, cocky, impatient, and dismissive, and his sharp elbows and bombastic outbursts left scars on everyone from mid-level staffers to top officials. He was wholly committed to his brother's success, and he didn't want anyone, or anything, to stand in the way.

Bobby's influence matched, if not exceeded, that of such famed presidential consiglieres as Wilson's Colonel House, FDR's Harry Hopkins, and Ike's Sherman Adams. He was the "man to see," the "Assistant President" or, as *LIFE* tabbed him for a cover piece in January of 1962, "The No. 2 Man in Washington." He was Jack's eyes and ears around the administration and even his voice, delivering the president's harsh assessments so that Jack wouldn't have to do so—such as when he angrily told Jack's foreign policy team a week after the Bay of Pigs that "we'd be better off if you just quit," while Jack sat quietly in a chair, tapping his front teeth with a pencil eraser.[17]

Though he was clearly a valued partner and a vital sounding board for Jack, Bobby's exalted stature brought out some of his worst qualities as the two brothers plotted their next move against Castro.

. . .

John F. Kennedy was fascinated by unconventional warfare, for it spoke to his sense of daring, his thirst for out-of-the-box thinking, and his desire to respond creatively to Khrushchev's national "wars of liberation." He was excited that the CIA was "experimenting with some of the gadgetry described in the fictional Bond adventures, such as the tiny radio beeper that could be attached to the underside of an escape car."[18]

Soon after assuming office, Jack ordered the Defense Department to develop "counter-guerilla" forces; authorized $19 million to train three thousand special forces (who became the Green Berets); sought more counterinsurgency funds from Congress; ordered U.S. ambassadors to support U.S. counterinsurgency efforts in the countries where they were stationed; directed Defense Secretary Robert McNamara to create academies to train Latin American police to confront communist guerillas; and removed Under Secretary of State Chester Bowles because he was a consistent skeptic of the administration's counterinsurgency plans. Jack created the "Special Group (CI)" of top security officials to "assure" the most effective administration effort "in preventing and resisting subversive insurgency and related forms of indirect aggression in friendly countries,"[19] and he authorized Operation Mongoose, which Bobby would run, to topple Castro.

For all of Jack's enthusiasm, however, Bobby was the administration's biggest fan of counterinsurgency, and he reportedly coined the term. To him, it was a mix of guerilla warfare and social do-goodism or, in his words, "social reform under pressure." Special forces would undermine communist governments or confront communist guerillas, but they also would help build roads, schools, and hospitals to improve living conditions and nourish support for Western values. "My idea," Bobby wrote in his notes of late 1961, around the time that Jack tapped him for Operation Mongoose, "is to stir things up on the island [of Cuba] with espionage, sabotage, general disorder, run & operated by Cubans themselves."[20] He had a naïve, romantic view of it all, with unrealistic expectations of what it could accomplish. But no one doubted his sincerity. He invited members of the special forces to his home, where they showed his kids how to swing from trees, and he kept a green beret on his desk at work.

Though the administration targeted countries as far away as Laos, South Vietnam, Thailand, and Burma for counterinsurgency, Bobby's big target was Cuba. He was obsessed with toppling Castro because the young revolutionary had bested his brother at the Bay of Pigs and also because U.S. national security officials feared that Castro would export his revolution across Latin America. He framed this challenge, as he did with so many others, in terms of good and evil. Bobby was "a wild man on this," the CIA's Richard Bissell remembered, calling the agency nearly every day for updates, pushing everyone to work harder, do more.[21] Impatient for results, dismissive of practical concerns, he would slam his papers on his desk or knock

"If It Wasn't for the Russians"

over a chair in frustration. He harshly cross-examined officials in front of others, and they often left the experience embittered. When Bowles raised concerns about the feasibility of this or that plan, Bobby caustically questioned his courage. That Castro outlasted both Jack and Bobby by many years spoke not only to the Cuban leader's wiliness but also to the dubious efforts to oust him.

Although, after the Bay of Pigs, Jack shared Bobby's view that Castro must go, the president was more concerned about how the fiasco made him look to Khrushchev, with whom he would meet in Vienna in June.

. . .

"It's so damned hard," a teary-eyed JFK said on Air Force One as he pondered the disastrous summit of days earlier at which Khrushchev threatened to close off West Berlin, which sat in East Germany but was under U.S. control.

Khrushchev baffled him, for neither rational discussion nor lighthearted charm—Jack's standbys to win arguments and nourish relationships—eased his hostility. Jack had, he later told a friend, "never come face-to-face with such evil."[22] His top Soviet experts and foreign leaders like France's Charles de Gaulle had advised him to expect a blustery Khrushchev in Vienna and ignore his histrionics. Jack, however, had reason to expect something better. In the months leading up to their summit, the two had agreed to communicate directly through private letters, congratulated one another on their countries' space launches that spring, and expressed hopes of making progress on issues of conflict and laying a stronger foundation for U.S.-Soviet peace. After their sharp private exchanges during the Bay of Pigs fiasco, the two agreed to set aside their differences over that issue and move ahead. In Vienna, however, Khrushchev was shockingly cold and unmovable. "I've never known anyone in politics like him," Jack said later.[23]

Berated by Khrushchev, who wagged his finger in his face as they strolled outside, Jack told friends, aides, and trusted reporters that he felt "savaged." He worried that, less than two months after he had chosen not to rescue the Bay of Pigs operation, the Soviet leader thought that he was too "weak" and "stupid" to defend America's interests. (Khrushchev suggested as much to his colleagues during the summit.) When Khrushchev repeated his threat to sign a peace treaty by December 31 with East Germany, which could then annex all of Berlin, Jack said that such a move would trigger a U.S. military response. Jack knew that he could stop the Soviets only by using nuclear weapons. Having experienced the horrors of war, the thought of igniting a nuclear World War III overwhelmed him. "If you could think only of yourself," he said, sitting in his undershorts on Air Force One, "it would be easy to say you'd press the button. And easy to press it, too. You can't just think about yourself. There are generations involved. It really doesn't matter as far as you and I are concerned. I've had a full life. What really matters is all the children."[24]

After returning to Washington, Jack grew obsessed with the Berlin crisis—"imprisoned" by it, as Interior Secretary Stewart Udall put it. Bobby used to ask Jack about once a week how he liked being president. Around this time, he routinely answered, "If it wasn't for the Russians, there's no question it would be the best job in the world."[25] Jack concluded that he couldn't back down over Berlin, even if that meant war. If forced from the city, the United States would lose all credibility with friends and foes alike. He, Bobby, and other top U.S. officials reiterated Washington's resolve through back channels to Khrushchev. While privately skeptical, the Soviet leader showcased his own resolve by announcing that he was cancelling a scheduled demobilization of 1.2 million of Moscow's three million men in uniform and boosting defense spending by a third.

"West Berlin . . . has now become—as never before—the great testing place of Western courage and will, a focal point where our solemn commitments stretching back over the years since 1945 and Soviet ambitions now meet in basic confrontation," Jack declared in a July 25 TV address from the Oval Office, marking his response to Khrushchev. "We cannot and will not permit the communists to drive us out of Berlin, either gradually or by force." He proposed a $3.25 billion boost for defense; increases in Army, Navy, and Air Force personnel; a tripling of draft calls; the authority to order reserves to active duty, extend tours, and call up other reserves; a reactivating of "many" ships and planes that were headed for "retirement"; and $207 million to fund civil defense measures that would better protect Americans in the event of nuclear attack. "To sum it all up," Jack said, "we seek peace—but we shall not surrender." Privately, Bobby pegged the chance of war at one in five.

As tensions mounted in the coming days, Khrushchev settled on a peaceful solution, though it offended America's sensibilities. For many months, thousands of East Berliners had been fleeing to the West, and heightened U.S.-Soviet tensions after Vienna boosted their numbers sharply. Jack and top U.S. officials knew that Khrushchev would have to curtail the exodus at some point. While J. William Fulbright, the Senate Foreign Relations Committee's chairman, expressed surprise on ABC's *Issues and Answers* on July 30 that the Soviets hadn't yet closed the border, Jack suggested privately that the Soviets might have to build a wall. When they began doing so on August 13, erecting barbed wire that they soon replaced with the Berlin Wall, he was more relieved than angered. "Why would Khrushchev put up a wall if he really intended to seize West Berlin?" he mused. "There wouldn't be any need of a wall if he occupied the whole city. This is his way out of his predicament. It's not a very nice solution, but a wall is a hell of a lot better than a war."[26]

As Jack savored the end of the Berlin crisis, his youngest brother was returning from a month-long trip to Latin America and preparing to relay his thoughts to his potential constituents—the good people of Massachusetts.

. . .

"Some 200 million human beings in Latin America are demanding membership in the 20th century," Ted Kennedy wrote in September of 1961 at the start of his five-part series for the *Boston Globe*. "They will no longer tolerate the ancient caste system under which most of them have lived lives of ordered frustration. They want freedom from poverty, ignorance, and indignity. They want opportunity and a degree of social justice. They may choose democracy. They would easily be seduced by communism."[27]

After Jack's election of nearly a year earlier, Ted hoped to influence America's foreign policy from within his brother's administration. "I was interested in arms control," Ted recalled. The Cold War had heated up in 1960 as U.S.-Soviet tensions grew over Berlin, the United States installed ballistic missiles in Italy, and the Soviets shot down a U-2 spy plane and paraded its pilot, Francis Gary Powers, before the world. Knowing that Jack would make arms control a high priority, Ted recalled, "I had this well-thought-out rationale." When he went to see Jack soon after the election, however, Jack turned him down. "You're interested in getting into elective politics, aren't you?" Jack asked. When Ted acknowledged that he was, Jack replied, "Well, you ought to leave right away and go back to Massachusetts."[28]

The president then had another thought. Before returning to Massachusetts, he told Ted, "go back to Africa."[29] Jack called the Senate Foreign Relations Committee and talked to Chief of Staff Carl Marcy, who told him that three Democratic senators had left on a fact-finding trip to Africa two days earlier and that if Ted left that night, he could catch up with them in Rhodesia (now Zimbabwe). Ted went home, gathered his things, and rushed to the airport. Once he landed overseas, U.S. reporters who were covering the trip of the three senators treated him kindly. "Mr. Kennedy is making the flight here from Washington at his brother's request," the *New York Times* reported, "and will report directly to the President-elect."[30] "Informed sources," United Press International wrote in a piece that appeared in the *Boston Globe*, "said Kennedy in particular made a favorable impression in Lagos and the American group's visit helped American prestige in Nigeria."[31]

Ted was eyeing a 1962 run for the Senate seat that Jack relinquished upon assuming the presidency; at Jack's request, the Massachusetts governor, Foster Furcolo, had appointed one of Jack's Harvard roommates to fill the seat until Ted (presumably) won it.

Over the next two years, Ted laid the groundwork in part by continuing his travels, enriching his knowledge of the world, and capitalizing on the publicity. In May of 1961, he and his wife, Joan, took a one-week "good will" trip to Italy for the centennial celebration of Italian unification, during which he met with the pope, Italy's president, and other notables.

Two months later, Ted set off on a four-week tour of nine Latin American countries and offered his impressions through the *Boston Globe*. He left in July, returned in August, and saw his pieces run in September.

. . .

"The crisis is today," Ted wrote about the region. "For democracy can win in Latin America, and cannot afford to lose."

Through his five-part series, he seemed every bit the Cold Warrior as Jack and Bobby, and he described U.S.-Soviet competition in the developing world in the same urgent terms. He also deployed the same sharp turn of phrase that marked his brothers' writings. "If Latin America is to raise itself by its own bootstraps," he wrote, "Uncle Sam realizes that it is first necessary to help provide straps for the boots." "The danger is great," he added. "Hunger, sickness, illiteracy and despair—the four horsemen of communism—are on the loose throughout most of the area." With Jack, in the summer of 1961, implementing his Alliance for Progress for the region, Ted reinforced Jack's view that raising living standards was key to convincing the masses to choose democracy over communism.

"Peasants in most of the nine countries I visited . . . spoke in anger and despair," he wrote.

One said simply: "To farm is to starve. . . ." I talked with men who literally had no roof to shelter their families . . . with women prematurely twisted into old age by deprivation . . . with homeless and parentless children living by their stealth and wits in the streets— and with one boy who had been sold by a mother who could not feed him. I read the medical report of . . . the more fortunate industrial workers who occupied a housing project. It showed: Ninety-five percent of those examined had intestinal parasites; 40 percent had hook worm; 60 percent had round worm; at least 40 percent were classed as "dangerously ill." Some were infected by as many as 12 different types of parasites.

Moreover, rampant lawlessness and corruption impeded efforts to reduce poverty and expand opportunity. "Why talk of laws?" a Columbian peasant asked Ted. "There are many land-reform laws in Latin America—but where is there any real land reform?" In Peru, Ted reported that 240 peasants received a landowner's permission to plant corn on unused land. But, with the help of armed guards, the landowner later seized the crops—and the peasants who protested were killed, wounded, or imprisoned. "The same problems, frustration, and distrust that have aroused peasants in Columbia and Peru," Ted wrote, "exist, in greater or less degree, in most parts of Latin America." The ramifications for America's regional interests were ominous, he suggested. "The frightful plight of the Latin-American peasant and the political confusion of the student groups offer obviously attractive opportunities for exploitation by the foes of democracy in the nations south of our border."

Just as Jack had blamed America's missteps for Soviet gains across Asia, Ted tied America's missteps to communist inroads in Latin America. U.S.-backed governments, he wrote, were "corrupt" or "inept"; industry was "poorly managed"; most labor unions were ineffective; and "much of our aid to the Latin American governments was being wasted in showy but impractical projects," with some "stolen by venal officials." Moscow, Beijing, and Havana were promoting communism through the schools they created and books they distributed, and Ted estimated that "the Communists" were spending four hundred times as much as the United States on propaganda literature. "You send food, which is necessary," a Latin American official told him, "and help build roads, which is commendable— but the Communists publish and supply most of the books, pamphlets, and other reading material. It is not enough to feed the body: democracy must also feed the Latin American mind."

"Given sufficient time," Ted summed, making the stakes for Washington crystal clear, "freedom will win. But will there be time—or has long neglect and poverty made the people of Latin America impatient for the kind of swift solution promised by Red propagandists? This is the decisive question."

. . .

By now, all three Kennedy brothers had witnessed America's competition with the Soviets across the developing world up close, and they all had expressed fears that Washington was losing the battle.

Jack recognized that the issue wasn't just what Washington offered the restive masses of Asia, Africa, and Latin America in economic aid, political support, and moral backing; it was also how, in its behavior at home and abroad, the United States was presenting itself to the world. His desire to improve America's global image shaped not only his foreign policy but his domestic policy as well.

7

"Whether a Free Society Can Compete"

"We are a goldfish bowl before the world," Jack Kennedy said during his second presidential debate with Richard Nixon. "We have to practice what we preach. We set a very high standard for ourselves. The communists do not. They set a low standard of materialism. We preach in the Declaration of Independence and in the Constitution, in the statements of our greatest leaders, we preach very high standards; and if we're not going to be charged before the world with hypocrisy, we have to meet those standards."

Focused on America's competition with the Soviets, Jack obsessed over its image. On his travels as a House member and senator, he found the nation's efforts to court global audiences severely wanting. Running for president, he argued that America must be a "beacon for all mankind," an example to emulate. "We defend freedom," he declared in Waterbury, Connecticut, just before Election Day. "If we succeed here, if we can build a strong and vital society, then the cause of freedom is strengthened. If we fail here, if we drift, if we lie at anchor, if we don't provide an example of what freedom can do in the 1960s, then we have betrayed not only ourselves and our destiny, but all those who desire to be free and are not free."

As president, Jack's interest in burnishing America's image shaped his appointments to top diplomatic positions, fueled his desire to create the Alliance for Progress and Peace Corps, and drove other key elements of his foreign policy. More strikingly, it also shaped much of his domestic agenda, in particular driving his response to the civil rights movement and his focus on the space program.

From his own travels, Bobby was every bit as concerned about America's image. After Jack's election, Bobby convinced him (after what he called a "rather strong argument") not to appoint J. William Fulbright, the Senate Foreign Relations Committee's chairman, as secretary of state—as Jack was considering—because Bobby thought that Fulbright's poor civil rights record would tarnish America's image among nations of color.[1] As attorney general, Bobby worked to prevent violence when blacks marched for civil rights or sought entry into segregated colleges, spoke around the nation about how America's racial problems were hurting its image overseas, and toured Europe and Asia to promote U.S.-led freedom over Soviet-led communism.

"We must be quite aware of the fact," Bobby declared at the University of Georgia Law School in May of 1961, "that 50 percent of the countries in the United Nations are not white; that around the world, in Africa, South America, and Asia, people whose skins are a different color than ours are on the move to gain their measure of freedom and liberty." They're deciding, he said, between "the evil promises of communist tyranny and the honorable promises of Anglo-American liberty."

. . .

"We preach freedom around the world, and we mean it," JFK declared in his landmark TV address of June 11, 1963, on civil rights, which he partly improvised because he didn't have a full draft in front of him, "and we cherish our freedom here at home, but are we to say to the world, and much more importantly, to each other that this is the land of the free except for the Negroes; that we have no second-class citizens except Negroes; that we have no class or caste system, no ghettoes, no master race except with respect to Negroes?"

Jack was not the first president to grapple with the global implications of America's race problems. In the late 1940s, blacks (including black soldiers who had served the nation in war) were beaten, maimed, or killed in waves of violence across the South. In a high-profile standoff in Arkansas in 1957, Governor Orval Faubus refused to let nine blacks attend Little Rock's Central High School, forcing Eisenhower to send paratroopers and federalize the Arkansas National Guard to reverse Faubus's decision. In the developing world, newspapers covered such events in great detail and Moscow exploited them to secure the loyalty of nonaligned countries. "The colour bar," a columnist in Ceylon (now Sri Lanka) wrote, "is the greatest propaganda gift any country could give the Kremlin in its persistent bid for the affections of the coloured races of the world."[2] The State Department and U.S. Information Agency fought Soviet propaganda by arguing, in printed materials and speeches around the world, that America was moving toward full equality.

As a senator, Jack sought ways for the United States to build stronger ties to foreign audiences of color. He pressed Eisenhower (to little avail) to reach out to African nationalist leaders, criticized the low number of educational scholarships that Washington was allocating for black Africa, arranged for the Joseph Kennedy Foundation (named for his older brother) to pay the travel of African students with scholarships to U.S. universities who lacked the funds to make the trip, and called for a new U.S. policy for Africa that focused on economic development. He envisioned a continent of independent nations instead of Western colonies, and he said the United States must support the aspirations of the African people if it hoped to secure their loyalty once they had won their independence.

Africans noticed Jack's efforts and were excited by his election as president. "Whenever our presence was known," Senator Frank Church said of his post-election trip to Africa with Senate colleagues in late 1960—the trip that Ted Kennedy joined late—"eager crowds would gather to shout 'Kennedy, Kennedy.'"[3]

At the time, the global implications of America's racial turmoil were growing because Jack took office amid an independence movement across Africa. With seventeen new nations established in 1960,

"Whether a Free Society Can Compete"

two in 1961, and four in 1962, more African leaders of color were watching how America treated its own people of color.

. . .

"Can't you get your goddamned friends off those buses?" Jack asked Harris Wofford, his special assistant for civil rights, in May of 1961.[4]

That month civil rights advocates decided to test the South's enforcement of recent Supreme Court decisions outlawing segregation in public transportation by launching "freedom rides," with people of different races traveling together on public buses and using the public facilities of terminals. The buses passed through the upper South without incident, but things changed dramatically as they rolled into the deep South. A "convoy of 50 cars" stopped one bus outside of Aniston, Alabama, and some two hundred white men yelled "Sieg, heil," beat the passengers with fists, bats, chains, clubs, pipes, and bottles, and threw a firebomb inside. In Birmingham— which was labeled the "Johannesburg of America" and reminded Edward R. Murrow, the famed CBS correspondent, of Nazi Germany—Ku Klux Klansmen pummeled the passengers of another bus with lead pipes as Police Commissioner Eugene "Bull" Connor ordered his forces to stand back. When, a week later, the bus that had stopped in Birmingham reached the bus depot in Montgomery, a mob of about two hundred shouted "filthy Communists, nigger lovers," and used pipes, bats, and bottles to bludgeon the riders as here, too, the police stood back.[5]

Jack and Bobby were especially pained by the timing of events, for the violence exploded less than a month before JFK would meet Khrushchev in Vienna. Covered prominently in leading newspapers at home and abroad, the violence gave Moscow an easy propaganda victory. "In Birmingham and Montgomery," the *New York Times* editorialized, "the United States has lost another battle in the global cold war. . . . In other lands they will see—if they have not done so already—the photographs of men beating Negroes or other unarmed white men and women. They will read the details— and there will be no need for the most skillful Red propaganda to embroider the facts—and they must be expected to ask themselves what the United States really stands for."[6] So concerned were Jack and Bobby about the photographs that they cut a quiet deal with Senator James Eastland of Mississippi, an avowed segregationist, to have the "freedom riders" arrested when they arrived in Jackson, avoiding more bloody confrontations.

Making matters worse, African leaders of color experienced America's race discrimination themselves. When, after landing in New York on their way to Washington, black diplomats drove on Route 40—which was dubbed the "Diplomatic Corridor" and stretched from the outskirts of Baltimore to the border of Delaware—restaurants along the route wouldn't serve them. The discrimination was so complete that, as the *Baltimore Afro-American* wrote at the time, the road "could be picked up and put down in Mississippi, and feel at home."[7] On his way to present his credentials to JFK in June of 1961, an ambassador from Chad was refused service when he stopped for coffee. Though such indignities occurred elsewhere, Route 40 was the big problem because so many foreign diplomats drove it.

Because he couldn't fix the problem by himself, Jack sought ways avoid it. "It's a hell of a road," he told aides. "I used to drive it years ago, but why would anybody want to drive it today when you can fly? Tell these ambassadors I wouldn't think of driving from New York to Washington. Tell them to fly!"[8]

. . .

As Jack knew, however, he needed real solutions to the challenge of America's race problem and global image.

With his first official appointment—that is, before announcing the names of any Cabinet members—Jack signaled his profound interest in Africa by naming "Soapy" Williams, Michigan's former progressive governor and a leading civil rights advocate, as assistant secretary for African affairs, terming it "a position of responsibility second to none in the new Administration."[9] After Williams caused an early stir by proclaiming "Africa for the Africans," raising alarms in Europe and among the State Department's "Europeanists" over

"Whether a Free Society Can Compete"

the implications for Europe's colonies, Jack defended him by telling reporters, "I do not know who else Africa should be for."

"I hope that the people of your continent recognize," Jack told African ambassadors at a White House reception for African Freedom Day in April of 1961, "that we wish to be associated intimately with them, that we wish for them the same things we wish for ourselves." Jack more than doubled economic aid to Africa in 1961, expanded the number of U.S. diplomats there, and met with eleven African leaders in 1961, ten in 1962, and seven in 1963. He scrapped Eisenhower's policy of deferring America's approach to Africa to the wishes of its European allies, and he pressured Portugal to free its African territories by reducing economic and military aid to Lisbon, backing a UN resolution urging reforms in Angola, and providing financial support to Angolan nationalists. The administration condemned South Africa over its apartheid policy of racial separation, expressed support for the anti-apartheid protestors who Pretoria had imprisoned, announced that Washington would stop selling arms to South Africa as long as it practiced apartheid, and voted for a UN resolution that called on every nation to stop arms sales to Pretoria.

At home Jack established a State Department Office of Special Protocol Services, which then convinced Maryland lawmakers to ban discrimination in public accommodations in the counties through which Route 40 passed. (The law exempted counties outside the "Diplomatic Corridor" on Maryland's eastern shore, making clear that the goal was to improve America's global image, not expand civil rights.) While working with Bobby to control civil-rights-related violence, Jack sent troops to enable black student James Meredith to attend the University of Mississippi, directed aides to work with officials in Birmingham to expand civil rights in that city, and ordered the Alabama National Guard to remove Governor George Wallace after he stood at the door of the University of Alabama and vowed to resist its integration.

How central was America's global image to Jack's civil rights concerns? After his civil rights bill came before the Senate Commerce

Committee in July of 1963, he tapped Secretary of State Dean Rusk to serve as the administration's lead witness and discuss its implications for America's foreign policy.

. . .

"Well, Ted, why can't we get this thing going right away?" Jack asked Ted Moscoso, the U.S. coordinator for his Alliance for Progress, early in his presidency. "Why is it taking so long for disbursements?"[10]

As in Africa, Jack sought to change America's image south of its border, and the Alliance for Progress was his main tool. With Ike backing right-wing dictators and deferring U.S. policy largely to American business interests in Latin America, grassroots feeling in the region was best symbolized by the violent protests that met Vice President Nixon on his 1958 trip to Caracas. Under the Alliance, the United States would facilitate $20 billion in loans to the region over the next decade and Latin American governments would launch economic and social reforms. After referencing the Alliance in his inaugural address, Jack announced it officially to more than two hundred Latin American diplomats in Washington in March, and U.S. officials wrote its charter with Latin finance ministers in August.

With a politician's desire to show that his initiatives were bearing fruit, Jack was unduly restless, if not naïve, about what the Alliance could achieve, and when. "He wanted instant development," Moscoso said later. "Well, you just can't get instant development. . . . You are dealing with distortions which are two, three hundred years old and you just don't eliminate them overnight." Some of the State Department's seasoned hands worried that the administration was overselling the Alliance to the public. Meanwhile, more than a few Latin leaders were reluctant to initiate reforms that could weaken their power, and they were skeptical that Washington understood the region to begin with. Traveling to Venezuela and Colombia in December of 1961, Jack seemed to make more headway in convincing their people of his good intentions than persuading their leaders to launch reforms. The Alliance died due to problems on Jack's watch and disinterest by his successors.

The Peace Corps—a concept that Jack began to articulate as far back as 1951—proved far more enduring. "I know that a lot of so-called hardened politicians are going to say, 'Oh, that's just a naïve kid dreaming of something just to try to make a splash in the campaign,'" Jack told a friend a week before Election Day of 1960, as he soaked in a hot bath in San Francisco, before proposing the Peace Corps in an evening speech.[11] He clearly felt strongly about the idea, and he wouldn't be deterred by any such criticism. "How many of you who are going to be doctors, are willing to spend your days in Ghana?" he had asked students two weeks earlier in impromptu remarks at the University of Michigan. "Technicians or engineers, how many of you are willing to work in the Foreign Service and spend your lives traveling around the world? On your willingness . . . to contribute part of your life to this country, I think will depend the answer whether a free society can compete. I think it can. And I think Americans are willing to contribute. But the effort must be far greater than we've ever made in the past."[12] Jack clearly touched a nerve. In the coming days—to cite one telling example—University of Michigan graduate students Alan and Judy Guskin would create the group Americans Committed to World Responsibility, gather signatures from hundreds of students who pledged to volunteer, present the signatures to Jack in Toledo two days before the election, and become Peace Corps volunteers themselves, in Thailand.

Because the Peace Corps was less prescriptive than the Alliance, demanding nothing of foreign governments in return, foreign officials were more inclined to accept its help. Under JFK's brother-in-law, Sargent Shriver, the Peace Corps established operations in scores of countries, and thousands of young Americans set off to serve as teachers, nurses, engineers, mechanics, and agricultural workers, nourishing trust by living among those they served. As Thanat Khoman, Thailand's foreign minister of the time, recalled,

It is well to have diplomats stationed in many parts of the world. But I think it is even more important for the people to come into contact with one another, to have first-hand knowledge, first-hand experience and also first-hand ideas about what we should do in this world to keep peace and to develop friendly relations between the nations of the world. . . . These young people who came here with no diplomatic privilege, no status whatsoever, but simply as young men and women, came with the only thing they can offer; that is goodwill, and indeed they offered us their goodwill and also their knowledge, their skill. And they came to live with our people not in hotels, not in sumptuous houses, but in our farmers' huts, sharing their food and the roof.[13]

Jack, too, recognized the need for "first-hand knowledge," which is why he traveled so much over the years. It's also why he sent Bobby around the world in early 1962 to make the case for America.

. . .

"We will defend our faith by affirmation, by argument and if necessary—and heaven forbid that it should become necessary—by arms," Bobby Kennedy told students at Japan's Nihon University in February of 1962. "It is our willingness to die for our ideals that makes it possible for these ideals to live."

On his month-long "good will" tour of Asia and Europe with his wife, Ethel, Bobby traveled to fourteen countries, including week-long stays in Japan and Indonesia. Spurred by Edwin Reischauer, America's ambassador to Tokyo, he sought to exploit his youthful looks to counter "the growing feeling," at least in Japan, "that the United States is a tired old country and that Communism and the Communists are developing young leaders for the future."[14] Wherever he went, he trumpeted freedom over communism, challenged communist sympathizers to confront the brutality of Soviet and Chinese rule, and answered tough questions about America's race relations. He heard from worried officials of friendly nations that Moscow was winning global hearts and minds more effectively than Washington.

"Whether a Free Society Can Compete"

"The important factor, and the one to which we are committed," Bobby told students at the University of Indonesia, "is that the state exists for man, that man is not a tool of the state. It is difficult for me to understand why the opposite ideology could appeal to any peace-loving nation or to a nation that takes—and rightly takes—a fierce pride in its independence." He visited some of the 1.5 million refugees in Hong Kong who had fled China, and he reassured Thailand's leaders that the United States would help their nation defend itself if communist guerillas infiltrated from Laos. In South Vietnam, to which Jack had sent thousands of military advisors, he vowed that "we will win . . . and we shall remain here until we do"—a stance that he would come to regret.

In West Berlin, Bobby received an enormous welcome that presaged Jack's triumphal visit of a year later. After the hot weather of Asia, Bobby found it hard to speak in Europe's bitter cold. As he ad-libbed from notes at a podium outside City Hall, Ethel rubbed his back to try to warm him. When East Germany sent four red flags on balloons over the crowd of 180,000, Bobby evoked a roar of approval by pointing upward and quipping, "The communists will let the balloons through but they won't let their people come through." Reinforcing America's commitment to the city, he declared, "An armed attack on West Berlin is the same as an armed attack on Chicago, or New York, or London, or Paris. You are our brothers and we stand by you." Speaking later at the Free University of Berlin, he repeated Jack's words of the previous July, "We do not want to fight, but we have fought before. We cannot and will not permit the communists to drive us out of Berlin, gradually or by force."

After returning home, Bobby wrote a best-selling book about his trip, *Just Friends and Brave Enemies*, in which he implored Americans to improve race relations at home to help their country nourish loyalty across the developing world. "The leaders of the nations—of Asia, Africa, South America, the Middle East—during the sixties, the seventies and the eighties will be the intellectuals, the college students, the labor leaders of today," he explained. "We cannot change their minds and interest them in democratic principles unless we are successfully practicing them at home."[15] To expand America's outreach to the developing world, Bobby donated the book's earnings to a scholarship fund for students from Japan, Indonesia, and West Berlin, and he encouraged book publishers to work with government agencies to make more of their books available around the world.

While Bobby promoted America's ideals to burnish its image, Jack showcased its technological prowess.

. . .

"Do we have a chance of beating the Soviets," Jack asked Vice President Johnson, who chaired his Space Council, in a memo of April 20, 1961, "by putting a laboratory in space, or by a trip around the moon, or by a rocket to land on the moon, or by a rocket to go to the moon and back with a man. Is there any other space program which promises dramatic results in which we could win? . . . Are we working 24 hours a day on existing programs. If not, why not? . . . Are we making maximum effort?"[16]

Jack viewed the space program "primarily in symbolic terms," recalled Ted Sorenson. "He had comparatively little interest in the substantive gains to be made from this kind of scientific inquiry. . . . Our lagging space effort was symbolic, he thought, of everything of which he complained in the Eisenhower administration: the lack of effort, the lack of initiative, the lack of imagination, vitality, and vision."[17]

Jack's memo to LBJ was hardly the first time he voiced concern about America's lagging space efforts. Days before his inauguration, the Ad Hoc Committee on Space that he created after his election sharply criticized NASA and the space program for lackluster leadership and activity. In March he pressed space officials for ways to catch the Soviets, and he sought more space-related funding from Congress. He was shaken on April 12 when Moscow launched Vostok I, with the first human in space on board.

That's why he was so anxious on the morning of May 5 as he waited through multiple delays before the United States launched its first manned mission to space, with astronaut Alan Shepard on board.

"Whether a Free Society Can Compete"

"It was," said Hale Boggs, an influential House Democrat who had breakfast with Jack that morning, "the only time I remember him being tense, and a little irritable."[18]

. . .

Jack's views about the space program evolved during his presidency, however, which showed just how "symbolic" they really were.

"If we are to win the battle that is now going on around the world between freedom and tyranny," he told Congress in May of 1961 when he announced the goal of a manned moon landing by the end of the 1960s, "the dramatic achievements in space which occurred in recent weeks should have made clear to us all, as did the Sputnik in 1957, the impact of this adventure on the minds of men everywhere, who are attempting to make a determination of which road they should take."

More than two years later—after U.S.-Soviet tensions had eased, the two nations had inked a nuclear test-ban treaty, and Jack no longer feared global perceptions that America was lagging behind the Soviets in space—he tied the space program less to defeating the Soviets than to cooperating with them.

At the United Nations in September of 1963, Jack proposed that Washington and Moscow collaborate more to address global challenges, such as by initiating "a joint expedition to the moon. . . . Why . . . should man's first flight to the moon be a matter of national competition? . . . Surely we should explore whether the scientists and astronauts of our two countries—indeed of all the world—cannot work together in the conquest of space, sending someday in this decade to the moon not the representatives of a single nation, but the representatives of all of our countries."

In other words, why beat the Soviets to the moon when Cold War necessities no longer dictated a competition?

. . .

The reduced tensions, test-ban treaty, and talk of a joint space mission came only after a frightening U.S.-Soviet confrontation that, for nearly two weeks, left the world on a precipice of nuclear catastrophe.

8

"R. Kennedy Was Very Upset"

"Doesn't that silly ass realize what I'm doing?" Jack asked a friend about George Anderson, the chief of naval operations for the Joint Chiefs, who was pressuring the president to take military action against Cuba.[1]

It was late October of 1962 and U.S. spy planes had discovered that, despite their repeated assurances to the contrary, the Soviets were installing offensive nuclear missiles in Cuba. Jack decided immediately that the missiles must go and most of his advisors agreed, but the question was how to remove them or convince Moscow to do so. The Joint Chiefs proposed a military strike (and Jack and most of his advisors initially agreed), perhaps accompanied by a land invasion, to wipe them out, leaving Moscow with a fait accompli. In fact, the brass viewed the missile crisis as an opportunity not just to destroy the missiles but, as Anderson recalled, "to get rid of the focus of infection of communism in the Western Hemisphere"—which was Castro. When Jack moved toward an embargo on Soviet military shipments to pressure Moscow while buying time for a peaceful resolution, Anderson warned him that that would risk a "large-scale war at sea" with "very serious loss of life and shipping to the United States and the Western world."[2]

After the Bay of Pigs, Jack had grown wary of advice from the brass, and he grew more concerned during the missile crisis as the generals pushed for military action and addressed their commander in chief with dismissive disdain. "You're in a pretty bad fix at the present time," the Air Force's chief of staff, Curtis LeMay, lectured him at one point, arguing that if Washington didn't respond militarily, Moscow would be tempted to challenge America's global interests in Berlin and elsewhere. "These brass hats," Jack later scoffed, "have one great advantage in their favor. If we listen to them, and do what they want us to do, none of us will be alive after to tell them that they were wrong."[3] Even after he resolved the crisis peacefully, the brass remained unmoved. "We lost!" LeMay told an incredulous Jack immediately afterward. "We ought to just go in there today and knock 'em off!"[4] Five years later, in an interview for the John F. Kennedy Library's Oral History Program, Anderson remained unconvinced by Jack's success and insisted he should have launched a "massive military intervention" to remove both the missiles and Castro.

To resolve the crisis, Jack viewed Khrushchev less as an implacable adversary than a fellow political leader, one who, like all political leaders, had constituencies to satisfy and critics to consider at home and abroad. Though chilled by Khrushchev's cold-bloodedness in Vienna, Jack nevertheless sought to find the human being within him, to understand what drove his decision to install the missiles, and to respond accordingly. Rather than bombs and bluster, as the brass was advising, Jack would walk the path of reason. Earlier that year he had read *The Guns of August*, Barbara Tuchman's classic about the miscalculations through which Europe's leaders stumbled into World War I. He was moved so much by what he learned that he summoned Army Secretary Elvis Stahr Jr. to the White House, gave him the book, and told him that he and "every officer in the Army" should read it.[5] Now, as he sought to solve the missile crisis, he was determined to avoid any miscalculation that could drive the superpowers to war. No one, he told Bobby at one point, would later write a book about how U.S. miscalculation had triggered a nuclear exchange.

"I've got a guy over there in Moscow who's in a corner," he mused about Khrushchev to a friend, "and I don't want to get him in a corner. I want to give him the opinion he can get out. Everything I'm saying, I'm speaking to Khrushchev and nobody else. I want to be able to get this thing solved and get the missiles out of Cuba. I've got to do it in such a way that this fellow can save face. If [George] Anderson doesn't realize that, it just shows he isn't as bright as I thought he was."

. . .

"In our discussions and exchanges on Berlin and other international questions," Jack wrote to Khrushchev in the early evening of October 22, about an hour before he told the American people about the Soviet missiles, "the one thing that has most concerned me has been the possibility that your Government would not correctly understand the will and determination of the United States in any given situation, since I have not assumed that you or any other sane man would, in this nuclear age, deliberately plunge the world into war which it is crystal clear no country could win and which could only result in catastrophic consequences to the whole world, including the aggressor."[6]

It was the first of about a dozen exchanges between the leaders through the last two weeks of October as Jack weighed his options. For about a week after he learned of the missiles on October 16, he kept the news a secret, maintained his public schedule, and met repeatedly with "EXCOMM"—an ad-hoc team of top military and diplomatic aides, "wise men" like the former secretary of state, Dean Acheson, and, most importantly, Bobby, on whom he leaned the most as he faced his gravest crisis. It was no easy secret to keep because Senator Kenneth Keating (the New York Republican whom Bobby would unseat in his run for the Senate two years later) had been complaining for weeks that Moscow was amassing troops and equipment in Cuba and building sites from which to launch missiles and Jack was doing nothing about it. With leaks from the CIA and State Department, leading newspapers and magazines were writing about the Soviet buildup.

Jack recognized the ramifications of Soviet nuclear warheads on what he called the "imprisoned island" of Cuba, just ninety miles from Florida. If they remained, Khrushchev could blanket America with nuclear bombs in minutes, forcing Washington to consider this frightening new threat before confronting the Soviets anywhere in the world. He could better protect Castro, his ally in Havana, against the threat of future U.S. action to topple him. He also could pressure Washington to abandon West Berlin, which would let the Soviets seize the city, close off its access to the West, and incorporate it into Soviet-dominated East Germany.

As Jack exchanged letters with Khrushchev and mulled his options, Bobby pushed Jack's advisors to consider all of the factors at play and crystallize the advice they were giving the president. He then played a key role in implementing the strategy that brought the crisis to an end.

. . .

"Oh, shit," Bobby exclaimed at about 9:00 a.m. on October 16, after viewing pictures of the Soviet missiles and launch sites in the White House office of National Security Advisor McGeorge Bundy, "shit, shit."[7]

Jack had called Bobby that morning, said "we have some big trouble," and ordered him to the White House. The pictures, which U.S. intelligence officials studied the night before, showed four missile launchers and eight "trailers" with missiles. The brothers immediately viewed Khrushchev's move as not just an enormous security challenge but also a personal affront. Republicans had been slamming Jack for weeks over his "weakness" as the Soviets poured military hardware and personnel into Cuba, and, as the *New York Times* reported in early October, they were "certain that the Administration's policies toward Cuba will be a net benefit to them" in the congressional elections in November.[8] Even some Democrats were growing antsy about JFK's reluctance to respond forcefully. Jack had stated more than once in September that he wouldn't stand idly by if the Soviets put *offensive* weapons in Cuba, saying they would raise the "gravest issues." Now, they had done so. "Those sons-a-bitches Russians," Bobby muttered.

Bobby understood Jack's fears that Moscow might miscalculate by dismissing his pledge to defend America's interests militarily, if necessary. While Jack had made that point in his letters to and conversations with Khrushchev, Bobby reinforced it through an important back channel. Sidestepping official diplomatic channels that ran through the State Department, Bobby met dozens of times with Georgi Bolshakov, a Washington correspondent for Soviet state publications over the years who, Bobby knew, was a KGB intelligence officer. They usually met at Bobby's Justice Department office, but they sometimes walked along the Washington Mall; Bobby also hosted Bolshakov at his home. Through Bolshakov (among other channels), Khrushchev assured Jack that he wouldn't place offensive weapons in Cuba, and Bolshakov apparently didn't know that Moscow was secretly doing so.

While EXCOMM, or subsets of it, met frequently through thirteen days of crisis—as its members slept fitfully, saw little of their families, and exchanged mordant asides at night about whether they'd be alive the next day—Jack often did not attend the discussions so that his advisors could argue among themselves rather than try to discern where Jack was leaning and then slavishly align themselves with him. When Jack wasn't there, Bobby served as the group's de facto chairman. "He sometimes wouldn't even sit at the conference table," McGeorge Bundy recalled. "I can remember times when he would deliberately put himself in one of the smaller chairs against the wall. . . . But it didn't make much difference."[9] Bobby asked questions, challenged assumptions, and tried to drive consensus.

Though Jack, Bobby, and most of the others initially supported a military strike, Jack soon harbored doubts. The brass couldn't promise that the air force could wipe out every missile, nor could anyone guarantee that Moscow wouldn't replace them with others. And whether it struck by air or land, the United States would likely kill not just many Cubans but also Russians, which could force Moscow to retaliate by seizing Berlin or even striking somewhere in the United States. Bobby soon harbored doubts as well. Early on, he suggested that Washington consider staging a military confronta-

"R. Kennedy Was Very Upset"

tion as a pretext to use force, akin to how the sinking of the USS *Maine* whipped up fervor for the Spanish-American War of 1898. Soon, however, the moral underpinning of his religious upbringing reshaped his thinking. He portrayed a U.S. strike on the missiles as "Pearl Harbor in reverse" and declared, "My brother isn't going to be the Tojo of the '60s." Though he found a sympathetic ear with Jack, the analogy made little sense, for it aligned an unprovoked Japanese attack on a U.S. naval base with a U.S. attack in response to a threatening Soviet move. Acheson, who remained among the strongest supporters of a military strike, told Jack that the analogy was "unworthy" of him.[10]

As Jack pursued delicate negotiations to end the crisis, he chose Bobby for the most delicate task of all.

. . .

"I should say that during our meeting," Anatoly Dobrynin, the Soviet ambassador to the United States, told the Kremlin after he met with Bobby on the evening of October 27, "R. Kennedy was very upset."[11]

Jack and Bobby were under enormous stress, with the former leaning on the latter more than ever. A few days earlier, news came that two Soviet ships were approaching the U.S. maritime blockade of Cuba. By then the Pentagon had raised the U.S. threat level to DefCon 2 (indicating its "full readiness for hostilities"), and Jack had put all U.S. nuclear bombers on alert and ordered one hundred thousand troops and more than five hundred combat aircraft to Florida. As a Soviet submarine moved between the ships, Bobby later wrote: Jack's "hand went up to his face and covered his mouth. He opened and closed his fist. His face seemed drawn, his eyes pained, almost gray. We stared at each other across the table."[12]

Suddenly, Moscow ordered its ships to turn back, avoiding a confrontation. The good news was short-lived, however. In ensuing days, the Soviets continued working on the missile sites and Washington let other Soviet ships through its blockade to sidestep a standoff. U.S.-Soviet talks were proving fruitless, and the brass was pressing harder than ever for military action. Earlier in the day that Bobby would meet with Dobrynin, all of the following happened: the FBI reported that the Soviet embassy in Washington was preparing to destroy papers, suggesting Moscow expected a war; U.S. aerial reconnaissance showed that the Soviets were continuing to assemble Il-28 bombers in Cuba; Moscow began moving ships back toward the quarantine line; U.S. and Soviet planes nearly exchanged gunfire as the Soviets chased a U-2 flight out of its airspace over Siberia; the Soviets shot down a U-2 flight over Cuba; and Cuba started shooting at low-flying U.S. aircraft over its airspace. That evening, Jack agreed to call up the reserves needed for an invasion and decided that he would respond militarily the next day if the Soviets or Cubans shot down another U-2.

Jack, however, proved wise to view Khrushchev as a politician with his own pressures, and not the "madman" that Acheson had labeled him.[13] As his letters made clear, the Soviet leader was as awed by the implications of a direct U.S.-Soviet conflict as Jack was, and he wrote to Jack on the evening of October 26 to offer a compromise: Moscow would remove the missiles in exchange for a U.S. commitment not to invade Cuba. But while a relieved Jack readied a positive response the next morning, Khrushchev sent another letter that added a tricky condition—that Washington remove its Jupiter missiles in Turkey that had become operational in April. It was the Soviet offer that Jack both expected and feared. Throughout the crisis he told his advisors that were the Soviets to make such an offer, most people would consider it a reasonable one. Through intermediaries, Bobby had floated the idea of such a trade with Moscow, though apparently without telling his brother. Walter Lippmann, the influential syndicated columnist, suggested the trade in a column two days before Khrushchev suggested it.[14] As the crisis reached its climax, Jack even told Secretary of State Dean Rusk to draft a statement that UN Secretary General U Thant might issue in his own name that would call for such a trade—in case Washington later needed it as political cover to resolve the crisis.

Nevertheless, for reasons both diplomatic and domestic, Jack didn't think he could accept a straight trade of Soviet missiles in

"R. Kennedy Was Very Upset"

Cuba for Jupiters in Turkey. The Turks rejected the idea privately when U.S. officials floated it with them on October 24 and publicly when Khrushchev offered it on October 27. While concerned about U.S.-Turkish relations, Washington also worried that withdrawing the Jupiters would cause tensions with NATO, which viewed them as a sign of U.S. resolve to defend Europe. At home, Republicans surely would vilify Jack for making concessions to Khrushchev in the face of his provocation. At the suggestion of advisors who included Bobby, Jack ignored Khrushchev's second letter and, in his response that evening, endorsed his first—that Moscow withdraw the missiles and Washington pledge not to threaten Cuba.

Meeting with Dobrynin that night, Bobby said that Jack was under enormous pressure from the military to strike the missile sites; warned that the two nations were close to war; and told him that Moscow must accept the terms of Khrushchev's earlier letter (of October 26) over the next day to avoid a military conflict. When Dobrynin asked about the Jupiters, Bobby promised that Washington would remove them in a few months but said the promise must remain a secret. When a dour Bobby—who didn't learn from Dobrynin that night how Khrushchev would respond—returned to the White House to brief his brother, Jack's pal Dave Powers was upstairs with him, eating roasted chicken. "God, Dave," Jack said, "the way you're eating up all that chicken and drinking up all my wine, anybody would think it was your last meal." "The way Bobby's been talking," Powers replied, "I thought it was my last meal."[15]

Fortunately, Khrushchev accepted the next day and, as the crisis ended, U.S.-Soviet relations took a brighter turn.

. . .

The morning after President Kennedy told the nation about the Soviet missiles and announced the embargo, Ted called him from Massachusetts, where he was running for the Senate.

Jack said that he couldn't provide details about the crisis over the phone, but he warned that, as Ted later put it, "the outcome was still far from certain." Ted wrote a statement about the crisis that he wanted to issue, but Jack's aides talked him out of it because, as the president's brother, Moscow might misinterpret whatever he said, complicating Jack's efforts to resolve the crisis. Ted was reduced, as he later put it, to "figuratively [pacing] the sidelines."[16]

At the time, another member of the Kennedy clan was less sensitive to the ramifications of unscripted activity. For years, Rose Kennedy had collected autographs from famous people, and during the crisis, she blithely wrote to Khrushchev to ask that he sign some pictures of him with Jack. When the Soviet leader signed and returned the pictures, she sent them to Jack, asked that he sign them, and mentioned that she planned to return some of the cosigned pictures to Khrushchev and distribute others to family members.

What exactly happened next is unclear. In his memoirs, Ted claimed the following: In Moscow, the KGB "burst through the door" of Khrushchev's office with Rose's letter, undoubtedly wondering what it could possibly signal. When Jack found out, he called his mother, asked "what in the world are you *doing*?!" and, after hearing her explanation, added, "The Russians won't assume this is innocent. They'll give it some interpretation. Now I have to get my CIA people speculating on what this interpretation might be! The strengths! The weaknesses! The contingencies!"[17]

How much of that actually occurred is uncertain. That's because nearly a week after the crisis ended, Jack wrote a calm letter to his mother that suggested he had only then learned what she had done. "Would you be sure," he asked her, "to let me know in the future any contacts you have with heads of state, etc. concerning requests for pictures, signatures, etc. Requests of this nature are subject to interpretations and therefore I would like to have you clear them before they are sent." A week later, a chastened Rose wrote back, "I understand very well your letter, although I had not thought of it before. . . . I can see that it was probably an error, and it will not happen again." Lightening the mood, she closed with humor. "As you know," she wrote, "Chancellor Adenauer and President Eisenhower autographed books for you last Christmas, and I have asked General de Gaulle to do so for this Christmas. I guess this clari-

"R. Kennedy Was Very Upset"

fies the situation. (When I ask for Castro's autograph, I shall let you know in advance!)" Nevertheless, she took Jack's admonition to heart, later asking his permission to seek the signature of India's prime minister, Jawaharlal Nehru. "Yes—go ahead," Jack replied, and she soon had it.[18]

Ted did nothing to complicate Jack's life. When the president resolved the crisis at the end of October, he and every other Democratic candidate for office reaped the political benefits a week later on Election Day.

. . .

"The fall of Berlin," Ted Kennedy declared on July 4, 1961, at Boston's historical Faneuil Hall, "could be a prelude to the fall of Boston."[19]

It was the kind of apocalyptic warning that Jack could have issued, showing that Ted was no less a Cold Warrior at that time than his brothers. "The hour is close to nine o'clock here in South Boston," he noted ominously while debating his Democratic primary opponent, Ed McCormack, in late August. "It's close to three o'clock in Berlin, and only in a few minutes from now the convoys will start on their way down the Autobahn. I wonder tonight whether this convoy will be stopped like it was last night."[20] He also attacked McCormack for advocating an end to U.S. nuclear weapons production.

Preparing for his Senate run, Ted traveled across Europe and the Middle East in early 1962 and, in Berlin, met up with Bobby, who was on the tail end of his global "good will" tour. Though traveling as a "private citizen," Ted secured meetings with top public and private officials. In Belgium he lunched with Foreign Minister Paul-Henri Spaak, conferred with the European Economic Community's president and officials from member nations, and met with labor leaders and students. In Israel he met with Prime Minister David Ben-Gurion and local leaders. In Greece he lunched with Crown Prince Constantine and dined with Prime Minister Constantine Caramanlis. In Poland he met with U.S. embassy officials and spent a night in Cracow's ancient Wawel Castle, courtesy of Poland's government. From West Berlin, he took a subway into communist-run

East Berlin and, upon his return, said the East was "sterile," with "no life, no action," and "the faces show the despair" of its people.[21] Together, Bobby and Ted met with West Germany's chancellor, Konrad Adenauer.

Though Ted cited his travels across Europe, Africa, and Latin America to validate his Senate credentials, Cuba was the foreign policy issue that dominated his race. After Ted won the Democratic nomination in September, his Republican opponent was George Cabot Lodge—the son of Henry Cabot Lodge Jr., who held the seat for six years until Jack ousted him in 1952. In the fall of 1962, George Cabot Lodge joined the GOP chorus by attacking Jack over the Soviet buildup in Cuba. After the missile crisis erupted and the country rallied around Jack, Lodge was forced to join Ted in expressing "support" for Jack's approach to resolving it. When Jack succeeded, Ted's election seemed even more assured.

In fact, on the very night that Jack told the nation about the Soviet missiles, Ted was scheduled to debate Lodge at a hall in Worcester, Massachusetts. As Jack spoke ominously of the crisis at hand, attendees watched on the TV sets that lined the walls as they ate their fruit cups. "Needless to say," Lodge reflected years later about the debate that would ensue over dessert, "I was at a slight disadvantage."[22]

Jack, too, sought to capitalize on his success, but not at home for political purposes. Instead, he hoped the peaceful resolution of a frightening big-power standoff would presage a U.S.-Soviet ban on nuclear testing.

. . .

"I had never seen him any madder than that," Harold Brown, a top Defense Department official at the time, said of Jack's reaction to the news of late 1961 that the Soviets would resume nuclear testing. "He was very, very angry. I think he obviously felt that he had been treated as a sucker by the Soviets."[23]

Jack was long troubled by nuclear weapons, though he recognized their essential place in America's defense arsenal. As a senator, he disparaged Eisenhower's New Look strategy of relying heavily on

"R. Kennedy Was Very Upset"

U.S. nuclear capabilities to deter adversaries, and he worried that the arms race raised the chances of a catastrophic conflict. "No sane society chooses to commit national suicide," he wrote on the eve of his campaign for president. "Yet that is the fate which the arms race has in store for us—unless we can find a way to stop it."[24] He proposed that Washington maintain the ban on nuclear testing that Ike had imposed while U.S. and Soviet negotiators were seeking a test-ban treaty in the late 1950s—as long as Moscow maintained the ban that it imposed after Ike's. He also proposed that, if Washington felt compelled to resume testing, it do so in limited ways; that it work harder to craft a permanent test-ban treaty; and that it learn more about the dangers of radioactive fallout and how to control it. He also worried about the grave implications of nuclear proliferation as more nations pursued nuclear weaponry.

Jack inherited the task of completing a treaty after U.S.-Soviet talks collapsed in May of 1960 when the Soviets shot down a U.S. spy plane and Eisenhower refused Khrushchev's demand that he apologize for the spying operation. When Jack took office, he extended the moratorium; appointed John McCloy (one of the postwar "wise men") to create an organizational structure for disarmament policy that later became the Arms Control and Disarmament Agency; and resumed talks with Moscow. Unfortunately, as Jack tried to inject some momentum into the talks in his early months, U.S.-Soviet tensions were rising over the Bay of Pigs in April; Vienna in June; and Berlin over the summer. Khrushchev's announcement of August 31 that the Soviets would resume testing came at the end of a month in which Washington and London (which was also a party to the talks) offered a series of proposals to the Soviets—including one on the very day of Khrushchev's announcement.

Rather than immediately resume U.S. testing, Jack sought to convince Khrushchev to reverse course and refocus on a treaty. Moscow began testing on September 1 and ignored Jack's entreaties for a full test ban. Its tests lasted until November 4 and included the largest H-bomb ever tested, generating enormous radioactive fallout around the world. After the third test of September, Jack felt compelled to announce that Washington would resume underground testing, which at least wouldn't cause the environmental damage of radioactive fallout. "What choice did we have?" a demoralized Jack asked his advisors. "They had spit in our eye three times. We couldn't possibly sit back and do nothing at all." Later in the conversation, he acknowledged that it might not be the right decision. "Who the hell knows?"[25] Treaty talks continued on and off through 1962, in different venues and at different levels of government. With the Soviets continuing atmospheric testing, however, Jack decided that he couldn't wait any longer to follow suit, lest he look weak next to Khrushchev and also let the Soviets make unilateral progress on the nuclear front. After warning in November of 1961 that Washington would prepare to resume atmospheric testing, Jack announced the following March that it would actually resume it.

The Cuban Missile Crisis, however, left both JFK and Khrushchev sobered by their close brush with a nuclear confrontation, and they emerged from it with a renewed desire to complete a treaty.

. . .

"As Americans, we find communism profoundly repugnant as a negation of personal freedom and dignity," Jack declared at American University in June of 1963. "But we can still hail the Russian people for their many achievements—in science and space, in economic and industrial growth, in culture and in acts of courage.... For, in the final analysis, our most basic common link is that we all inhabit this small planet. We all breathe the same air. We all cherish our children's future. And we are all mortal."

In his most moving address, Jack sought to refashion the Cold War by promoting global peace—"genuine peace, the kind of peace that makes life on earth worth living, the kind that enables men and nations to grow and to hope and to build a better life for their children, not merely peace for Americans but peace for all men and women, not merely peace in our time but peace for all time." Jack wanted to move out in a bold new direction and considered the speech so important that he directed close White House aides not to show a draft to top Defense Department or State Department officials, who normally would have much time to weigh in, until it was too late to discuss major changes. That some top military officials opposed a test ban undoubtedly drove Jack's secretive approach as well.

What had changed, Jack explained at American University, was not the brutal nature of Soviet rule, the inherent frictions of international relations, or the reality of a very imperfect human nature. Indeed, in his landmark address in Berlin just two weeks later, Jack stressed the ideological divides that made U.S.-Soviet cooperation so difficult. "There are many people in the world who really don't understand, or say they don't, what is the great issue between the free world and the communist world," he told more than 150,000 wildly enthusiastic people of West Berlin who gathered on a windswept day to hear their American hero proclaim that he wouldn't abandon them. "Let them come to Berlin." Jack denounced the Berlin Wall as "an offense against humanity," praised the "vitality . . . force . . . hope . . . [and] determination" of West Berlin, and described the great "pride" of Americans in supporting the besieged city. "All free men, wherever they may live," he declared, "are citizens of Berlin, and, therefore, as a free man, I take pride in the words, 'Ich bin ein Berliner.'"

What had changed instead were the frightening implications of war in the nuclear age. As the Cuban Missile Crisis was ending, Jack suggested in a letter to Khrushchev that the two "give priority . . . to the great effort for a nuclear test ban" and Khrushchev replied that "we have now conditions ripe for finalizing the agreement on signing a treaty."[26] Eight months later at American University, Jack described peace as the product not of "a sudden revolution in human nature" but of "concrete actions and effective agreements"; said that "the one major area" of U.S.-British-Soviet arms control talks "where the end is in sight, yet where a fresh start is badly needed, is in a treaty to outlaw nuclear tests"; announced that high-level talks to complete a treaty would begin shortly in Moscow; and declared that Washington would not conduct further tests in the atmosphere as long as other nations did not. Just a month after he spoke at American University and then in Berlin, the United States, Soviet Union, and Great Britain completed a treaty that banned tests in space, in the atmosphere, and underwater (allowing them underground), and, two months later, the Senate ratified it on an 80–19 vote.

That summer, after the treaty was completed, Jack was having drinks with his negotiators and other key advisors one evening in Hyannis Port when he termed the treaty his biggest accomplishment to date.

. . .

As Jack was savoring the test-ban treaty and anticipating further progress in reducing U.S.-Soviet tensions, he was shifting course on a quintessential Cold War venture in the jungles of Southeast Asia.

"R. Kennedy Was Very Upset"

9

"George, You're Just Crazier Than Hell!"

The United States should do all it can to help South Vietnam with political support, economic aid, and military equipment, Jack told Roger Hilsman, his nominee for assistant secretary of state for far eastern affairs, in the spring of 1963. But if the South couldn't win with this help, then America should withdraw. What we should *not* do was send troops to fight or widen the war by bombing the North.[1]

Of all the what-ifs about Jack, Vietnam remains the most intriguing. In an interview with CBS's Walter Cronkite in September of 1963, Jack made clear that he was growing impatient with President Ngo Dinh Diem's failure to make the reforms necessary to bolster his domestic support and rally his country around the war. In early November, and with quiet U.S. backing, the South's military chiefs ousted Diem and his powerful brother, Ngo Dinh Nhu, replacing them with what became a succession of military governments over the next few years that proved no better. By then, Jack had signaled more than once that he would withdraw from Vietnam altogether after he (presumably) won reelection in 1964.

Nothing better reflects the conflicting strains of Jack's foreign policy than Vietnam. With the young president fearing that Khrushchev viewed him as weak and stupid after the Bay of Pigs and Vienna, he sought to "make a stand" against communist expansionism thousands of miles from home. Recognizing, however, that a sizable American military presence would ignite the anti-Western fervor in the developing world about which he had long warned, he sent advisors rather than combat troops and limited their numbers, visibility, and role. Not surprisingly, his views about what to do, and whether to cut his losses when problems grew, tilted this way and that as diplomatic and military advisors offered conflicting perspectives about the chances for success and how best to achieve it. That, more than two years into his term, Jack felt compelled to enunciate his policy in Vietnam to Hilsman, who was already a key State Department official, was striking.

Bobby and Ted did what they could to support Jack. But, they, too, found themselves in the last months of Jack's life caught between the Cold War goal of containing Soviet-led communism and the reality of South Vietnam's challenges. Bobby publicly pledged America's commitment to victory while privately helping Jack think through a withdrawal. Ted endured an ugly confrontation with the South's most notorious figure as she defended her government, trashed its critics, and complained about the U.S. effort.

That Jack was so focused on Vietnam in the last months of his life was striking as well, for it did not seem like America's biggest challenge in Southeast Asia when he took office. Back then, all eyes were on Laos.

. . .

"This," President Eisenhower told President-elect Kennedy, "is one of the problems I'm leaving you that I'm not happy about."

It was January 19, 1961, the day before Jack would take office, and he and Ike were meeting a second time since the election. Eisenhower reviewed communist activity across Southeast Asia but focused on Laos, which he called "the cork in the bottle of the Far East," reflecting the "domino theory" that he had enunciated years earlier—that one nation's fall to the communists would trigger the fall of its neighbors. Laos was not a new concern for Washington. After France abandoned its colonial control in 1954, the communist Pathet Lao fought against U.S.-backed government forces in hopes of seizing power. Through 1960, Washington and Moscow had grown more vested in the struggle, and Eisenhower showered

"George, You're Just Crazier Than Hell!"

the U.S. side with hundreds of millions in economic and military aid. If the communists now seized Laos, Ike told Jack, South Vietnam, Cambodia, Thailand, and Burma would fall to them, maybe even the Philippines and Formosa (now Taiwan). "We may have to fight" in Laos, he warned. When Jack asked how long it would take to move a division (about ten thousand troops) there, Ike's defense secretary, Thomas Gates, said twelve to seventeen days. When Jack asked Eisenhower why he hadn't acted more forcefully if he considered the situation "so critical," Ike said that he didn't feel comfortable committing U.S. troops just before ceding power to his successor.[2]

Jack would have been happier to inherit a war that he could blame on his predecessor than launch a new one, as he noted privately, but—in the early days of his administration, when all seemed possible—the new president nevertheless laid the groundwork for action. In his State of the Union address of January 30, he declared, "We seek in Laos . . . freedom for the people and independence for the government." In late March he opened a news conference with a long discussion of Laos, using a map to show where Soviet-backed communists were advancing and explain America's interests in the conflict. Washington sought a "neutral" and "independent" Laos, he said, not one in which the communists had forcefully seized power. At the time, his military advisors were recommending bold steps—to bomb the Pathet Lao or send upward of sixty thousand troops. Because Laos was a landlocked country with poor communications routes through Thailand or South Vietnam, officials concluded that Washington couldn't succeed militarily without a sizable commitment of forces. While rejecting such measures, Jack sent the Seventh Fleet to the Gulf of Thailand and helicopters and personnel to a nearby airfield to showcase America's interest in the conflict and threaten its adversaries with possible intervention.

As Jack was mulling his next steps in Laos, the Bay of Pigs fiasco unfolded. For all the embarrassment it brought him, Jack thought it had one salutary effect: in its aftermath, he viewed Laos in a wholly different light. If the predictions of his military chieftains had proven so wrong about a communist challenge just ninety miles from Florida, why should he trust their predictions about a far more complicated challenge halfway around the world? "Thank God the Bay of Pigs happened when it did," Jack told Ted Sorenson. "Otherwise, we would be in Laos by now—and that would be a hundred times worse."[3] Nor, because Jack had refused to send forces to rescue the Bay of Pigs operation, did he think he could justify military action in Laos. "I don't see how," he told Richard Nixon in April, "we can make any move in Laos which is 5,000 miles away if we don't make a move in Cuba which is 90 miles away."[4]

Fortunately, Khrushchev sent early signals that he wasn't any more interested in a U.S.-Soviet military confrontation over Laos than Jack was. In response, Jack directed Averell Harriman, his assistant secretary of state for East Asian and Pacific affairs (and another of the postwar "wise men"), to spearhead negotiations that prompted a cease-fire and, by the summer of 1962, established a "neutral" government that included both U.S.-backed and communist elements.

With other considerations in mind, Jack viewed Vietnam through a wholly different lens.

. . .

"George, you're just crazier than hell!" Jack told Undersecretary of State George Ball in late 1961, after Ball said that by sending more military advisors to Vietnam, the president was creating the conditions under which the United States would have three hundred thousand troops there in five years. "This decision doesn't mean that. We're not going to have 300,000 men in Asia."[5]

Jack dismissed Ball's prediction—which proved eerily prophetic under LBJ—for multiple reasons. Not only did he expect to still be president in five years and still deciding where U.S. troops were stationed, but he was also keenly sensitive to the downsides of a big American military footprint in the developing world. Nor was Jack alone in his forebodings about a U.S. combat role in Southeast Asia. When he sought the advice of General Douglas MacArthur about Laos in April of 1961, MacArthur warned him not only that America should not fight there but that "anyone wanting to

"George, You're Just Crazier Than Hell!"

commit ground troops to Asia should have his head examined."[6] MacArthur's warning helped Jack rebuff calls to send troops to Vietnam. "Whenever he'd get this military advice from the Joint Chiefs or from me or anyone else," General Maxwell Taylor recalled, "he'd say, 'Well, now, you gentlemen, you go back and convince General MacArthur, then I'll be convinced.'"[7]

Nevertheless, Jack told his top aides more than once in the spring of 1961 that, after the Bay of Pigs and Vienna, he would make a stand in Vietnam. To Jack and his team, Vietnam was now, in Ike's phrase, the "cork in the bottle." As Bobby recalled years later, JFK feared "the loss of all of Southeast Asia if you lost Vietnam. I think everybody was quite clear that the rest of Southeast Asia would fall."[8] Rather than do the fighting, however, the United States would teach the South Vietnamese how to fight so they could win the war. Unlike in Laos, where Jack wasn't sure that Washington had an effective leader with whom to work, he had viewed Diem as a good partner ever since Diem deployed American aid effectively, in the late 1950s, to build his country and nourish support among his people. When, at Jack's direction, Vice President Johnson flew to Saigon to meet with Diem in May, he carried a letter from Jack that offered more aid and closer collaboration; LBJ reinforced Jack's warm feelings by publicly labeling Diem the "Winston Churchill of Asia." Unlike Laos, South Vietnam also offered a long coastline on which to land U.S. personnel and supplies.

As Jack knew, however, America's challenges in the South were mounting as he took office. Though effective in the past, Diem was growing more remote from his people and less tolerant of dissent, and he stoked grassroots anger by ignoring calls for reforms that would reduce his power. Army officers tried to topple him in a coup attempt in late 1960, reflecting the growing unhappiness among those close to him, and he responded by arresting fifty thousand "enemies" and torturing or killing many of them.

A week into his presidency, Jack read a report from Edward Lansdale, the model for a main character in *The Ugly American*, suggesting that U.S. officials needed a new approach to Diem. Lansdale described him as a proud man who resented Washington's way of ordering him around rather than seeking to work with him. Though he was becoming more difficult, Lansdale warned, Washington had no realistic alternative.

. . .

In May of 1961, Jack sent four hundred Green Berets to train South Vietnamese troops, reflecting his enthusiasm for counterinsurgency.

For most of 1961, however, his advisors were focused more on Laos, the Bay of Pigs, Vienna, and Berlin, and they didn't pay enough attention to Vietnam, as several later acknowledged. After twenty-six thousand Vietcong launched several successful attacks against the South in the fall, alarming U.S. officials, Jack sent Maxwell Taylor and Walt Rostow, his deputy national security advisor, to Vietnam in October to assess the situation. They returned two weeks later to express ominous concerns about the South's future, warn that its fall would make nearby nations more susceptible to communist takeovers, and recommend that Jack send more advisors and up to eight thousand troops and give the troops a combat role. While Defense Secretary Robert McNamara and the Joint Chiefs backed the call for troops, they scoffed at the eight thousand figure and suggested two hundred thousand, to make the U.S. commitment clear not just in Hanoi but in Moscow and Beijing as well.

Jack sent more advisors (who numbered just over two thousand by year-end), along with helicopter units to help guide South Vietnamese troops. Rejecting the call for troops, however, he mocked the very idea. "The troops will march in; the crowds will cheer; and in four days everyone will have forgotten," he told Arthur Schlesinger Jr. in late 1961. "Then we will be told that we have to send in more troops. It is like taking a drink. The effect wears off, and you have to take another."[9]

At times he was even forced to remind those in the field that they were there to provide advice, not fight the war. Sailing on the *Honey Fitz*, the presidential yacht that he named for his grandfather, off the coast of Newport one day, he picked up the phone to hear

"George, You're Just Crazier Than Hell!"

from an aide that some marines wanted to mount an attack under what they considered ideal conditions. Jack left his swivel chair on the deck, picked up a phone in a private area, and made clear that he wanted no such action to occur.

While Jack worked to limit the U.S. role in Vietnam, Bobby stressed America's commitment to the broad effort.

. . .

President Kennedy "has been extremely impressed with the courage and determination of the people of your country," Bobby said during a two-hour refueling stop in Saigon during his global tour of early 1962, "and he has pledged the United States to stand by the side of Vietnam through this very difficult and troublesome time."

In such a setting, Bobby's expression of robust support—"We will win in Vietnam and we shall remain here until we do"—was hardly surprising. He was greeted at the airport by Ngo Dinh Nhu, Diem's brother and chief political advisor, and, through the reporters on hand, addressed his remarks to the people of that war-torn country at a time when Vietcong attacks were escalating. When a British reporter noted that "American boys are dying out here" and asked whether the American people understood and supported U.S. involvement, Bobby responded in Churchillian tones. "I think the American people understand and fully support this struggle," he said. "Americans have great affection for the people of Vietnam. I think the United States will do what is necessary to help a country that is trying to repel aggression with its own blood, tears and sweat."[10]

The war had special meaning to Bobby because, by the time of his global tour, he was deeply enmeshed in the administration's counterinsurgency strategy and viewed Vietnam as a place to deploy it. In *Just Friends and Brave Enemies*, his book about the tour, he wrote of Vietnam, "It is war in the very real sense of the word, yet it is a war fought not by massive divisions but secretly by terror, assassination, ambush, and infiltration."[11] America's counterinsurgency effort in Vietnam, however, suffered from two big drawbacks. First, to a great extent, American military officials in Washington and advisors in South Vietnam didn't buy into the concept, and the advisors were largely training the South's troops in conventional warfare. Second, Diem was resisting the political and social reform, which Washington was urging, that would nourish more domestic support for him and, in turn, the war effort.

At the very time that Bobby was pledging that America will "win" and "remain here until we do," his brother was starting to mull a sizable shift in direction. In light of the South's mounting military losses, Washington's growing problems with Diem, and the rising calls for troops that were making him wary, Jack was wondering whether a Laos-like solution would make more sense. In April of 1962, he discussed the war with John Kenneth Galbraith, America's ambassador to India and a friend, on a farm in Virginia. He then directed Galbraith to work through Indian officials to send a peace feeler to Hanoi, offering to reduce U.S. activity if the North scaled back its guerilla operations.

But Averell Harriman, the assistant secretary of state, convinced Jack to delay the overture, and he never gave Galbraith the final go-ahead.

. . .

"We don't have a prayer of staying in Vietnam," Jack told a friend in April of 1963, around the time he was advising Hilsman to maintain the U.S. effort. "Those people hate us. They are going to throw our asses out of there at almost any point. But I can't give up a piece of territory like that to the communists and then get the American people to reelect me."[12]

Publicly, Jack insisted that he didn't think the United States should withdraw from South Vietnam; privately, he suggested more than once that his end game was a postelection withdrawal. In July of 1962, he directed McNamara to plan for a phased withdrawal that would stretch through the end of 1965 and transition South Vietnam's troops, as trained by American advisors, to assume all on-the-ground responsibility. Then, while relaxing in Florida over the Christmas holidays, he referenced the "Who lost China?" fervor

"George, You're Just Crazier Than Hell!"

that he helped fuel as a House member in the late 1940s to explain why a U.S. withdrawal from Vietnam would have to wait. "If I tried to pull out completely now from Vietnam," he told White House aide Kenny O'Donnell, "we would have another Joe McCarthy red scare on our hands, but I can do it after I'm reelected. So we had better make damn sure that I *am* reelected."[13]

At the end of 1962, America had 11,500 military advisors in Vietnam, but real progress was hard to find. It was a depressing end to a year that began with far brighter hopes, with Jack and his advisors investing more energy and devising new strategies to turn things around. Jack issued a directive in January to enable some advisors to engage in combat operations (while continuing to deny publicly that any U.S. personnel were doing so), and he launched a "strategic hamlet" program in March that was supposed to protect hamlets (i.e., small areas) from the Vietcong and persuade the peasants to support the South's efforts. After visiting the South, McNamara proclaimed in May that "we are winning the war." By year-end, however, the North was showing no sign of troop shortages; the Vietcong were handling the South's military tactics more effectively; the strategic hamlet program (which Diem gave his brother to run) was failing because, as the CIA told Jack, "the six thousand hamlets were more like concentration camps than fortified villages of patriots"; and Diem was growing more isolated.[14] In a report in December, Hilsman labeled the notion that "the tide is now turning" as "premature." "At best," he wrote, "it appears that the rate of deterioration has decelerated."[15]

Meanwhile, Jack's allies on Capitol Hill were getting antsy. When, at his request, Senate Majority Leader Mike Mansfield visited South Vietnam in late November of 1962, he refused to issue a statement (which America's embassy in Saigon drafted) that said he was "encouraged" by the progress.[16] The South "can" make progress, he told Jack in a written report in December, if its challenges didn't grow and both Saigon and Washington implemented effective on-the-ground strategies. Otherwise, he said, "It is difficult to conceive of alternatives, with the possible exception of a truly massive commitment of American military personnel and other resources—in short, going to war fully ourselves against the guerillas—and the establishment of some form of neocolonial rule in South Vietnam."[17] When the two met in Florida just before New Year's Eve, Jack angrily told Mansfield that he was hearing something different from "my people." The president wasn't naïve, however. It was after meeting with Mansfield that he discussed a postelection withdrawal with O'Donnell.

As Jack, in late 1963, mulled a withdrawal, his youngest brother tangled with Saigon's most notorious figure.

. . .

"Listening to Madame Nhu," Ted Kennedy told the Advertising Club of Boston in September of 1963, referring to Diem's powerful sister-in-law, "did not change my feeling that no government which pursues a policy of religious persecution, a policy that sets group against group and causes so much strife, can hope to keep the confidence of the people that is so necessary to their fight against communism."[18]

That month, Ted had "listened" to Madame Ngo Dinh Nhu in Belgrade while the two attended an Inter-Parliamentary Union conference. Serving as a U.S. delegate, Ted would talk about race in America at a timely moment—just three weeks after Martin Luther King delivered his "I Have A Dream" speech in Washington. Echoing the sentiments of Jack and Bobby, Ted said that America held itself to a high standard due to its values, acknowledged that it had fallen short on race, but noted that Jack's election showed that it was making progress by overcoming the "No Irish Need Apply" bigotry of its earlier years. Ted's remarks, however, were overshadowed by his encounter with Nhu.

The caustic, flamboyant, embittered, and altogether dishonest Nhu unexpectedly plopped herself down next to Ted at a lunch in Belgrade and delivered what he later called a "ninety-minute tirade" that whitewashed Diem's human rights abuses and disparaged the Buddhists protesting Saigon's crackdown on them. In Washington,

"George, You're Just Crazier Than Hell!"

Jack was alarmed that Nhu had cornered his brother because their encounter, which the *New York Times* covered on its front page, came at a particularly sensitive moment—as JFK and Diem were tangling publicly over how Saigon could best win the war. Nhu had sought out Ted, and another U.S. delegate steered her to a seat next to him.

That fall, Jack's Vietnam policy was under attack on several fronts. Diem, the Catholic ruler of a mostly Buddhist nation, had used deadly force against Buddhist demonstrators over the spring and summer, and several Buddhist monks burned themselves to death in gruesome protests that were splashed across the front pages of America's newspapers and aired on TV. As Diem imposed martial law and his brother, Ngo Dinh Nhu, sent special forces to target Buddhist sanctuaries, Buddhist leaders pressured Jack to cut ties with Diem. The president found the Buddhist crisis particularly painful. "Mike, I just cannot have a religious war out there," Jack told Michael Forrestal, a top White House foreign policy advisor. "It isn't just that I'm a Catholic myself, and therefore in an immensely difficult position. It's just that to add to all our other difficulties in Vietnam the prospects of a religious conflict will make this problem completely unmanageable."[19] At Jack's direction, U.S. officials in Saigon pressured Diem to fire his brother and institute reforms, but he steadfastly refused.

Meanwhile, Madame Nhu called Buddhist self-immolations "barbeques," earning her the "Dragon Lady" sobriquet, and she offered to provide more gasoline and "clap" if more Buddhists wanted to burn themselves to death. Her stop in Belgrade, where she headed Saigon's five-member delegation, was part of a U.S. and European tour in which she defended Diem and her husband. Responding to Jack's calls for reforms, she termed him a "politician" trying to "appease" his critics, said he was "misinformed," insisted that Saigon respected human rights, criticized Washington for not effectively helping the South in its war, and dismissed reporters as "spoiled children" who were plotting against Diem's government.[20]

. . .

"The two of you did visit the same country, didn't you?" Jack asked General Victor Krulak and the State Department's Joseph Mendenhall after they briefed him about South Vietnam in September of 1963.[21]

At Jack's direction, Krulak and Mendenhall flew to South Vietnam to assess the situation, but they would do so from different vantage points; Mendenhall interviewed U.S. officials in Saigon, Hue, and Da Nang, while Krulak traveled across the provinces. Briefing the president and more than a dozen other top officials on September 10, Krulak was upbeat: the South was making military progress and, despite Diem, would win "if the current U.S. military and sociological programs are pursued." Mendenhall was not: the war against the Vietcong, he said, was now "secondary to the 'war' against the regime"; Buddhists and Catholics were close to civil war; a "pervasive atmosphere of fear and hate" engulfed Saigon; and the South couldn't win if Ngo Dinh Nhu remained.

Jack was torn between Diem's refusal to reform and his own reluctance to withdraw precipitously. By the time of the briefing, however, he was mulling not whether to pursue a post-reelection withdrawal but, instead, how to orchestrate it. When, in his interview with Cronkite, the CBS anchor asked him an open-ended question about Vietnam, he blurted, "I don't think that unless a greater effort is made by the government to win popular support that the war can be won out there. In the final analysis, it is their war." Only after criticizing Diem at greater length did he volunteer the other side of the equation. "I don't agree with those who say we should withdraw," he said. "That would be a great mistake." His sharp tone about Diem was striking: just two months earlier, he had called Saigon's crackdown on the Buddhists merely "unfortunate" because it came just as "the military struggle has been going better than it has been going in many months."

In early October, Maxwell Taylor, who was now chairing the Joint Chiefs, and McNamara returned from a fact-finding trip to South Vietnam. Meeting with Jack in the Oval Office, they told him that the South was making military progress, recommended that he with-

"George, You're Just Crazier Than Hell!"

draw one thousand of the nearly eighteen thousand U.S. military advisors, and assured him (as Taylor put it) that the South could reduce "this urgency to little more than sporadic incidents" in most places by 1964.[22] Jack agreed to bring one thousand advisors home and set a target date of 1965 for a full withdrawal. Whether, in light of the gloomier assessments he had received, he really thought that the South was making much progress remains unclear.

Also unclear is how Jack would have orchestrated a full withdrawal. At one point he suggested that Saigon might simply ask the United States to leave. At other times he and Bobby pointed to Laos and pondered whether negotiations could establish a "neutral" government in Vietnam as well.

. . .

After Jack's death, Vietnam was among the myriad global challenges that Bobby and Ted would address in the years to come. As they increasingly opposed LBJ's Vietnam strategy, they played a huge role in undermining the Cold War consensus and pushing America's empire in strikingly new directions.

PART 2

10

"I Wouldn't Be My Grandfather's Grandson"

"[Polish leader Wladyslaw] Gomulka would never have done a thing like that," Jozef Winiewicz, Poland's deputy foreign minister, told Bobby Kennedy in June of 1964, denouncing him for milling among the Polish people in Warsaw, Cracow, and other cities. "Well," Bobby replied, "maybe that's what's wrong with Gomulka."[1]

The tense exchange, over dinner at the U.S. embassy in Warsaw, came at the end of Bobby's week-long visit to Germany and Poland with Ethel, three of their children, and aides. Bobby marked the one-year anniversary of Jack's "Ich bin ein Berliner" speech in Berlin by addressing seventy thousand West Berliners on the same spot where Jack had spoken and dedicating a plaque to his slain brother. From that gut-wrenching experience, he traveled to Poland to promote U.S.-Polish ties. While behind the Iron Curtain, he ignored protocol; met with Warsaw's most feared critics; and waded into crowds that gathered wherever he went to cheer him and, when they were close enough, grab and kiss him. He angered communist leaders who feared that he was stoking the freedom-starved Polish people to anger against their government, and he embarrassed U.S. officials who were stationed in Poland and followed the rules they had worked out with the regime.

The year 1964 was a tumultuous one for Bobby as he mulled what to do next in the aftermath of Jack's death, and it was a frightening one for Ted. Just a week before Bobby left for Europe, Ted almost died when the seven-seat, twin-engine plane that was carrying him from Washington to Massachusetts for a political event crashed in an apple orchard outside Springfield, Massachusetts. After driving all night from Hyannis Port to the hospital in Northampton to see Ted, who lay with a broken back, a punctured lung, and cracked ribs, Bobby took a walk with Walter Sheridan, a family friend who had rushed to the hospital from Washington. When, after strolling across a field near the hospital, the two men laid down on the grass, Bobby lamented, "Somebody up there doesn't like me."[2]

As he continued recovering from Jack's death, participating in more events in the early months of 1964, Bobby remained a hearty Cold Warrior. On St. Patrick's Day in Scranton, Pennsylvania, he quoted the Irish poet John O'Reilly—as Jack had done—to warn that "the world is small when your enemy is loose on the other side," adding, "The greatest enemy of freedom today, of course, is communism, a tyranny that holds its captives in vise-like subjugation on a global scale." A month later in Toronto, he called for a stronger U.S. commitment to a "war of ideals" to defeat communism, saying, "We have not been as tough, aggressive, or articulate as we might have been" in promoting freedom. In June at the California Institute of Technology, he called for better training for "foreign nationals to defend themselves against communist terrorism and guerilla penetration" but, more importantly, for "progressive political programs which wipe out the poverty, misery, and discontent on which [communism] thrives." In Berlin his words were eerily similar to Jack's as he explained why communist advances anywhere threatened freedom everywhere and how the West could prevent them. Two weeks before leaving for Germany and Poland, he wrote LBJ to offer to serve as America's ambassador to Saigon, an offer that LBJ seemed to appreciate but rejected out of fear for Bobby's safety in a war zone.

With summer ending and Ted immobilized but recovering, Bobby resigned as attorney general to run for a Senate seat from New York. He easily won the Democratic nomination and handily defeated GOP incumbent Kenneth Keating, with whom Jack had tangled over Cuba in 1962. As Bobby told friends, however, he didn't want to be a senator. He remained anguished by the circumstances that forced him to ponder life after Jack, and he recognized that, with his natural impatience, he would find it hard to transition from an executive role in which he could make things happen on his own to a legislative role in which he would have to build consensus among his colleagues to advance legislation. (Even when he worked in Jack's administration in the early 1960s, he couldn't stomach the demands of retail politics. After helping Jack schmooze lawmakers on the presidential yacht one evening, Bobby plopped into an aide's car, loosened his tie, and sighed, "What a shitty job this is."[3]) Nevertheless, after LBJ told him in demeaning fashion at a tense White House meeting in late July of 1964 that he wouldn't choose him to run for vice president that year, Bobby decided that the Senate was his best path for political rebirth—and a future White House run.

Bobby's first trip abroad to shape foreign policy after Jack's death wasn't the one to Europe, however; it was a trip to Asia in early 1964. Oddly enough, it was the hostile LBJ who sent him on the peace mission that, if it went well, would prevent war between Indonesia and Malaysia and also revive Bobby's spirits.

. . .

"He's functioning again," a relieved companion said after Bobby landed on January 17 at western Tokyo's Yokota Air base, laid a wreath at a ten-foot granite memorial to JFK that Japanese employees had built, grew teary-eyed as he studied it, and gave his tie pin to the employee who led the drive to build it.[4]

Bobby was two days into his peace mission to the Far East, and his entourage was buoyed by his energy. Since Jack's murder, he had been largely absent in both mind and body—"shattered," as more than one friend put it. He was still the attorney general, but he didn't go to work, leaving his top aides to run the Justice Department. To those who saw him, he seemed in physical pain. His eyes were hollow, the bags under them pronounced, the wrinkles in his face etched more deeply. He stared into space, started sentences without finishing them, couldn't focus, lost interest, and cracked morbid jokes. That many people who had immediately returned his calls when he was the "Assistant President" now took their time made him feel even more lost. As his weight fell, suits sagged on his body and shirt collars wobbled around his neck.

As friends sought to reinvigorate him, a few top foreign policy officials decided that a mission to resolve a border conflict in the Far East, which was years in the making, might help. At the urging of Britain, a colonial power in the region, Malaya joined with Singapore and two former British protectorates in Borneo to create the Federation of Malaysia in September of 1963. The parties had been talking up their plans to create the federation since the spring of 1961 but, in February of 1963, Indonesia's president, Sukarno, declared his opposition due to suspicions about British motives and fears that the federation would complicate his plans to create a Greater Indonesia. After the federation was born in September, Sukarno launched his "Crush Malaysia" campaign, with Indonesia-backed guerrillas launching attacks across its border with Malaysia, on the island of Borneo. Complicating matters further, the Philippines refused to recognize the federation due to an old territorial dispute.

A day after Sukarno voiced his opposition to the federation in early 1963, Jack voiced his support because he considered Malaysia an important Cold War bulwark against communist China. "It is," he told reporters, "the best hope of security for that very vital part of the world."[5] Upon its creation in September, he sent his deputy undersecretary of state, Alexis Johnson, to the celebration as his representative. Just days before his death in November, he told U.S. diplomatic officials that they could tell Sukarno that, if he ended his dispute with Malaysia, Washington would boost its aid to Indonesia and he would visit the following spring. As the conflict simmered in the weeks after Jack's death, raising prospects for open war, Washington found itself in a tricky spot—between a troublesome ally in Indonesia, which was the most populous country of Southeast Asia, and a new pro-Western, anti-communist ally in Malaysia. Moreover, due to America's treaty commitments, Washington might face the question of whether it must intervene if war broke out and drew in, say, the nearby military forces of Australia or New Zealand.

"I Wouldn't Be My Grandfather's Grandson"

If LBJ needed to send an emissary to the region to ease tensions, Bobby Kennedy was a logical choice. He had spent a week in Indonesia during his global tour of early 1962 and, while there, convinced Sukarno to stop threatening military action against Netherlands New Guinea by assuring him that his dispute with the Dutch over the territory would be resolved in his favor (which it later was). In early 1964, America's ambassador to Indonesia, Howard Jones, recommended that LBJ send Bobby, and the idea gained support from such top foreign policy officials (and Kennedy-ites) as Averell Harriman, Roger Hilsman, Michael Forrestal, and McGeorge Bundy.

LBJ agreed only reluctantly, for he already felt a hatred for Bobby that would only grow in the coming years.

. . .

"Bob is very warm," Sukarno later told the writer Cindy Adams. "He is like his brother. I loved his brother."[6]

After a forty-five-minute chat with LBJ in the White House, Bobby set off with Ethel on a trip of almost two weeks. He met with Sukarno in Tokyo, where the Indonesian autocrat was vacationing, and, while there, he also met with Japan's premier, Hayato Ikeda, and Emperor Hirohito. After a side trip to South Korea to visit America's troops, he flew to Manila for a two-and-a-half-hour meeting with the Philippines' president, Diosdado Macapagal, at the Malacanang Palace, a historic structure where the president lived and worked. He was next off to Kuala Lumpur, where he met with Prince Abdul Rahman, Malaysia's prime minister. From there he flew to Jakarta for more talks with Sukarno.

With a nod to what all three Kennedy brothers had learned from their travels across the developing world, Bobby made clear that he hadn't come to impose an American solution to the conflict. "This is an Asian dispute," he said more than once, "and should be decided by Asian countries." Instead, he was there to nudge the parties toward peace, to "take this controversy out of the jungle, out of the warfare that is now taking place, and put it around the conference table."[7]

Sukarno was key to resolving the conflict, for he had ignited it with his "Crush Malaysia" campaign, and, fortunately, Bobby had some leverage over him. A new U.S. foreign aid law required that Washington end its $12 million in annual education and other aid to Indonesia unless the president declared that maintaining it remained in America's interest, and LBJ had sent word to Sukarno that he'd be hard-pressed to do so if Indonesia continued its action against Malaysia. By then Washington had already ended its $2.5 million in military aid. After a week of shuttle diplomacy across the region, Bobby won a ceasefire between Indonesia and Malaysia and a commitment by those countries and the Philippines for talks to begin in February on a final solution.

Bobby was reinvigorated by the diplomatic accomplishment and warm welcomes. In Tokyo, he returned to Waseda University, where communist students had heckled him in 1962. This time, ten thousand students cheered wildly as a teary-eyed Bobby eulogized Jack as "not only President of one nation" but "President of young people around the world."[8] When Bobby landed at the airport in Manila, he was met by five hundred people on the field and five thousand more on a rooftop observation area. Before he left Manila, students at Philippine Women's University greeted him enthusiastically.

"I hadn't wanted to go on that trip," he later told journalist Murray Kempton, "but afterwards I was glad I had."[9] Decades later, Ted wrote that it "restored [Bobby's] faith that life was worth living after all."[10]

. . .

"The man from Pittsburgh is not free until the man from Peking is free," Bobby told seventy thousand West Berliners on June 26, on the very spot from which Jack had spoken exactly a year earlier, in what was now John F. Kennedy Square, with words that echoed the "Ich bin ein Berliner" message of JFK's moving address. "The man from West Berlin is not free until his brother from East Berlin is also free."

While in Germany, Bobby met with President Heinrich Lubke, Chancellor Ludwig Erhard, Foreign Minister Gerhard Schroeder,

"I Wouldn't Be My Grandfather's Grandson"

and former Chancellor Konrad Adenauer; donned a helmet as he took a "bone-shaking ride in a tank that stopped occasionally to fire a volley of blank shells"; delivered the John F. Kennedy Memorial Lecture at the Free University of Berlin; spoke at Heidelberg University; and toured a school, a factory, and a U.S. military housing development.[11] As with Jack a year earlier, the German people welcomed Bobby in rousing fashion. "Bobby, Bobby," eight hundred people chanted when he arrived at Frankfurt Airport. Some three hundred thousand people lined the streets as his motorcade wound its way through West Berlin, on the same route that Jack had taken, while Bobby stood in the passenger seat of an open convertible and waved. At City Hall the seventy thousand in attendance chanted "Kennedy, Kennedy" when he appeared on stage with Mayor Willy Brandt, a police band played the German tune "I Had a Comrade," and the crowd cheered heartily when he said that the name West Berlin was a "password of freedom."[12]

He had come to West Germany at a timely moment. Two weeks earlier, the Soviets had signed a new twenty-year treaty of friendship with East Germany that accorded it the same status as other members of the Soviets' Eastern European bloc. Ever since the allies partitioned Germany after World War II, Western officials were sensitive to any moves by Moscow that would further implant East Germany in the Soviet orbit rather than move toward the German reunification that the West supported. In fact, on the day Bobby spoke in Berlin, the United States, Great Britain, and France issued a joint statement to denounce the treaty for seeking to "perpetuate the arbitrary division of Germany." In response Moscow sent notes to the three Western capitals that stressed its commitment to defend East Germany, denounced West Berlin's participation in West Germany's presidential election, and stated, "It is well known that West Berlin never belonged and does not belong" to West Germany.[13] U.S.-Soviet tensions raised the stakes for Bobby's remarks.

One can only imagine the emotion that a still-grieving, thirty-eight-year-old Bobby must have felt when he mounted the stage outside City Hall to pay homage to his beloved brother on the one-year anniversary of an iconic JFK moment. Bobby had dedicated most of his adult life to John Fitzgerald Kennedy: volunteering for his House campaign of 1946, directing his uphill Senate victory of 1952, driving his long-shot quest for the vice presidential nomination in 1956, running his campaign for president in 1960, and serving as his confidante in his administration. A month after Jack's death, Bobby told a friend that, for the first time, he needed to find a goal for himself because his goal up to then was always to advance his brother's career. Perhaps to draw comfort for himself, Bobby tailored his remarks in Germany to what Jack had said in Berlin and throughout his career. In the years to come, his aides kept Jack's speeches nearby as they drafted Bobby's.

In Berlin in 1963, Jack closed by saying, "All free men, wherever they may live, are citizens of Berlin, and, therefore, as a free man, I take pride in the words 'Ich bin ein Berliner.'" A year later, Bobby closed by saying that on behalf of his brother, his family, and the American people, "we are proud to be among you as free citizens of the world." In proposing the Peace Corps while running for president, Jack challenged young people to "spend your days in Ghana" or work in the Foreign Service. At Heidelberg University, Bobby told students that "the carpeted office of the medical specialist has little relationship to the ailing peasant child in Latin America" and asked them whether, once they prospered, they would "lend your talents to the service of your society—and of all societies on this shrinking planet."

West Germany's leaders welcomed Bobby's reassuring words about the rock-solid American commitment to defend their country. He received a far cooler reception when he expressed himself in Poland.

. . .

In defying Warsaw's efforts to force him to follow protocol, Bobby explained, "I wouldn't be my grandfather's grandson if I didn't."

He was surely referring to the often-defiant Honey Fitz, who lived until Bobby was almost twenty-five and with whom he shared a middle name: Francis. On this trip, however, he was just as much his

"I Wouldn't Be My Grandfather's Grandson"

father's son, for he displayed all the audacity that Joe had exhibited as America's ambassador in London. For three tumultuous days in Poland, he clashed repeatedly with the authorities. After it ended, wrote the *New York Times*'s Arthur J. Olsen, who followed him across Poland, he left behind "a United States embassy in a state of shock, a half-angry, half-bewildered Polish Government and a good many thousand ordinary Poles in a state of euphoria. . . . In the short run the Kennedy visit certainly did harm to Polish-United States relations. In the long run the Kennedy invasion of Poland may well be remembered as an act of unorthodox statesmanship. Using deliberate shock tactics, he assaulted the complacencies of diplomats and Communist functionaries."[14]

As the brother of a beloved president and an unofficial ambassador from the world of freedom, Bobby was mobbed wherever he went. He landed in Warsaw on June 27 after flying on a U.S. Air Force plane that took a three-hundred-mile detour to avoid flying over East Germany because the United States didn't officially recognize that country. At the airport, he was met by a crowd of two hundred, with men and women throwing flowers at him and yelling "sto lat," a traditional Polish wish for someone to live one hundred years. When he stepped outside his limousine to shake hands after the crowd blocked its path, three men "gave him the Slavic embrace with a resounding kiss on the side of the face."[15] When, that night, he stepped into Crocodile, Warsaw's nicest restaurant, he wound up sitting with a celebrating bride and her friends, offering her good wishes ("May you have as many children as we have—eight"), and waltzing with her.[16] The next day, two thousand cheering, clapping, bouquet-bearing people followed Bobby and Ethel as they walked to church where they received Holy Communion, and the crowd grew to ten thousand before they reemerged. They climbed aboard the roof of Ambassador John Moors Cabot's car to speak to the boisterous throng. Bobby ignored the warnings of Cabot, who was sitting inside, that the roof was caving in. He then spoke to five hundred raucous students at Warsaw University before making unscheduled stops at the Tomb of the Unknown Soldier and

Slaski Park. When he and Ethel visited the ancient square in Cracow, the Irish couple delighted the crowd by improvising an off-key rendition of "When Polish Eyes Are Smiling."

As the Polish people fell for Bobby, the authorities sought to limit his impact. Before he and Ethel arrived at an orphanage amid a blinding rainstorm to distribute copies of Charles Schulz's *Happiness Is a Warm Puppy*, officials whisked the children away to another location. Bobby ignored a government warning that a meeting with Stefan Cardinal Wyszynski, the Catholic primate, would damage U.S.-Polish relations due to Warsaw's clashes with the Church over religious freedom. When he actually met with Wyszynski in Czestochowa, the authorities reversed course and accommodated him. Warsaw relaxed its regulations that normally put the city off limits to U.S. embassy officials and let two officials travel with him and use an embassy car.

The Polish leg of Bobby's trip further revived his spirits. He displayed the boyish wonder, mischievous wit, stubborn impatience, and dogged independence that defined him before Jack's death. After returning home, he launched the next phase of his career, with vast implications for America's global role.

. . .

"I see the foreign policy of the United States," New York's Democratic candidate for Senate declared in late September of 1964, "as an opportunity to turn adversaries into friends and ancient allies into modern partners."[17]

In his campaign, Bobby focused heavily on foreign policy partly because he wanted to promote Jack's successes as a blueprint for his own foreign policy and partly because Republican incumbent Kenneth Keating was attacking Bobby's performance on the issue. Bobby advocated negotiations with Moscow to ease tensions, highlighting the Cuban Missile Crisis and nuclear test-ban treaty as successful examples, and he suggested that Washington explore whether "recent advances in the art of detection" would enable the two sides to expand Jack's limited nuclear test-ban treaty by banning

"I Wouldn't Be My Grandfather's Grandson"

underground testing.[18] Highlighting the Alliance for Progress and JFK's outreach to progressive leaders across the developing world, Bobby renewed Jack's call to loosen ties to right-wing dictators and put America on the side of political reform to nourish democracy.

Bobby and Keating clashed repeatedly on foreign policy. Bobby charged that Keating's efforts of early 1963 to promote a relentlessly tough anti-Soviet stance jeopardized Jack's efforts to complete a test-ban treaty—and that Keating ridiculed the treaty itself, speaking in its favor only when the Senate seemed certain to ratify it. Keating called Bobby's charges "a complete and utter distortion," saying he consistently supported the treaty.[19] The Republican incumbent mocked Bobby's efforts to make peace between Indonesia and Malaysia, noting that the parties didn't carry out the agreement he had fashioned.

Bobby's former colleagues defended him when Keating attacked. "Kennedy was a major participant in every important foreign policy action of his brother's Administration, from Berlin to the test ban," Abram Chayes, the State Department's former legal advisor, wrote in a long letter in the *New York Times*. "He contributed responsible counsel that met the test in the crucible of decision, not the public talk that is often so cheap and easy."[20]

As Bobby pursued public office in the aftermath of Jack's death, his younger brother sought his own personal recovery.

. . .

In the spring of 1964, Ted Kennedy traveled abroad in search of solace after the loss of his beloved older brother.

"Today is a day of joy and sadness for me," Ted told a swarming crowd in spur-of-the-moment remarks outside a Dublin presbytery after a memorial service for Jack, who had visited Ireland for three rousing days the previous summer. "Joy because I am in Ireland on a beautiful spring day, sadness because today is the President's birthday. My brother will not be able to come back and enjoy any more spring days here." At that point, he choked up and his eyes filled with tears, evoking tears in many who were listening. "In all the time I've known him," a close friend said later, "I've never seen Ted as deeply moved. He just stopped. And then he got hold of himself and went on."[21]

After the memorial service, Ted visited the U.S. ambassador, Matthew McCloskey, at his Phoenix Park residence, where Ted spoke with "ruddy-cheeked youngsters" who were waiting at the gates and then went inside to where the Irish people had sent mail, rosaries, poems, and donations to what would become the John F. Kennedy Library and Museum, in Cambridge, Massachusetts. He lunched with businessmen; visited Lord Mayor Sean Moore at Dublin's City Hall; was mobbed as he walked the streets; attended an evening reception that Ireland's prime minister, Sean Lemass, threw for him at Iveagh House; followed up that night with a half pint of stout at a pub; drank tea at another pub the next morning; distributed autographs and PT-109 pins to children after his morning tea; visited the "clan of Fitzgerald" (his mother's ancestors) in Adare; and spoke to forty thousand people in Limerick.

Ted's trip to Ireland was part of a larger European tour to raise funds for the JFK Library. He met with British, French, German, and Italian leaders as well as Pope Paul VI. In London, Harold Macmillan, the former prime minister, broke down in tears as he spoke to Ted about his relationship with Jack.

At City Hall in Dublin, Ted noted that Jack's three days in Ireland were "the happiest days in the president's life." Indeed, Jack and the Irish people had showered one another with love. "Some of us who came on this trip," Jack said as it was ending, "could come home and—here to Ireland—and feel ourselves at home and not feel ourselves in a strange country, but feel ourselves among neighbors, even though we are separated by generations, by time, and by thousands of miles." Even more striking, he said, "This is not the land of my birth, but it is the land for which I hold the greatest affection, and I certainly will come back in the springtime."

It was Jack's promise about the springtime to which Ted referred in Dublin and that brought him to tears.

"I Wouldn't Be My Grandfather's Grandson"

. . .

From a hospital in Boston more than two months later after his plane crash, Ted announced his support for the Gulf of Tonkin resolution, through which Congress authorized LBJ to "take all necessary measures [in Vietnam] to repel any armed attack against the forces of the United States and to prevent further aggression."

The resolution, which only two senators and no House members opposed, would prove controversial in the years to come for the unlimited power it gave LBJ to escalate the war, and for the mounting questions over whether the White House had accurately portrayed the underlying Gulf of Tonkin incident as an act of North Vietnamese aggression. Four decades later, Ted cited the resolution as he explained why he opposed the 2003 U.S.-led war in Iraq. In the summer of 1964, however, the resolution merely made him antsy to return to work. "Events of the past few days," he wrote to Ralph Yarborough, a Texas senator, during the debate, "made me wish more than ever that I was down in the Senate in the midst of the goings on."[22]

During his six-month recuperation, his body in a Stryker frame, Ted stayed abreast of public matters with the help of his staff and officials who briefed him and professors who conducted seminars on foreign and domestic issues. Those who stopped by to educate him included Defense Secretary Robert McNamara, Assistant Labor Secretary Daniel Patrick Moynihan, Harvard's John Kenneth Galbraith, and MIT's Jerome Wiesner.

. . .

A day after they won their Senate races, Bobby and Ted Kennedy posed for pictures at the hospital.

"Step back a little," a photographer told Bobby, who was standing alongside Ted's bed, "you're casting a shadow on Ted."

"It's going to be the same in Washington," the younger brother cracked.[23]

He wasn't far off.

11

"Are These People for Real?"

"What should I say about the Dominican crisis?" Bobby Kennedy asked at a State Department briefing in late 1965 as he prepared to tour South America.

President Johnson had sent thirty thousand troops to the Dominican Republic in the spring to quell an insurrection that he claimed was communist driven—a claim that soon became a matter of serious debate in Washington. Rebels had launched an uprising in the capital city of Santo Domingo to topple the military-backed junta of J. Donald Reid Cabral and, they said, restore the constitutional government of President Juan Bosch, who was ousted in a coup two years earlier. Within days, LBJ ordered American citizens to evacuate the capital and sent troops to assist their departure and prevent a communist takeover.

Bobby opposed the move, criticized LBJ for acting unilaterally rather than coordinating a response with America's regional allies, and questioned how much of the uprising was communist driven as opposed to a populist effort to address "injustice and oppression." LBJ's action bore all the markings of an old-style American effort to impose its will by force—in a region that had seen all too much of that over the years—and Bobby was sure that it would ignite resentment toward the United States. Now that he was preparing to travel to the region, he wanted to be ready for the questions that he thought were inevitable.

"Nobody will ask you about it," Jack Vaughn, LBJ's assistant secretary of state for inter-American affairs, replied gruffly to Bobby's question, "because they don't care about that issue."[1] Vaughn's dismissive response, which was one of several that left the senator justifiably fuming, came amid a tense briefing that reflected a widening breach between LBJ and Bobby over Latin America. Over the next few years, the president and the senator would battle in increasingly open, bitter, and personal terms over Vietnam, leaving the two barely speaking to one another. But it was over Latin America that the first big breach between them on foreign policy occurred.

In the Dominican Republic, however, Bobby criticized LBJ for doing some of the very same things that he and Jack had done in the region—making clear that their dispute was as much personal as substantive.

. . .

America's "determination" to prevent a communist revolution in Latin America, Bobby told the Senate on May 6 in reference to the Dominican crisis, "must not be construed as opposition to popular uprisings against injustice and oppression just because the targets of such popular uprisings say they are communist-inspired or communist-led, or even because known communists take part in them."

By the 1960s, Washington had been deeply involved in Dominican affairs for many decades. Woodrow Wilson sent in the marines in 1916 when the Dominican Republic balked at U.S. demands for economic, political, and military reforms, and U.S. civilian and military officials ruled the nation until an elected government took over in 1924. When, in May of 1961, rebels assassinated the brutal dictator Rafael Trujillo after U.S. encouragement that began under Eisenhower, Jack and his team worked closely with different factions to help the country transition back to constitutional democracy with Juan Bosch's election in December of 1962. Washington provided economic assistance and threatened military intervention more than once to prevent Trujillo's family and military officials from reimposing autocratic rule. When Bosch was ousted in late 1963,

Washington reluctantly recognized the new military government in exchange for its vague promise to hold national elections in 1965.

Then came the tumult under LBJ. It was April 24, 1965, when the rebellion erupted in Santo Domingo. A day later, junta leader Donald Reid resigned and the rebels swore in an acting leader to rule until Bosch would return to take his place. Led by military officials, however, loyalist forces opened fire on the rebels, sending the nation into chaos. On April 27, LBJ ordered Americans to evacuate and, a day later, announced that he had sent four hundred marines to help and told congressional leaders that the rebel command was full of communists. Over the next week, the president sent growing numbers of military personnel so that by May 6, thirty thousand troops were on the ground or manning thirty U.S. ships and 275 aircraft nearby. While Washington worked with its regional allies to create a provisional government until Bosch's return in September, America's military exchanged gunfire with the loyalists.

To be sure, LBJ was sincerely concerned about a communist takeover. "I sure don't want to wake up," he told National Security Advisor McGeorge Bundy privately, "and find out Castro's in charge."[2] After Washington tried unsuccessfully to engineer a ceasefire, the president said in a TV address on the evening of May 2: "The revolutionary movement took a tragic turn. Communist leaders, many of them trained in Cuba, seeing a chance to increase disorder, to gain a foothold, joined the revolution. They took increasing control. And what began as a popular democratic revolution, committed to democracy and social justice, very shortly moved and was taken over and really seized and placed into the hands of a band of communist conspirators." Enunciating what became the Johnson Doctrine, he declared, "The American nations cannot, must not, and will not permit the establishment of another communist government in the Western Hemisphere."

Bobby watched the unfolding events with growing "outrage," in the words of Arthur Schlesinger Jr., who had spoken with him.[3] He was concerned that Washington acted on its own rather than in concert with its regional allies and that its large-scale military action would trigger a backlash that would drive "genuine demo-crats" into the hands of the communists. But it was the next line from Johnson that made the dispute far more personal for Bobby. "This," Johnson said of his doctrine, "is what our beloved President John F. Kennedy meant when, less than a week before his death, he told us, 'We in this hemisphere must use every resource at our command to prevent the establishment of another Cuba in this hemisphere.'" In other words, LBJ was suggesting that Jack would have done the same thing.

Also rankling Bobby was a slap that LBJ seemed to take at Jack a day after his TV address. Speaking to a labor conference in Washington, he said, "We don't propose to sit here in our rocking chair with our hands folded and let the communists set up any government in the Western Hemisphere." That Jack used a rocking chair in the Oval Office was widely known in establishment circles.

"We all understand," said Gerald Ford, the House Republican leader, "the innuendo of that statement."[4]

. . .

To Bobby's great dismay, LBJ didn't share Jack's views about American policy for the developing world.

Lyndon Baines Johnson was an old-school Cold Warrior in the mold of Eisenhower. As the Senate's majority leader in the 1950s, he worked closely with Ike on foreign policy and, eyeing a presidential run, strengthened his foreign policy credentials by speaking to the United Nations, traveling abroad, and welcoming foreign leaders to his Texas ranch. As he sought the Democratic nomination for president in 1960, he tried to derail Jack's candidacy by portraying him as young, inexperienced, and naive on foreign affairs. For the developing world, he was far more sympathetic to Ike's policy of backing right-wing dictators than Jack's notion of pushing political reform and building stronger ties to grassroots populations.

Bobby had no intention of abandoning Jack's approach because the two shared the same views about the developing world. In the aftermath of LBJ's action in the Dominican Republic, Bobby talked about rising expectations and deep-seated yearnings across the developing world, and about America's urgent need to promote economic and political reform. "We cannot win with mere military force," he said about guerilla warfare, speaking to Green Berets at Fort Bragg, North Carolina on May 29, 1965 (Jack's birthday), "for guns cannot fill empty stomachs, napalm cannot cure the sick and bombs cannot teach a child to read." In June he told the graduating class of Queen's College in New York, "Around the world—from the Straits of Magellan to the Straits of Malacca, from the Nile Delta to the Amazon basin, in Jaipur and Johannesburg—the dispossessed people of the world are demanding their place in the sun. . . . We have shown them that a better life is possible. We have not done enough to make it a reality." A month later, he told the International Police Academy graduation in Washington, "The great struggle of the coming decades is one for the hearts and minds of men."

Less than a month after Jack's death, LBJ appointed diplomat Thomas Mann—who shared the new president's view of American policy for the developing world and was a skeptic of Jack's Alliance for Progress—as assistant secretary of state for inter-American affairs. It was a shot across the bow of Jack's Latin American policy. In fact, Mann's arrival, in the words of William Rogers, the Alliance's deputy administrator at the time, brought "a more dramatic shift in tone and style of U.S. Alliance leadership [than] would have been difficult to imagine."[5] The following March, Mann directed American diplomats in the region to support right-wing dictators if they treated American businesses well. A year later, LBJ promoted Mann to undersecretary of state for economic affairs.

Notwithstanding their sharp differences over U.S. policy toward the developing world, LBJ had a point when he invoked Jack's name to justify his intervention in the Dominican Republic. The Johnson Doctrine was a mere variation on the Kennedy Doctrine that Jack had enunciated in a speech in Miami just four days before his death. Months earlier, Jack had directed a White House task force to develop a doctrine to make clear to the Soviets and to Latin American nations that the United States would not accept a "second Cas-

"Are These People for Real?"

tro" in the Western Hemisphere.[6] After declaring in Miami that we "must ... use every resource ... to prevent ... another Cuba," Jack explained that "if there is one principle which has run through the long history of this hemisphere, it is our common determination to prevent the rule of foreign systems or nations in the Americas."

Nevertheless, LBJ took some liberties in tying his action to Jack's pronouncement, which undoubtedly fueled Bobby's outrage. After all, Jack's vow "to prevent ... another Cuba" came in a speech in which he was promoting the Alliance for Progress—the centerpiece of his Latin American policy—which LBJ was now undermining.

But if LBJ took some liberties in justifying his action in the Dominican Republic, Bobby took a few in criticizing it.

. . .

"I am sure," Bobby told the Senate in his speech of May 6, "that every member of this body agrees with President Johnson in his determination to prevent the establishment of a new communist state in this hemisphere."

"But," he cautioned, "this cannot mean that we plan to act on our own without regard to our friends and allies in the Organization of American States. We are all involved in the struggle for free government in the hemisphere together. . . . Of course, unilateral action is easier than collective action; but we are much stronger when we act in concert with the rest of the hemisphere than when we act alone; and consultation is the price we must pay for the extra strength our alliances give us." He stressed the same point a day later in an interview that the *New York Times* carried on its front page.

To distinguish JFK from LBJ, Bobby noted that Jack secured approval from the Organization of American States (OAS), a hemispheric group, before implementing his strategy during the Cuban Missile Crisis. Jack did, in fact, respect the OAS far more than LBJ did. Of it the latter once said, "It couldn't pour piss out of a boot if the instructions were written on the heel."[7] Four days after the Dominican rebellion began, LBJ justified his decision to violate the noninterventionist pledges of Franklin Roosevelt's "Good Neighbor" policy and the OAS charter by saying, "OAS is a phantom—they are taking a siesta while this is on fire."[8]

Nevertheless, Bobby's criticism was a bit rich. On the Cuban Missile Crisis, Jack worked for a week in complete secrecy with a small group of top aides, keeping Washington and the wider world in the dark. As for the OAS, he told its members what he planned to do. He didn't seek their input, nor would he likely have changed direction much in the face of their opposition. Nor should he have, for while the Cuban Missile Crisis had clear implications for the region, it was a direct conflict between the world's two superpowers that only they could resolve. When reporters asked Bobby whether JFK had secured OAS approval before the Bay of Pigs, he acknowledged that Jack had not, adding weakly, "I don't think we handled the Bay of Pigs very well."[9]

As Bobby criticized the military nature of LBJ's action in the Dominican Republic, he was on even shakier ground.

. . .

When Bobby spoke to the Senate about the Dominican crisis, he inserted into the *Congressional Record*—the official daily compendium of House and Senate proceedings—a story from the *Christian Science Monitor* that warned about a growing backlash against the presence of American troops.

"U.S. presence in the Dominican Republic, to the extent of 15,000 troops, is viewed with growing alarm by the rebels," the story stated. "There is clear good will and even an understanding of President Johnson's decision to safeguard American lives. 'But we understand you've removed these Americans,' said a rebel major who added, 'Isn't it time for you to get out and allow us the opportunity to win the struggle against the forces of those opposed to constitutionalism?'"

If Bobby was concerned about American troops in the Dominican Republic under LBJ, he had few such concerns in the aftermath of Trujillo's assassination in May of 1961 when Jack was president. Earlier that year, Jack had shared Ike's view that Washington should find a way to push Trujillo out because, officials feared, his increasingly harsh crackdown on moderate opponents was creating a political vacuum in the country that, if he were toppled, a revolutionary leftist (i.e., a "second Castro") would fill. But the Bay of Pigs fiasco gave Jack great pause in approving any action by U.S.-backed dissidents against Trujillo that could be traced to Washington. In early May, Jack told his foreign policy team that Washington must not "initiate the overthrow of Trujillo before knowing what government would succeed him."[10] Nevertheless, he also directed the Pentagon to prepare to invade the Dominican Republic, if necessary, to prevent a communist takeover, which he deemed the least desirable of all possible outcomes.

In late May, U.S. officials received word from the dissidents that efforts to assassinate Trujillo were imminent. With Jack mulling his next step, Bobby led the charge within the administration for Washington to take strong action after the assassination to push the country in the right direction. With Secretary of State Dean Rusk in Paris, Chester Bowles was serving as acting secretary in Washington. "Bobby," Bowles recalled later, "put on very heavy pressure for the U.S. to move in," perhaps by blowing up the American consulate in order to create the rationale for a U.S. invasion. Bowles, who considered Bobby's invasion idea "very dangerous" and feared another Bay of Pigs, suggested a low-key deployment of U.S. ships thirty miles from shore in case they were needed later, prompting Bobby to term him a "gutless bastard."[11] Bowles called Jack, who backed his low-key approach. "Am I Acting Secretary or is your brother?" an angry Bowles asked. "You are," Jack replied. "Well," he then asked, "will you call your brother and let him know that?"—which Jack later did.[12]

Why in 1965 did Bobby express concern about thirty thousand troops in the Dominican Republic when four years earlier he was ready to launch a full-scale invasion? Perhaps he was just older and more seasoned by then. At least as likely, however, LBJ provided an irresistible target.

. . .

"Are these people for real?" Bobby asked Frank Mankiewicz, the Peace Corps' Latin American director, after the State Department briefing for his South America trip. "Do they really believe that stuff, or do they just talk that way?"[13]

In the summer of 1965, Fred Dutton, a top political aide to Bobby, suggested that he travel abroad that fall and visit a foreign university "as a platform for your projecting moral and intellectual leadership."[14] The one place that Dutton said he should *not* go was Latin America, where feelings over LBJ's action in the Dominican Republic remained raw. It was also a region in great tumult, where coups had toppled governments of one kind or another in El Salvador in 1961, Argentina and Peru in 1962, Guatemala, Ecuador, the Dominican Republic, and Honduras in 1963, and Brazil and Bolivia in 1964. Rather than avoid the hostility that might trigger violence, however, Bobby gravitated to it. Facing the prospect of danger, the trip would give the middle child within him another opportunity to prove his courage. Just a few months earlier, he became the first man to climb what Canada's government named "Mt. Kennedy" to honor the slain president, a cathartic trek of nearly fourteen thousand feet that left him pained and exhausted but also exhilarated. For the fall, he accepted an invitation to speak in Brazil and, around that speech, put together a broader trip to the region.

For Bobby, the State Department briefing proved an eye-opening, infuriating, and depressing waste of time. LBJ's appointees took great pleasure in telling one Robert F. Kennedy that the Latin American policies of his brother were no longer in favor. The meeting wreaked of hostility, from the optics in the room to the words exchanged. Flanked by a few aides, Bobby sat in the middle of one side of a long table and smoked a cigar while balancing his chair precariously on its back legs. About ten State Department officials sat on the other side, and behind them was a row of about another sixteen, then a row of about ten, then a row of about five, and then a sprinkling of others. One State Department official moved to Bobby's side in hopes that others would follow and ease tensions, but none did.

Jack Vaughn, the assistant secretary of state, not only defended LBJ's policies but, as he glared at Bobby, derided Jack's policies and referred to the former president dismissively as "your brother." (That

"Are These People for Real?"

the normally affable Vaughn was exuding such hostility prompted Bobby's aides to suspect, without proof, that LBJ must have directed it.) When the discussion turned to Peru, Bobby and Vaughn first clashed over Jack's decision to suspend U.S. relations in 1962 in the aftermath of a military coup. They clashed again over LBJ's subsequent decision to suspend aid to what was then a democratic government in Peru over its dispute with the International Petroleum Company (a subsidiary of Standard Oil of New Jersey). When Bobby asked about Brazil, where the regime was cracking down on political rights and civil liberties, a State Department official suggested that he express regret for the turn of events. When Bobby derided that idea, Vaughn suggested, "Well, why don't you just say nothing?"[15]

"Well, Mr. Vaughn," Bobby sniffed, "as I see it, then what the Alliance for Progress has come down to is that you can abolish political parties and close down the congress and take away the basic freedoms of the people and deny your political opponents any rights at all and banish them from the country and you'll get a lot of our money. But if you mess around with an American oil company, we'll cut you off without a penny. Is that it?" After mulling the question, Vaughn responded, "That's about the size of it."[16] Before long, Vaughn stood up and said, "I'm very sorry but I've got another meeting. I've already been here far too long, and I've got to leave. You will excuse me."[17]

He left without shaking hands.

. . .

"A revolution is coming," Bobby declared in Latin America in what became his refrain about the developing world until his death, "a revolution that will be peaceful if we are wise enough, compassionate if we care enough, successful if we are fortunate enough, but a revolution will come whether we will it or not."

Three weeks across the tumultuous region brought out the emerging revolutionary in Bobby Kennedy. It was a rollicking, sleep-deprived, somewhat spontaneous, sometimes dangerous journey to Peru, Chile, Argentina, Brazil, and Venezuela with Ethel and a few aides. Bobby was met by deliriously welcoming crowds of thousands, but he also was the target of eggs, tomatoes, and spit from communist students. He delivered inspiring speeches that urged vast political and economic change, and he inspected dilapidated homes, sewage-clogged streets, and dangerous mines in poverty-strewn areas that local officials openly ignored.

Bobby met with the region's most powerful officials and most powerless residents. In Peru he visited schools, factories, farms, and orphanages, spoke with university students in Lima, distributed PT-109 tie clips to the poor in that city's harsh slums, met with Peruvian intellectuals at the home of artist Fernando Seizlo, and spoke with Indians and Peace Corps volunteers in Cuzco after he was scraped on the cheek when a crowd of two thousand broke through a barbed wire fence. In Chile he lunched with its Christian Democratic president and visited the farming town of Linares, where almost all of its eight thousand people came to see him, women threw flowers at his open car, and children ran alongside it. In Argentina he was greeted by more than one thousand people at the Buenos Aires airport and thousands more at the home of America's ambassador.

In Brazil he attended Mass and met with barefoot children in the desperately poor town of Bahia, spoke to more than a thousand people from atop a truck in Natal, harangued Brazil's president and business leaders for not paying poor sugar cane cutters the legal minimum wage, answered questions from a thousand students in Recife, and attended a soccer match and spoke with students in Rio de Janeiro. He toured the Amazon in a wagon, fell into the bushes, borrowed a bicycle to finish the tour, and flew deeper into the Amazon to ride the rapids and swim in piranha-filled waters. In Venezuela he debated communist students in Caracas, where he also spoke to labor leaders and toured the slums with the country's president while more than a thousand people followed behind.

"Why does he want to see all this?" an impatient Peruvian official complained while Bobby walked through the shacks of Lima. "I've lived here all my life and I've never been in one of these places."[18]

"Are These People for Real?"

"You lose the bet," Bobby cabled Jack Vaughn from Lima, Peru, where he had landed to start his adventure.

When, in his State Department briefing, Vaughn told Bobby that no one would ask about the Dominican crisis, Bobby replied, "I'll bet you're wrong" and predicted it would be the topic of one of his first questions.[19] Sure enough, when local reporters greeted him at the airport, one quickly asked him about it.

At the time Bobby was hoping to reduce tensions with LBJ, not inflame them. News of his State Department briefing leaked, and leading newspapers wrote accounts that included excruciating detail. So, notwithstanding his concerns about LBJ's actions, he did his best to close the gap between himself and the president. "If," he told a communist student in Concepcion, Chile, "a country votes to have a communist government—and no country has voted for one since World War II—then there would be no intervention like there was in the Dominican Republic." In prepared remarks and responses to questions, he carefully explained his feelings: "I disagreed with the intervention, but it must be seen in perspective. The United States does not want to dominate the Dominican Republic. It wants no military base there. If the people vote for a communist government, we will stay out."

Bobby acknowledged America's imperfect history in the region, but he challenged his audiences to neither blame his country for their troubles nor rely on it for their salvation. Just as he pushed students back home to join the Peace Corps or find other ways to serve, so too did he challenge Latin American students to build their own futures. "And what I have asked students in Lima and Mendoza, in Santiago and Recife," he said at Rio de Janeiro's Catholic University, "I now ask you: what leadership will you give to the great question of our time—whether the traditions of freedom can survive in an era of unprecedented change; whether man's great unsatisfied yearning for economic progress and social justice can be answered by free men within a framework of democratic institutions; whether, in the words of the great Mexican patriot Benito Juarez, 'Democracy is the destiny of future humanity.'"

While publicly expressing strong confidence that no one would opt for communism by choice, Bobby suggested quite the opposite in a private moment after surveying local hardships.

. . .

"If these kids are going to be revolutionaries," Bobby told an aide, "they're going to have to improve their aim."

About a week into his trip, Bobby was in Concepcion, Chile, where communist students visited him at his hotel and threatened to drown him out in protest if he spoke that night at the local university. "We do not condemn you personally," a student leader told him, "but as a representative of a government whose hands are stained with blood."[20] Bobby scoffed at the notion of blood-stained hands, said he visited Chile because he was interested in its future, reminded them that Chile received more American aid per person than any other Latin American country, suggested the students weren't confident enough in their views to let him speak, and challenged them to listen to what he had to say.

When they left after refusing his request to speak without interference, aides advised him not to go that night because the police would adhere to local custom and stay off the university campus— and no one would be there to guarantee his safety. He chose otherwise because two Christian Democratic students visited him after the communist students left and said his absence would leave the communists victorious. It was on his way into the packed gymnasium, as communists pelted his aides with eggs but missed him, that he snickered about their "aim." After jumping atop a table, he struggled to speak above the jeers; the communists sang the national anthems of Chile and Cuba while some of them burned the American flag. When they refused his invitation to leave the stands and debate him, he tried to climb the stands to reach them. After they still refused to quiet down and one spat in his eye, he left to the roars of an overwhelmingly sympathetic crowd of perhaps two thousand.

"Are These People for Real?"

Intrigued by the communist students in Concepcion, he brushed aside concerns for his safety early one morning and visited coal mines where workers toiled in dangerous conditions 1,500 feet underground. "If I worked in this mine," he said after reemerging at ground level, "I'd be a communist, too."[21]

. . .

"I can't really approve of all this invasion of privacy," a U.S. embassy official in Rio de Janeiro observed as Bobby toured a slum. "But I must say his humble way of admitting our own mistakes has done a lot to blur anti-American feelings."[22]

No matter how much Bobby defended LBJ on his trip, he couldn't change a basic reality: across Latin America, Lyndon Johnson was no match for a Kennedy. In life and now in death, Jack was revered for his outreach to the region and his Alliance for Progress. U.S. relations with Latin America cooled considerably under LBJ, due to his different approach to the region and his appointees.

Reflecting hostility to Bobby, administration officials ordered America's embassies in the countries he visited not to publicize his trip very much. Nevertheless, huge crowds formed once word spread that Bobby was in the area. They showered him with love, as much because he was the brother of their slain hero as for anything he said or did. "Viva Kennedy!" they shouted. He was often asked when he'd be America's president, and he was sometimes introduced as the next one.

Not surprisingly, his trip did nothing to improve his relations with the sensitive president back home. When he returned, the two would tangle more directly over America's expanding military effort in Vietnam.

12

"Not by Escalation, but by De-escalation"

"You haven't said anything for a year," Jack Newfield, an anti-war activist and, later, Bobby's biographer, admonished him in December of 1966 in reference to Vietnam. "When will you talk again?"

"If I become convinced," Bobby replied, "that by making another speech that I could do some good, I would make it tomorrow. But the last time I spoke I didn't have any influence on policy, and I was hurt politically. I'm afraid that by speaking out I just make Lyndon do the opposite, out of spite. He hates me so much that if I asked for snow, he would make rain, just because it was me."[1]

Their hatred for one another, which was growing worse by the month, was years in the making. Like his father, Bobby was a man of long memories and bitter grudges, particularly in matters involving the Kennedy clan; Joe Kennedy reportedly said that of his children, Bobby was the most like him because "he hates like me."[2] Bobby never forgot that LBJ rejected his father's offer of 1955 to finance a presidential run for him if he would make Jack his running mate. When JFK and LBJ vied for the 1960 Democratic nomination, LBJ angered Bobby by deriding his father as a Nazi-appeasing "Chamberlain umbrella man" and suggesting Jack was disease ridden. Bobby stewed over LBJ's penchant for calling him "son" to his face and much worse behind his back. After Jack died, Bobby told a columnist who had pushed Jack to run with LBJ, "Now you've made that damn fellow President of the United States."[3] Bobby also resented LBJ's purported remark that Jack's murder was perhaps "divine retribution" because Jack reportedly ordered the murder of foreign leaders.[4] LBJ, meanwhile, resented Bobby's effort at the 1960 Democratic convention to reverse Jack's decision to pick him. LBJ knew that, at the White House and Hickory Hill (Bobby's home in Northern Virginia), he was the frequent butt of cruel mocking by Bobby and his friends, all of whom considered him crude. Ethel and others called him "Uncle Corn Pone." All told, Bobby thought that LBJ was "mean, bitter, vicious—an animal in many ways" and a pathological liar, while LBJ viewed Bobby as a "grandstanding little runt" and a "little shitass."[5] Their mutual hatred exacerbated their clashes over Vietnam because as LBJ militarized the war and Bobby denounced it, each suspected that the other was driven by personal animus.

In his dispute with LBJ, Bobby revealed his most audacious side. To put it bluntly, Jack was dead and some top administration officials who had served him were now serving a new president with his own ideas about foreign policy and, like all presidents, the authority to make final decisions. To Bobby, however, the JFK holdovers who toed LBJ's line were somehow acting disloyally to his slain brother. Just months after Jack's death, Bobby said, "Those who were closely identified with President Kennedy who came to work for Lyndon Johnson—I thought that they felt: 'The king was dead, and long live the king.'" Moreover, he thought that LBJ was getting credit for things that Jack had done and some JFK holdovers, "like Bob McNamara and Mac Bundy," weren't correcting the record. Democratic elder statesman Clark Clifford called Bobby's attitude "curious . . . completely illogical, wholly emotional," while Kennedy intimate Milton Gwirtzman acknowledged, "I don't think that Robert Kennedy at that time could appreciate the fact that other people could make the same claim of loyalty on subordinates that his family could."[6]

Bobby and Ted Kennedy confronted LBJ over Vietnam in two stages. In the first, through the end of 1966, they sought to convince him to change course by suggesting, in public speeches and private counsel, alternatives to his efforts to overwhelm the North with bombs and bullets. In the second, starting in early 1967, they broke more openly with him after concluding that he was unmovable. They were not the first lawmakers to express concern about the president's Vietnam policies. But whether it was Bobby alone or the brothers together, their sentiments carried outsized weight because their views attracted outsized attention from the media, the Washington establishment, and the country.

As they worried more about Vietnam, they worried less about the Cold War, which was once their greatest concern.

. . .

"I vote for this resolution," Bobby told the Senate in May of 1965 in connection with LBJ's request for $700 million for the war, "because our fighting forces in Vietnam and elsewhere deserve the unstinting support of the American government and the American people. I do in the understanding that . . . it is not a blank check."

Just a few months into his Senate career, Bobby was already raising concerns about LBJ's Vietnam strategy, which represented a sharp break with Jack's. In March, with twenty-three thousand U.S. military advisors in Vietnam, LBJ sent the first combat forces—3,500 Marines to defend America's air base at Da Nang—largely in response to a Vietcong attack on the U.S. compound at Pleiku that killed eight Americans. Also that month, LBJ launched Operation Rolling Thunder, an expanded bombing campaign that was designed to last eight weeks but continued on and off for three years. Lyndon Johnson had no appetite for the graceful withdrawal from Vietnam that Jack Kennedy was contemplating before his death. He compared an American appeasement of North Vietnamese aggression to Chamberlain's appeasement of Hitler, and he worried about the political impact of a "who lost Vietnam?" backlash—which he imagined that Bobby Kennedy would help drive.

Though LBJ was a commanding figure at the time, with an enormous mandate from his landslide reelection of November and broad public support for America's effort in Vietnam, discontent was festering in important quarters. Fears were spreading on and off Capitol Hill that Vietnam would become a quagmire, drain funds that would be better spent at home, threaten the economy, and jeopar-

"Not by Escalation, but by De-escalation"

dize hopes for better U.S.-Soviet relations in the aftermath of JFK's test-ban treaty. Senate Majority Leader Mike Mansfield sent multiple memos to LBJ opposing ground troops, while Richard Russell, the Senate Armed Services Committee's chairman and a commanding figure in Washington on military matters, advised LBJ to seek an early exit. Influential columnists like the syndicated Walter Lippmann and the *New York Times*'s Arthur Krock were starting to air their concerns and advise the president to pursue a negotiated settlement. In April, Students for a Democratic Society sponsored the first national protest against the war, attracting twenty thousand people to Washington.

Also in April, LBJ outlined a nonmilitary plan for Vietnam that he thought would bring a swift peace. Most striking was a new initiative that seemed straight out of the Kennedy counterinsurgency playbook—$1 billion for the Mekong River area to provide food and water, build schools, and expand the reach of medicine. Along with it was an expanded program of using U.S. farm surpluses to help feed and clothe "the needy in Asia." "This war, like most wars," he explained at Johns Hopkins University in Baltimore, "is filled with terrible irony. For what do the people of North Vietnam want? They want what their neighbors also desire: food for their hunger; health for their bodies; a chance to learn; progress for their country; and an end to the bondage of material misery. And they would find all these things far more readily in peaceful association with others than in the endless course of battle." It was the kind of package that Jack and Bobby routinely proposed to help the needy across the developing world and nourish support for the United States. LBJ, however, viewed his plan as less a Kennedy-style effort to address rising nationalism than a deal to cut with a fellow politician. A legendary wheeler-dealer when he served as the Senate's majority leader, LBJ predicted that his initiative would bring peace because North Vietnam's Ho Chi Minh would find the $1 billion impossible to refuse. "Old Ho can't turn me down," LBJ told Press Secretary Bill Moyers while they flew back to Washington from Baltimore.[7] "Old Ho" turned him down a day later, however, putting LBJ and Bobby back on a collision course over Vietnam.

In early May, the president sent his request for the $700 million to Congress, which Bobby viewed as less a legitimate request for needed funding than as an LBJ effort to force the Senate to endorse his Vietnam strategy. Bobby wanted to oppose it, but he wasn't ready to split so openly with the president. Instead, he framed LBJ's request on his own terms. "We confront three possible courses in Vietnam," he told the Senate. The United States could withdraw, he said, but that would repudiate "commitments undertaken and confirmed by three administrations" and "gravely—perhaps irreparably—weaken the democratic position in Asia." It could "enlarg[e]" the war, but that would require hundreds of thousands of U.S. troops in Vietnam, risk China's entry, force the Soviets to provide "major assistance" to Hanoi, and perhaps "revive" relations between Beijing and Moscow. Or it could pursue "honorable negotiation," which he understood was "the policy of the administration, the policy we are endorsing today."

Later that month, Bobby privately urged LBJ to halt the bombing, arguing that it "would do no harm, and maybe something useful would come of it." The president did so in mid-May, but his heart wasn't in it as he privately disparaged the halt as "Bobby Kennedy's bombing pause" and resumed bombing about a week later.

. . .

"Bob Kennedy Urges Share for Reds in Saigon Regime," the *Los Angeles Times* headlined its front-page story of February 20, 1966. Bobby's controversial suggestion of a day earlier that Washington offer the Vietcong a power-sharing role in South Vietnam in hopes of a peace deal garnered front-page coverage by the *New York Times* and *Washington Post* as well.[8]

Weeks earlier, Senator George McGovern, a dovish Democrat of rising prominence, suggested to Bobby that he "continue to raise questions about Vietnam" because his "voice" was "one of the very few that is powerful enough to help steer us away from catastrophe."[9] That Bobby's idea attracted such notice and received such scorn—including from some of LBJ's foreign policy advisors with whom he had worked closely under Jack—was particularly striking, since J. William Fulbright, the Senate Foreign Relations Committee's chairman, had suggested the same thing more than once. At the time, Bobby and Ted were exerting more influence over America's foreign policy debate. Their political stock was rising in Washington and around the country just as LBJ's Vietnam strategy was growing more controversial.

"By hoary tradition," *Newsweek* wrote about the brothers in January of 1966, with the face of each adorning its cover, "the freshman senator from New York and the junior senator from Massachusetts ought to be invisible men in a chamber that cleaves to the seniority rule as religiously as the bricklayers' union. Yet, if a senator must finally be judged for what he does, a Kennedy must be measured here and now for what he is: the inheritor of a magic name, an uncompleted mission, a deep-rooted family mystique of ambition and competition and power."[10] The brothers attracted more media attention than other senators, were allotted more space when they wrote articles for leading magazines, received more daily mail, drew more attention from their colleagues when they spoke in the Senate, garnered more speaking invitations around the country, attracted bigger crowds, and joined LBJ and Vice President Hubert Humphrey as the only Democrats who were guaranteed to sell out a party fundraiser. As congressional elections approached in the fall of 1966, Bobby's stock soared even higher as he campaigned for Democrats from coast to coast.

As senators, the brothers operated very differently. Bobby viewed the Senate as a necessary stop on the road to an inevitable presidential run (though, at the time, he presumed that wouldn't come until 1972). To his colleagues, he was often cold, brusque, abrasive, and moody. "One day it would be a warm, fun conversation," recalled Walter Mondale, who served with him in the Senate. "The next day the shop was closed."[11] Not surprisingly, Bobby was a bit of a Senate loner, as Jack had been in the 1950s. While he developed relationships with such fellow backbenchers as Mondale and Fred Harris and retained others from his days as attorney general, he couldn't hide his impatience with the peculiar norms of a stuffy institution, such as the tradition by which senators called one another "the honorable" and "my friend"—no matter how they viewed one another. Bobby dispensed with such norms by leaving committee hearings in open disgust as debates dragged on, subjecting his opponents' views to withering criticism, and questioning the intelligence of his colleagues.

Ted, by contrast, was invariably warm, cheerful, and convivial—a "Senator's Senator," as McGovern put it, happy in his role and respectful of the institution.[12] Ironically, it was Jack who suggested that, upon Ted's arrival in 1963, he pay courtesy calls on such senior senators as Richard Russell—the kind of step that Jack himself wouldn't take after assuming his House seat as an arrogant twenty-nine-year-old. Though, like his brothers, Ted ran for the Senate with an expectation that higher office lay ahead, he quickly came to appreciate the Senate and savor a career there. He grew interested in those who had held his seat—including such giants as Charles Sumner and Daniel Webster—and, mining the historical resources of the legendary Boston bookstore Goodspeed's, he collected and framed photos, letters, and speeches of his famous predecessors, displaying the artifacts at home. From his earliest days on the job, he prepared painstakingly for committee hearings, sat through them to the end, exchanged back slaps and banter with fellow senators, and learned the chamber's arcane rules so that he could convert his ideas into policy. That as an accomplished senator he could distinguish himself from his brothers surely shaped his path as well; as a young adult, he privately expressed fears about whether he would measure up as a Kennedy.

For Bobby and Ted, their outsized influence complicated their efforts to convince LBJ—who was sensitive under the best of situations but suspicious of Bobby to the point of paranoia—to change direction on Vietnam.

. . .

Bobby's call to offer the Vietcong a governing role in the South, which Ted echoed on NBC's *Meet the Press* two weeks later, was not his first war-related remark to stoke controversy.

"Not by Escalation, but by De-escalation"

In July of 1965—two months after he reluctantly supported LBJ's request for $700 million—Bobby sought to nudge America's war effort away from bombing and toward the counterinsurgency that he and Jack favored for the developing world. "The essence of successful counter-insurgency is not to kill," he said at the International Policy Academy's graduation ceremony, "but to bring the insurgent back into the national life." The prior two decades, he said, had shown "beyond doubt that our approach to revolutionary war must be political—political first, political last, political always. Victory in a revolutionary war is won not by escalation, but by de-escalation."[13] That year Bobby discussed the need for counterinsurgency at Fort Bragg, North Carolina, in May and in commencement addresses across New York in June. But, at the International Police Academy in July, he tied his views about counterinsurgency to Vietnam and, not surprisingly, angered LBJ by what the president viewed as a direct attack on his war policy.

Bobby wasn't ready to elevate the dispute any further. (In fact, the words he delivered that day in July were less critical of LBJ than the text that his staff released to reporters a day earlier because, in between, White House officials convinced him to cut the sharpest language.) So, he didn't deliver another major address on Vietnam for several months, even with anti-war rallies taking place in forty cities in October and U.S. troop levels rising to 185,000 by year's end. His off-the-cuff remarks that fall, however, reflected his evolving views, leftward drift, and growing concerns. The more he broke with LBJ's war stewardship, the more comfortable he grew with the increasingly outlandish tactics of anti-war activists. He defended Rutgers University historian Eugene Genovese's right to express hope for a Vietcong victory (for which Bobby earned a public scolding from Richard Nixon), he defended the rights of young Americans to burn their draft cards, and—in his most controversial suggestion to that point—he expressed support for the idea of giving blood to the North Vietnamese. "Even to the North Vietnamese?" a reporter followed up, giving Bobby a chance to reconsider his outlandish statement. "Yes," he replied, undeterred.

Critics pounced. Senator Barry Goldwater, the hardline conservative Republican who had worked with Jack in the Senate and maintained cordial relations with him as the two prepared to run for president against each other in 1964, called Bobby's remarks "closer to treason than academic freedom." "If," the *New York Daily News* asked, "you feel strongly enough for the enemy to give him a pint of your blood every ninety days or so, then why not go the whole hog? Why not light out for the enemy country and join its armed forces? Bobby Kennedy is young, strong and virile, and financially able to provide for his wife and children while he is away at war."[14]

While Bobby was stoking the growing anti-war efforts at home, his brother was assessing the war up close.

. . .

"The best we can possibly say about the situation," Ted Kennedy told reporters after five days in South Vietnam in late 1965, "is that we're hopeful about it."[15]

Ted was moving in the same direction as Bobby on Vietnam, but at a more measured pace for reasons both personal and political. "I had a basic presumption," he relayed years later, "in favor of decisions that my brother [Jack] made" in Vietnam. Not only did he have "enormous confidence [and] . . . a great belief in him," but he had heard Jack discuss Vietnam at family gatherings while he was president.[16] Then, when LBJ took over and changed the nature of America's involvement, Ted—like most of his colleagues at that time—was reluctant to second-guess a president on war-related matters. That the more audacious Bobby was less reluctant is not surprising.

Through 1965, Ted supported LBJ's goals in Vietnam, even as he found more to criticize with American and South Vietnamese tactics. When, in the spring, Boston University held a teach-in on Vietnam—as many universities were doing at the time—that drew two thousand people, Ted warned in a letter to the event that a U.S. pullout "would permanently undermine our credit with other nations in the area which are trying to remain independent of the historic and powerful influence exerted by China."[17] He expressed support for the U.S. bombing, which he said was designed to strengthen Saigon's bargaining position with Hanoi. Visiting schools around his state that fall, he remained true to the cause. Calling the war "the fundamental moral question facing the United States," he asked in one speech, "Are we concerned at all about people in a far and distant land? Do we want to defend freedom?" "We do," he answered, "because this is our commitment, our heritage, our destiny."[18]

By summer, as Ted grew more concerned about America's progress in the war, he was mulling a trip to Vietnam to evaluate the situation up close. After deciding to go in the fall, he landed in Saigon on October 23 with three other Democratic lawmakers and, even before looking around, immediately aligned himself with LBJ. "I feel that the overwhelming majority of the American people are committed to the policy of President Johnson and are willing to see a long and difficult struggle here," he told reporters. A day later he watched the "battle of Pleime," with the Vietcong surrounding a U.S. Special Forces camp south of Pleiku, from aboard a C-47 military aircraft about ten miles from the fighting. "Can we circle around and get closer?" he asked the pilot, who was understandably careful to keep the senator out of harm's way.[19] On the ground later that day, dressed in battle fatigues, he placed a wreath at a site near Pleiku and spoke with injured soldiers. Two days later, helicopters that were escorting the one in which Ted and his colleagues were flying to another Special Forces camp came under fire from snipers on the ground, prompting the escorts to respond with rockets and machine gun-fire as Ted watched the battle.

"I supported the war when I arrived in Vietnam," Ted recalled decades later, and "I still supported it upon my return." U.S. military and diplomatic officials told him and the other lawmakers that America was making progress, and he recalled, "I was impressed and accepted" what he heard.[20]

Nevertheless, he returned with concerns.

. . .

While Bobby critiqued big-picture strategic issues, Ted focused on the collateral human damage of America's war efforts.

On a topic to which he would devote enormous attention in the coming years, in Vietnam and other countries, he focused on refugees. Earlier in 1965, as chairman of the Senate Judiciary Subcommittee on Refugees and Escapees, he held thirteen hearings and heard from forty witnesses over the course of four months about how America's war effort was affecting Vietnam's people. After witnessing the situation up close, he relayed his thoughts in a *LOOK* magazine piece that appeared in early February of 1966.

"That really represents my best judgment" of the time, Ted said years later about the *LOOK* piece.[21] Perhaps, but he almost wrote a much different article. After returning from Vietnam, he planned to write a piece that reflected what he had heard from military officials about how the "domino theory" related to Vietnam—that America needed to stay there or the South, and then the region, would fall to the communists. He wasn't ready to break with LBJ over Vietnam or shed his Cold War-centric outlook. Ted's top aides, however, thought he should write about the concerns that the trip had raised in him—specifically, about Saigon's problems in rallying South Vietnam's people around the war. His aides were concerned enough about what Ted was planning that they phoned Rep. John Tunney, a pal of Ted's and one of the three other lawmakers on the trip, who rushed to Ted's office and convinced him to follow his aides' advice.

"We have been involved in two conflicts in Vietnam," Ted wrote in the piece that made its way into print.

> One has been the battle against the terror brought in the name of revolution by the Vietcong guerillas and the forces from the North. . . . Our Government has taken a position in this endeavor that has been clear and firm. . . . The second conflict in Vietnam—the struggle for the hearts and minds of the Vietnamese people themselves—has not been waged with the same ferocity. There has been no one firm humanitarian policy understood throughout our nation or the world. The struggle in Vietnam has not been one that has produced a

"Not by Escalation, but by De-escalation"

concern for the most important element in the Vietnam situation—the welfare of the Vietnamese people themselves.[22]

Ted chronicled the bleak mismatch between South Vietnam's growing needs and its miniscule capacity to address them. The "vast majority" of Vietnam's sixteen million people were illiterate, its rural school system was "nearly destroyed," 80 percent of its children suffered from worms, its local government was "decimated," none of its sixteen thousand villages or their leaders had "escaped assassination or terror," and refugees by then totaled about a million (six percent of its population). Meanwhile, South Vietnam had only eight hundred doctors, five hundred of whom were in the military; seventeen of the twenty-eight hospitals that were equipped to do surgery were "idle" because they lacked physicians; one camp of more than six hundred refugees that he visited had no working toilet; and a nation that once produced enough rice to export some of it was now forced to import it to feed its people.

Ted praised LBJ for recognizing this "second conflict" in his Johns Hopkins speech of April, for establishing "Project Vietnam" to encourage America's civilian doctors to volunteer their services in South Vietnam, and for sending a doctor there to assess the nation's needs. Nevertheless, he suggested that Washington launch a humanitarian effort to rival its military effort and, as part of it, help rebuild "democratic political action" by Vietnam's people, appoint a high-ranking refugee official at America's embassy in Saigon, recruit experts from other nations to help address the refugee problem, and create an international force to nurture the developing areas of Southeast Asia.

"To the extent that we leave Vietnam one day with more to mark our presence than destruction," he concluded, "we will have met our true commitment to the Vietnamese."

. . .

"I thought," Bobby wrote to LBJ in late January of 1966, "it might give you some comfort to look again at another President, Abraham Lincoln, and some of the identical problems and situations that he faced that you are now meeting."

With his four-page, hand-written letter, Bobby sent a copy of *Never Call Retreat*, the third volume of Bruce Catton's classic Civil War trilogy. Bobby was hoping to convince LBJ, who had ordered another bombing halt about a month earlier, to rebuff the military's call to resume bombing. "In closing," he wrote, "let me say how impressed I have been with the most recent efforts to find a peaceful solution to Vietnam. Our position within the United States and around the world has improved immeasurably as we face the difficult decisions of this year." In a note drafted by White House aide Jack Valenti, LBJ responded warmly a few days later, telling Bobby that his letter had arrived at "one of those hours when I felt alone, prayerfully alone. I remembered so well how President Kennedy had to face, by himself, the agony of the Cuba missile crisis." LBJ also relayed that, while meeting with congressional leaders, he read a paragraph from the book that Bobby had marked about Lincoln's responsibilities, adding, "I knew exactly how Lincoln felt."[23]

The exchange of warm letters had no discernable effect on LBJ's thinking, however, and it came at a moment when America's divides over Vietnam were growing. On January 28, a day after LBJ replied to Bobby, the Senate Foreign Relations Committee launched its televised hearings on Vietnam, with Secretary of State Dean Rusk as the first witness. LBJ resented the hearings, which ran for three weeks and attracted some twenty-two million viewers, and everything they represented—for the Democrat-controlled Senate committee was investigating the war strategy of a Democratic president. Two days after they began, LBJ told congressional leaders in a White House meeting that he would resume the bombing. When Fulbright, the Foreign Relations Committee chairman, began to offer his views, LBJ turned away to chat with Defense Secretary McNamara. In a clear effort, a few days later, to distract attention from the hearings, the president announced that he would fly to Honolulu for meetings with South Vietnam's leaders.

Strikingly, Rusk suggested in his testimony that LBJ's approach to Vietnam, which was increasingly tearing the nation apart, actually reflected America's Cold War consensus. "In March 1947," he stated in reference to the Truman Doctrine, "in connection with our then assistance to Greece, President Truman stated that 'I believe that it must be the policy of the U.S. to support free peoples who are resisting attempted subjugation by armed minorities or by outside pressures.' That is the policy we are applying in Vietnam in connection with specific commitments which we have taken in connection with that country." The Truman Doctrine provided the philosophical underpinning for the containment strategy against the Soviets that Truman devised and successive presidents implemented. By 1966, however, Bobby and Ted were questioning whether Vietnam was as central to America's Cold War effort as they had believed.

When the bombing resumed on January 31, Bobby responded the same day on the Senate floor, criticizing the decision in ominous terms. "If we regard bombing as the answer in Vietnam," he declared, "we are headed straight for disaster. In the past, bombing has not proved a decisive weapon against a rural economy—or against a guerrilla army. And the temptation will now be to argue that if limited bombing does not produce a solution, that further bombing, more extended military action, is the answer. The danger is that the decision to resume may become the first in a series of steps on a road from which there is no turning back—a road which leads to catastrophe for all mankind."

Bobby never served on the Senate Foreign Relations Committee, but he was keenly interested in its Vietnam hearings. He watched from the back of the room or on TV from his office, where he "paced the floor . . . occasionally catching himself 'talking back to the screen.'"[24] After Rusk's return testimony of February 18, the last day of the hearings, Bobby decided to hold a news conference the next morning and suggest a governing role for the Vietcong in South Vietnam.

. . .

"If negotiation is our aim, as we have so clearly said it is," Bobby told reporters that Saturday morning, then "each side must concede matters that are important in order to preserve positions that are essential."

Privately, Bobby was wondering whether negotiation was, in fact, "our aim." The previous November, Ho Chi Minh had told Italian officials that he would "go anywhere; to meet anyone" and offered terms of negotiations that reflected the 1954 global agreement that split Vietnam in two. As Rusk reacted skeptically to Ho's offer and Washington delayed a response, the North sent word that a U.S. bombing of Hanoi or Haiphong would kill any hope of negotiations. In December, nevertheless, LBJ ordered the bombing of a power plant near Haiphong. "Why didn't we accept the . . . message positively, agreeing to [Ho's] four points and offering our own interpretation," Bobby wondered aloud at a Christmas party at his home a few days later. "Then the onus would be on Hanoi to refuse. This would make us look good whether the offer was real or not. But to dismiss it out of hand is disastrous. We lose all credibility. . . . If we had acted that way in the Cuban crisis we might have had war."[25]

Now, two months later, Bobby's proposed concession—to include the Vietcong in a coalition government—set off a firestorm that widened the gap between the president and the senator. "This," Vice President Humphrey said, "is more or less like putting a fox in a chicken coop" or "an arsonist in the fire department," adding, "I do not believe in writing a prescription for the ills of South Vietnam which includes a dose of arsenic." National Security Advisor McGeorge Bundy and Undersecretary of State George Ball, both JFK holdovers, also assailed the idea. Like Jack, Bundy said on NBC's *Meet the Press*, he had little faith in popular fronts like the Vietcong. "That subject was on his mind," Bundy said of Jack, "and what he said was 'I am not impressed by the opportunities open to popular fronts throughout the world. I do not believe that any Democrat can successfully ride that tiger.'"[26] In his inaugural address, Jack had urged the new governments of the developing world to "remember that, in the past, those who foolishly sought power by riding

"Not by Escalation, but by De-escalation"

the back of the tiger ended up inside." Bundy was now using Jack's words to attack Bobby.

Though Bobby was losing support around LBJ, he was gaining it around the country, giving him more political leverage and portending poorly for LBJ and his Cold War approach to Vietnam. "Senator Robert F. Kennedy is becoming the new hero of the Democratic left," the *New York Times* wrote after he proposed his governing coalition. It was, as the *Times* noted, an ironic development, reflecting the changes in both Bobby and the nation. "Some self-described liberals who formerly regarded him as a ruthless, cold-blooded and even unprincipled political operative now look to him increasingly as the symbol and exponent of their dissatisfactions with the Johnson Administration."[27]

Bobby's next effort, on which he was joined by Ted, did nothing to dampen liberal enthusiasm: he called for a new U.S. approach to communist China.

13

"We Live in the Same World with China"

"We have striven to isolate China from the world and treat it with unremitting hostility," Bobby Kennedy told a University of Chicago conference of China experts in early February of 1967. "That, however, is not a policy. It is an attitude founded upon fear and passion and wishful hopes."

In the 1960s—as U.S.-Soviet tensions cooled, Soviet-Chinese tensions escalated, and Vietnam undermined the Cold War consensus—Bobby and Ted helped drive an emerging debate about whether Washington should overhaul its hardline policy of isolating mainland China. In June of 1965, Bobby began pushing LBJ to include Beijing in nuclear-arms talks with Moscow and in global disarmament talks. The following May, Ted called for a blue-ribbon panel to reassess America's policy toward China and, that July, proposed that Washington reverse its opposition to Beijing's admission to the United Nations and adopt a "two China" policy in which the mainland and Taiwan would each have a seat.

On China, the Kennedy brothers had come a long way. As a House member in 1949, Jack chastised Truman for letting Mao's communists topple Chiang's U.S.-backed nationalists, forcing the latter to flee to Taiwan. As a Senate aide in 1953, Bobby slammed America's allies for trading with China at a time when Beijing was backing the North during the Korean War. Now, Bobby and Ted were promoting ideas for the U.S.-China relationship that, not many years earlier, would have evoked outrage from all three brothers.

Bobby and Ted's ability to help reshape America's policy toward China also reflected a shifting landscape of U.S. foreign policy-making. In the early 1960s, Jack began to wonder whether isolating China still made sense, though he limited his comments to private conversation. He responded enthusiastically when Chester Bowles showed him a draft of his article for the April 1960 issue of *Foreign Affairs* in which he recommended China's admission to the United Nations. Just before Jack assumed the presidency, however, Eisenhower warned him that he would publicly oppose steps to recognize the communist government or give it a UN seat. As a result, Jack relegated any such initiatives to his second term because he wanted to retain Ike's support for his foreign policy. Nevertheless, Jack approved Bowles's suggestion that, during his trip to Asia in early 1962, he work through Burma's president, U Nu, to offer to sell rice and wheat to a famine-plagued China if Beijing would ease its expansionism in the region and agree not to attack Taiwan. Bowles's mission, however, fell victim to a revolution in Burma that toppled Nu before he arrived.

By the mid-1960s, Bobby and Ted were working in a much different foreign policymaking environment, and they laid the groundwork for presidents Nixon and Carter to rewrite America's China policy in the years to come.

. . .

"In all our efforts," Bobby told the Senate in June of 1965 after outlining a plan to stop the spread of nuclear weapons, "we will have to deal with one of the most perplexing and difficult questions affecting American foreign policy: China."

Bobby's entry point into the China debate was nuclear nonproliferation, and he sought to continue the work that Jack began with his limited test-ban treaty. Bobby called the "mounting threat posed by the spread of nuclear weapons" the "most vital issue now facing this nation and the world." He quoted Jack on the frightening prospect of "nuclear weapons in so many hands, in the hands of countries large and small, stable and unstable, responsible and irresponsible, scattered throughout the world." He called for multilateral talks on a global nonproliferation treaty, "nuclear-free zones" around the world, a more comprehensive test-ban treaty, a freeze on U.S. and Soviet nuclear capabilities, a stronger International Atomic Energy Agency, and less U.S. reliance on nuclear weapons in its defense strategy. When Bobby finished, sixteen senators each rose to praise his remarks.

His proposal to include China in nonproliferation talks attracted the most attention and stoked the most controversy. "It is difficult to negotiate on any question with the intransigent leaders of communist China," he acknowledged as he sought to convince the China hardliners around LBJ, on Capitol Hill, and in the foreign policy establishment. "And it is doubly difficult when we are engaged in South Vietnam. China is profoundly suspicious of and hostile to us—as we are highly and rightly suspicious of her. But China is there. China will have nuclear weapons. And without her participation it will be infinitely more difficult, perhaps impossible in the long run, to prevent nuclear proliferation." He noted that at the UN's Disarmament Commission a week earlier, seventy nations "urged that China be included" in any nonproliferation agreement; that LBJ had "repeatedly offered to negotiate with any government in the world as to the peace of Southeast Asia"; and that Americans had "voted overwhelmingly in a recent poll" for negotiations with China.

At the White House, Bobby's ideas fell victim to LBJ's personal resentments and policy differences. The president had devoted considerable time to nuclear nonproliferation, and a special committee that he appointed in the fall of 1964 to study the issue had completed its "top secret" report. Now that Bobby was focusing on the issue, LBJ concluded that Bobby was finding fault with the president's efforts. What particularly irked LBJ, however, was the timing of Bobby's speech. LBJ had planned a major address on nonproliferation for June 25 as part of the UN's twentieth anniversary celebration in San Francisco—and it was scheduled before Bobby decided to address the subject two days earlier. After top administration officials sought in vain to dissuade Bobby from delivering

"We Live in the Same World with China"

his speech on that day, LBJ ordered his advisors to shift the focus of his UN speech to avoid echoing Bobby. "Of course," LBJ's press secretary, George Reedy, sniffed after Bobby's speech, "we are glad Senator Kennedy is also interested in this field."[1]

Bobby continued to push for China's participation in nonproliferation talks, and LBJ continued to resist. When, in October of 1965, Bobby suggested in a Senate speech that Washington invite Beijing to global disarmament talks that were scheduled to resume the following January in Geneva, the State Department reiterated longstanding administration policy that China wouldn't be included until it changed its "hostile policy."[2] The following May, Bobby proposed again that Washington invite Beijing to disarmament talks after the State Department confirmed that the administration had rejected a private suggestion from the communist government that each declare that it wouldn't use nuclear weapons against the other.

By the spring of 1966, Bobby wasn't the only Kennedy making waves on America's China policy.

. . .

In early May, Ted proposed a "major reassessment" of China policy; said the United States needed to know (among other things) whether "there are any changes we can make in our policy toward the Chinese that will make her a more responsible nation and improve the prospects of peace and stability in Asia"; urged LBJ to appoint a blue-ribbon panel to recommend "new directions in our China policy"; and echoed Bobby's call to include China in global disarmament talks.

Ted's proposal arose from his discussions with Jerome Cohen, a Harvard Law School professor and China expert, who was pushing Washington to "normalize" relations with the mainland—that is, to establish full diplomatic relations with it. In his Senate speech, Ted bemoaned the previous fifteen years during which no "meaningful political discussion" on rewriting America's China policy had occurred for the "fundamental reason ... that, as a nation, we are still unprepared to face up to the realities of China." It was an interesting slap at the time when Jack's hardline views about China prevailed (and when Bobby and Ted shared them). Now, in noting the "realities of China," Ted echoed Bobby's comment of a year earlier that "China is there" and Washington should stop trying to isolate it and explore the possibilities of engagement.

Ted tip-toed around the issue of China's admission to the United Nations. "If," he said, "a system of representation were devised which would allow a seat for mainland China and still preserve Taiwan's rights, it should receive serious consideration." He warned that America's policy was dangerously static because, in 1965, the UN's General Assembly cast a tie vote on admitting mainland China and giving it Taiwan's seat. That, Ted said, suggested that Washington was losing support for its hardline opposition to China's admission. In July he cast aside his caution over a "two China" policy and called for UN seats for both the mainland and Taiwan. He also suggested that LBJ himself had opened the door to a new approach to China because, a week earlier, he had urged reconciliation between China, its neighbors, and the United States.

President Johnson didn't criticize Ted's call for a blue-ribbon panel and Vice President Humphrey actually praised the idea, which suggested that LBJ was ready to reconsider his hardline views. But LBJ reacted harshly to Ted's "two China" proposal. Just a few hours after Ted unveiled it in a Senate speech, he told reporters that he wouldn't reverse Washington's opposition to China's UN admittance or ease its trade embargo until Beijing showed that it would live by the UN's charter.

While Bobby and Ted were planting the seeds of a new U.S. policy for China in the years ahead, LBJ was looking like an increasingly obstinate Cold Warrior at a time when the Cold War consensus was fraying.

. . .

With their proposals, Bobby and Ted helped to drive a soul-searching debate in Washington about how America should approach China.

In early 1966 LBJ, Humphrey, McNamara, and Dean Rusk each

issued statements that, as the *New York Times* put it, "pictured a relentlessly expansionist China, dedicated to spreading communism and Chinese power throughout the world, advancing toward threatening nuclear strength, and needing to be stopped now—in Vietnam—as the world should have stopped Hitler on the Rhine." They based their views on such factors as China's continued development of nuclear weapons as well as a doctrine—which China's defense minister, Lin Piao, enunciated the previous September—under which China's global revolution would conquer the U.S.-led West as well as the Soviet Union. LBJ and his team assumed that Beijing was driving North Vietnam's aggression against the South. "In the forties and fifties," LBJ said in Honolulu, "we took our stand in Europe to protect the freedom of those threatened by aggression. Now the center of attention has shifted to another part of the world where aggression is on the march. Our stand must be as firm as ever." Rusk said that Lin Piao's doctrine was "as candid as Hitler's 'Mein Kampf.'"[3]

At the Senate Foreign Relations Committee, Fulbright launched hearings in March of 1966 about America's China policy in order to reduce the "fatal expectancy" in Washington and Beijing that war between them was inevitable.[4] What the committee heard was far different than what LBJ and his team were peddling—mostly, calls to reconsider U.S. efforts to "isolate" China, particularly by opposing its UN membership. No China expert who testified at the hearings denied the need to "contain" China, but most thought that Washington should replace isolation with outreach to lower tensions and increase understanding. They called for Washington to consider recognizing the communist regime as China's legitimate government, support its UN admission, and scale back America's trade embargo against it. (In the midst of the hearings, 198 China experts issued a document that reflected those sentiments.)

The hearings showcased a remarkable transformation in the nation's capital that, with their speeches and writings, Bobby and Ted helped to nourish. Referring to the longstanding fears of elected officials, dating back to the McCarthy era, that they not appear "soft" on communism, one leading reporter wrote, "A heresy is being exorcised before the Senate Foreign Relations Committee.... The curtain of taboo on discussing China since it fell under communist rule in 1949, is lifting."[5]

While debate over a new U.S. policy for China raged throughout 1966, Bobby challenged the Cold War consensus on another front as he traveled to Africa and confronted one of America's most reliable Cold War allies.

. . .

In May of 1966 the influential Democratic activist Allard Lowenstein was preparing to fly with socialist leader Norman Thomas to the Dominican Republic, where they would observe elections, when he received a message to call Bobby.

"I'm going to make this speech in Cape Town," Bobby told Lowenstein by phone from his New York apartment when Lowenstein called him from an airport in New York, "and I need to talk to you about it." When Lowenstein said they could talk after he returned from the Dominican Republic in three days, Bobby told him that he was leaving for South Africa before then. When Lowenstein explained that he was taking Thomas, an eighty-one-year-old man with poor eyesight and an unsteady walk, as part of an official delegation of observers, Bobby blurted, "Oh, for heaven's sakes, someone else can take Norman Thomas to the Dominican Republic."[6] Lowenstein quickly passed Thomas off to another observer at the airport and rushed to Bobby's apartment.

Bobby reached out to Lowenstein and others because he knew how much was at stake with his trip. The previous fall the National Union of South African Students invited him to speak at its annual "Day of Reaffirmation of Academic and Human Freedom," which the union established after the government closed its "open" universities to non-whites in 1959. The union—which, with its 19,500 members, was the nation's largest multiracial organization outside of churches—invited Bobby because he worked on human rights issues as attorney general and he represented a younger generation

"We Live in the Same World with China"

of leaders. The invitation put South Africa's government in a tough spot: approve his visa and watch him energize the anti-apartheid movement, or deny his visa and garner global scorn. Top officials and government-backed newspapers denounced the invitation from what Justice Minister Balthazar Vorster called "a damnable and detestable organization" and, although the government eventually approved the visa, it refused Bobby's request to visit in May of 1966, delaying his trip until June.[7] Officials prevented the union's twenty-one-year-old president, Ian Robertson, from attending Bobby's speech and rejected requests from all American reporters (reportedly as many as thirty) who wanted to accompany Bobby on his four-day visit.

Bobby's trip nourished more tension with LBJ because the president thought that the senator was trying to upstage him on foreign policy. A week before Bobby boarded his plane, LBJ tried to divert attention from his trip by delivering his own speech on Africa— his only one as president, as it turned out. More importantly, the two disagreed about South Africa's role in America's foreign policy. LBJ, who was far less interested in Africa than any of the Kennedy brothers, was comfortable with the pre-JFK policy of backing anti-communist governments of all stripes and deferring U.S. policy to European nations with colonial holdings. South Africa was a particularly important anti-communist bulwark on the continent and, though LBJ opposed apartheid, he didn't want Bobby to weaken America's relationship with South Africa by denouncing its government. (President Reagan would voice the same concern two decades later when Ted led the fight for U.S. sanctions over apartheid.) Bobby, however, was now less concerned about the Cold War and more concerned about America's approach to great moral issues, and he wanted to put Washington squarely on the side of human rights.

Bobby left little to chance. After letting Lowenstein and other trusted advisors rewrite his Cape Town speech at his New York apartment, he took more suggestions on the draft from Britain's Lord Harlech, a family friend whom Bobby visited in London on his way to South Africa.

. . .

"Each time a man stands up for an ideal," Bobby told thousands of students and faculty at the University of Cape Town, "or acts to improve the lot of others, or strikes out against injustice, he sends forth a tiny ripple of hope, and crossing each other from a million different centers of energy and daring, those ripples build a current which can sweep down the mightiest walls of oppression and resistance."

Bobby's "ripple of hope" speech, perhaps his most compelling on foreign affairs, reflected his continuing evolution from hardcore Cold Warrior to liberal humanitarian. To be sure, he remained a fierce critic of communism. In his remarks, he said he's "unalterably opposed" to it "because it exalts the state over the individual and over the family; and because its system contains a lack of freedom of speech, of protest, of religion, and of the press, which is characteristic of a totalitarian regime." With that in mind, however, he criticized South Africa's government for suppressing freedom, smearing its opponents as communists, and—in denying freedom— strengthening "the very communism it claims to oppose."

South African officials were right to worry about the attention Bobby would attract. Though no outside reporters were allowed into South Africa to cover his trip, some fifty reporters who were already there (South African reporters or foreign correspondents of U.S. and other news outlets who were based there) did so. When he and Ethel landed in Johannesburg's Jan Smuts Airport on the evening of June 4, two thousand students mobbed them for a half-hour, some with banners reading "We Love You, Bobby." When he arrived two nights later to speak at the University of Cape Town, eighteen thousand school officials and students had been waiting outside in the bitter cold and wind, some of them for nearly three hours. After wading through the crowd for a half-hour, he entered the hall behind a symbolic procession in which a student carried "the extinguished torch of academic freedom." As he reached the stage, he passed an empty chair that was left for Robertson.

"We Live in the Same World with China"

Over the next three days, Bobby debated apartheid-backing students at Stellenbosch University; warned an audience of twenty thousand at the University of Natal that South Africa's failure to address its racial issue would generate "major crises"; stood atop a car to sing "We Shall Overcome" to a huge crowd; hosted a multiracial dinner with leading South African political, cultural, and religious leaders; visited Robertson and gave him a copy of JFK's *Profiles in Courage* that Jackie Kennedy had inscribed; met with Nobel Peace Prize winner Albert Luthuli, whom the government had confined to his farm in the town of Stanger; visited the Soweto district of struggling black townships; and received thunderous applause when he denounced apartheid in soaring language in a final speech at Johannesburg's Witwatersrand University. It was his "ripple of hope" speech, however, that left the greatest impact.

When he returned home, Bobby shifted his attention again to the rising power in Asia that had long bedeviled Washington.

. . .

"It is safe to say," Bobby told the China experts who had gathered in Chicago in early 1967, "that there is no aspect of American foreign policy so important and yet uncertain—no country so seemingly menacing about which we know so little—as China."

In the global affairs of that time, Bobby sensed an opportunity for Washington. In China, he said, the chaotic Cultural Revolution that Mao launched in 1966 to purify the country of revisionist elements and recommit it to communist fervor "insures" that Beijing would focus "on internal matters for at least the immediate future." In America, meanwhile, a Cold War that had "calmed" in the West would enable Washington "to divert some energy and thought to this part of the world." As Bobby saw it, America's policymakers now had a rare and precious commodity—time—to rethink its future with China.

Though Bobby didn't outline a comprehensive new policy, he offered a framework for one. "Our policy," he said, "must rest on the knowledge that we cannot predict the possibility of Chinese military expansion." The United States should be prepared to defend itself but not presume that armed conflict was inevitable; should welcome U.S. contacts with China so that Washington faces a "rational or informed China," not an "irrational and ignorant one"; and should consider a Marshall Plan for Asia that—as with the Soviet Union in Europe two decades earlier—could help contain China by strengthening the nations around it. Seeking a policy to nourish friendlier ties with China, he echoed Jack's words at American University when he promoted "genuine peace" with the Soviets. "Policy," Bobby said, "demands a conscious and open recognition that we live in the same world and move in the same continent with China. . . . Only when we accept this reality can we work toward our central task—to bring about Chinese acceptance of the fact that it too must live with us and the other nations of the world."

That Bobby helped shape the debate in foreign policy circles about China grew clear when, in the fall of 1967, Richard Nixon penned a long piece about China for *Foreign Affairs*. He, too, called for less isolation and more outreach, arguing that "we simply cannot leave China forever outside the family of nations, there to nurture its fantasies, cherish its hates and threaten its neighbors."[8] He, too, called for U.S. measures to strengthen its allies in Asia so that, as with the Soviets in Europe, China would choose to live with its neighbors rather than seek to conquer them. With Bobby Kennedy and Richard Nixon both promoting a new approach to China in 1967, the unanswered question is whether Bobby would have pursued it at the same pace, and in the same way, that Nixon did—had Bobby won the presidency in 1968 after another Kennedy-Nixon race.

Around the time that Bobby spoke in Chicago about China, a rush of events related to Vietnam forced his final big break with LBJ and, in the months to come, would leave the Cold War consensus in tatters.

14

"Not Very Different Than What Hitler Did to the Jews"

"These are the children not of the Cold War, but of the thaw," Bobby said of America's youth in February of 1967.

These young people, he observed in a speech to the liberal group Americans for Democratic Action, knew nothing of Stalin's "purges and death camps," of the Soviet invasion of Hungary in 1956 to suppress a populist uprising, or of a monolithic communist movement bent on world conquest. They were living in a far different world, a world of growing Soviet-Chinese discord, a world in which "communism is certainly no better, but perhaps no worse, than many other evil and repressive dictatorships all around the world—with which we conclude alliances when that is felt to be in our interest." And even, he said, as Washington was seeking to "build bridges" to the new communist world, "they see us, in the name of anti-communism, devastating the land of those we call our friends ... they see us willing to fight a war for freedom in Vietnam, but unwilling to fight with one-hundredth the money or force or effort to secure freedom in Mississippi or Alabama or the ghettos of the North."

Bobby had come of age amid the Cold War consensus, and he had assumed the role of a Cold Warrior with enthusiasm: slamming FDR for caving to Stalin at Yalta, chastising America's allies for trading with communist China during the Korean War, denouncing communist rule after traveling across the Soviet republics, and vowing that the United States would "win" in Vietnam.

But if Bobby and the "children" grew up in different eras, the truth was that, by the late 1960s, their views were converging. Bobby was questioning where the hardcore anti-communism of his earlier days had taken his country in Vietnam and elsewhere. "The erosion of his old views and the looming of the new ones," Allard Lowenstein marveled, "was something quite phenomenal to experience."[1]

As Bobby continued to evolve, he helped fuel growing doubts about America's military venture far from home.

. . .

"It was the first time that I remember him specifically questioning whether Johnson was really sane," Lowenstein said years later of Bobby, after he and LBJ confronted one another in a brutal stand-off in the Oval Office in February of 1967. "I don't remember if he used the word 'sane,' but the question [was] whether he was really in control of himself then. What did this portend and what should he do now that he had been through this?"[2]

Bobby had traveled to Europe for ten days in late January for business and pleasure, and—ironically, as it turned out—he told aides beforehand that he wanted to keep the trip low-key so that it wouldn't attract lots of media attention. In Paris he and a U.S. embassy official met with French diplomat Etienne Manac'h. Though Bobby didn't realize it at the time, largely because the other two were speaking French to one another, Hanoi was sending a message through Manac'h to Washington that it was ready for peace talks if Washington halted its bombing. With a leak from a State Department official about Hanoi's overture, *Newsweek* wrote up the story and the *New York Times* followed with one of its own.

LBJ read the front-page *Times* story, exploded over what he considered Bobby's inappropriate diplomacy, summoned him to the Oval Office, accused him of leaking the story, told him that America's forces were winning in Vietnam, said that Washington didn't need to negotiate, and warned him that "I'll destroy you and every one of your dove friends in six months. You'll be dead politically in six months." "Look," Bobby replied, as he stood up to leave, "I don't have to take that from you."[3]

"Not Very Different"

With that, Bobby decided to end his public silence over Vietnam that had rankled Jack Newfield and other leading anti-war activists. As LBJ recommitted himself to the military effort, Bobby escalated his fight with the president. He decided to deliver a major speech about the war in early March and polished it until 3:30 a.m. on the day he spoke.

Bobby teed up his speech beforehand with reporters, who dutifully publicized his plans to speak. With such prior notice, LBJ did his best to distract attention from the speech by delivering two unscheduled speeches himself that day, holding a news conference, and confirming that his daughter was pregnant.

. . .

"Three presidents have taken action in Vietnam," Bobby told the Senate in the late afternoon of March 2, with many senators in the chamber to hear him. "As one who was involved in many of those decisions, I can testify that if fault is to be found or responsibility assessed, there is enough to go around for all—including myself."

It was a startling admission, implicating both him and Jack. Though he mostly blamed the war on the North for pursuing "relentless and unyielding conquest with obdurate unconcern for mounting desolation," he also said that it was "partly our responsibility." His most moving words concerned the innocent. Beyond the "valor" and "righteousness" of combat, he said, the war was "the vacant moment of amazed fear as a mother and child watch death by fire fall from the improbable machine sent by a country they barely comprehend . . . the sudden terror of the official or the civil guard absorbed in the work of his village as he realizes the Vietcong assassin is about to take his life . . . the refugees wandering, homeless, from villages now obliterated, leaving behind only those who did not live to flee . . . the young men, Vietnamese and American, who in an instant sense the night of death destroying yesterday's promise of family and land and home."

Bobby bemoaned the geopolitical costs as well. By destroying villages and rural areas and eroding "the fabric of that society," he said, the war was making the challenge of eventual reconstruction that much bigger. For Washington it was preventing "fresh understanding and diminishing tensions" with Moscow and draining Washington's energy from the important task of leading the West.

Noting that top Soviet and North Vietnamese officials had suggested in recent weeks that a U.S. bombing halt would prompt peace talks, Bobby urged a halt to test Hanoi's sincerity, comparing that approach to Jack's decision to probe Khrushchev's most promising statements for resolving the Cuban Missile Crisis. LBJ knew that Bobby would call for a bombing halt—he had already done so publicly and during their Oval Office confrontation—so he dispatched his top team to mock the idea in the days leading up to Bobby's speech. Rather than halt the bombing, LBJ escalated it that spring.

While Bobby battled with LBJ over war strategy, his brother sought to address another aspect of the war's collateral damage.

. . .

"We have a system," Ted Kennedy said of the Vietnam draft in a National Press Club speech of January 12, 1967,

> which sends tens of thousands of young men into the Army simply because they cannot afford to go to college; and which lets 75 percent of those wealthy enough or bright enough to go on to graduate school to escape military service completely. We have a system which allows professional athletes to join National Guard units which neither train nor guard. We have a system of local boards which apply widely different rules—which result in calling up married men in some states, while tens of thousands of single men in other states remain untouched; which conscript nineteen-year-olds in one city and twenty-two-year-olds in another; which put returning Peace Corps volunteers at the top of the list in one area, and at the bottom in another.

At the time, Bobby and Ted were both devoting more attention to the draft. Bobby, who nurtured Ted's interest in the draft by pin-

"Not Very Different"

pointing its unfairness, was offended by the well-to-do young Americans who called for stronger U.S. military action in Vietnam while securing draft deferments that left the fighting disproportionately to poor minorities. Two weeks after his March 2 speech, he spoke to five thousand students at the University of Oklahoma and called for ending draft deferments for college students. After some boos and hisses, he asked how many of the students in attendance supported a U.S. withdrawal from Vietnam, how many backed LBJ's policies, how many wanted more military action, and how many supported draft deferments for students. After the students expressed their strongest support for both more military action and deferments, he asked, "How many of you who voted for escalation of the war also voted for the exemption of students from the draft?" After some stunned silence, the students began to applaud.[4]

While both brothers bemoaned the unfairness of draft deferments that shielded the well-to-do, it was, not surprisingly, Ted who sought to change the system through legislation. In early 1966 he testified before the House Armed Services Committee and appeared on ABC's Sunday morning news show *Issues and Answers* to propose a lottery to replace the draft. Opposed, however, by the head of the Selective Service System, who had served in that post since before World War II, his proposal went nowhere that year. But he resurrected it in his National Press Club speech the following January.

With Ted, not Bobby, proposing a lottery, LBJ expressed no knee-jerk opposition. In the early months of 1967, the president appointed a commission to study a lottery; the commission recommended one; LBJ then called for one; Ted held hearings as a Senate subcommittee chairman; the head of the Selective Service System changed his mind and became a supporter; and the Senate voted overwhelmingly for legislation to let the president establish a lottery. But the House drafted a competing bill that prohibited the president from doing so, and Richard Russell, the Senate Armed Services Committee chairman and a lottery skeptic, convinced the Senate to accept the House provisions.

Though Ted lost that battle, he laid the groundwork for Congress to approve the request of President Nixon—who assumed office in January of 1969—to establish a lottery, which he did later that year.

. . .

"Don't you realize," Bobby told several hundred students at New York's Marymount College in December of 1967, "that what we are doing to the Vietnamese is not very different than what Hitler did to the Jews?"[5]

With LBJ committed to military victory throughout 1967 and inclined to do the opposite of whatever Bobby recommended, both Bobby and Ted grew more anguished and lashed out more expressively (as witnessed by Bobby's outlandish allusion to the Holocaust). They drove, and were driven by, growing domestic opposition to the war. In the spring, as America's forces launched their largest military offensive of the war, four hundred thousand protested in New York and seventy-five thousand marched in San Francisco. Over the summer, as Allard Lowenstein launched a "Dump Johnson" movement to convince Democrats to nominate someone else for president in 1968, Defense Secretary Robert McNamara admitted to a Senate committee that bombing wasn't working. General William Westmoreland, America's military commander in Vietnam, asked LBJ for two hundred thousand more troops, which would have swelled U.S. forces to six hundred seventy-five thousand, but the president limited the increase to forty-five thousand. In October, as one hundred thousand people protested at the Lincoln Memorial, polls showed that 46 percent of Americans believed the war was a "mistake" and most Americans thought the nation should "win or get out."

Bobby continued to argue that, in Vietnam and across the developing world, America's success would come less from military force than political reform. By the summer of 1967, however, he was questioning the entire U.S. effort in Vietnam, the very *raison d'etre* behind American's involvement. That's because the government in Saigon was signaling that, whatever the results of elections scheduled for

September, it didn't plan to relinquish power. Of America's purpose in Vietnam, Bobby told the Senate in August, "It is, most fundamentally and honorably, to protect and insure the right of the South Vietnamese people to govern themselves; to determine the nature of their society; and to select their leaders free from external control and internal violence." But, he said, the government was kicking some candidates off the ballot, harassing others, jailing dissidents, censoring media, and barring Buddhists and trade unionists from full political participation. Saigon's military government also was creating a Military Affairs Council, which seemed like a move to "perpetuate its power, regardless of the voting." And all of this was occurring, Bobby said, as America's military effort was expanding while the South's was shrinking.

Without free elections, Bobby concluded, "We would no longer have a common purpose with the government of Vietnam. For our commitment is to the Vietnamese *people*—not to any government, not to any generals, not to the powerful and privileged few." In other words, Jack's decision to "make a stand" against communist expansionism in Vietnam no longer made sense if Washington was defending a corrupt, authoritarian regime that was little if any better than a communist alternative.

. . .

While Bobby questioned America's entire effort in Vietnam, Ted maintained his focus on its human costs.

In April of 1967 he secured an administration promise to build three American military hospitals in South Vietnam for wounded civilians (although the administration never followed through). A month later he said that civilian casualties were running at least twice as high as official government figures. Pressed by Ted, the administration sent doctors to South Vietnam in July to assess its medical care. Though, in their report in September, they called for more U.S. spending on medical care, they opposed Ted's call for three new hospitals, saying that would slow medical advances in Vietnam.

The senator responded vigorously when he met privately with

the doctors. To their claim, quoted in a White House press release, that "hospitals appear to be sufficient in number and well located for our peacetime needs," Ted made the obvious point that "We are not in peace over there, and as far as I myself have been able—I don't see what in the world that has to do with what the problems are." As the doctors defended themselves, he responded, "We are the ones that are ripping that country up. And the question is what we are going to do about it."[6] He held hearings in October, airing his disagreement with the doctors before turning to the issue of the rising numbers of refugees. Government and private experts testified that refugees were now more likely fleeing America's military than the Vietcong and that, due to American combat tactics, the Vietcong were gaining more in recruits than they were losing on the battlefield.

Ted ended the year with a low-profile trip to Vietnam, arriving on January 1, 1968, and meeting over the next twelve days with military officials, war fighters, war correspondents, doctors, and international volunteers. After many months of sparring with administration officials over casualty and refugee figures, and of learning that America's war effort wasn't progressing nearly as well as LBJ and his team suggested, he was now determined to dig below the surface of what he later termed "canned pronouncements and packaged tours." Before leaving for Vietnam, he sent a team of experienced investigators to scour the country for refugee camps and hospitals for him to visit. After arriving, he ignored the agenda that America's embassy in Saigon had prepared for him; pursued the path that his investigators recommended; and changed his schedule on the fly as he discovered more places to see. His improvisation may have saved his life because after he rescheduled a dinner with a young American volunteer who was teaching farming to peasants, a bomb blew out the front of the building in which they were supposed to dine—and at the time of their scheduled meal.

Ted kept reporters largely at bay so they wouldn't disrupt the trip and make it harder for him to gather information. It was a wild two weeks, as Ted drove across a jungle at midnight in a fruitless search for a notorious mental hospital where patients were fed garbage; talked to a weeping U.S. air controller who located bombing targets for fighter pilots but admitted that he couldn't know from the air whether the figures in black pajamas were Vietcong fighters or civilians; found pictures of JFK on the walls of "tarpaper shacks" in Saigon; and lambasted the U.S. military officials who offered happy talk that contradicted what he had just seen with his own eyes. When his trip ended, Ted recalled years later, he decided that he could no longer support "this atrocity of a war" and, anguished by what he saw, "drank a great deal of liquor on the flight home."[7] In his thoughts about the war, he was now where Bobby had arrived months earlier.

Ted flew home, briefed a hostile LBJ, and delivered his findings in a high-profile speech.

. . .

"Negotiations will not be a quick or painless solution to the Vietnam War," Ted told an audience of five hundred at Boston's World Affairs Council in late January of 1968, "but the sooner they begin, the sooner men of peace, rather than those concerned solely with military victory, will begin bringing their influence to bear on the ultimate result."

After two weeks in Vietnam, he concluded that America's military effort wasn't worth the cost. In a sharp, graphic, often moving thirty-minute address, he explained that Washington was doing too much to win the war; Saigon was doing too little; the South's government, police, and other institutions were thoroughly corrupt; its people were suffering cruel deaths or cowering in fear in cities, villages, and hamlets; Saigon was doing little to help the mounting numbers of refugees; and American refugee aid was going largely to waste. Washington and Saigon, he said, should seek negotiations with Hanoi and, if they did not begin promptly, Washington should rethink its military goals and significantly scale back its efforts.

Though more subtle than Bobby's *mea culpa* of the previous March, Ted's remarks offered a whiff of an apology for his previous support for the Vietnam venture. Noting that he left Saigon in late 1965 "feeling things were going to get better" or "at least with the hope that some real progress was on the horizon," he made clear that he now felt otherwise. "I am forced to conclude," he said,

> that the objectives we set forth to justify our initial involvement in that conflict, while still defensible, are now less clear and less attainable than they seemed in the past. And I believe that if current policies relating to the nature of the war are not changed, and the assumptions underlying civilian programs are not revised, then the prospects for individual freedom and political stability in Vietnam in the foreseeable future are dim. In essence, I found that the kind of war we are fighting in Vietnam will not gain our long-range objectives; that the pattern of destruction we are creating can only make a workable political future more difficult; and that the government we are supporting has given us no indication and promises little, that it can win the lasting confidence of its own people.

He described Saigon residents "forced to live in graveyards" or "hollowed out tombs"; rural areas in which the "scorched outlines of houses burned to the ground" covered more than half of a province; pediatric wards with "rats in the rafters and filth on the floors, windows without screens, children wide-eyed with pain, and no Vietnamese personnel to comfort them or care for them"; government officials more interested in maintaining power than treating war victims; corruption that "pervades all aspects of Vietnamese life"; a people who "do not fully have their hearts in this struggle"; and a government "that does not have its heart in the cause of the people." He urged a "confrontation" in which Washington would tell Saigon that if it didn't root out its corruption and build support among its people, Americans would "rightfully" demand a new U.S. approach to Vietnam.[8]

Six days after Ted spoke, the North launched the Tet Offensive, attacking one hundred cities and towns. It sparked Bobby's response a week later in Chicago in what's known as his "Unwinnable War" speech. While echoing major themes of Ted's Boston remarks, he declared that Tet "shattered the mask of official illusion with which

"Not Very Different"

we have concealed our true circumstances, even from ourselves," by showing that "half a million American soldiers with seven hundred thousand Vietnamese allies, with total command of the air, total command of the sea, backed by huge resources and the most modern weapons, are unable to secure even a single city from the attacks of an enemy whose total strength is about two hundred fifty thousand."

As Bobby, Ted, and, later in February, CBS anchor Walter Cronkite suggested negotiations to end the war, the question was whether one Robert F. Kennedy would run for president to make them happen.

. . .

For months, as pressure mounted on Bobby to run, he hesitated because, among other things, he worried that LBJ would respond by digging in further, recommitting himself to the troops and the bombs.

When he finally announced his candidacy in March, he called unconditionally for the war's end. Comparing America's turmoil to the Civil War era, he told fifteen thousand students at Kansas State University that Vietnam "has divided Americans as they have not been divided since your state was called Bloody Kansas." The war, he said, "must be ended, and it can be ended in a peace for brave men who have fought each other with a terrible fury, each believing that he alone was in the right."

The young firebrands around Bobby hoped that, as he ran, he would lean on them rather than on older advisors with whom Bobby worked under Jack and remained close, men like Ted Sorenson. That's because the firebrands thought very differently about America's global challenges. What Bobby had said about the nation's youth was true of them: "They were children not of the Cold War, but of the thaw." The Cold War consensus was gone, and the firebrands disparaged the Cold Warriors in their midst. "Don't forget," one of them said, "that JFK campaigned in '60 on . . . that Cold War crap."[9]

With Bobby's murder in June, it was now Ted who would lead the anti-war effort and continue to reshape America's global role.

1. Joe Kennedy, center, America's ambassador to Great Britain, arrives in Southampton, England, in July of 1938 with Joe Kennedy Jr., left, and Jack. JFK Presidential Library and Museum, Presidential Collection.

2. Jack, right, in 1943 with his crew of the PT-109 in the Pacific, where he received national acclaim for his heroic efforts. Richard W. Sears/U.S. Signal Corps via JFK Presidential Library and Museum, vol. 83, p. 24.

3. Bobby with Supreme Court Justice William Douglas in Stalingrad in September of 1955, at the tail end of their six-week trip across the Soviet Union.
Courtesy of the Associated Press.

4. The brothers with, from left, Jean, Rose, Joe, Pat, and Eunice in Hyannis Port, circa 1948—the year that Jack turned 31; Bobby, 23; and Ted, 16. JFK Presidential Library and Museum, Presidential Collection.

5. Bobby, Jack, and Ted in Palm Beach, Florida, in April of 1957. Douglas Jones / *Look* magazine via JFK Presidential Library.

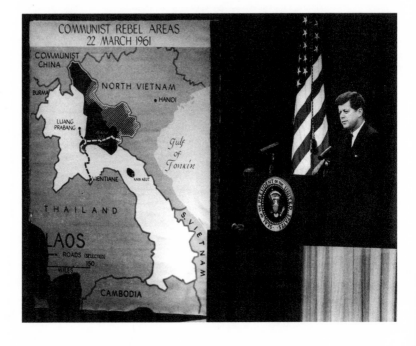

MEMORANDUM FOR

VICE PRESIDENT

In accordance with our conversation I would like
for you as Chairman of the Space Council to be in charge of
making an overall survey of where we stand in space.

1. Do we have a chance of beating the Soviets by
putting a laboratory in space, or by a trip
around the moon, or by a rocket to land on the
moon, or by a rocket to go to the moon and
back with a man. Is there any other space
program which promises dramatic results in
which we could win?

2. How much additional would it cost?

3. Are we working 24 hours a day on existing
programs. If not, why not? If not, will you
make recommendations to me as to how
work can be speeded up.

4. In building large boosters should we put our
emphasis on nuclear, chemical or liquid fuel,
or a combination of these three?

5. Are we making maximum effort? Are we
achieving necessary results?

I have asked Jim Webb, Dr. Weisner, Secretary
McNamara and other responsible officials to cooperate with
you fully. I would appreciate a report on this at the
earliest possible moment.

6. (*opposite top*) Jack meets with Adlai Stevenson, America's ambassador to the United Nations, in the Oval Office in March of 1961. JFK Presidential Library and Museum, White House Collection. Photograph by Abbie Rowe.

7. (*opposite bottom*) Jack discusses the conflict in Laos, where his advisors were recommending that he send upward of sixty thousand troops, at a news conference in March of 1961. JFK Presidential Library and Museum, White House Collection. Photograph by Abbie Rowe.

8. (*above*) Jack's memo to Vice President Lyndon Johnson, who chaired the Space Council, in April of 1961: "Do we have a chance of beating the Soviets"? JFK Presidential Library and Museum, White House Collection. Photograph by Abbie Rowe.

9. Ted and Joan Kennedy visit Rome in May of 1961 on Ted's "good will" tour of Italy, a year before he successfully ran for the Senate. Courtesy of the Associated Press.

10. (*opposite top*) Jack and Jackie Kennedy watch astronaut Alan B. Shepard's liftoff in the office of Jack's secretary, Evelyn Lincoln, in May of 1961. JFK Presidential Library and Museum, White House Collection. Photograph by Cecil Stoughton.

11. (*opposite bottom*) Jack with Soviet Premier Nikita Khrushchev in June of 1961 in Vienna, where their summit turned contentious. Courtesy of the Associated Press.

12. (*opposite top*) Jack meets with, from left, Prime Minister Julius Nyerere of Tanganyika (which later became part of Tanzania) and "Soapy" Williams, his assistant secretary of state for African affairs, at the White House in July of 1961. JFK Presidential Library and Museum, White House Collection. Photograph by Robert Knudsen.

13. (*opposite bottom*) Jack meets with his new U.S. ambassadors in July of 1961, before they leave for their overseas posts. JFK Presidential Library and Museum, White House Collection. Photograph by Abbie Rowe.

14. (*above*) Jack addresses the nation by TV and radio to discuss the crisis in Berlin in July of 1961, when war with the Soviets seemed a distinct possibility. JFK Presidential Library and Museum, White House Collection. Photograph by Abbie Rowe.

15. Jack with Chester Bowles, his special representative on African, Asian, and Latin American affairs, in December of 1961. JFK Presidential Library and Museum, White House Collection. Photograph by Abbie Rowe.

16. (*opposite top*) Bobby and Ethel Kennedy with Ambassador George Frederick Reinhardt in Rome in February of 1962, on the European leg of Bobby's global "good will" tour. JFK Presidential Library and Museum, Edwin O. Guthman Collection.

17. (*opposite bottom*) With West Berlin's mayor, Willy Brandt, alongside him and photographers in the background, Bobby peers over the Berlin Wall in February of 1962. Courtesy of the Associated Press, Picture-Alliance/DPA.

18. (*opposite top*) Bobby briefs Jack and, from left, Secretary of State Dean Rusk and Vice President Lyndon Johnson in late February of 1962 after returning from his global "good will" tour. JFK Presidential Library and Museum, White House Collection. Photograph by Abbie Rowe.

19. (*opposite bottom*) Jack signs a proclamation to order U.S. forces to "interdict . . . the delivery of offensive weapons and associated materiel to Cuba" during the Cuban Missile Crisis in October of 1962. JFK Presidential Library, White House Collection. Photograph by Abbie Rowe.

20. (*above*) Jack meets with Bobby and the rest of EXCOMM, his ad-hoc group of top advisors during the Cuban Missile Crisis in October of 1962. JFK Presidential Library and Museum, White House Collection. Photograph by Abbie Rowe.

21. Bobby meets with civil rights leaders at the White House in June of 1963, at a time when he and Jack worried that violence against blacks in America was hurting the nation's image in the developing world. JFK Presidential Library and Museum, White House Collection. Photograph by Abbie Rowe.

22. (*opposite top*) Jack delivers the commencement address at American University in June of 1963, outlining his vision of "genuine peace." JFK Presidential Library and Museum, White House Collection. Photograph by Cecil Stoughton.

23. (*opposite bottom*) Jack at Eyre Square in Galway, Ireland, during his triumphant visit to his ancestral home in June of 1963. JFK Presidential Library and Museum, White House Collection. Photograph by Robert Knudsen.

24. Jack meets with America's ambassador to South Vietnam, Henry Cabot Lodge Jr., in August of 1963. JFK Presidential Library and Museum, White House Collection. Photograph by Abbie Rowe.

25. (*opposite top*) Jack discusses Vietnam with CBS anchor Walter Cronkite in Hyannis Port over the Labor Day weekend of 1963. JFK Presidential Library and Museum, White House Collection. Photograph by Cecil Stoughton.

26. (*opposite bottom*) Bobby and Ethel Kennedy tour Warsaw in August of 1964, where Bobby tangled with Poland's communist leaders. JFK Presidential Library and Museum, Edward O. Guthman Collection.

27. Senators Bobby and Ted Kennedy descend the steps of the U.S. Capitol in October of 1965. Courtesy of the Associated Press. Photograph by Henry Griffin.

28. (*opposite top*) Ted visits a U.S. Army soldier during his trip to South Vietnam in January of 1968, after which he decided to no longer support "this atrocity of a war." JFK Presidential Library and Museum, Edward M. Kennedy press kit.

29. (*opposite bottom*) Bobby in California in the spring of 1968, as he ran for president in hopes of ending the Vietnam War. JFK Presidential Library and Museum, Sven Walnum Collection.

30. Ted attends a NATO meeting in Bonn in November of 1972 and visits with, at right, his wife, Joan, and Horst Ehmke, West Germany's minister of the chancellery. The man to the left is unidentified. Courtesy of the Associated Press.

31. Ted meets with China's foreign minister, Huang Hua, in Beijing in January of 1978. Courtesy of the Associated Press.

32. Surrounded by well-wishers, Ted tours Soweto in January of 1985 during his trip to South Africa to raise global consciousness about apartheid. Courtesy of the Associated Press.

33. Ted meets Soviet leader Mikhail Gorbachev, right, in February of 1986 in Moscow, where he helped secure the release of Soviet refusenik Natan Sharansky. Courtesy of the Associated Press. Photograph by Boris Yurchenko.

34. Ted speaks alongside Mo Mowlam, Northern Ireland's secretary, in Belfast in October of 1998 during his visit to promote an end to "the troubles." Courtesy of the Associated Press. Photograph by Stefan Rousseau.

35. Ted launches his campaign against what became the 2003 war in Iraq with a September 2002 speech at the Johns Hopkins School of Advanced International Studies in Washington. Courtesy of the Associated Press. Photograph by Ron Thomas.

PART 3

15

"Dear God, Help Us, This War Must End"

"The world," Senator Edward M. Kennedy wrote in the summer of 1969, "is in a state of flux; we and the other nuclear powers stand ready to open a vast Pandora's box of new nuclear weapons systems."[1]

The Senate was debating President Nixon's request for $5.5 billion for an antiballistic missile (ABM) system that—by destroying incoming ballistic missiles—would protect America's cities from nuclear attack, and Ted was leading the opposition. He thought not only that it wouldn't work, but that it would risk the safety of communities that housed the ABM sites, divert huge sums from domestic needs, and, most of all, reignite the arms race—pushing Moscow to develop more powerful weapons to overcome the ABM, which would push Washington to develop more powerful weapons to keep pace, and so on, leaving the world more dangerous.

A year earlier, Bobby's death had shattered Ted in the same way that Jack's death shattered Bobby. Ted was much closer with Bobby than Jack when the boys were growing up, and he grew especially close to him when they were both senators. After Bobby's death, Ted said years later, "The bottom just dropped out, and I just sort of checked out."[2] He secluded himself, grew a beard, and spent much of his time on the seas, sailing along the coast of Maine. He paid little attention to politics in the turbulent summer of 1968, ignoring Democratic entreaties to run for president or vice president.

Just as Bobby's peacemaking trip to Asia in early 1964 helped revive his spirits, so, too, did an issue of foreign policy—Vietnam—

help reinvigorate Ted. "There is no safety in hiding," he declared in late August of 1968 in his first speech after Bobby's murder, rejecting the kind-hearted advice of others that he retreat to private life to protect himself and care for his family. In a nationally televised address to a "hushed audience of 1000" at Holy Cross College in Worcester, Massachusetts, he called the war "the tragedy of our generation" and urged that "we now resolve" to end it "as quickly as it is physically possible . . . and extricate our men and our future from this bottomless pit." He proposed an unconditional U.S. bombing halt, a reduced military effort, negotiations with Hanoi to reduce troop levels, and steps to help Saigon build "a viable political, economic and legal structure that will not promptly collapse upon our departure."[3]

As Ted began confronting Nixon over Vietnam in the spring of 1969, he also pursued arms control, making the ABM his first target.

. . .

"I want to improve the human condition," Ted once told a reporter who had inquired about his plans.[4]

Ted Kennedy, the wayward soul of yesteryear, was just thirty-six when Bobby died. But, as the lone Kennedy brother, he was now America's most influential liberal. He wasn't nearly the public speaker that Jack was, nor as magnetic as Bobby. Politically, though, he was far more skilled than either of them. For the next four decades, with his skills at hand and his brothers in mind, he would exert an influence over America's global role that, in its long-term impact, would exceed that of either Jack or Bobby.

As he sought to "improve the human condition" abroad, Ted was no foreign policy visionary in the mold of Jack. He did not develop a broad U.S. approach to the world akin to Jack's "flexible response." Nor was he a fiery revolutionary in the mold of Bobby, traveling the world and predicting the populist overthrow of ossified regimes. Instead, Ted pursued a defined set of priorities while seizing opportunities as they arose.

He worked to build on Jack's arms control legacy by achieving more U.S.-Soviet arms reductions, and to build on Bobby's human rights legacy by promoting democracy across the developing world and securing freedom for dissidents in the Soviet Union, China, and elsewhere. While pursuing these broad priorities, he worked to reshape U.S.-China relations; impose sanctions on South Africa over apartheid; withdraw from Vietnam; end America's proxy wars with the Soviets across Latin America; prevent war in Iraq; and make peace in Northern Ireland. Like his brothers, he believed that America could be a moral beacon, an example to which other nations could aspire.

Ted didn't talk incessantly about Jack or Bobby, publicly or privately, but he noted on occasion that their work influenced his pursuits. Sometimes he mused about his brothers in more personal terms. Late at night, perhaps on a flight home, he would relay a story about one of them to a trusted aide. At that point he would stop and sit silently for a moment, revealing the pain that never fully left him.

. . .

Among Ted Kennedy's favorite expressions was the Irish proverb, "Strangers are just friends you haven't met."[5]

Working the halls of Congress, deploying the skills he inherited from Honey Fitz, Ted was the lawmaker as everyman, a warm, jovial, down-to-earth colleague who sought to develop personal relationships with politicians of all persuasions and to capitalize on them when he sought support for his ideas. "It's something that you learn very quickly in a family of 11," he said later, "especially when you're the youngest child: you just have to get along with other people."[6] While always pursuing bipartisan support to help usher his proposals through the Senate, he sometimes took the unusual step (for a senator) of visiting House members in their offices to help move his proposals through the House. Unlike his restless brothers when they were senators, he was unceasingly patient, willing to pursue an initiative year after year until he gathered the requisite support to bring it to fruition. He accepted the world of public policy as it was: slow, grinding, and complicated, a system of highs and lows, advances and setbacks—in his words, a "river" that he tried to bend in his direction.[7] Nevertheless, he brought a sense of urgency to his pursuits. Ted was no lukewarm advocate of the kind who would outline the reasonable views on all sides and explain why he chose one path over another. Once he took a position—sometimes after consultations with experts that might include dinner seminars at his home—he argued for it in strident terms, deploying sharp language and a thunderous voice, from his desk near the back of the Senate. At those moments, he seemed far more like the passionate Bobby than the cerebral Jack.

While doggedly working the ins and outs of retail politics, Ted also exploited the unique power that he could wield simply because he was a Kennedy. He was a magnet for media attention, enough so that like-minded lawmakers often let him take the lead on issues even as they envied the attention he attracted. More enraging to other senators was when he seized an issue on which they had been working—including major issues of foreign policy—such as by delivering a big speech and proposing his own solution. "We got used to it," recalled Walter Mondale, his former Senate colleague.[8] Not every senator was so forgiving, however, and Ted's forays into major issues were sometimes followed by an angry phone call from an embittered colleague or clashes between staffs.

Ted also wielded outsized influence abroad as foreign leaders sought him out when he was overseas or they were passing through Washington—because they had known Jack or Bobby, or they were intrigued by the Kennedy mystique, or they assumed that, in Ted, they were investing in a future president. He met with the leaders of democracies and autocracies and, with the latter, insisted on seeing opposition figures and visiting the communities of oppressed populations. Like his brothers, he was a magnet for grassroots attention, drawing huge crowds in Europe, Asia, and Latin America, whether delivering a speech or walking the streets. Also irritating to some senators was when foreign leaders contacted him, rather than his more senior colleagues. When, for instance, Hanoi sent signals to Ted in late 1970 that they would give him a list of the POWs they were holding and he sent a former JFK aide to Paris to get it, Chair-

"Dear God, Help Us, This War Must End"

man J. William Fulbright took umbrage that Ted hadn't turned the matter over to his Senate Foreign Relations Committee. On Ted's travels abroad, he also raised the hackles of American ambassadors by refusing to let them attend his meetings with foreign officials because, he said, those officials would speak far more candidly with him if they weren't there.

Everybody "wanted to touch him," an aide summed, and he leveraged his stature as he tried to bend the "river."[9]

. . .

"We know today that we can build a mighty nation, able to conquer any military threat, by any power," Ted wrote in early 1968. "But we also know that this might has brought us neither peace nor security; that we must find alternatives to the constant amassing of armed might if we are to live in peace."[10]

That January, as Kennedy watchers focused on whether Bobby would run for president, Ted put the finishing touches on *Decisions for a Decade*, his book about what the nation would likely face in the 1970s. Long forgotten by now, the book nevertheless offers a telling window into the thinking that would guide him for the next four decades. He proposed steps to help end the Cold War, limit future American military activity in Asia, nourish ties with communist China, turn Latin American revolutions toward democracy rather than totalitarianism, and secure peace by promoting global prosperity. That he was deeply concerned about America's global challenges is clear: not only did he devote considerable space in his book to foreign affairs, but he also asked diplomat George Kennan to write its preface. Also clear is how much Jack and Bobby had influenced him to that point; if you didn't know better, you might have thought that they had written some of his words.

Like Jack, Ted described America's challenges in dire terms, questioned whether the nation would find the wherewithal to meet them, and disparaged its efforts to date. "The men who signed the Declaration of Independence in 1776," he wrote, "were fired by the conviction that free men could build a great nation, governed by their own wisdom. The coming decade will bring grave challenges to this conviction." It was the same concern that Jack constantly raised from the time he wrote *Why England Slept*. Of America's failure to confront its challenges sufficiently over the previous two decades—"to settle for gradual progress where swift and bold change was required"—Ted wrote in JFK-ish fashion, "In the words of a French leader after France fell to the Nazis: 'We wanted to *have* more than we wanted to *give*. We spared effort, and met disaster.'"[11]

Ted also brought Bobby's passion to his pages, particularly about the developing world. "In Latin America," he wrote, echoing Bobby's prophesies of revolution and pleas for U.S. wisdom, "we face a continent where decisions *are* imminent; where the coming decade *will* be critical. Here, as on no other continent, the 1970s will determine whether we are right in asserting that fundamental and rapid change can take place without violent, bloody disruption." Like Bobby, he advised Washington not to robotically oppose all leftist movements because they might pave the way for communist takeovers. "Radical revolutionary movements, subject to Communist influence, might succeed in a Latin American country," he wrote, "and vigilance is necessary. However, if we assume that all radical movements are subversive; if we curtail aid to governments because they promise swift change; if we deprive them of our markets and our resources, we ourselves may force them to look elsewhere."[12]

As the events of later years revealed, he was clearly wrong on some key assumptions. Urging an end to the Cold War, for instance, he argued that Soviet control over Eastern Europe had largely ended. "Twenty years ago," he wrote, "the Soviet Union commanded a string of satellite states, totally submissive to her economic and political wishes. Today, with the exception of East Germany, Russia has no more satellites."[13] Just months after he put the finishing touches on *Decisions for a Decade*, however, the Soviets invaded Czechoslovakia to rein in Prague's reformist government, reminding everyone that East Germany was hardly Moscow's lone satellite in Europe.

. . .

In the winter of 1969, Jerome Wiesner, Jack's former science advisor who was then serving as MIT's provost, called Ted to express concerns about the ABM system that Nixon planned to build.

The ABM was many years in the making. Eisenhower and JFK opposed it because they doubted it would work, but interest in an ABM rose among policymakers in the late 1960s as its technological possibilities grew more promising; as the Soviets developed their own limited ABM system; and as the Chinese tested increasingly sophisticated nuclear weaponry. Defense Secretary Robert McNamara, who had convinced Jack to reject the military's plea for an ABM, couldn't convince LBJ to do the same and, at his behest in September of 1967, McNamara announced plans to build one. A year later President Johnson persuaded Congress to provide $1.9 billion to build the ABM's missile and radar instillations—at a time when Ted was still recovering from Bobby's murder and away from Capitol Hill. Included among more than a dozen proposed sites was one in Reading, Massachusetts, and many of Ted's constituents there complained to his office.

When, in early 1969, key senators of both parties renewed their efforts to kill the ABM in response to Nixon's request for $5.5 billion, Ted joined them. Nixon believed that because the Soviets had an ABM system and were developing more powerful nuclear weapons, the United States needed one as a "bargaining chip" for arms control talks.[14] Ted strongly disagreed. In February he wrote to Defense Secretary Melvin Laird to express concerns that the system wouldn't work and, rather than drive arms control, would reignite the arms race. By then anti-ABM protestors had demonstrated in Boston, Chicago, and other cities where the Pentagon was buying land for antiballistic missile sites. Although Ted convinced Laird to suspend work on the ABM, Laird acknowledged that he still supported it. More importantly, Nixon remained fully committed to it.

At the time Ted Kennedy was wielding more power than ever in the Senate because, in January of 1969, he unseated Louisiana's Russell Long as Senate majority whip, the second-highest ranking position among Senate Democrats. At just thirty-six, he had mastered the mores of the "world's greatest deliberative body," and he viewed a leadership position as a logical next step in his career. He lost that position two years later in the aftermath of Chappaquiddick, when a young woman died after the car he was driving with her in it plunged off a narrow bridge into Poucha Pond on Martha's Vineyard. Chappaquiddick would plague Ted Kennedy not only at home for decades to come but also abroad, where his adversaries sometimes mocked him with ugly signs about the scandal or hinted at it by questioning his morality. However painful that scandal must have proved to Ted, losing that Senate leadership position seems, in retrospect, a blessing in disguise. Without it, he would still wield extraordinary power as both a Kennedy and a politically gifted senator. But, free of the demands that came with it, he could devote more time to studying issues, holding hearings, building coalitions, and moving legislation to reshape America's global role.

To influence the ABM debate, he took a particularly audacious step in early 1969. Expressing doubt that the Pentagon, which was conducting a study of the ABM, would provide an honest assessment for lawmakers, he announced that he would commission a study from a group that Wiesner would cochair with Abram Chayes, the State Department's legal advisor under Jack. In reality his study would be no more objective than the Pentagon's, for Wiesner and Chayes were well-known ABM critics and Ted stacked the group with such allies as JFK Counsel Ted Sorenson, JFK defense official Adam Yarmolinsky, JFK national security official Carl Kaysen, and JFK Labor Secretary Arthur Goldberg.

Whether, as president, Jack would have taken kindly to a comparable challenge to his own Pentagon is highly debatable.

. . .

"There is nothing sacrosanct about the recommendations of the Department of Defense," Ted wrote in his introduction to the ABM study he had commissioned. "The Congress should put them to the same scrutiny it applies to all other government programs."[15]

By the time Harper & Row published *ABM: An Evaluation of the*

Decision to Deploy an Antiballistic Missile System (its book version of the study) that summer, printed two hundred thousand copies, and sold each for ninety-five cents, Washington's debate over the system had grown fiercer. In the spring the Senate Armed Services Committee and a Senate Foreign Relations subcommittee held hearings on the ABM, with Wiesner, Kaysen, and other members of Ted's study group battling such high-profile ABM supporters as Laird, former Deputy Defense Secretary Paul Nitze, and Edward Teller, who worked on the Manhattan Project and was considered the "father of the hydrogen bomb."

The ABM, Ted wrote, "is to be built in response to some potential threat to the United States—but the precise nature of the threat cannot be told to the American people for security reasons"; it will cost about $7 billion, but that figure didn't include "the billions for nuclear warheads, the billions for research and development nor the billions for customary defense contract cost underestimates"; it is "the single most complex undertaking" in history, "but if experience with previous national defense projects teaches any lesson, it will be years late in completion and may never work at all"; and it is "virtually certain to force our potential enemies to take steps to counteract it, just as we would—and have in the past—taken steps to counteract a defensive system constructed by our enemies."[16]

As the debate grew nastier, Ted butted heads directly with Nixon. When, in June, Nixon labeled his foreign policy critics "new isolationists," Ted devoted his commencement address at New York's Fordham University largely to defending them. He also disparaged a book that the conservative Hudson Institute wrote to rebut Ted's study. Though Nixon won the ABM fight when the Senate defeated proposals in August of 1969 to kill its deployment, Ted had signaled that he would target entire weapons systems as part of his broader arms control agenda.

By then Ted was also battling Nixon—who had promised peace in Vietnam—over how he was conducting the war.

. . .

"It is both senseless and irresponsible," Ted told the Senate on May 20, 1969, "to continue to send our young men to their deaths to capture hills and positions that have no relation to ending this conflict."

That morning, American military officials were on TV from Vietnam, claiming a huge victory after capturing Ap Bia Mountain, a ridge near Laos that soldiers called "Hamburger Hill" for the way it turned them into meat. The battle lasted ten days and required a dozen U.S. assaults on the mountain, where the Army "dropped more than 1,088 tons of bombs, 142 tons of napalm, 31,000 rounds of 20mm shells, and 513 tons of teargas on North Vietnamese forces."[17] Though U.S forces had killed 630 troops from the North, the battle also left 72 Americans dead and more than 370 wounded. Ted's criticism signaled a change in his approach to Vietnam. In the early months of 1969, he gave Nixon space to pursue peace. He was soon sorely disappointed with the new president's approach, however. Not only did Nixon say that he would maintain current military operations to strengthen America's position at the Paris Peace Talks, but he also was mounting operations that, to Ted, made little sense. That America's forces abandoned Ap Bia Mountain two weeks later (a quick exit that Ted later said he had predicted) seemed to confirm his judgment.

With the White House and congressional Republicans assuming that Ted was gearing up to run against Nixon in 1972, their response was sharp. Senate Republican whip Hugh Scott attacked him for second-guessing America's commanders and, as Ted repeated his complaints in the coming days, he was attacked by Laird, military officials, and Nixon's press secretary. Senate Republican leader Everett Dirksen said that with Hanoi broadcasting Ted's words by radio, he had dampened U.S. troop morale.

Ted remained undeterred. After two months of seclusion prompted by Chappaquiddick in July of 1969, he reemerged in September to call for a coalition government in South Vietnam that would include communists—akin to Bobby's call for a coalition government that would include the Vietcong. On the anti-war movement's "Moratorium Day" a month later, he told one hun-

"Dear God, Help Us, This War Must End"

dred thousand protestors on the Boston Common that Washington should withdraw all American troops within a year and stop all air and naval support by the end of 1972.

. . .

"Our prayer is a simple one," Ted said in May of 1970 at a memorial service for four Kent State students who were gunned down by the Ohio National Guard during an anti-war protest on campus. "Dear God, help us, this war must end."[18]

As casualties mounted in Vietnam and protests proliferated across America, Ted grew more emotional in his language and absolutist in his goals. Unequivocally opposed to the war by now and determined to end it, he disparaged Nixon's "Vietnamization" policy—American troop withdrawals over time as Saigon took over more of the war—because it would end America's operations too gradually. "The strange and tragic fascination of military victory in Vietnam," he said in the spring of 1970, "has cast its mad spell over two successive presidents and thousands of young Americans have gone to their death."[19] Running for reelection that year, he routinely said of the war, "I'm opposed to our involvement in Southeast Asia. I think we should get out of Southeast Asia, lock, stock, and barrel."[20] A year later he told POW families that their men were "rotting" as prisoners and that, were he president, he'd "crawl" into the Paris Peace Talks to get them home.[21]

That he was helping to turn America against the war was lost to no one. "I address you," syndicated columnist Joseph Alsop, a JFK confidante who continued to support America's military effort in Vietnam in these later years, wrote in an open letter to Ted a few days after the Kent State memorial service, "because the events of the last weekend seemed to indicate the widespread prevalence of sheer political lunacy in this poor country of ours, and because I suspect that you, almost alone, have it in your power to bring many people back to their senses." By "political lunacy," Alsop meant the massive protests in Washington after Nixon sent troops into Cambodia in April to attack communist sanctuaries. But if Alsop hoped to sway Ted, he must have come away sorely disappointed.

"Though I am flattered," Ted responded in his own open letter that newspapers could publish, "that you imply I may have the capacity to bring this land to some unanimity of view in these difficult moments, neither I nor anyone except the President of the United States can bring this nation together. And he can do so only by ending the war." As for the suggestion of "political lunacy" driving the protestors, Ted came to their strong defense. "'Political lunacy' it was," he wrote, "that brought upon us the events of the past two weeks. Yet I would not place the charge against those who came to Washington but to those who caused them to come here. As a nation we have had enough of war, and death, and divisiveness."[22]

Ted continued to use the Senate Judiciary Subcommittee on Refugees and Escapees, which he chaired, to highlight Vietnam's human toll—including the rise in civilian casualties and refugees. Through the early 1970s, the subcommittee held hearings and conducted studies and, based on what it learned, increased its estimates of the numbers of casualties that the war had caused and refugees it had created. In December of 1969, as Ted called the war "a human tragedy of the greatest dimensions and proportions," he reported that it had caused by then more than a million casualties, including three hundred thousand deaths.[23] Three years later, he raised the figures to more than 1.25 million casualties and almost four hundred thousand deaths.

In his rhetoric, however, Ted Kennedy sometimes went too far for other top Democrats. When he accused Nixon in 1971 of slowing peace efforts so that the president could show more progress a year later when he ran for reelection, Hubert Humphrey dismissed Ted's assertion and defended Nixon.

. . .

"I think it would be the height of folly," America's ambassador in Saigon, Graham Martin, told Henry Kissinger in early 1974, "to permit Kennedy, whose staff will spearhead this effort [to cut U.S.

"Dear God, Help Us, This War Must End"

aid to the South], the tactical advantage of an honest and detailed answer to questions of substance raised in his letter."

Ted had written to Kissinger, who at the time was serving as both national security advisor and secretary of state, to ask him to explain America's obligations in Indochina—since the Vietnam War had supposedly ended in January of 1973—and Martin was suggesting that Kissinger ignore the inquiry. Martin's cable was confidential, but a State Department employee sent it to Ted's office in Washington. "The list of questions," he complained, "is cleverly drawn to thoroughly mix apples and oranges. Any substantive answer would permit another calculated campaign of distortion that would preempt the attention the presentation of the Administration's case should receive."[24]

However outrageous was Martin's suggestion that Kissinger ignore Ted's letter, as Kissinger acknowledged by sending Ted a fourteen-page response, it was a testament to Ted's influence. Over time he had undermined the case for war, showcased its human toll, and energized the anti-war movement. In early 1973 he convinced Senate Democrats to call for ending all U.S. military operations and rejecting future funding for them. When, later that year, Washington was still arming the South and bombing Cambodia, he led a successful effort to convince Congress to cut Nixon's proposed funding for the South.

As the war wound down, Ted geared up to address global challenges of a different nature that were festering much closer to home.

16

"Help Us, Kennedy!"

"You were there for us when human rights were being massively and systematically violated," Chile's president, Michelle Bachelet, told Ted in late 2008 as she visited the ailing senator in Hyannis Port and presented him with the Order to the Merit of Chile, her government's highest civilian honor.[1]

In no Latin American country did Ted Kennedy devote more time and wield more influence than Chile. In September of 1973 General Augusto Pinochet ousted the democratically elected president, Salvador Allende, in a violent coup and ruled for the next seventeen years with an iron fist, severely abusing human rights. Ted opposed Nixon's support for Pinochet, held hearings on his abuses, confronted him in speeches and letters, supported opposition figures who were seeking to restore democracy, and convinced Congress to end military aid to the regime. Due to the "Kennedy amendment" of 1976 to cut off military aid, Pinochet later labeled him a Chilean "enemy."

In the 1970s and '80s, Ted's influence over U.S. policy in Latin America extended far beyond Chile, however. He battled Nixon, Ford, and Reagan over their support for right-wing regimes that backed Washington but abused human rights (the Eisenhower approach to the developing world that Jack had overhauled). He then worked to end Reagan's proxy wars with the Soviets across the region. Reagan—who restored a hardline U.S. approach to Moscow in an effort to win the Cold War, not end it through greater U.S.-

Soviet understanding—sought to topple the Soviet-backed left-ist Daniel Ortega in Nicaragua, and he supported the right-wing government in El Salvador that was battling leftist insurgents. Ted, who thought that Reagan's Cold War efforts were dangerously mis-guided, sought to promote human rights in Latin America; loosen ties to rights-abusing regimes; steer aid to democratic nations; and prevent American military intervention.

Before launching these efforts, however, Ted needed to rediscover the region to which his brothers had devoted so much attention.

. . .

"It is a personal tragedy," Ted told a University of Montana audi-ence in April of 1970, "that I can repeat nearly the same somber facts about Latin America that President Kennedy cited in 1960 and that Robert Kennedy cited in 1966."

Ted Kennedy traveled to, and wrote from, Latin America before his Senate days but, once in office, he hadn't done much to influ-ence American policy in the region. That was very much on his mind in 1970. "My brothers both understood that Latin America was important to the United States," Ted told a young man seeking a job with him early that year, "and I haven't done enough."[2] He was scheduled to deliver the University of Montana's annual Mansfield lecture that spring at the invitation of Senate Majority Leader Mike Mansfield, and he decided to use the occasion to critique American policy in the region. The speech was important enough to him that Ted Sorenson and Arthur Schlesinger Jr. were among the Kennedy intimates who labored over the draft.

His blistering broadside of April 17 spared no one—not even Jack. "We began the decade of the sixties," he recalled, "by joining with the Latin American nations in a call to hemispheric action, a call to promote a better life for millions of Latin Americans who are forced to endure both poverty and oppression. . . . In March of 1961, the sound of a revolutionary trumpet echoed to the govern-ments and to the people of Latin America, calling on them to join with us in a new Alliance for Progress. Yet," he went on, "barely a month later on April 17, 1961—nine years ago tonight—we launched the Bay of Pigs invasion," an "embarrassing reminder of our history of gunboat diplomacy toward the hemisphere," showing that "we had not yet learned the lesson that we have no divine right to intervene, forcibly or otherwise, in the internal affairs of Latin American nations. Rarely in our history have two events, coming so close together, so clearly symbolized the best and worst in American foreign policy. Time and again over the past decade, we have seen the noble goals of the Alliance for Progress perverted by the Cold War philosophy symbolized by the Bay of Pigs."

Reviewing the region's dire social conditions, stunted economic growth, concentrated land ownership, and proliferation of military governments, Ted called the Alliance a failure for not driving the progressive change that Jack had envisioned. He urged Washington to end its military missions in the region; reserve its economic assistance for programs designed to produce social justice; ensure that private investment contributes more to the region's development; and, in another slap at Jack's Cold War approach, rethink its trade and travel restrictions with Cuba.

He also echoed Bobby's refrain that change in Latin America was inevitable and the only question was whether "with intelligence and compassion we can accelerate peaceful change, and avoid a more violent and destructive transformation." For the United States in the 1970s, he said, "the vital decision . . . must be how to reform our own efforts so that they complement the Latin Americans' struggle to modernize."

. . .

"I heard one suspect being led into the room and the door closed behind him," an eyewitness told Ted when his refugee subcommittee held hearings on Pinochet's human rights crackdown two weeks after his coup of September 1973.

Thereafter I heard people beating him with some sort of an object so loudly that you could hear the impact of this object on human flesh. . . . The beating went on and I began to hear animal moans. Then I heard no noise at all; I presume that the person lost consciousness. Thereafter the beating began again and I heard the same sort of terrible animal moans. . . . Then I heard a series of six shootings which were isolated, not six shots one after another. Then I heard no noise at all. Then I heard the moans again and a little bit more beating, one final shot, then I heard the door open, people leave, the door close.

The coup that brought Pinochet to power, which began on the morning of September 11, 1973, came after three years of cool relations between Nixon, a hardcore Cold Warrior of many years, and Allende, a vocal leftist. The CIA had sprinkled dollars around Chile in an unsuccessful effort to prevent Allende's election in 1970 due to American concerns that he would establish a communist government; after taking office, he did, in fact, nationalize domestic and foreign-owned companies. Nixon and his team severely limited aid to Santiago to make its economy "scream" (as CIA Director Richard Helms put it at the time), launched propaganda campaigns and other covert activities to weaken Allende, assisted opposition parties and groups, boosted military aid to strengthen America's ties to Chile's military, and debated whether to organize a coup—though Washington wasn't directly involved in the one that occurred. After the coup ended forty-six years of Chilean democracy, Nixon embraced Pinochet, was slow to condemn his abuses, and increased economic aid.

While Nixon stroked the dictator, Ted confronted him. The abuses on which he shed light, through hearings and speeches, were chilling. Pinochet rounded up Allende's supporters and other "extremists" by the thousands, housed them in stadiums, and locked them in cramped cells, leaving them with no room to sit and no food for days; many were beaten savagely or gunned down as they stood with their hands behind their heads or backs. Dead bodies piled up at city morgues, hundreds at a time, many with slit chests and crushed heads, as the harsh smell of decomposing bodies filled the air. Troops swarmed cities and towns and ransacked homes, forcing residents to their knees at gunpoint. At night Chileans sat in fear that a "knock at the door" would mean the arrest of a loved one. The regime closed newspapers and magazines and killed their editors, purged universities of leftist instructors, and seized tens of thousands of books—by Mao, Marx, Marcuse, and others—from homes, bookstores, and libraries and burned them in bonfires.

Ted highlighted Pinochet's abuse in hearings in September of 1973, July of 1974, and October of 1975.

. . .

"I have read [Ted's letter of January 31, 1974]," Pinochet wrote in response two months later, "with deliberateness and interest because it comes from a political personality such as yourself, widely known throughout the world and because the name Kennedy awakens in Chile very deep and profound memories, given the understanding and friendship that your brothers always showed my country."

"I also have read it with concern," he went on, "because the very object of your letter demonstrates that the extremely active campaign that international Marxism has loosed abroad against Chile has succeeded in influencing politicians of your importance. While I can understand that Marxism would launch such a campaign of calumny and defamation against my country on seeing itself, for the first time in history, expelled from power, it is difficult, on the other hand, to understand how it has been able to convince and confuse the views of eminently democratic personalities."

Ted had written to Pinochet about human rights, and Pinochet was dismissing the issue as Marxist-driven fiction, an effort by Allende's backers to tarnish the regime. Nobody took Pinochet's assertions seriously; the evidence of abuse was overwhelming. Nevertheless, his argument about "international Marxism" proved useful to Nixon, Ford, Kissinger, and the administration officials who testified at Ted's hearings. Though they didn't dismiss Pinochet's abuses, they argued that geopolitical concerns (i.e., possible communist inroads in Latin America) were more important. As "realists," Nixon, Ford, and Kissinger believed that Washington should deal with other governments as they were and, thus, that human rights concerns shouldn't complicate government-to-government relations. When David Popper, America's ambassador to Chile, raised such concerns to Chilean officials, Kissinger told him to "cut out the political science lectures."[3]

Nixon and Ford's reluctance to criticize other governments over human rights gave autocrats more leeway to abuse them and, not coincidentally, the world witnessed some particularly egregious instances of humanitarian horror. In Cambodia, Pol Pot's Khmer Rouge killed a fifth of the population (1.7 million people) through starvation, persecution, execution, and torture. In Vietnam hundreds of thousands of fleeing "boat people" died on the seas after the North won the war and imposed its brutal rule. After Indonesia invaded East Timor, 150,000 died from genocide and a resulting famine. On Capitol Hill sentiment turned increasingly against the realists, and Ted seized the chance to elevate the issue of human rights in American foreign policymaking.

At his initiative Congress voted to bar arms sales to Chile in 1976, marking the first time (after Ford signed the bill that included the provision) that Washington ended military aid to another country over human rights. Kissinger fumed privately that Ted's arms cutoff was "insane" and surmised that the senator was "on some ego trip."[4] He was no happier when, with Ted leading the Senate part of the effort, Congress passed bills over White House objections in the mid-1970s that forced the State Department to report each year on every country's human rights record and required the administration to consider that record as it decided where to allocate foreign aid.

A decade later Ted battled another Republican president over Washington's policy in Latin America—this time a president who sought to rein in Soviet, Cuban, Nicaraguan, Grenadian, and other leftist forces.

. . .

"We know the evasions, the rationalizations, the fabrications," Ted told the Senate in April of 1984, "for we have heard them from this administration until they have become as tattered as they are untrue."

Ted was seeking Senate support for his resolution stating that Washington should not spend any more federal money to mine "the ports and territorial waters of Nicaragua." Days earlier, the *Wall Street Journal* had broken the explosive story that the Reagan administration had secretly mined the harbors of Nicaragua, where it was providing arms and money to the Contra rebels who were trying to overthrow Daniel Ortega's Sandinista government. Reagan's team didn't brief Congress beforehand about the mining and Barry Goldwater, the Senate Intelligence Committee chairman, told William Casey, the CIA director, that he was "pissed off" and labeled America's action "an act of war" that would be hard to explain.[5]

The mining controversy came amid a swirling debate in Washington about America's global role that set Ronald Reagan and Ted Kennedy sharply against one another. Two decades after it had disintegrated over Vietnam, Reagan sought to rebuild the Cold War consensus—or at least refocus his nation's attention on the Cold War as America's top global concern. "The national security of all the Americas is at stake in Central America," Reagan told a joint session of Congress in April of 1983, framing the regional challenge in Cold War terms. Just as Secretary of State Dean Rusk had quoted the Truman Doctrine to explain America's military effort in Vietnam, so, too, did Reagan quote it to explain U.S. policy in Latin America—that "nearly every nation must choose between alternative ways of life," that our way is "based upon the will of the majority and is distinguished by free institutions," that the alternative "is based upon the will of a minority forcibly imposed upon the majority," and that "it must be the policy of the United States to support free peoples who are resisting attempted subjugation by armed minorities or by outside pressures."

After assuming office in January of 1981, Reagan moved quickly to strengthen ties to right-wing military regimes in Chile, Brazil, and Argentina; confront the Soviets in the region; support the Contras; train Salvadoran soldiers and junior officers who were battling leftist insurgents; and threaten military action to stop Cuba from arming Salvador's insurgents. In June he approved a new policy of economic and military aid to fight the region's poverty and "counter . . . Cuban and Soviet subversion."[6] Reagan's team looked the other way as Nicaraguan, Cuban, and Panamanian exiles trained in the United States to prepare to overthrow their governments—raising questions about whether, by allowing the training, the administration was violating federal and international law.

With a desire for more U.S.-Soviet understanding, not less, Ted did what he could to derail Reagan's policies.

. . .

At first, his efforts achieved little.

Year after year Ted sought to block American military aid to El Salvador over human rights, cut off support for Nicaragua's Contras, and prevent Reagan from sending troops to the region without Congress's approval. He disparaged Reagan's Latin American policies as "a prescription for a wider war" and denounced a commission, chaired by Henry Kissinger, that in January of 1984 expressed support for Reagan's covert activities against Nicaragua's Sandinistas and military aid for El Salvador.[7]

Though a sizable number of Democrats supported Ted's proposals, the Republican-run Senate routinely rejected them. It was when the administration mined Nicaragua's harbors that the tide turned.

"The Senate took a first step to halt President Reagan's secret war in Nicaragua," Ted declared after the Senate voted 84–12 for his resolution, which the House overwhelmingly approved two days later.[8] Though it was nonbinding—an exaltation, not an enforceable directive—Reagan read the tea leaves of congressional sentiment and stopped the mining. When, two months later, the Senate voted 88–1 to block more aid for the Contras, Ted added, "This is a historic day, the day the tide was turned against the secret war in Nicaragua."[9]

More than a decade after Pinochet's coup, however, the tide had not turned in Chile, prompting a visit by Ted to confront the regime and its supporters.

. . .

"Help us, Kennedy!" a crowd around Ted shouted as he toured Santiago, Chile's capital, in January of 1986.

Ted was on the last leg of a week-long trip to the region, where he celebrated new democracies that had replaced military governments in Brazil, Uruguay, Argentina, and Peru, and he was now promoting a return to democracy in Chile. After labeling him a Chilean "enemy" due to the "Kennedy amendment" that cut off military aid, Pinochet refused to meet with him. Instead the regime and its thuggish supporters sought to rattle him personally while disrupting his visit. Upon his arrival, he was forced to leave Santiago's airport by police helicopter because two hundred demonstrators blocked the highway and police on the ground did little to clear a path for his motorcade. Some demonstrators donned life preservers with the word "Chappaquiddick" on them, carried pictures of Mary Jo Kopechne (the woman who drowned), and distributed a leaflet that asked about *her* human rights. Later that day, demonstrators hit Ted's car with rocks and eggs after he toured a rehabilitation center, and some carried signs that read "Death to Kennedy."[10]

For more than a decade after pushing his military aid cutoff through Congress, Ted pressed his own government to confront Pinochet more forcefully. In late 1978 he urged the Carter administration to join an international investigation after twenty-five "mutilated" bodies were discovered in a Chilean mineshaft. A year later he criticized Carter for merely scaling back Washington's ties to Chile after its Supreme Court refused to extradite three former secret police officers who were allegedly tied to the murder of Orlando Letelier—the exiled Chilean leader who was killed in Washington in 1976 when a bomb exploded under his car. A former top official under Allende, Letelier was one of Pinochet's fiercest critics and, ten days before his murder, the regime stripped him of his citizenship. Letelier was driving along Washington's Embassy Row to meet with one of Ted's top aides when the bomb went off. When, in 1980, Pinochet's regime planned a national plebiscite, Ted termed

it a fraud and urged Washington "to disassociate itself both publicly and privately" from the regime.[11]

Even before Ted's visit to Chile in 1986, signals mounted that it
would be a rocky, if not dangerous, one. "Who would dare shake
hands with the No. 1 enemy of Chile?" full-page newspaper ads
asked. Meanwhile, the CIA's station chief in Buenos Aires told Ted
that Chile's military had organized demonstrations and provided
signs. "I am told," Ted said at the airport upon his arrival, undeterred by the chaos around him, "that there are some people who
regard me as an enemy of Chile. I am not an enemy of Chileans. I
am an enemy of kidnapping, murder and arbitrary arrests." After
cancelling visits that day to the offices of opposition politicians
and human rights activists due to fears over more violence, he used
a social club for his meetings. He also promoted Chile's return to
democracy in impromptu remarks in a downtown park.

"I have come to a country which has proven anew that the fire
of freedom cannot be extinguished," he told about eight hundred
government opponents, all of whom risked the regime's retribution
for attending, in a moving evening speech in an auditorium, "even
when the darkness descends, when dictators rule and law is lost,
the flame still warms and moves millions of individual indomita-
ble hearts. The spark still passes from soul to soul, connecting one
person with another, across vast expanses of space and time, with
each for a few moments or miles carrying and passing on freedom's
torch—so that one day the light finally shines out again across the
land."[12] His words echoed Bobby's "ripple of hope" message of two
decades earlier in South Africa.

He would return to Chile four years later, under far warmer, more
welcoming, more satisfying circumstances.

. . .

"Vice President Dan Quayle got the photo opportunities in Chile,"
the *Boston Globe* wrote in March of 1990, "but Sen. Edward M. Kennedy got the rave reviews during the visit both men made last weekend to the inauguration of Chile's new president, Patricio Aylwin."[13]

With a nod to his work of many years to promote human rights in Chile, Quayle invited Ted to fly on Air Force Two to Santiago and witness the inauguration of Aylwin, marking Chile's return to democracy. Aylwin beat Pinochet in an election that Pinochet finally allowed, paving the way for his ouster.

As Quayle met with Pinochet, Ted attended a church meeting with human rights activists and the family members of some Pinochet opponents who remained missing. The senator lauded them for their battles against the dictator and expressed his joy that he could "breathe free air in Chile at last."[14]

. . .

As Ted battled Pinochet in the 1970s and '80s, he sought to nourish warmer U.S. ties with Moscow and Beijing.

17

"Nothing More nor Less Than Voodoo Arms Control"

"One survivor of Hiroshima, opening a shelter door minutes after the blast, exclaimed: 'Oh, God,'" Ted Kennedy wrote in *Freeze!*, his 1982 book with Senator Mark Hatfield, an Oregon Republican, on how to prevent nuclear war. "Almost the same words came from the copilot of the *Enola Gay*, who screamed 'My God,' as the bomb exploded from a tiny purple dot into a mammoth churning fireball. For both the pilot and the survivor, the words were a plea, a prayer, a cry of despair and hope."[1]

Ted sought U.S.-Soviet arms control until the Soviet empire crumbled in the early 1990s, wrote books and articles to promote it, and traveled multiple times to Moscow to advance it. To help bring China into arms control efforts, he continued the work that he and Bobby began in the 1960s to end China's isolation and nourish stronger U.S.-China ties. After Nixon's historic trip to China of 1972, Ted pushed Carter in the late 1970s to fully normalize U.S.-China relations and, when Carter did, he paved the way for Congress to support it.

In the early 1980s, Ted paid particularly close attention to the nuclear freeze movement that had erupted across the West in response to Reagan's arms buildup, his plan to deploy new intermediate-range missiles in Europe, and the astonishing belief of some of his top aides that America could survive a nuclear war with the Soviet Union and that Washington should prepare to win one. "If there are enough shovels to go around," a top Reagan Pentagon official told the *Los Angeles Times*'s Robert Scheer in late 1981, "everybody's going to make it." As this official explained it, urban dwellers who fled to the countryside with the onset of nuclear war would dig holes in the ground, covered by doors and three feet of dirt, to protect themselves. "It's the dirt that does it," he said.[2] "The notion," Kennedy and Hatfield wrote in response, "that nuclear war is survivable and winnable, in any meaningful sense, has become increasingly and dangerously fashionable."[3]

After Ted decided not to run for president in 1984, he recommitted himself to the Senate. To expand his venues for reshaping America's global role, he took a seat on the Senate Armed Services Committee—which most of his Democratic colleagues were eager to give him so they could fight Reagan's arms buildup more effectively. When Howard Metzenbaum, an ornery Senate Democrat from Ohio, asked why Ted should get a third major committee assignment when Democratic rules limited each member to two, Missouri's Tom Eagleton replied, "Oh, Kennedy is Kennedy."[4]

Indeed.

. . .

"If you were President of the United States now," Soviet Premier Leonid Brezhnev told Ted in their April 1974 meeting in Moscow, to which Ted brought a draft treaty to ban all U.S. and Soviet nuclear testing, "I would ask you to sit over here in front of this fireplace. We would light a fire, and we would have some vodka, and both of us would sign it and celebrate a great step toward halting nuclear expansion."[5]

After the Kremlin invited him for a visit and high-level meetings that would include Brezhnev, Ted flew to Moscow with Joan, two of their three kids, and aides for six days of talks on arms control and other matters. With the Watergate scandal raging, Nixon's days as president looking numbered, and Soviet leaders wondering how a post-Nixon Washington might deal with Moscow, Ted sought to assure the Kremlin that Democrats were just as committed to détente (i.e., less U.S.-Soviet tension) as the besieged president. With Kissinger at the time pursuing more arms control with the Soviets, Ted told the Senate days before his trip, "We do not believe that domestic political developments [i.e., Watergate] should be permitted to slow the progress of arriving at such agreements."

Brezhnev assumed that, with Ted Kennedy, he was speaking to a future president and treated him accordingly. He met with the senator for four hours—a time commitment that he normally reserved for heads of state and large delegations. In Moscow Ted assumed a presidential posture as well. After his meeting with Brezhnev, his office issued a statement that read like a communique from a head of state: "Both Senator Kennedy and General Secretary Brezhnev expressed the deep commitment of their two countries to maintain peace between them, to bring the arms race firmly under control and to working out productive relations in a host of other areas."[6]

In fact, all of Ted's global travels that year assumed a presidential air. On the weekend before he set off for Moscow, he flew to Bonn to confer with West Germany's chancellor, Willy Brandt, about America's role in Europe and to celebrate a quarter century of German democracy. On his trip to the Soviet Union, Ted also visited Yugoslavia and Romania, where he secured audiences with Presidents Josip Broz Tito and Nicolae Ceausescu, respectively. "Many today see in Edward Kennedy," wrote *Borba*, a leading Belgrade daily, "the main candidate of the Democratic party in the 1976 presidential elections and, maybe, the future occupant of the White House."[7] Later that year, he traveled across Europe and the Middle East—attending a NATO meeting in London; lunching with France's president, Valery Giscard d'Estaing; and also meeting with Egypt's prime minister, Anwar Sadat; Israel's prime minister, Yitzhak Rabin (and his predecessor, Golda Meir); Portugal's president, Francisco da Costa Gomes; and Jordan's King Hussein.

Though Ted pushed for warmer U.S.-Soviet ties—for a deeper relationship that would transcend détente—he never grew naïve about the nature of Soviet rule. He considered Brezhnev "a classic Russian strongman" and, when they met, Ted "subtly tried to keep my grip as firm as his."[8] As his family settled in at one of Moscow's big government guest houses, he gathered them in a bathroom, ran the showers and faucets, and flushed the toilet so that listening devices wouldn't pick up his words. He then reminded everyone to watch what they say because the Kremlin was surely listening.

. . .

"The first phase of improving U.S.-Soviet relations, which developed over more than a decade, provided a buffer against the cold war and greatly reduced the risks of nuclear war and confrontation," Ted wrote in a piece for *Foreign Policy* in the fall of 1974. "But that first phase is now over." On a hopeful note, he suggested that "a new phase is just beginning—going beyond détente."[9]

He had made much the same pitch in Moscow. Though Nixon and Brezhnev had inked the SALT I treaty two years earlier—capping U.S. and Soviet intercontinental and submarine-launched ballistic missiles and incorporating an ABM treaty that sharply limited U.S. and Soviet national missile defense systems—Washington was concerned that Moscow continued to test nuclear weapons. Ted relayed those concerns and promoted arms control in speeches that the Kremlin let him deliver, including one at Moscow State University that marked the first speech on that site by an elected American official (though the Soviets moved it to a Sunday to reduce student participation).

When he met Brezhnev, the Soviet leader insisted that the Soviet Union wasn't threatening the United States and argued that Washington was restricting the travel of Soviet visitors to America far more than Moscow was restricting the travel of U.S. visitors. "Let me show you," Brezhnev said as the two rose from their chairs and Ted followed him to a map of the Soviet Union, "Americans cannot go here or here," he said, pointing at different spots. "Or here, or here. Or here. But outside of that, Americans are able to go any place they want."[10] When, after returning home, Ted told a military expert where Brezhnev had pointed, he learned that the Soviet leader had identified top-secret missile sites.

In his piece for *Foreign Policy*, Ted echoed the sentiments of Jack's "peace speech" at American University. Jack had said, "Let us not

"Voodoo Arms Control"

be blind to our differences, but let us also direct attention to our common interests and to the means by which those differences can be resolved." In the same spirit Ted wrote, "The superpowers must join in recognizing their common involvement in the outside world, and their shared responsibilities for meeting the demands of global problems." To move "beyond détente," he suggested that the two sides "begin with even greater efforts to end the strategic arms race"—with (among other things) both sides disclosing their weapons doctrines and programs, both eschewing arms programs that suggested that they hoped to survive nuclear war, and Washington no longer building "unneeded" weapons systems to use as "bargaining chips" for arms control.

After 1974 Ted returned to Moscow on several occasions to push for more arms control and less tension. With the same goals in mind for China, he sought a new U.S. posture toward Beijing.

. . .

"If I were able to go back to my constituents," Ted told Deng Xiaoping, China's ascendant leader, in early January of 1978, "and to the United States Senate and to say that I was completely convinced that people in Taiwan would be able to live in peace and prosperity, that would have an impact on American opinion."[11]

Ted's trip to China was years in the making. In a speech to the National Committee on United States-China Relations in March of 1969, to which the *New York Times* gave front-page coverage, he called on Washington to lift its travel and trade restrictions to China; stop opposing Beijing's entry into the United Nations as China's representative; reestablish a consular office in China; include China in global arms control talks; discuss full diplomatic relations with Beijing; and stoke Beijing's interest in such relations by withdrawing American forces from Taiwan. "If nothing changes," he warned, "we Americans will have to live with the consequences of arms and fear and war. We owe ourselves, we owe the future, a heavy obligation to try."[12] Two years later, Ted decided that he wanted to visit China, hoping to do so before any other major American political figure.

When, in July of 1971, the news broke that Kissinger had just returned from a secret trip to China and Nixon would visit the following February, Ted still hoped to get there before Nixon. In September he flew secretly to Ottawa and spoke for several hours with Huang Hua, China's ambassador to Canada, which had established full diplomatic relations with Beijing a year earlier. Hua indicated that Beijing might let Ted visit if he stated publicly that Taiwan was part of China and should be incorporated into it. As Hua reached into his jacket pocket, signaling that he would provide a visa if he liked what he heard, Ted refused to take the bait and reiterated that China should not incorporate Taiwan unless most Taiwanese residents supported the idea.

Maintaining his hard line, Ted attacked Nixon sharply a month after his trip to Ottawa. As Kissinger was visiting China a second time in October, the United Nations was voting on China's seat in the body. After rejecting a U.S. proposal to give seats to both the mainland and Taiwan, the United Nations voted to give Taiwan's seat to Beijing and expel Taiwan. After a few days of bipartisan outrage in Washington, Ted blasted Nixon for not speaking out to ease the concerns of Americans. Then, before 2,500 people at a New York conference on the United States and China, Ted aired his suspicions about Nixon's silence—that it was part of an unseemly deal between Washington and Beijing. "Perhaps the timing was a coincidence, and perhaps not," he said. "We shall probably never know whether this was a gesture, exacted . . . as the price of the President's coming visit."[13] In response a top Nixon aide said that Ted had "exhibited a degree of pettiness unbecoming of a United States Senator."[14]

After Beijing denied Ted a visit due to his views on Taiwan, he wouldn't make it to China for nearly seven more years.

. . .

Deng, Ted later recalled, was "a diminutive person, not well, [a] chain smoker, [who] spit all the time."

The senator's hopes for U.S.-China normalization received a big boost with the election of Carter, who had promised to pursue it.

"Voodoo Arms Control"

Though Nixon had broken the ice of more than two decades between Washington and Beijing by flying to China, normalization would mark a more fundamental change in American foreign policy. Ted proposed it in an August 1977 speech at Boston's World Affairs Council. He worked on the speech privately with White House and State Department officials who hoped that it would prod Carter to act. In remarks that garnered front-page *Washington Post* coverage, he said that while it was up to the mainland and Taiwan to resolve their differences, they should do so peacefully. When Ted noted that Secretary of State Cyrus Vance was due to visit China a week later, China watchers assumed that Ted's words presaged what Vance would say in Beijing.

When Beijing let Ted visit and he flew to China in late December of 1977 with lots of family and a few aides, Deng rejected Ted's suggestion that he reassure Americans that China would leave Taiwan alone. Their meeting came after a few days of tense uncertainty. Once Ted had landed, Chinese officials suggested that Deng, a hardheaded pragmatist who was consolidating power in the aftermath of Mao's death, was too ill or busy to see him. Ted made clear that he had received assurances before he boarded his plane that he would see Deng and he expected Beijing to follow through. To help move things along, a China expert who had traveled with Ted called his wife and, assuming that Chinese officials were listening in, raised concerns that Beijing wasn't treating the senator with the respect he deserved.

When Ted met with Deng, a spittoon was situated on the floor between their chairs. As Ted spoke, Deng would gather up a huge wad of phlegm and spit it in the pot, prompting giggles from some of the Kennedy kids who attended the meeting.

Deng was all business, however, and Ted described his answers as "very vigorous . . . very curt . . . very strong, [and] definitive."[15]

. . .

America has a "continuing interest" in the "peaceful resolution of the Taiwan issue," Ted wrote in words for Congress to approve, "and expects that the Taiwan issue will be settled peacefully by the Chinese themselves."

Before Carter announced in December of 1978 that the United States would establish full diplomatic ties with China and break them with Taiwan, Ted received a heads-up from Secretary of State Vance. He was one of very few lawmakers who knew beforehand, however. Other than Senate Majority Leader Robert Byrd, Carter gave no lawmaker any advance notice, and Carter announced his policy when Congress wasn't in session and lawmakers weren't in Washington. It created a firestorm among conservatives who were outraged that Washington would abandon Taiwan and among liberals who didn't know how to explain the policy to their constituents.

Nor did Carter, who considered Ted as much a political rival as an ally, feel any obligation to acknowledge his years of work on U.S.-China relations that paved the way for Carter's action. When Deng flew to Washington for a nine-day visit in late January of 1979, marking the first visit by a Chinese leader since Mao founded the People's Republic thirty years earlier, Carter left Ted off the guest list for his state dinner for Deng. Only Vance's intervention prompted Carter to change his mind. Nevertheless, with both parties in an uproar over Carter's announcement, Ted stepped in to help quell the rebellion on Capitol Hill.

Democrats and Republicans alike wanted to send a strong signal that while Washington was scrapping its defense treaty with Taiwan, closing its embassy, and bringing its troops home, it remained concerned about Taiwan's security. But the language it would approve had to pass muster with Beijing, which considered Taiwan part of China, and Carter, who didn't think he needed Congress's help to reassure Taiwan to begin with.

Over dinner at his house, Ted wrote the language with Carter's aides and the head of China's liaison office in Washington, and it was enacted as part of legislation to implement America's new relationship with Taiwan.

. . .

When Ted returned to Washington after Congress's winter break of late 1982, he shocked aides with the news that he wasn't running for president (including aides who were planning a campaign) and told them he wanted to serve on a Senate foreign policy-related committee. They assumed that he meant the Foreign Relations Committee.

After all, the Senate Foreign Relations Committee was a prestigious panel with a gloried past. In the nineteenth century it was chaired by such legendary figures as Henry Clay, Thomas Benton, and Charles Sumner. In the twentieth, it was the perch from which Henry Cabot Lodge convinced the Senate to reject the Treaty of Versailles and, with it, America's entry into the League of Nations; from which Arthur Vandenberg worked with President Truman to enact America's containment strategy; and from which J. William Fulbright held his Vietnam hearings. In the late 1950s Jack used his committee seat to raise his profile on foreign affairs as he eyed the White House.

Ted had another idea, however. By the early 1980s he needed no such perch to raise his profile. He was a Kennedy serving in the afterglow of Jack and Bobby, and he also was a national figure in his own right, a magnet for media attention, and a seasoned lawmaker who had already helped shape America's global role. He could deliver a speech or hold a press conference and attract all the attention he wanted. And for all of its prestige, Foreign Relations did not do much of the one thing he loved, which was to legislate.

Jack's experience at the Foreign Relations Committee showed just how differently he and Ted viewed the Senate, and why Ted decided more than two decades later that that wasn't the right place for him. Musing about Jack's participation at the committee, a frustrated Fulbright once blurted, "When he comes to the committee meetings, what does he do? He sits down at the foot of the table autographing pictures of himself."[16] Moreover, while Jack was a member, the committee decided to create a subcommittee focused on Africa. Jack was keenly interested in Africa, of course, but he wasn't very interested in the nuts and bolts of legislating. When the committee's chief of staff, Carl Marcy, asked Jack whether he'd chair the subcommittee, Jack asked in return, "Well, if I take it, will it ever have to meet?"[17] Assured that it wouldn't, he agreed to serve as chairman.

The very notion of chairing a subcommittee that never met, or serving on a committee that was more of a debating society than a legislative venue, would have proved anathema to Ted. Rather than Foreign Relations, he took a seat on the Senate Armed Services Committee, which exerted enormous influence over the Pentagon's budget and its component parts: weapons systems, military operations, research and development, personnel, and so on. At Armed Services, he could question defense secretaries who were promoting weapons systems, grill military chieftains who were advocating combat operations, vote on the Pentagon budget, and influence the votes of others.

. . .

"In the devastation that follows a full-scale nuclear attack on the United States," Ted Kennedy wrote in *Freeze!*, "little or no health care will be available to any who survive; the burned and wounded will quickly come to regard the dead as the lucky ones."[18]

It was a variation of a remark that Jack had attributed to Khrushchev years earlier—"the survivors will envy the dead"—though there's no evidence that the Soviet leader ever uttered those words.[19] It was Herman Kahn who popularized the sentiment when, in his 1960 book, *On Thermonuclear War*, he titled a chapter "Will the Survivors Envy the Dead?" That Ted expressed a sentiment about nuclear war that Jack helped to popularize is not surprising; Ted viewed his nuclear freeze as a logical extension of Jack's limited test-ban treaty. "In effect," Ted wrote, "a freeze would . . . be a comprehensive test ban between the superpowers. They could then move to expand it into more formal sanctions against all nuclear tests or explosions."[20]

On arms control, the decade before *Freeze!* was published in 1982 was a frustrating one for Ted. Though U.S.-Soviet talks over SALT II began in late 1972, and though Ford and Brezhnev agreed to the framework of a treaty in Vladivostok in late 1974, it wasn't until

"Voodoo Arms Control"

June of 1979 that Carter and Brezhnev signed a treaty in Vienna. Then, after the Soviets invaded Afghanistan that December, Carter asked the Senate to delay its debate over ratifying SALT II and the Senate never ratified it. While Washington and Moscow largely adhered to its terms until it expired at the end of 1985, both SALT treaties only limited arms rather than reducing them. Ted's efforts to build on Jack's limited test-ban treaty and convince both sides to craft a comprehensive test ban proved as elusive as ever.

Not long after Reagan took office, his defense buildup, missile plans for Europe, and thoughts about nuclear war galvanized a grassroots movement across America and Europe to freeze nuclear arms. Kennedy and Hatfield proposed a freeze in March of 1982 and, three months later, one hundred thousand people rallied for one in New York City. With polls showing that Americans feared the consequences of Reagan's arms buildup, the president decided to support an alternative freeze proposal from Senators John Warner and Henry "Scoop" Jackson: Washington would first build its nuclear arsenal to close its alleged gap with Moscow and then negotiate a freeze. Ted viewed the buildup as (1) unnecessary—he didn't perceive a gap, (2) irrational—he thought both sides had enough weapons to blow each other up many times over, and (3) misguided—he thought it would further fuel the arms race. "The President says, in effect, that we have to build more nuclear bombs now in order to reduce their number in the future," Ted told a union convention in June. "The Reagan approach is nothing more nor less than voodoo arms control—which says that you must have more in order to have less."[21]

As the Senate rejected Ted's freeze in late 1983, he was fighting Reagan's defense buildup on another front. After Reagan proposed his Strategic Defense Initiative (SDI)—a high-tech, space-based, missile defense system to protect America from nuclear attack—in a televised address in March of 1983, Ted blasted his "misleading Red-scare tactics and reckless Star War schemes." The "Star Wars" moniker stuck, and Ted used it to nourish opposition to SDI. After disparaging Reagan's "Star Wars scheme for outer space" that would "open another trip wire for nuclear war," he told a Brown University forum in June that "we must reject the preposterous notion of a Lone Ranger in the sky, firing silver laser bullets and shooting missiles out of the hands of Soviet outlaws."[22] Despite his passionate opposition, Congress provided research funds for SDI before the Soviet empire crumbled and Reagan's successors canceled the project.

After his arms control setbacks of the early 1980s, Ted's doggedness drove an important breakthrough later in the decade.

. . .

When Soviet officials signaled Washington that they wanted to use Ted as a back channel for U.S.-Soviet arms control talks—two decades after JFK and Khrushchev had used Bobby to send messages to one another—Reagan's arms negotiator, Max Kampelman, liked the idea.

"The Soviets were as fascinated by the Kennedy family as any American aficionado," Kampelman wrote later; they viewed the Kennedys as "millionaires, presidents and senators, glamorous celebrities of legend." Moreover, Ted had close ties to Anatoly Dobrynin, Moscow's long-time ambassador in Washington; the Soviets liked to work through back channels; and Kampelman liked Ted, even if they often disagreed. Kampelman had come to know him more intimately in the 1980s because Ted served on the Senate Arms Control Observers Group that traveled to Geneva, where Kampelman was leading U.S. arms control talks with the Soviets. Some Reagan aides were wary of deploying Ted as a conduit, fearing a "self-aggrandizing effort," but Kampelman wasn't one of them. He brought the idea to Secretary of State George Shultz, who brought it to Reagan, who supported it. The back channel proved fruitful; Ted told Kampelman whatever he heard from Dobrynin, and Kampelman told him what to say in return.

Ted proved his worth as Washington and Moscow sought a treaty to limit intermediate-range nuclear forces (INF). Before flying to the Soviet Union in February of 1986 to meet its young, dynamic new leader, Mikhail Gorbachev, who had assumed power less than a

"Voodoo Arms Control"

year earlier, he met with Reagan and other top officials at the White House to coordinate strategy. While in Moscow he insisted on Soviet TV that Reagan was deeply interested in securing an arms control agreement. The most important moment of Ted's visit, however, was when Gorbachev surprised him with the news that he would pursue an INF treaty with Reagan even if the two leaders didn't resolve their dispute over SDI, which Gorbachev bitterly opposed. That Ted had disparaged SDI so stridently made him a trusted conduit in Gorbachev's eyes. U.S.-Soviet talks expanded later that year to all U.S. and Soviet intermediate-range missiles, culminating in the INF Treaty that Reagan and Gorbachev signed in December of 1987.

Years earlier, Kampelman recalled in his memoirs, Henry "Scoop" Jackson asked him "to participate in a private seminar with Ted on the Soviet Union, which is when I first talked seriously to him. Scoop . . . told me at the time that Ted was much more knowledgeable and sophisticated about the Soviet Union than he sometimes conveyed publicly, and I realized that in those first meetings."[23]

. . .

Three days after Ted left the Soviet Union, Gorbachev freed Soviet dissident Natan Sharansky. The timing was not coincidental.

18

"This Year in Be'er Sheva"

"I need to talk to you," Ted Kennedy told Boris Katz at about 1:00 a.m. on a September morning of 1978 in Moscow. "Privately."

Not long before, Ted had arrived at the tiny walk-up apartment of Alexander Lerner, a noted Soviet scientist, to meet with a dozen Jewish "refuseniks"—Soviet citizens who were refused permission to emigrate. Four years after meeting with Brezhnev, Ted returned to Moscow to push for more arms control and continue his efforts to persuade the Kremlin to free some refuseniks. Ascending the stairs to Lerner's apartment, he was accompanied by a contingent of KGB officers who had followed him on his drive and—this being the Soviet Union—thought that they'd monitor the meeting. Ted thought otherwise. "It's a private meeting," he told them as he entered the apartment, with the refuseniks looking on in startled admiration. "Could you please leave?"

After the KGB left and Ted introduced himself to each refusenik, he and Katz slipped away to talk in Lerner's kitchen. He first asked Katz about his infant daughter, who was suffering from malabsorption syndrome—an intestinal malady that, without special baby formula that Katz and his wife were smuggling in from the United States, could have left the young girl starving to death. He then told Katz that he had had "a discussion with the authorities" and "they agreed to let you go." Katz wouldn't let himself believe the good news. Nor would his wife, Nataly, when he told her after returning home a few hours later. "I wouldn't have been surprised if it hadn't happened," she recalled years later. "I had a sliver of hope, but it definitely wasn't a sure thing for me at the time."[1]

Ted harbored fewer doubts because in the weeks before his trip, his staff had negotiated with Soviet officials for the release of eighteen families and, after he met with Brezhnev and pressed the matter, the Soviet leader agreed to let them go. It was a victory for which he sought little public praise, for he believed that quiet diplomacy was the best way to convince Moscow to free its refuseniks.

It was a strategy that he had pursued four years earlier in Moscow to great effect, and that he pursued elsewhere around the world.

. . .

Asked to describe Ted Kennedy's view of America's global role, a former advisor said, "stand up to the bullies."[2]

Ted rarely rejected an opportunity to write a letter or deliver a speech to publicize the plight of a political prisoner. Sometimes, an aide would mention a dissident in an authoritarian society who was languishing in a faraway prison, isolated and lonely. Other times, constituents who were fortunate enough to escape to America would plead the cases of family members left behind.

Ted knew that he wielded far more influence in foreign capitals than an average senator, or even than a senior member of a congressional foreign policy committee. He enjoyed a built-in connection to officials in Moscow, Paris, Jerusalem, Pretoria, and numerous other capitals who remembered Jack and Bobby and wanted to know him. He also knew that, as a perennial would-be president, he enjoyed considerable leverage with foreign leaders who wanted to curry favor with him.

While he frequently wrote letters and delivered speeches about individuals on the front lines of battle over human rights, his most consequential work may have been his quiet diplomacy to free them. He knew that Soviet and Chinese leaders wanted him to visit so they could size him up, do business with him in the short term, and nourish ties that would prove important if he made it to the Oval Office. So, he conditioned his visits on what Moscow and Beijing surely considered a brazen demand—their promise to release a number of their political prisoners in exchange. Dozens of families that had lived under authoritarian regimes later owed their freedom to him.

On nearly a half century of travel abroad as a senator, Ted celebrated new democracies; pressured autocrats to free imprisoned dissidents; and praised activists, journalists, unionists, teachers, women, and others who were working to bring more freedom to their oppressed societies.

. . .

"Even though the United States government does not recognize you," Ted told eight thousand people in early 1972 in what became Dhaka, the capital of Bangladesh, "the people of the world do recognize you."[3]

The previous August he flew to South Asia to visit East Pakistani refugee camps in India, accused Pakistan of committing genocide as it tried to suppress an independence movement in the east, and urged Washington to cut off military and economic aid until the conflict ended. After India defeated Pakistan in their war over what became Bangladesh, Ted received a hero's welcome when he visited the new state in February of 1972. He compared Bangladesh's liberation to the American Revolution and urged President Nixon to extend diplomatic relations, which he did months later.

After celebrating a quarter century of West German democracy in Berlin in April of 1974, Ted flew to Portugal in the fall to encourage its new leaders to create a new democracy. Military officials had toppled a longstanding dictatorship in Lisbon, and President Ford (who had replaced Nixon by then) and Kissinger feared that the government would turn communist, which gave Ted some pause about visiting. After discussing the issue with Kissinger, he proceeded with his visit and met with Portugal's new president, was hosted at a dinner by its foreign minister, spoke with army officers and socialists, and announced that he would push for American aid for the fledgling democracy but warned that it wouldn't come if the government turned communist. After returning to Washington, he convinced

　　　　　　　　　　　　　　　　"This Year in Be'er Sheva"

Congress to provide $55 million. "I believe that the United States should support efforts by Portuguese democrats to forge popular institutions in their country," he told the Senate. "Let it not be said that this experiment was jeopardized because we turned a blind eye to what is happening in Portugal, because we failed to demonstrate our concern for what these people are trying to do."

Three years later in China, Ted gave the authorities in Beijing a list of twenty-two people who weren't allowed to leave the country—a list that his staff compiled after discussions with outside groups. Among them was Johnny Foo, a tuberculosis sufferer who wanted to visit his parents in Massachusetts. Officials allowed Ted to see Foo while he was in China, but they refused to discuss the list of twenty-two with him. Nevertheless, in another sign of Ted's influence, Beijing later let all twenty-two leave. In the summer of 1978, with Ted on hand to witness the event, Foo and his wife arrived at Boston's Logan Airport to see his parents for the first time in twenty years and carried visas that let them stay in America.

"I am a Pole," Ted declared nearly a decade later in Gdansk, Poland, echoing Jack's iconic "I am a Berliner" declaration.[4] With more than a dozen members of the Kennedy clan, he had flown to Poland in 1987 to present the Robert F. Kennedy Human Rights Award to two leaders of its Solidarity movement who had spent time in prison. They won the award in 1986, but Poland's communist regime prohibited their travel to Boston to receive it and rejected Ted's request that year to visit Poland. With U.S.-Polish relations improving, however, he convinced Warsaw to change course after pressing Polish officials in Washington. As Ted met with Solidarity founder Lech Walesa at a church in Gdansk, thousands gathered outside and called for them to appear. They went outside and stood on a doorstep when, amid impromptu remarks, Ted declared, "Jestem Polakiem" (I am a Pole).

It was in Moscow, however, where Ted had his biggest impact in securing freedom for political prisoners.

. . .

When Ted flew to Moscow in 1974, Washington was engaged in a fierce debate over how best to convince the Soviets to let more of their people go.

At the time, Jewish refuseniks were playing a more central role in U.S.-Soviet relations. New organizations had sprung up across America to highlight their plight, making them an issue of growing political importance. Meanwhile, the Kremlin was responding harshly to the refuseniks' increasingly bold tactics. When, in 1970, a group of Jews tried to steal a plane and fly it out of the country, the authorities sentenced two of them to death before commuting the sentences in response to a global outcry. Two years later, the refusenik issue took center stage in Washington when the Kremlin imposed an enormous "exit fee" on Jews who wanted to leave, supposedly to pay for the education they had received.

With the Soviet Union craving "most favored nation" trading status (i.e., normal trade relations) with the United States, Senator Henry "Scoop" Jackson, an anti-Soviet hardliner, argued that Washington should condition that status on Moscow's behavior toward its Jews and other persecuted minorities. He teamed with Rep. Charles Vanik on the Jackson-Vanik amendment to a 1974 trade bill, which denied "most favored nation" status to "non-market economies" that refused to let people emigrate; though they cloaked their target in the generic language of "non-market economies," everyone knew that it was Moscow. The Kremlin withdrew the exit fee, but Jackson and Vanik pushed ahead with their amendment because Moscow continued to tightly restrict Jewish and other emigration.

Nixon and Kissinger were pursuing détente at the time and, as foreign policy realists, arguing that the Kremlin's human rights record should play no role in Washington's policy toward Moscow. While Soviet leaders and American business interests lobbied Congress to reject Jackson-Vanik, Nixon and Kissinger warned that the measure would backfire because, to show the world that it wouldn't succumb to outside pressure, Moscow would restrict emigration even more. Rather than economic pressure, Nixon and Kissinger suggested that quiet consultation would prove more effective.

In the debate over how best to help the refuseniks, Ted came down decidedly on the quiet side.

. . .

Ted didn't object when the Senate voted in late 1974 to attach Jackson-Vanik to that year's trade bill.

In one sense it was an easy call because leading Soviet dissidents supported the measure. In an open letter a year earlier, Soviet physicist and human rights activist Andrei Sakharov urged Congress to enact Jackson-Vanik because doing otherwise would mean "a betrayal of the thousands of Jews and non-Jews who want to emigrate, of the hundreds in camps and mental hospitals [because they had sought to emigrate], of the victims of the Berlin Wall." Rather than prompt Moscow to ease up on would-be emigrants, Sakharov said, congressional rejection of Jackson-Vanik "would lead to stronger repressions on ideological grounds. It would be tantamount to total capitulation of democratic principles in [the] face of blackmail, deceit and violence. The consequences of such a capitulation for international confidence, détente and the entire future of mankind are difficult to predict."[5]

Ted was no crusader for Jackson-Vanik, however; neither he nor his brothers sought to condition U.S.-Soviet relations on human rights. While each denounced communism—articulately and repeatedly—for denying freedom to the individual, they each sought ways to reduce big-power tensions, which they clearly thought was more important. That was the spirit of Jack's peace speech at American University, of Bobby's push to end China's isolation, and of Ted's plea that Washington move "beyond détente" with the Soviets.

To win freedom for refuseniks, was Ted right to favor quiet diplomacy over public pressure? In the short run, Nixon and Kissinger proved prophetic in predicting that Jackson-Vanik would drive the Soviets to restrict Jewish emigration even more. After Moscow boosted the number of Jews that it allowed to leave from just eight thousand between 1965 and 1970 to thirty-five thousand in 1973 alone, it cut the number to twenty-one thousand in 1974 and thirteen thousand a year later. In later years the number rose and fell with the state of U.S.-Soviet relations.

Nevertheless, Natan Sharansky and other leading refuseniks and human rights activists considered Jackson-Vanik a major factor in the Soviet Union's collapse less than two decades later because it denied Moscow the trade benefits that it needed economically, put the Kremlin on the defensive globally, and emboldened the refuseniks.

. . .

In April of 1974 Ted was nearing the end of his meeting with Brezhnev when he asked for an exit visa for Mstislav Rostropovich—the great Russian cellist and conductor who was exiled in the Soviet Union, unable to perform or leave, because he had befriended Aleksandr Solzhenitsyn, the dissident Russian writer.

Joan Kennedy, who was trained as a classical musician, was well acquainted with Rostropovich, and she helped lay the ground for Ted's formal request—and Brezhnev's decision to grant it. Leonard Bernstein, the conductor who attended Harvard with Jack and became a friend of his after they graduated, was close to Rostropovich and, according to Joan, had conducted him in Vienna. Bernstein called Ted before his trip and urged him to press Brezhnev to release the Russian cellist.

The evening before Ted met with Brezhnev, he and Joan dined with Soviet officials at Moscow's Rossiya Hotel and, while Ted talked with officials about various matters, Joan talked with others about the cellist. At one point during the trip, she even went to the Moscow Conservatory in a futile attempt to find him. At a picture-taking ceremony before Ted met with Brezhnev, Joan raised the issue directly with the Soviet leader—which, she said later, angered Ted, who glared at her, apparently for stealing his thunder.

To both Ted and Joan, Brezhnev was noncommittal about Rostropovich but promised to give them an answer before too long. As their plane was returning to Washington, the Soviet ambassador called with the news that Moscow was, in fact, releasing Rostropovich and his wife. After the couple emigrated to the United

States, the Kennedys hosted a welcoming party at their home in McLean, Virginia. "I can never thank you enough for helping me get out of the Soviet Union," a teary-eyed Rostropovich told Ted.[6] The cellist went on to become the musical director and conductor of the National Symphony Orchestra in Washington, and Reagan awarded him the Medal of Freedom in 1987.

In November of 1989 Rostropovich was in Paris when he heard that demonstrators had gathered at the Berlin Wall. He phoned a friend who owned a jet, and they immediately flew to Berlin and went to the wall. After his friend grabbed a chair from a guard, Rostropovich sat at the crossing point known as "Checkpoint Charlie" and played Bach's Second Suite for cello as demonstrators dismantled the brick.

The Soviets restored Rostropovich's citizenship in 1990 and, while he celebrated his eightieth birthday at the Kremlin in 2007, Vladimir Putin presented him with the Order of Service to the Fatherland.

. . .

During that same trip of 1974, Ted flew to Leningrad where he toured a cemetery and other sites and where he wanted to meet with Polina Epelman, a Jew seeking an exit visa to join her husband in Israel.

After the U.S. general consul arranged for the meeting but before it occurred, Ted received word that Epelman had yelled out the window to a neighbor that the KGB barricaded her in her apartment. Furious, Ted told aides that he wanted to drive to her apartment right then, but they talked him out of it, explaining that before he arrived, the KGB would have taken her elsewhere. When his plane landed on its return to Moscow, he reamed out Brezhnev's aide for how he was treated, how Epelman was treated, and how Soviet Jews were treated. "And," Robert Hunter, Ted's foreign policy advisor of the time, recalled later, "that guy got out of the plane absolutely ashen."[7]

Ted also told Brezhnev's aide that, in Moscow, he wanted to meet with Jews who wanted exit visas. The two argued, but he insisted. With his staff's help, he arranged a late-night meeting with a small group of refuseniks at Alexander Lerner's apartment. When, in the meeting, the dissidents urged continued American protests about their plight, saying the publicity gave them some protection from Soviet abuse, he promised to speak publicly on their behalf. "They were at peace with themselves," Ted reflected later, "all had suffered, but nothing could be done to them that was going to interrupt their own kind of mindset, and the fixture of their soul and their hearts as to what they believed, and what was at risk."[8] Catering to Ted, Moscow eventually let some of them leave.

A few months later Ted traveled to Israel as part of his broader trip to Europe and the Middle East. By then Moscow had allowed Polina Epelman to leave for the Holy Land, and she settled in Be'er Sheva, a large city in the south. Coincidentally, Ted was scheduled to speak at Ben Gurion University, located in that very city. His aide found the Epelmans, and Ted visited them in their apartment. When he asked Polina how she felt, she looked out the window and said, "It isn't Russia. We are a family again."

At Ben Gurion University, a proud Ted declared, "So for the Epelmans, 'next year in Jerusalem' is this year in Be'er Sheva."[9]

. . .

By the time Ted returned to Moscow in September of 1978, Moscow had agreed to release more refuseniks.

Before the trip, Ted peppered Brezhnev with private messages that requested better treatment for refuseniks and dissidents, while his staff negotiated the list of eighteen families that Moscow later allowed to leave. When Ted met with Brezhnev, it was a far different get-together than in 1974. The Soviet leader was in declining health, and, rather than banter with Ted, he read a long statement that the Kremlin later gave to Ted's staff. He disparaged those who pressed Moscow on human rights, calling the issue "a deliberate line pursued by those who want to poison the atmosphere, to undermine trust and, generally, to frustrate or, at least, to seriously impede the positive development of relations between the USSR and the USA." "This is," he said, "a crude attempt to interfere in our internal affairs and to bring pressure to bear upon us."[10] When Brezhnev's eyes began to close, Soviet officials cut the meeting short. His bluster was a sideshow, however, for the Kremlin had already cut its deal with Ted on who it would release.

When Ted returned to Lerner's apartment early the next morning, those waiting for him included Sakharov and his wife, Yelena Bonner, and the mother and brother of Natan Sharansky, who was sentenced to hard labor in 1978 over his human rights activism. As Sakharov and other leading dissidents had when Congress debated Jackson-Vanik in 1974, they praised the measure. Along with Boris Katz, Ted told Lev David Roitburg, another refusenik, that he was among those destined for freedom. Rather than adopt the wait-and-see attitude of Boris and Nataly Katz, Roitburg wept with joy.

It wasn't until Ted returned to Moscow in early 1986 to see Gorbachev that he secured Sharansky's release.

. . .

As Brezhnev had done when Ted pressed him on human rights, Gorbachev erupted when he raised the issue, pounding the table and criticizing America for its homeless, crime, and other social maladies.

At least in part, Gorbachev was going through the motions, for he had already decided to release Sharansky. For months before Ted's trip, a top aide had flown to Moscow and elsewhere to meet with Soviet officials, securing an agreement that the Kremlin would release nine families that he had inquired about—and also would release Sharansky in the near future. When, in the weeks leading up to Ted's trip to Moscow, his staff felt sure that Gorbachev would fulfill the Kremlin's promise to release Sharansky, Ted delivered the news by phone to Sharansky's wife, Avital, who had campaigned around the world for his release ever since Moscow let her leave for Israel in 1974.

A few days after Ted was back in Washington, the Soviets released Sharansky, letting him walk across the Glienicke Bridge that connected East Germany and West Berlin. Reagan received the credit, and, to be sure, the president had pressed Gorbachev about Sharansky and other political prisoners—and, when Ted pushed for Sharansky's release, he was working in concert with the president.

Nevertheless, Ted played a major role for which he neither sought nor received much public adulation.

. . .

In Washington, Ted resumed his work that would lead to the release of another iconic political prisoner—Nelson Mandela.

19

"The Echoes of My Brother Bob's Trip"

"This is one of those moments that will live in our history," Ted Kennedy told the Senate in the late afternoon of October 2, 1986, "that each of us will remember, as long as we live—the day America set its policy right on one of the great issues of our time, the cause of a free South Africa."

Minutes later, the Senate closed a high-stakes, impassioned, topsy-turvy debate of two years by voting 78–21 to override President Reagan's veto of legislation to impose sanctions on South Africa over apartheid. Following a House vote of a few days earlier, the Senate vote marked the first time that Congress had overridden a president on an issue of foreign policy in eleven years—and, even in a Republican-controlled Senate, no one had done more than the Democratic senator from Massachusetts to make it happen.

During those two years, he traveled to South Africa; sparred with top U.S. and South African officials and business leaders; drafted sanctions legislation; coordinated strategy with like-minded senators and House members; testified before Senate and House committees; debated his opponents heatedly on the Senate floor; aired his views on the Sunday morning TV news shows and leading op-ed pages; and delivered moving speeches at the United Nations and elsewhere. He worked out front and behind the scenes, sweet-talking some colleagues while pressuring others. He led the Democrats and exploited a wedge that opened between a Republican president who wanted to stand by a key Cold War ally and Republican lawmakers who increasingly preferred to be on the enlightened side of civil rights.

However notable was Ted's achievement, the Senate vote on that hot autumn day marked far more than the tactical victory of one senator. It culminated decades of effort by all three Kennedy brothers.

. . .

When Bishop Desmond Tutu and fellow South African cleric Allan Boesak asked Ted in October of 1984 to visit their country and focus more global attention on apartheid, he was initially hesitant to go, fearful that he could never equal Bobby's dramatic performance of 1966.

"I could still hear the echoes of my brother Bob's trip . . . which was enormously successful in terms of taking on the problems of racism," Ted recalled. "Robert Kennedy was the right person at the right time to make the right speeches, and he had the right schedule and interaction with the students and with the leaders there."[1]

Despite his doubts about a trip, Ted was eager to help on the apartheid fight and, by then, had become more involved. Earlier that year he compared apartheid to Nazism in a moving UN speech, denounced Pretoria in multiple Senate floor statements, and met with South African activists and journalists when they passed through Washington. He even met with the African National Congress's president, Oliver Tambo, which no other senator would do because the group had used violence and the Reagan administration designated it a terrorist organization. Tutu and Boesak were in Washington to speak at a forum that Ted had organized on apartheid (though he canceled it at the last minute because he needed to be in the Senate, which was then debating arms control policy).

Their request, which they relayed to Ted over lunch in his office after the Senate finished its debate, came at a key moment. The antiapartheid movement was gathering steam around the world, with protests and arrests at South Africa's embassy in Washington and grassroots pressure forcing state and local governments, businesses,

"The Echoes of My Brother Bob's Trip"

and colleges to "reassess their ties to the apartheid state."[2] South African activists, however, were frustrated that the nation's president, P. W. Botha, was still welcome in Washington and European capitals. In the same month that Tutu and Boesak visited Washington, the United States abstained on a Security Council resolution to condemn Pretoria's apartheid policies. Nor, to Ted's dismay, did Reagan's policy toward South Africa play any discernable role in that year's presidential campaign, in which he won a landslide reelection.

With his invitation from Tutu and Boesak, Ted could further extend the Kennedy legacy on South Africa. As president, Jack repeatedly condemned Pretoria over apartheid and, in 1963, banned U.S. arms sales to the nation as long as apartheid remained in place. With his dramatic trip of 1966, Bobby was among the first Western figures to denounce apartheid while in South Africa. In his UN speech of June of 1984, Ted quoted both of his brothers as he made the case for stronger U.S. action.

Nevertheless, Ted was fretful enough about not measuring up to Bobby that he wouldn't commit to a visit when he saw Tutu and Boesak, telling them merely that he was interested. It was only after Tutu won the Nobel Peace Prize a few days later and phoned Ted, again urging him to come, that he accepted.

. . .

In fighting apartheid, Ted once again ran headfirst into Reagan's Cold War-centric outlook on foreign policy.

As in Latin America, Reagan thought the Soviets and Cubans were on the move in southern Africa, sending troops and weapons to help insurgents convert pro-Western governments into communist regimes. Perhaps sensing American weakness under Carter (who had disparaged America's "inordinate fear of communism" just months after taking office), they sent troops or weapons in the late 1970s to incite revolution in, among other places, Angola, Ethiopia, Namibia, and Rhodesia (now Zimbabwe). Reagan hoped to stem Soviet and Cuban adventurism, and he viewed South Africa as a key anti-Soviet bulwark in the region. South Africa viewed itself the same way and, in fact, Pretoria sent troops and conducted air strikes to fight the communist-driven effort in Angola. With that in mind, Reagan pursued "constructive engagement" with South Africa, which involved teaming with its government on regional challenges while working quietly to convince officials to provide more rights to its black population.

"Our credibility in Moscow and Havana," Chester Crocker, who would serve as Reagan's assistant secretary of state for African affairs, wrote in a piece for *Foreign Affairs* that ran in December of 1980, just a month before Reagan took office, "depends on adopting a strong line against the principle of introducing external combat forces into the region. . . . There can be no presumed communist right to exploit and militarize regional tensions, particularly in this region where important Western economic, resource and strategic interests are exposed." As for constructive engagement, Crocker urged American support for "a regional climate conducive to compromise and accommodation in the face of concerted attempts to discredit evolutionary change." The West, he said, should eschew "trade and investment sanctions" and recognize that "engagement" with South Africa's economy "can be constructive for the [black] majority."[3]

Constructive engagement dramatically altered Washington's policy toward Pretoria. Dismissing the public criticism and pressure campaign of Carter and his top team, Reagan praised Pretoria as a worthy ally; vetoed critical Security Council resolutions; boosted U.S. trade and investment; lifted U.S. restrictions on providing military equipment; expanded Washington's diplomatic, military, and intelligence relations; welcomed back Pretoria's military attaches; and refused to take sides in disputes between government officials and black leaders—thus, implicitly equating the oppressed with their oppressors. None of that, however, seemed to improve prospects for the black majority.

To Ted and a growing number of congressional Republicans, South Africa was more of a human rights challenge than a geopolitical one. Rather than quietly prod Pretoria to change, Ted wanted to force it to do so through the pressure of public shaming and the

"The Echoes of My Brother Bob's Trip"

pain of economic sanctions. Rather than support Reagan's call for patience, Ted shared the activists' desire for speedy transformation.

Ted traveled to South Africa in January of 1985 and, despite his concerns about measuring up to Bobby, he need not have worried. His trip matched Bobby's in drama and, in the end, far exceeded it in impact.

. . .

"What's going on?" Ted asked an aide when South African police stopped his motorcade, jumped out of their cars, pulled out their Uzis, and told Ted's staffers that they couldn't continue their drive to Soweto because rioting had erupted there.[4]

Ted had just landed at Jan Smuts Airport in Johannesburg for an eight-day visit, and he was headed to Soweto with Tutu and his wife, who would host him that evening at their home in the black ghetto—where whites needed government permits to visit (Ted didn't bother getting one) and only rarely spent the night (Ted was reportedly the first foreign dignitary to do so). With at least tacit assent from Reagan administration officials on the ground, South African authorities felt no obligation to welcome Ted as a distinguished guest. Quite the contrary, they imposed a host of roadblocks right from the start. ("Participating in the effort to make [the trip] fail," one of his top aides recalled, "were the American embassy and the ambassador!"[5]) At the airport, police did little to control about a hundred demonstrators from the Azanian People's Organization (AZAPO), a "black consciousness" group that opposed the visit of Ted—who they dismissed as a millionaire representative of an "imperialist" country and who, they believed, was legitimizing South Africa's government with his visit. "Kennedy go home," they chanted as he walked through the terminal.

Advised that he couldn't go to Soweto because it wasn't safe, Ted told an aide, "no, no, no, I'm going" and continued his drive to the Tutu home. Police, however, prevented two buses of reporters who were covering his trip from following, leaving them to report only about the mixed greeting he received at the airport. The authorities also jammed the phone lines, preventing aides who were with Ted from speaking to other aides who flew in earlier and were now at Tutu's home. (Ted's aides also tangled with State Department officials who were serving as liaisons between the Kennedy entourage and South African officials, prompting a heated phone conversation between the senator and Herman Nickel, the U.S. ambassador, after Nickel's aides complained to him.)

The police announcement about rioting in Soweto was nonsense, as Ted may well have suspected. When he and the Tutus reached Soweto, they were met not by violence but by hundreds of people holding candles and singing songs. That night, Ted recalled years later, a choir from Tutu's church sang "soft" songs to lull him to sleep in Tutu's bed, next to his Nobel Peace Prize.[6] Tutu stayed up with the choir until dawn before grabbing an hour or two of sleep in a chair.

It wasn't the only time that the authorities warned about violence, or stoked it, to complicate Ted's trip.

. . .

"This," Ted said after touring a Soweto hostel for migrant laborers, "is one of the most distressing and despairing visits that I have made to any facility in my lifetime."[7]

The Nancefield hostel, one of South Africa's "oldest and most run-down," was home to six thousand men who lived in cubicles. Under the nation's migrant worker system, blacks lived in camps far from home eleven months of the year, traveling in long blue buses to work in cities each morning; sleeping in cramped quarters each night; and working on contracts that were renewed a year at a time. That was the only way they could save enough money to provide for their families, many of which lived far away in tribal homelands. "The worst part is the loneliness," a fifty-four-year-old worker told Ted.[8] "Here," Ted said after his tour, "individuals are caught up between trying to provide for their families or living with their families, and I don't really know of any other place in the world where that kind of cruel, harsh, difficult choice has to be made by people who believe in family life."[9]

Over the next week Ted sparred with South Africa's foreign minister, "Pik" Botha, in a tense ninety-minute meeting in Pretoria; he endured harsh criticism from government-backing newspapers and state-run TV that dismissed his visit as a precursor to a presidential run and taunted him about Chappaquiddick and his Harvard cheating scandal; he rejected a meeting with the imprisoned Nelson Mandela because officials conditioned it on his promise to publicly denounce violence by anti-apartheid activists and he didn't want to give Pretoria a propaganda victory; he visited Mandela's wife, Winnie, in a remote black ghetto to which the government banished her a decade earlier and restricted her freedom; he sparred with Nickel before a Johannesburg luncheon of business leaders about the most appropriate American policy toward South Africa; he spoke to thousands in Cape Town; and he was forced to cancel his concluding address in Soweto's Regina Mundi Cathedral because Tutu feared that protestors would resort to violence. Ted had hoped that that address would echo Bobby's "ripple of hope" speech.

For all their similarities, the contrast between Ted's trip and Bobby's of two decades earlier was striking. Bobby had come to South Africa to evangelize for change, to speak to the better angels of its white residents, to appeal to their consciences and convince them to do better. Ted adopted a more confrontational tone, highlighting the horrid conditions of blacks while lecturing their white masters. It was among the reasons why he endured far more criticism in South Africa than Bobby had.

The more consequential contrast between the trips, however, was their aftermath. After Bobby raised consciousness about apartheid, he returned home to devote more time to Vietnam. Before Ted had even left South Africa, he was talking about the changes in American policy that he hoped to push through Congress.

. . .

In his push for sanctions, Ted echoed the worries about America's policy toward the developing world that he had long shared with Jack and Bobby.

In testimony and Senate speeches, Ted expressed concern that Reagan's support for Pretoria was tarnishing America's global image. "When Robert Kennedy visited South Africa," he told the Senate Banking Committee in April of 1985, "the United States was recognized as a role model for millions of whites and blacks alike for being able to achieve some of the most basic and fundamental rights. The United States had faced this issue, and we had really set an example for the world. That concept and model has been crushed, dashed, and destroyed. . . . The United States now is thoroughly and completely identified with the policy of constructive engagement. . . . The hostility to the United States is increasing dramatically."

Ted expressed another concern about constructive engagement, a concern that Jack expressed about Eisenhower's policies in Africa and Bobby expressed about LBJ's policies in Latin America: its impact on America's relationship with South Africa over the long term. "South Africa will be free some day," he said, "and, make no mistake about it, those in that government when it is free are going to ask whether the United States was the last country to go down with apartheid. And it certainly appears to blacks in South Africa today that this is the case."

As Jack stated about Vietnam, and Bobby about Malaysia, Ted stressed that it was up to the people of South Africa to build their own future, not for Washington to impose it on them. With constructive engagement, however, Ted charged that America's ability to "have some influence over that process" was shrinking. What Washington needed, he explained, was a new policy that would restore America's credibility with the forces of change, not continue to associate it with the forces of retrenchment.

. . .

"This tactic is beneath the dignity of the Senate," Ted charged in September of 1985 after the Foreign Relations Committee's chairman, Richard Lugar, removed the printed version of a sanctions bill from the Senate chamber, preventing a vote on it.

To Ted it was an outrageous way (what he called "this trickery

and . . . abuse of the Senate rules") for Republican leaders to protect Reagan, who opposed the bill, from a legislative defeat. It also
was a disheartening end to more than six months of work to push
a strong sanctions bill through Congress. He had introduced a bill
in March with Lowell Weicker, a Republican senator from Connecticut, that would have barred new U.S. bank loans to Pretoria;
prohibited new U.S. investment in South Africa; prevented U.S.
imports of South African gold coins; and blocked sales of U.S. com-
puters to South Africa. He testified about the legislation a month
later before both the Senate Foreign Relations and Banking committees, and he helped gather the Senate votes in July for Lugar's
modified version that the Foreign Relations Committee approved.

Congressional Republicans were reluctant to split with a popular
president of their own party, especially after his landslide reelection
of a year earlier, and especially on an issue of foreign policy (because a
defeat on foreign policy could tarnish the president's image abroad).
But with Pretoria enforcing apartheid in ever-more brutal fashion, killing hundreds of blacks and torturing thousands of political
opponents, Senate Republicans were growing antsy about constructive engagement. Just after Reagan's reelection, Lugar (a skeptical
supporter of constructive engagement from the start) and Nancy
Kassebaum (another influential Senate Republican voice on foreign
policy) wrote him a private letter to urge him to reassess his policy.

By the summer of 1985 the Senate and House had passed separate
sanctions bills, a House-Senate conference committee had ironed
out a final version, and the House had passed that bill as well. Facing
almost certain Senate approval of a sanctions bill that he opposed,
Reagan tried to avoid it by announcing that he would implement
many of the bill's provisions through an executive order—that is,
through action that he could take on his own. At that point Senate
Republicans rallied around Reagan, supported his executive order,
and rebuffed Ted's call to pass the bill as a broader sign of American
opposition to apartheid. As Ted was urging his colleagues to pass
the bill, Lugar conspired with Senate Republican leader Bob Dole
to prevent a vote on it by taking the bill itself from the chamber.

The sanctions bill of 1985 had died, but, as Pretoria dug in to maintain apartheid, Ted was eager to try again.

. . .

"Without exception," Ted wrote in a *New York Times* op-ed in July of 1986, "every time that he has been questioned about South Africa since taking office, President Reagan has defended the white minority regime."[10]

Washington was debating sanctions legislation again, but, nearly a year after the previous version had died, Ted was better positioned to force this one into law. Senate Republicans were now antsier about constructive engagement, leaving Reagan more isolated. That's because his executive order did little to persuade Pretoria to rethink apartheid. Quite the contrary, as Ted noted in testimony and speeches throughout 1986, the regime was cracking down harder on black protestors and government critics.

In June Pretoria declared a state of emergency, and, by August, as Ted promoted sanctions legislation that the Foreign Relations Committee had crafted, he told the Senate, "12,000 political leaders have been arrested and detained" and "the entire leadership of the black South African trade unions are in jail or in hiding at this very moment." Citing a University of Cape Town study of detainees, he added, "83 percent . . . reported some form of physical torture by the security policy" including "punching, kicking, slapping, beating with a whip, forced standing, excrement abuse, maintaining abnormal body positions, electric shocks to genitals, arms and feet, strangulation by hand or by means of a cloth or towel, legs chained around the neck, pulling out or burning hair or beard, genital abuse, beating the soles of the feet, burning matchsticks under nails, fingernails being crushed by a brick, breasts squeezed, petrol poured over body and set alight, sleep deprivation, hooding and blindfolding, drugs, sham executions, the use of animals such as dogs, spiders and snakes." The most "heavily tortured" South Africans were younger than twenty.

As Pretoria cracked down harder, Ted denounced its ally in the

"The Echoes of My Brother Bob's Trip"

White House more sharply. A day after his *New York Times* op-ed, he told the Foreign Relations Committee, "The policy of the administration is a disgrace. It is an embarrassment. . . . Constructive engagement has become synonymous with aid and comfort to racism in South Africa, and instead of the last best hope of earth, the United States of America has become the last best friend of apartheid. . . . No matter what the South African government does . . . the administration clings to a bankrupt policy that puts the United States on the side of apartheid and transforms our country into the second most detested government in the eyes of all Africa."

Nevertheless, prospects for sanctions legislation remained problematic. By a voice vote in June, the Democrat-controlled House passed a bill "imposing a trade embargo on South Africa and requiring all American companies . . . to leave within 180 days."[11] House Republicans mused hopefully that the bill was so extreme that it might kill efforts to enact a sanctions bill for another year. After the Senate voted 84–14 for a more moderate bill, the question was how to push a final bill quickly through Congress before it adjourned for the year. If sanctions proponents failed, they would have to start all over again when the next Congress assembled in January.

Rather than take the time to draft a new compromise bill, the only viable option was for the House to pass the Senate version intact, which would send it to the White House. Someone would have to convince key House Democrats to go along, and, with his leadership on the issue and his stature among Democrats, Ted was the logical choice. He met with the Congressional Black Caucus, an influential organization of African American lawmakers, and convinced its leaders after about twenty minutes of discussion. The House passed the Senate bill, sending it to the White House. After Reagan vetoed it, the House and Senate voted to override the veto and turn the bill into law.

. . .

After spearheading success in South Africa, Ted returned to the trickier task of ending bloodshed in Northern Ireland.

20

"He's Not Going to Hug Gerry Adams"

Among Ted Kennedy's favorite songs was "The Town I Loved So Well," a sad and sweet ballad about growing up in Derry, a city in Northern Ireland, and how the "troubles" of the late twentieth century upended its simple lifestyle.[1]

It was, as singer and songwriter Phil Coulter described it in his ballad of 1973, a town where, not many years earlier, happy children played ball and ran home in the rain; music filled the air; and men and women endured through good times and bad. Now, however, it was a town "brought to its knees" by "armoured cars" and "bombed-out bars," and by tanks, guns, and barbed wire.[2]

The words are poignant, and they resonated with Ted because, like his brothers, he took his Irish heritage seriously. Jack traveled to Ireland as a journalist in 1945, as a House freshman in 1947 (when he visited his sister, Kick, and drove for hours to reach the home of distant relatives), with Jackie in 1955, and then as president on his triumphant visit of 1963. As Jack had wanted, Jackie Kennedy later renamed their Virginia home "Wexford" to honor the county in Ireland from which his ancestors had come. Ted stopped in Ireland during his European trip of 1962, returned in 1964 in a heart-wrenching visit to retrace Jack's steps of a year earlier, and flew to Dublin in 1970 to speak at Trinity College. In later years he returned to Ireland and traveled to Northern Ireland in search of peace.

While all three brothers were proud of their Irish roots, and all three inherited their father's resentments over the anti-Irish prejudice of his day, Ted was the most outwardly Irish of the three. He was the most like his colorful grandfather, Honey Fitz, so, not surprisingly, he was far more eager than the reserved Jack or the awkward Bobby to mount a table and break into an Irish song. He never missed the annual St. Patrick's Day celebrations on Capitol Hill, and as he sought the help of presidents to bring peace to Northern Ireland, he convinced them to attend those celebrations as well.

Ted spent far more time on the "troubles," which left 3,600 dead and more than thirty thousand wounded over the course of three decades, than any other global challenge. After centuries of English domination of Ireland, Anglo-Irish treaties of the early 1920s split the land in two, creating the "Irish Free State" (later known as Ireland) and leaving six mostly Protestant counties of Northern Ireland under British control. By the late 1960s the North's Catholic minority began to protest decades of discrimination in employment, housing, and voting rights, and violence erupted between (mostly Catholic) Irish republicans who sought a united Ireland and (mostly Protestant) unionists who wanted to remain within Britain. Ted began pursuing a solution soon after the "troubles" began, at a time when he was also seeking peace in Vietnam, a new approach to China, and better relations with the Soviets.

His decades of work—culminating in the "Good Friday Agreement" of 1998 that officially ended the conflict as well as the "Miracle of Stormont" of 2007 that ushered in a coalition government of once-bitter foes—showcased his skills as a Senate operative of unmatched effectiveness.

. . .

"In recent months, we have witnessed appalling outbreaks of civil strife in Northern Ireland—the worst in the entire half-century since Ireland was partitioned," Ted told the Senate in October of 1971, as he proposed a resolution that Britain withdraw its troops from the North and that a united Ireland take shape.

"The soaring toll of death and violence," he said, "is uncontrolled. Thousands flee their homes in terror. Businesses are bombed, and factories close down. Barbed wire roadblocks imprison every street corner. Young children stand on curbstones and shout shrill insults filled with hate. A child is slain returning from an errand for his parents. A priest is killed as he kneels over a desperately wounded victim. A lorry backfires, and the driver is cut down in a wanton hail of military bullets."

A month earlier, Ted was in London when an Irish woman stopped him on the street to ask why the human-rights-minded senator, who had denounced the killing of four students at Kent State the previous year, hadn't said anything about Britain's harsh rule in Northern Ireland. At the time, Northern Ireland's local government had begun detaining hundreds of suspects without trial, virtually all of them Catholic. New York's Hugh Carey, a House Democrat who was among a handful of Irish American political figures with whom Ted would work closely on the issue for years to come, returned from a visit to Belfast in August and told him that the government was torturing its detainees.

Ted spoke out as both an Irishman and a human-rights-minded leader. Americans should care about the "troubles," he said, because "the Irish have had a monumental impact on the America we know today." Not only have they "built our railroads, dug our coal, erected our buildings and our churches . . . organized our unions and our businesses . . . [and] fought in all our wars," but they have also produced such cultural giants as Eugene O'Neill, F. Scott Fitzgerald, George M. Cohan, John L. Sullivan, Connie Mack, Cardinal Cushing, and George Meany. Ted, however, stressed that he'd be speaking out even if he weren't Irish, for "the conscience of America cannot keep silent when men and women of Ireland are dying." At the time, he was denouncing injustice on multiple fronts at home and abroad, so, as he put it years later, "my nerve endings were heightened and sharpened and obviously, with my emotional attachment to Ireland, this became front and center for me."[3]

Like his brothers, he knew how to draw attention to make his point. "The tragedy of Ulster is the tragedy of America in Indochina," he told the Senate. "For Ulster is becoming Britain's Vietnam." Jack

"He's Not Going to Hug Gerry Adams"

had outraged the French by denouncing their rule in Algeria, while Bobby had compared America's action in Vietnam to the Holocaust. Now, with the audacity he inherited from his father and shared with his brothers, Ted was harshly criticizing a close American ally and framing the issue in graphic terms. The British weren't accustomed to lectures from Washington, however, and Nixon—the realist who didn't think that Washington should worry about the human rights record of *any* government, friend or foe—wasn't criticizing London for its actions. Not surprisingly, the British expressed outrage over Ted's comments; Prime Minister Ted Heath termed them "an ignorant outburst" while, in a nasty reference to Chappaquiddick, a conservative parliamentarian chastised the senator for "expressing moral judgments on anything."[4]

Ted, however, would not be deterred. In a snippy letter to the *Times of London* a few days later, he wrote, "It is difficult to believe that my proposal would have generated such fervor if Britain, one of the great symbols of freedom and democracy to us Americans, did not have a guilty conscience over Ulster."[5]

. . .

"My understanding of the situation in Northern Ireland," Ted wrote years later, "really began to evolve after I met John Hume, a brilliant young member of parliament from Northern Ireland."[6]

At Ted's request, they met in late 1972 in Bonn, where Ted was attending a NATO meeting. An Irish Catholic from Derry and the eldest of seven children, Hume was a founding member of Northern Ireland's Social Democratic and Labour Party and, from 1979 to 2001, its leader. In the same month that Ted called "Ulster . . . Britain's Vietnam," Hume conducted a forty-eight-hour hunger strike to protest the North's internment of hundreds of Irish republicans. At a time when most leaders were taking sides between the Irish Republican Army (IRA) terrorist campaign to force the British from Northern Ireland and Britain's brutal retaliation, Hume was pushing for a peaceful resolution. An advocate of nonviolence, he went on to win the Nobel Peace Prize in 1998, the year of the

Good Friday Agreement. Hume convinced Ted—who, to that point, had spoken far more about Britain's crackdown than the IRA killings—to adopt a more even-handed opposition to violence, lest he legitimize the IRA's behavior.

Hume influenced him only gradually, however. In February of 1972 Ted testified before a House Foreign Affairs subcommittee about his Senate resolution of the previous year that urged Britain to withdraw, which he had proposed with Abe Ribicoff, a Senate Democrat from Connecticut. "The nation that gave Magna Carta and habeas corpus and due process to the world," he told the House panel, "imprisons hundreds of innocent citizens of Northern Ireland, without warrant, charge or trial." He quoted an official British inquiry that found prisoners "deprived of food and sleep . . . spread-eagled against the wall for up to 48 hours at a time . . . shrouded in heavy black hoods, to induce a sense of desperation . . . [and] forced to suffer through the intense loud hissing noise of machines designed to surpass human endurance." He denounced the "escalating military violence" that "culminated" in Britain's "wanton killings of Bloody Sunday at Londonderry," when British troops gunned down Catholic protestors during a march against internment. He also criticized Nixon for his silence. Though he condemned both British and IRA violence, he focused overwhelmingly on the former. In a *Foreign Policy* article in the summer of 1973, he largely echoed his Senate remarks and House testimony.

By the late 1970s Ted was espousing a far more balanced view of the conflict. With Hume urging him to encourage America's Irish diaspora to stop financing the IRA, Ted joined with Senator Daniel Patrick Moynihan, House Speaker Tip O'Neill, and Carey—the all-Irish group soon immortalized as the "Four Horsemen"—on a St. Patrick's Day statement of 1977 urging "all organizations engaged in violence to renounce their campaigns of death and destruction and return to the path of life and peace" and "our fellow Americans . . . to renounce any action that promotes the current violence or provides support or encouragement for organizations engaged in violence." At the urging of Ted, the other "Horsemen," and Hume, President

"He's Not Going to Hug Gerry Adams"

Carter echoed the sentiment in a public statement in August and promised that, if the two sides moved toward peace, Washington would help boost investment in Northern Ireland. Ted lauded Carter publicly and in a private, handwritten note.

In the early 1980s Ted pushed Reagan, who was proud of his own Irish heritage on his father's side, to prod Britain's prime minister, Margaret Thatcher, a hardliner on the "troubles" with whom Reagan was close, to take steps to ease the conflict. When, in 1985, she and Garret FitzGerald, Ireland's prime minister, inked the Anglo-Irish Agreement, giving Ireland an advisory role on human rights and police issues in Northern Ireland, Ted called Hume with some good news: "We keep our promises."[7]

Fulfilling Carter's pledge of nearly a decade earlier, the United States contributed to the new International Fund for Ireland, which Britain and Ireland created "to promote economic and social advance as well as encourage contact and dialogue between nationalists and unionists throughout Ireland."

. . .

Ted was waiting at Boston's Logan Airport to meet Gerry Adams, the controversial leader of Sinn Fein—the Irish republican party with close ties to the IRA—when an aide advised him that, with media on hand, "whatever you do, don't let [him] hug you." As Ted smiled, Vicki Kennedy (his second wife) quipped, "He's Irish. They barely hug their wives. He's not going to hug Gerry Adams."[8]

It was September of 1994, and Adams's arrival would culminate his two-year push, in which Ted was a central player, to secure a visa to visit America. With the election of President Clinton, who had promised to pursue a peace deal to end the "troubles," two years earlier, Ted positioned himself to exert far more influence over America's peace-making efforts. He first convinced Clinton to appoint his sister, Jean Kennedy Smith, as America's ambassador to Ireland—where she broke the mold of her predecessors by involving herself in the "troubles" that, since they weren't in Ireland, weren't technically within her jurisdiction. (She apparently inherited a bit of her father's audacity as well.) Ted felt a special bond with his sister, with whom he was closest in age among his siblings and shared years together at the kiddie table at dinner while the older children discussed global events at the main table. Ted also convinced Clinton to appoint one of his top foreign policy advisors, Nancy Soderberg, as deputy national security advisor. Clinton, who needed Ted's support of health reform and a raft of other priorities, was happy to oblige. Ted now had close allies in the White House and in Dublin with whom to work for peace.

Adams's support was key to fashioning an enduring peace, but whether he should get a visa was a subject of great controversy, and one with which Ted struggled. Adams was reportedly a top IRA strategist for nearly two decades by then, though he always downplayed his ties to the group. He spent much of the 1970s in prison, though he was never convicted of the IRA-related charges against him, and he survived a shooting in 1984, allegedly by unionist adversaries. In the late 1970s he began pushing for a more political, less violent, strategy for Northern Ireland's Catholics to achieve their goals. Hume, Smith, and Soderberg all supported a visa for Adams, convincing Ted that the risk of embarrassment if he later engaged in violent action was worth the potential upside of involving him more intensively in peace-making efforts. Clinton rejected Adams's visa request in late 1993, citing evidence of his continuing close ties to the IRA, before granting him a forty-eight-hour visa to visit New York City in early 1994.

When the visa idea first arose in early 1993, Ted rejected it out of hand, dismissing Adams as a terrorist. IRA bombings that fall did nothing to change his mind. What convinced him was his trip to Dublin with Vicki at year's end to visit Jean, who had lost her husband a year earlier, over the holidays. Rather than relax with her brother, Jean Kennedy Smith ran him to meetings with key officials, all of whom reinforced her view that a visa for Adams could help advance peace. He spent ninety minutes with Albert Reynolds, Ireland's taoiseach (i.e., leader), who said he was convinced by British intelligence that Adams was now committed to nonviolence. Ted

"He's Not Going to Hug Gerry Adams"

heard much the same from Tim Pat Coogan, a noted Irish writer with whom he had lunch. Hume swung by for a visit, stressing his support for a visa. After Adams applied for one in January of 1994, Ted made the case for it to Clinton at the White House.

When, after more prodding from Ted, Clinton approved a visa for Adams in September of 1994, Ted met him at Logan Airport and came away thinking that he was "very able, gifted . . . talented" and "charismatic."[9] As Adams advanced, albeit somewhat inconsistently, toward a more political, less violent, approach to end the "troubles," Ted advocated for him more forcefully. At Ted's urging, Clinton in 1994 lifted a ban on official U.S. contacts with Sinn Fein and on Adams's fundraising for Sinn Fein in the United States and, a year later, invited Adams to his annual lunch with Ireland's taoiseach. Later in 1995 Ted and top White House officials met with Adams as he visited Washington during another trip to America.

Ted's support for Adams was not unconditional, however. After the IRA broke a ceasefire in early 1996, bombing a London wharf and killing two, Ted refused to see him a month later.

. . .

"Today, we stand at a defining moment in the modern epic of this land," Ted Kennedy told hundreds of officials, republicans, and unionists at the University of Ulster in January of 1998. "The talks that are about to resume offer both a challenge and an opportunity. In the coming crucial weeks, the parties will determine whether this is a genuine way forward, or just another failed station on the way to sorrows."

Three months before the parties inked the Good Friday Agreement, Ted was scheduled to deliver the university's "Tip O'Neill Memorial Lecture" (for the House speaker who had died four years earlier), and he hoped to use the opportunity to help revive the stalled peace talks. That peace had not yet come—in fact, Irish Catholic assassins had gunned down a prominent unionist terror leader just weeks earlier—raised all sorts of security issues around Ted's trip. Like his brothers, Ted was both brave and fateful, determined to operate on the public stage without undue restraint and willing to let fate decide how and when he would die. Those around him, however, did not share his carefree attitude, and their efforts—driven in large part by Vicki—to protect him from attack by a disgruntled individual on either side sent them scurrying in multiple directions.

For starters, he wouldn't always wear the heavy bulletproof vest that his staff had secured for him. The bigger problem was how to screen the large audience that would attend his well-publicized speech to ensure that no one entered with a weapon. Vicki was insisting that attendees pass through magnetometers at the speech site. When his staff landed in Northern Ireland a week before the speech, they pressed security officials for the machines. At one point officials told them that they (the staffers) had erred in the invitations they distributed: they hadn't specified that attendees "should leave their personal weapons at home." That's because with tensions so high and violence so random, many people carried guns to protect themselves. The security forces eventually came through with two old magnetometers, though one didn't work, causing a long backup into the event. As attendees passed through the machines, the security forces found that many were, in fact, carrying guns, but they waived many of them through, vouching for their character. When staffers told Ted about it, he took the news in stride but suggested that they not tell his wife.

In his remarks Ted grew unusually personal as he sought to spur the parties toward peace. "Like so many of you here," he said in closing, "my family has been touched by tragedy. I know that the feelings of grief and loss are immediate—and they are enduring. The best way to ease these feelings is to forgive, and to carry on—not to lash out in fury, but to reach out in trust and hope." He then quoted from a letter that Joe Kennedy had written in 1958—at a time when Joe Jr. had been gone for more than a decade—to a friend who had just lost a son. "When one of your children goes out of your life," he wrote, "you think of what he might have done with a few more years and you wonder what you are going to do with the rest of yours. Then one day, because there is a world to be lived in, you

"He's Not Going to Hug Gerry Adams"

find yourself a part of it again, trying to accomplish something—something that he did not have time enough to do. And, perhaps, that is the reason for it all. I hope so."

When the parties completed their negotiations and announced their agreement on Good Friday of April 10, they launched a final phase of peacemaking that would climax in 2007, with Ted once more in Northern Ireland.

. . .

"You're very welcome here," Eileen Paisley, wife of the Rev. Ian Paisley, told Ted as they sat to witness the historic establishment of a coalition government in Northern Ireland.[10]

It was a startling sign of very changed times. For decades, as the *Boston Globe* put it, Paisley considered Ted "the embodiment of the interloping Irish-American politician who was biased in favor of Irish nationalists and against British loyalists such as Paisley." On May 8, 2007, however, Ted was warmly welcomed at the Stormont Assembly building in Belfast where he had come to watch Paisley (who ran the main political party of Northern Ireland's Protestants) and Martin McGuinness (a leading figure in Sinn Fein) be sworn in as first minister and deputy first minister, respectively, of Northern Ireland. President George W. Bush asked Ted to represent the United States at the ceremony, and he was among a mere handful of Americans in attendance.

The Good Friday Agreement announced peace, but it did not actually bring peace. An agreement between the British and Irish governments and a host of political parties in Northern Ireland, it called for a new executive and legislature for Northern Ireland to decide local issues and new institutions to foster cooperation between Ireland and Northern Ireland and between Ireland and Britain. Voters in Ireland and Northern Ireland approved the agreement overwhelmingly in May of 1998, but it was challenged almost immediately as the parties were slow to fulfill their obligations. The IRA refused to lay down its arms, and the unionists refused to form a government until it did. That August, an IRA-related bombing killed twenty-nine.

After three decades of effort to make peace, however, Ted refused to let it slip away. Publicly and behind the scenes, he pressed all sides to fulfill their obligations. "Teddy was a huge show of strength," recalled Bertie Ahern, Ireland's taoiseach at the time.[11] He worked the phones, pressing the IRA to abandon its weapons and the British to relinquish power. He also convinced Bush, who assumed office in 2001, to maintain Clinton's efforts and press all sides. When the IRA was linked to the gruesome murder of Robert McCartney, a thirty-three-year-old father of two, in January of 2005, Ted made a point of seeing McCartney's sisters when they were in Washington on St. Patrick's Day and refusing to see Adams, who was also in town.

Addressing a joint session of Congress in March of 2009, British Prime Minister Gordon Brown chose to say a few words about Ted, who was suffering from brain cancer and not on hand. "Northern Ireland today is at peace," Brown said, "more Americans have health care, children around the world are going to school, and for all those things, we owe a great debt to the life and course of Senator Edward Kennedy." Four decades earlier, Ted had outraged the British by calling "Ulster" their "Vietnam." Now, Brown announced, Queen Elizabeth II would bestow an honorary knighthood on him.

. . .

As Ted was celebrating peace at the Stormont ceremony, he was still trying to end America's war in Iraq.

21

"Can't Be a Bully in the World Schoolyard"

"This is Sharon!" Ted Kennedy roared one morning in the summer of 2002 inside a crowded Washington DC metro station during rush hour, as his unsuspecting foreign policy aide, Sharon Waxman, rode down the escalator. "She's going to stop the war!"[1]

Like Jack and Bobby, Ted liked to have fun. His humor was somewhat different than theirs, however. Jack's was usually sophisticated, surfacing in a wry comment or witty observation. Bobby's was often self-deprecating. Ted could be sophisticated and he could be self-deprecating but, far more often than his brothers, he was rollicking, if not outrageous. When, for instance, he was driving with family and staff to one of President Clinton's St. Patrick's Day parties at the White House, he announced, "You know what? I'm going in the front door. I used to go in the front gate when Jack was president and I'm going in the front gate."[2] When, rather than the visitor's gate, Ted's van reached the front, the guards looked inside, saw him in the front passenger seat, and, not surprisingly, waved him through.

Now he was savoring an unexpected opportunity to have some fun at a time when George W. Bush was beginning to hint at war with Iraq. Ted was heading to Washington from suburban Maryland, where he had attended a political event for his nephew, Mark Shriver, a candidate for Congress. Waxman, who was heading to her office, didn't know that he would be at the metro station and, after his good-natured teasing before a throng of commuters, she would now have to ride a train with him for ten stops until they reached Union Station, the stop nearest the Senate. "Can you imagine?" she later asked lightheartedly.[3]

For Ted it was an amusing moment at an ominous time. As he listened to President Bush, Vice President Cheney, and other top officials in the summer and fall of 2002, he feared a rerun of some of America's worst moments on the world stage. With the nation still shaken by the September 11 terrorist attacks of a year earlier, the White House was painting Iraq's Saddam Hussein as a dire threat to peace due to his chemical weapons and nuclear aspirations. Ted was particularly shaken by Cheney's speech in late August to the Veterans of Foreign Wars in which he warned that Saddam was enhancing his chemical and biological weapons and pursuing nuclear weapons with which to threaten his adversaries, and that he would "acquire nuclear weapons fairly soon."[4] To Ted, America was preparing to do battle in a land about which Washington had firmer beliefs than knowledge. Surveying the landscape, he thought about all that he had learned about the developing world since he set out for Africa in the 1950s, and about the fears, lies, ignorance, and blunders that drove the horror of Vietnam.

He must have considered the odds of stopping Bush's march to war as quite long because, a decade earlier, at a far less fearful time, he couldn't derail the efforts of an earlier Bush to make war with Iraq.

. . .

"I urge the Senate to reject the Orwellian argument that the only real hope for peace is for Congress to threaten war," Ted declared. "That is brinkmanship of the worst sort, and the U.S. Senate should not be an accomplice to it."

It was January 12, 1991, and the Senate was debating whether to authorize the first President Bush to use force to push Iraq's army out of Kuwait, which it had invaded the prior August. With the Cold War over after the Soviet collapse, Bush sought to create a "New World Order" under which the United States would preside as the world's lone superpower but also cooperate with other

"Can't Be a Bully"

powers to enforce the rule of law and maintain the peace. Reflecting that vision, Bush nourished a broad coalition of nations to support a U.S.-led military operation against Iraq. After convincing the UN Security Council to impose sanctions against Iraq and sending hundreds of thousands of troops to the Persian Gulf to protect Saudi Arabia and its oil fields (which could have been Saddam's next target), Bush set a January 15 deadline for Iraq to withdraw from Kuwait or face possible military action. When, a few days before the deadline, the Senate voted 52–47 to authorize military action, following a Security Council authorization in November, no one doubted what was coming next if Saddam didn't retreat.

With thoughts of Vietnam swirling in his head, Ted had announced his opposition to military action months earlier. When, in the early fall of 1990, the Foreign Relations Committee brought a resolution to the Senate to endorse Bush's actions to date, Ted was one of only three senators to oppose it as he raised the specter of a "Tonkin Gulf resolution for the Persian Gulf." When, in November, Bush sent more troops to the region, Ted warned against "a headlong course toward war."[5] In January he denounced the war authorization and thought that Washington should give sanctions more time to work—for he had seen sanctions work in South Africa, which by then had freed Nelson Mandela and was starting to chip away at apartheid. He also sharply criticized the diplomacy of Reagan and Bush that, he said, helped fuel the problem at hand. Under them, he said, America had cozied up to Saddam to counter Moscow's regional influence; sold him arms to counter Iran's regional ascendance; turned a blind's eye when he used poison gas on his own people; opposed congressional efforts to sanction him over his brutal human rights record; and suggested to him privately that it wouldn't respond if he invaded Kuwait.

"It is said," Ted told the Senate, "that the United States, with all our ideals and all our heritage and all our history, has now become the country that beats the drums of war, while other nations hold forth the olive branch of peace." It was not much different than what he and Bobby had said about Vietnam and what each had said about U.S. military action that they opposed in different parts of Latin America. Dismissing Bush's high-minded notion of a New World Order, Ted declared, "the principal reason driving the president's policy of war can be spelled out in three other letters: O-I-L—oil. Does anyone anywhere in this country seriously believe that 400,000 American troops would be stationed in the Persian Gulf on the brink of war today if there were no oil wells in Kuwait?"

After forty-two days of bombing and a ground invasion, the U.S.-led coalition forced Iraq from Kuwait in an overwhelmingly successful operation that caused few American casualties. Ted's fears of a Vietnam-style quagmire proved more prophetic when a second Bush ordered a second attack on Iraq.

. . .

"Maybe I should give a speech," Ted Kennedy mused to an aide on the Friday before Labor Day in 2002.[6]

He was growing antsy over White House signals that suggested the need for another military venture in Iraq. The terrorist attacks of a year earlier had left the nation reeling and Washington wondering how best to confront this kind of unconventional warfare, in which just one terrorist with, say, chemical weapons could wreak havoc. (Terrorism had been around for decades by then, causing death and destruction across the world, but mainland America had been largely untouched by it.) Even more frightening was the prospect that terrorists or terror-sponsoring states could acquire nuclear weapons and, with America as their target, kill millions and paralyze the nation.

What became far more controversial were administration efforts to tie al Qaeda's attacks of September 11 to Saddam. And what made the White House signals in the summer and fall of 2002 far more ominous was that Bush's foreign policy team included officials who thought that the first Bush had erred in not toppling Saddam in 1991—that, in essence, Saddam was a piece of unfinished business. "Bush, Cheney, [Deputy Defense Secretary Paul] Wolfowitz, and [Defense Secretary Donald] Rumsfeld, all had their eye on Saddam

"Can't Be a Bully"

Hussein," Ted said years later, "and were looking for an opportunity to topple him."[7] Nor was Ted assuaged by private assurances that summer from Clinton and Britain's chancellor of the exchequer, Gordon Brown, that Britain's prime minister, Tony Blair, had convinced Bush to take the issue of Saddam's weapons to the United Nations.

That summer and fall Ted acknowledged more than once that Saddam represented a clear danger, that he had used weapons of mass destruction before and could do so again, and that the world needed to deal with him. The issue was whether to maintain the UN search for his weapons or invade Iraq and take them by force. Under what scenario would Saddam more likely use those weapons: when he faced military action or when he didn't? That question took center stage when Ted interrogated Defense Secretary Donald Rumsfeld at a Senate Armed Services Committee hearing on September 19:

KENNEDY: What is the basis of your judgment that there's a higher risk if we don't go to war than if we do, since many [analysts] believe that Saddam will use the weapons of mass destruction if his back is against the wall and his regime is about to fall?

RUMSFELD: If the argument goes 'one must not do anything because he has weapons of sufficient power that they could impose destruction on us that would be at an unacceptable level,' then the next step would be that, if that's the conclusion, then in one year, two years, three years, and he has even more powerful weapons, a nuclear weapon, and longer-range capabilities, then he is able to use those weapons of terror to terrorize the rest of the world, including the United States. It's kind of like feeding an alligator hoping it eats you last.

KENNEDY: Many of the analysts believe, that when his back is against the wall, he'll throw everything at us, including weapons of mass destruction.

RUMSFELD: It's possible.

KENNEDY: It's very possible, you recognize. So it is possible; we'll leave it at that.

Three days of committee hearings in late September, with current and former military officials testifying, went a long way toward convincing Ted that Bush had not made the case for war. So, too, did scores of private conversations that he began holding with top military and diplomatic figures across the political spectrum—including Madeleine Albright, the former secretary of state; William Perry, the former defense secretary; Brent Scowcroft, Zbigniew Brzezinski, and Anthony Lake, all former national security advisors; John Deutch, the former CIA director; Generals Joseph Hoar, John Abizaid, and Wesley Clark; UN Secretary-General Kofi Annan; and a wide range of private experts.

After the public hearings and private conversations, Ted was sure that he wanted to speak out against military action.

. . .

"America should not go to war against Iraq," Ted declared on September 27 at the Johns Hopkins School of Advanced International Studies (SAIS) in Washington, "unless and until other reasonable alternatives are exhausted."

It was the first of several high-profile speeches that he would deliver both before and after the U.S.-led invasion in March of 2003. At the time of his speech at SAIS, he was a somewhat isolated figure in his party and the country. Facing congressional elections in November, Democrats worried about the political fallout as one of their leading figures opposed a popular president on an issue of war and peace. Perhaps swept up by the patriotic fervor of the time, the national media largely ignored his speech and dismissed his concerns. Bush was telling the nation that Saddam, his weapons, and his nuclear ambitions represented an unacceptable risk. Ted disagreed, and he wouldn't let the political exigencies of the time deter him.

"There is clearly a threat from Iraq," he said, "and there is clearly a danger, but the administration has not made a convincing case that we face such an imminent threat to our national security that a unilateral, pre-emptive American strike and an immediate war are necessary." He raised concerns that such a strike would threaten the

"Can't Be a Bully"

coalition of ninety nations that were helping the United States in Afghanistan; would shift America's "focus, resources, and energy" to Iraq before it had eliminated the threat from al Qaeda and assured a strong post-Taliban government in Kabul; and, as a largely unilateral American war in the Muslim world, would serve as a rallying cry for al Qaeda and other terrorist groups in their recruiting efforts. In the Senate Armed Services Committee hearings, Ted said, he saw no "persuasive evidence" that Saddam was about to acquire nuclear weapons or would transfer biological or chemical weapons to terrorists. Nor did he doubt that, with its overwhelming might, the United States could contain Iraq.

Ten days before Ted spoke at SAIS, Bush unveiled his new National Security Strategy, which stated that—due to the toxic mix of proliferating weapons of mass destruction and fanatical terrorists who might get their hands on them—Washington should not hesitate to take preemptive military action to address growing threats to its national security, that "in the new world we have entered, the only path to peace and security is the path of action."[8] Making the case against preemptive action, Ted recalled the frightening days in late October of 1962 when JFK learned that the Soviets had installed offensive nuclear missiles in Cuba. Just as Jack ignored the urgent calls of his military advisors to conduct airstrikes, took more measured steps, and brought the crisis to a peaceful conclusion, Ted argued that so, too, should the nation's leaders now take more measured steps to address Saddam's chemical weapons and nuclear aspirations.

Years later Ted said that his views about the war in Iraq largely reflected his views about war in general. They derived from the teachings of Saint Augustine, who established the theory of a "just war" in the fifth century, and Saint Thomas Aquinas, who fleshed out the theory further in the thirteenth century. War, Ted believed, "must have a just cause . . . must be declared by a legitimate authority . . . must be driven by the right intention . . . must be a last resort . . . must be proportional . . . [and] must have a reasonable chance of success."[9] The 2003 war in Iraq, he believed, failed on virtually every measure.

Ted's case didn't change much from the run-up to war in the fall of 2002 to the chaos that ensued after the U.S.-led coalition invaded the following March, toppled Saddam, and tried to create a new democratic government. What did change, dramatically, was his view of the motives of those who sent America's troops into battle.

· · ·

"Let me say it plainly," Ted declared at the start of his SAIS speech in September of 2002. "I not only concede, but I am convinced that President Bush believes genuinely in the course he urges upon us."

Around that time, Ted applauded when Bush announced that he would take his case against Saddam to the United Nations and when he chose to make his case for war in a televised address to the nation. In a Senate speech of October, he echoed the words of his SAIS speech in vouching for Bush's motives.

Nevertheless, Ted was worried by the signs that Bush planned to exploit the war issue that fall to help Republicans pick up congressional seats in the November elections. That Bush forced Congress to vote before the elections on whether to authorize him to use force, that the Senate passed the measure on a 77–23 vote on October 10 (with Ted in the minority), that Bush's operatives questioned the character of Democrats who criticized his march to war, and that Republicans picked up two Senate seats and eight House seats that fall (bucking historical trends in which the president's party usually loses seats in mid-term congressional elections) left Ted fuming.

The events of that fall so distressed him, in fact, that he developed a distinct nostalgia for how the first President Bush shepherded the nation to war a decade earlier—however strongly Ted opposed that war as well. "In 1991," he wrote years later, "the administration of the first President Bush timed the vote on the use of military force against Iraq to occur *after* midterm elections, in order to de-politicize the decision."[10]

"Can't Be a Bully"

Frustrated by the rush to war, unconvinced by the arguments for it, embittered by the politics around it, and fearful of the global consequences, Ted lashed out at Bush and his team in increasingly fiery language.

. . .

"This was made up in Texas, announced in January to the Republican leadership that war was going to take place and was going to be good politically," Ted told the Associated Press in September of 2003, as Iraq was unraveling six months after the invasion. "This whole thing was a fraud."[11]

Like water surging through a dam, Ted's frustration of the previous year burst forth. As the nation approached and then went to war, he denounced it in ever-angrier terms. At the National Press Club in January of 2003, he warned that Iraq would be "the wrong war at the wrong time" by distracting America from the far more immediate threat of terrorism and North Korea's nuclear progress.[12] Days later at Harvard, he dismissed Bush's approach to Iraq as "chip-on-the-shoulder foreign policy" and said the administration's "case for war would be laughed out of the courtroom."[13]

When, at the United Nations in February, Secretary of State Colin Powell outlined the evidence that, with his weapons of mass destruction, Saddam had violated UN resolutions, Ted praised Powell but called on the administration to explain the likely human costs of war in terms of American lives lost and Iraqi refugees created. When Bush tied his efforts to defend America from Saddam to JFK's efforts to defend America from the Soviets during the Cuban Missile Crisis, Ted explained that, unlike Bush, Jack understood that "war must always be the last resort."[14] As Bush, in March, vowed to disarm Saddam with or without UN backing, Ted declared that America "cannot be a bully in the world schoolyard and expect cooperation [and] support from the rest of the world."[15]

The administration's failure to plan adequately for the aftermath of Saddam's fall, and the failure of coalition forces to find his weapons of mass destruction, triggered even fiercer denunciations from the senator. In July he returned to SAIS to condemn a "case for war . . . based on shoddy intelligence, hyped intelligence, and even false intelligence." He said that Bush's postwar policy was "built on a quicksand of false assumptions," and that America's troops were like "police officers in a shooting gallery" who were paying the price for the administration's "ideological pride."[16] By then, it was but a short step to Ted's audacious remark of September about the "fraud" of war. In June of 2006, he told a Massachusetts Democratic Party convention, "My vote against this misbegotten war is the best vote I have cast in the United States Senate since I was elected in 1962."

As with Vietnam, he never lost sight of the war's collateral damage—the lives disrupted and refugees created—and, despite his anger, he worked with the administration in 2007 to address a key aspect of that damage.

. . .

"My son and I were dragged out of the cab of our truck," a former Iraqi driver who had delivered water to America's troops told Ted at his Senate Judiciary subcommittee hearing in January of 2007.

"We were positioned face down on the side of the road by a group of terrorists. . . . They kept saying to me, 'Don't work with the Americans,' and one of them struck me in the face with the butt of his gun, permanently damaging my jaw. Another man twisted my son's arm so severely that he broke it. They knew my name and instructed me that this was a warning and that I would be killed if I continued assisting the Americans. After they made their threat they departed, leaving us bloodied on the side of the road."

Notwithstanding his views about the war, Ted believed that, as he said at the hearing, "we owe a special duty to protect all of [the Iraqis] and their loved ones who are being targeted by insurgents and sectarian death squads because of their faith or their association with the United States." He held the hearing as part of his drive to boost the number of Iraqi refugees—the millions of people who fled or were forced from their homes—that America would accept and to

"Can't Be a Bully"

give special preference to the drivers, cooks, translators, interpreters, and others who risked their lives to help the troops.

He aired the issue in a *Washington Post* op-ed in late 2006, calling for a U.S. and global effort. He met with Secretary of State Condoleezza Rice to float the idea of an international meeting on the refugees, and, with her support, he arranged to see UN Secretary General Ban Ki-moon in New York. Upon learning in the meantime that, as a teenager, Ban had met President Kennedy, Ted mailed him a framed picture of the two that his staff found at the JFK Library. After Ted's subsequent get-together with Ban, during which Ban regaled him with warm memories of Jack, the United Nations held its international meeting on the refugees, which top State Department officials attended, in April of 2007 in Geneva. Ted introduced legislation; secured bipartisan support; worked quietly with Ryan Crocker, America's ambassador to Iraq; and secured the assistance of such disparate figures as Ken Bacon, president of Refugees International, and David Keene, president of the American Conservative Union.

In January of 2008 President Bush signed legislation to make it easier for Iraqis to resettle in America and to give special consideration for those who risked their lives to help the United States.

. . .

After months of blasting Bush, questioning his honesty, motives, and judgment, Ted Kennedy received a letter from the president's father, George H. W. Bush, who wrote to say that the criticism was unduly harsh.

Rather than write back, Ted decided to call. He told the elder Bush by phone that he appreciated the letter, understood why the former president felt that way, and would keep his thoughts in mind as the debate ensued.

The elder Bush, who had endured his share of political battles over the years, held no personal animus toward Ted, however. Less than a month after he termed the war a "fraud," the Bush Presidential Library Foundation announced that Ted would receive the 2003

George Bush Award for Excellence in Public Service—and that the former president would present the $20,000 prize and crystal trophy to him. "Senator Kennedy has consistently and courageously fought for his principles," said the foundation's executive director, Roman Popadiuk, "and has rightly earned the respect of his Senate colleagues on both sides of the aisle. His commitment to excellence in public policy and his devotion to public service serve as an inspiration to all Americans."[17]

Nor, for all his cutting words about George W. Bush, did Ted hold a grudge against the president. However deeply he opposed the war, he saw an opportunity to work with the administration, with lawmakers of both parties, and with influential figures in the private sector to address Iraq's mounting refugee crisis and the injustice faced by those who had helped America's troops.

With one more chance to shape America's global role, Ted Kennedy used all the skills he inherited from Honey Fitz to bring it to fruition.

Epilogue

What If?

With the first two gunned down in the prime of life and the third struck down by cancer while old but hardly enfeebled, the "what if" questions about Jack, Bobby, and Ted surface quickly in any discussion of their lives.

We don't know for sure what they would have done later about the challenges they were facing, or the challenges to come, or other challenges they might have created through their own actions. Nevertheless, their hopes and fears, personalities and propensities, and beliefs and activities suggest that they might well have shaped America's empire in significantly different ways than their successors and that, alas, America might—might—have sidestepped a fiasco or two.

For Jack, the biggest "what if" involves Vietnam. A Cold Warrior to the end, he was always concerned about communism's advances and freedom's losses around the world, so he would have been reluctant to withdraw without some confidence that the South could stand on its own. For more than a decade before his death, however, he was keenly concerned about rising nationalism across the developing world, and about the grassroots resentment that a sizable U.S. military footprint in Asia, Africa, or Latin America would nourish. In the months before his death, he relayed his intention to withdraw from Vietnam after his reelection to top administration officials and senior lawmakers, and he directed officials to plan for it.

At the time Jack hoped to capitalize on his limited test-ban treaty to nourish more U.S.-Soviet arms control and reduce big-power tension. He also expressed interest in, and took tentative steps toward, outreach to communist China. In a second term Jack may have spearheaded (thus, speeding up) the debate that Bobby and Ted later drove about rewriting America's hardline policies toward China.

With both Moscow and Beijing supporting the North in Vietnam, making the war a sizable obstacle to Jack's big-power agenda, he might have considered an American withdrawal from Vietnam a necessary step toward the "genuine peace" that he envisioned at American University.

· · ·

Jack would have been seventy-two in 1989, the year that the Soviet empire began to crumble, bringing the Cold War to an end shortly thereafter.

Amid the euphoria, he likely would have cautioned against predictions of the "end of history"—a popular hope of the time—with U.S.-led freedom and democracy likely to sweep the world, ushering in greater peace and prosperity.[1] A student of history and a keen observer of different cultures, he likely would have warned that freedom and democracy were not inevitable, certainly not in the short term, in Russia; in the former Soviet republics; in Eastern Europe; or in the developing world.

He also might have reminded everyone that China remained in communist hands, that Beijing had just cracked down brutally on freedom at Tiananmen Square, and that, despite the conventional wisdom of the time, economic liberalization in China might not inevitably force political freedom.

· · ·

In late 1990, as the first President Bush was laying the groundwork for ousting Saddam from Iraq, Jack would have been seventy-three and, that November, Bobby would have turned sixty-five. How they would have viewed Bush's efforts is an interesting question.

If Jack had withdrawn from Vietnam, and America had avoided the horror of war that it experienced under LBJ and Nixon, then perhaps all three Kennedy brothers would have thought better of Bush's decision to use force than Ted actually did at the time. They would have weighed the benefits of ensuring global order against the uncertainty of a large American military footprint in the turbulent world of the Middle East.

In late 2002, as the second President Bush was beating the drums for another U.S.-led invasion of Iraq—this time as part of a "war on terror"—Jack would have been eighty-five and, that November, Bobby would have turned seventy-seven. A year earlier they surely would have joined Ted in supporting America's military action in Afghanistan in response to the terrorist attacks of September 11. Since they were UN enthusiasts, they just as surely would have supported Bush's efforts to highlight Saddam's flouting of UN resolutions about his weapons of mass destruction. Nevertheless, like Ted, they would have raised serious questions about whether the United States should take preemptive military action against Iraq, what it would cost in lives and treasure, and what might follow Saddam's demise.

In the absence of a Vietnam horror, however, and in the aftermath of the first Bush's success in Iraq, they might not have feared a second Iraq venture as much as Ted actually did at the time.

. . .

The Arab Spring, which began in late 2010 in Tunisia and spread from northern Africa to the Middle East, would have excited Jack (if he were still alive at ninety-three), Bobby (at eighty-five), and Ted (at seventy-eight).

They would have recognized what Jack, back in 1957 in connection with Algeria, had called "man's eternal desire to be free and independent," and they likely would have supported the pro-democracy protestors with more verbal vigor and behind-the-scenes help than President Obama actually did.

The progression from Jack's Alliance for Progress and outreach to Africa, to Bobby's denunciation of Soviet rule and "ripple of hope" speech in Cape Town, to Ted's efforts to restore democracy in Chile and secure freedom for dissidents in authoritarian lands, and—then—to the brothers' support for millions of people seeking better lives during the Arab Spring is an easy one to envision.

. . .

With the rise of a hostile, revanchist Russia under Vladimir Putin, all three brothers certainly would have derided President Trump's refusal to recognize Russian interference in America's elections and, especially, his vocal support for Putin's denials over the conclusions of U.S. intelligence agencies.

Presuming that Ted had lived long enough to witness Trump's immigration-related actions at America's southern border, he surely would have denounced family separation and child abuse from a humanitarian perspective. He would have denounced them from a geopolitical perspective as well by arguing that Trump's policies were damaging America's global image, thus undermining its ability to promote freedom and democracy around the world.

Whether Jack, as an ex-president; Bobby, as a senator after Jack's second term or in another line of work; or Ted, from his Senate perch, would have wielded enough influence to reshape America's action in Iraq, during the Arab Spring, or at the southern border are still more "what ifs" to ponder.

. . .

Iconic figures in their own time, we are left to consider what might have been—how Jack and Bobby might have further remade America's empire if they were not struck down in the spring of their lives, and how Ted might have continued doing so if the autumn of his life had lasted a bit longer.

Notes

Prologue

1. Frank R. Kelley, "*Athenia* Survivors Angrily Shout for U.S. Warship Convoy Home," *New York Herald Tribune*, September 8, 1939, 1; "*Athenia* Survivors Demand a Convoy," *New York Times*, September 8, 1939, 14.

2. Renehan, *Kennedys at War*, 111–12.

3. Kelley, "*Athenia* Survivors Angrily Shout," 1; "*Athenia* Survivors Demand," 14.

4. Amanda Smith, *Hostage to Fortune*, 370.

5. Renehan, *Kennedys at War*, 111–13; Swift, *Kennedys Amidst*, 192–93.

6. Schlesinger, *Robert Kennedy and His Times*, 12.

7. Although America's leading media called China's capital by the Westernized name of "Peking" until well into the 1980s, I am using the name "Beijing," which China itself adopted much earlier, throughout the book to avoid confusion.

1. "Like Carbonated Water"

1. Amanda Smith, *Hostage to Fortune*, 468–71.

2. Schlesinger, *A Thousand Days*, 79.

3. Rose Kennedy, *Times to Remember*, 112.

4. Rose Kennedy, *Times to Remember*, 7.

5. Jean Kennedy Smith, *The Nine of Us*, 23.

6. Kevin Cullen, "An Upbringing That Groomed the Clan for Public Service," *Irish Times*, August 27, 2009, https://www.irishtimes.com/news/an-upbringing-that-groomed-the-clan-for-public-service-1.726414?mode=print&ot=example.AjaxPageLayout.ot.

7. Kirk LeMoyne Billings, recorded interview by Dan B. Jacobs, March 25, 1964, 13–14, John F. Kennedy Library Oral History Program.

8. Lincoln, *My Twelve Years*, 97.

9. Amanda Smith, *Hostage to Fortune*, xxv.

10. Bzdek, *Kennedy Legacy*, 17.

11. Charles Spalding, recorded interview by John F. Stewart, on March 14, 1968, 3, John F. Kennedy Library Oral History Program.

12. Rose Kennedy, *Times to Remember*, 372.

13. Pitts, *Jack and Lem*, 74.

14. Amanda Smith, *Hostage to Fortune*, 190.

15. Amanda Smith, *Hostage to Fortune*, 318.

16. Renehan, *Kennedys at War*, 101.

17. Dallek, *An Unfinished Life*, 3.

18. Edward M. Gallagher, recorded interview by Ed Martin, January 8, 1965, 22, John F. Kennedy Library Oral History Program.

19. Amanda Smith, *Hostage to Fortune*, 161.

20. Goodwin, *Fitzgeralds and the Kennedys*, 550.

21. Arthur Krock, recorded interview by Charles Bartlett, May 10, 1964, 14, John F. Kennedy Library Oral History Program.

22. Schlesinger, *Robert Kennedy and His Times*, 14.

23. Edward M. Gallagher, recorded interview.

24. Amanda Smith, *Hostage to Fortune*, 227–28.

25. Swift, *Kennedys Amidst*, 220.

26. Goodwin, *Fitzgeralds and the Kennedys*, 713.

2. "My Experience Was the War"

1. Shaw, *JFK in the Senate*, 15.

2. Arthur Krock, "Trial Loan for Year Suggested for Europe," *New York Times*, September 14, 1947, E3.

3. Krock, "Trial Loan for Year," E3.

4. Amanda Smith, *Hostage to Fortune*, 538.

5. Rose Kennedy, *Times to Remember*, 283.

6. Charles Spalding, recorded interview by John F. Stewart, on March 14, 1968, 4, John F. Kennedy Library Oral History Program; Matthews, *Bobby Kennedy*, 7.

7. Aldous, *Schlesinger*, 281.

8. Rose Kennedy, *Times to Remember*, 100–101.

9. Dallek, *An Unfinished Life*, 70.

10. Renehan, *Kennedys at War*, 11.

11. Rose Kennedy, *Times to Remember*, 123.

12. Amanda Smith, *Hostage to Fortune*, 120, 147.

13. Rose Kennedy, *Times to Remember*, 169.

14. Cari Beauchamp, "Two Sons, One Destiny," *Vanity Fair*, December 2004, https://www.vanityfair.com/news/2004/12/kennedy-200412.

15. Goodwin, *Fitzgeralds and the Kennedys*, 306.

16. Amanda Smith, *Hostage to Fortune*, 96.

17. Amanda Smith, *Hostage to Fortune*, 410.

18. Schlesinger, *Robert Kennedy and His Times*, 13.

19. Library Foundation, *Rose Kennedy's Family Album*, 71.

20. Rose Kennedy, *Times to Remember*, 304.

21. Goodwin, *Fitzgeralds and the Kennedys*, 807.

22. John F. Kennedy, *Profiles in Courage*, 9–10.

23. George Tames, Oral History Project, United States Senate, https://www.senate .gov/artandhistory/history/oral_history/George_Tames.htm.

24. Leamer, *The Kennedy Men*, 101.

25. John F. Kennedy, *Why England Slept*, 182.

26. Jean Kennedy Smith, *The Nine of Us*, 21–22.

27. John F. Kennedy, *Prelude to Leadership*, 119.

28. Leamer, *The Kennedy Men*, 122.

29. "Peace in Our Time," *Harvard Crimson*, October 9, 1939, https://www.thecrimson .com/article/1939/10/9/peace-in-our-time-pmilitant-democratic/. The opening sentence of the online copy reads, "Militant democratic sympathy brands immediately as heresy and concessions to the ogre Hitler," but that's neither grammatical nor understandable. Reflecting the spirit of the piece, the word "and" was likely supposed to be "any."

30. John F. Kennedy, *Why England Slept*, 18.

31. John F. Kennedy, *Why England Slept*, 22.

32. John F. Kennedy, *Why England Slept*, 100.

33. John F. Kennedy, *Prelude to Leadership*, xxiv.

34. Schlesinger, *A Thousand Days*, 87.

35. Amanda Smith, *Hostage to Fortune*, 551.

36. Schlesinger, *A Thousand Days*, 86.

37. "John F. Kennedy and PT 109," John F. Kennedy Presidential Library and Museum, https://www.jfklibrary.org/JFK/JFK-in-History/John-F-Kennedy-and-PT109.aspx.

38. Leamer, *The Kennedy Men*, 194.

39. Amanda Smith, *Hostage to Fortune*, 553–54.

40. Shaw, *JFK in the Senate*, 15–16.

41. John F. Kennedy, *Prelude to Leadership*, 49.

42. John F. Kennedy, *Prelude to Leadership*, Appendix C.

43. Papers of John F. Kennedy. Personal Papers. Boston Office, 1940–1956: Personal File. Hearst Newspapers, International News Service, April 25–July 28, 1945, and John F. Kennedy, *Prelude to Leadership*, 6.

44. Dallek, *An Unfinished Life*, 51.

45. John F. Kennedy, *Prelude to Leadership*, 58.

3. "Like a Seventeenth-Century Jesuit Priest"

1. Amanda Smith, *Hostage to Fortune*, 97.

2. Fay, *Pleasure of His Company*, 156–57.

3. Amanda Smith, *Hostage to Fortune*, 635.

4. Thomas, *Robert Kennedy*, 30.

5. Edward M. Kennedy, *True Compass*, 28.

6. Schlesinger, *Robert Kennedy and His Times*, 63.

7. Newfield, *Robert Kennedy*, 18.

8. Schlesinger, *Robert Kennedy and His Times*, 23.

9. Thomas, *Robert Kennedy*, 53.

10. Richard Nixon, interviewed by Pat Buchanan, "Crossfire," CNN, November 9, 1982, https://www.youtube.com/watch?v=MacmN1EtIPQ.

11. Robert F. Kennedy, "A Critical Analysis of the Conference at Yalta, February 4–11, 1945," University of Virginia Law School, n.d..

12. Robert Kennedy, "British Hated by Both Sides," *Boston Post*, June 3, 1948, 1; Robert Kennedy, "Jews Have Fine Fighting Force," *Boston Post*, June 4, 1948, 1; Robert Kennedy, "British Position Hit in Palestine," *Boston Post*, June 5, 1948, 1; and Robert Kennedy, "Communism Not to Get Foothold," *Boston Post*, June 6, 1948, 1.

13. Hersh, *Edward Kennedy*, 57–58.

14. Papers of John F. Kennedy. Personal Papers. Boston Office, 1940–1956: Personal File. 1951 travel journal: bk. 2, October–November, 1951.

4. "The Knife Itself Is Still in His Fist"

1. Senate Subcommittee, "Control of Trade," 18.

2. Dallek, *An Unfinished Life*, 221.

3. "Robert Kennedy Urges U.S. Caution in Russian Deals," *Daily Boston Globe*, September 16, 1955, 9.

4. Harry Schwartz, "Russia's Iron Curtain Lifting—Just a Little," *New York Times*, August 7, 1955, E3.

5. Robert F. Kennedy, "The Soviet Brand of Colonialism," *New York Times Magazine*, April 8, 1956, SM15.

6. John Harris, "Iron Curtain Lifted for 2 Americans," *Daily Boston Globe*, July 17, 1955, C1.

7. "Robert Kennedy Finds Segregation in Soviet Schools," *Daily Boston Globe*, October 18, 1955, 5.

8. John F. Kennedy, "Report on Communist-Controlled Poland."

5. "The Hour Is Late"

1. Amanda Smith, *Hostage to Fortune*, 643.

2. Edward M. Kennedy, "Newly-Independent Morocco Undergoes the Painful Adjustments of Freedom," International News Service Features, September 17, 1956, Box 033, Joseph P. Kennedy Personal papers, John F. Kennedy Presidential Library and Museum.

3. Hersh, *Edward Kennedy*, xi.

4. Clymer, *Edward M. Kennedy*, 13.

5. Hersh, *Edward Kennedy*, 113.

6. Bzdek, *Kennedy Legacy*, 30.

7. Amanda Smith, *Hostage to Fortune*, 471.

8. Leamer, *The Kennedy Men*, 165.

9. Library Foundation, *Rose Kennedy's Family Album*, 287.

10. Rose Kennedy, *Times to Remember*, 356.

11. Library Foundation, *Rose Kennedy's Family Album*, 268.

12. Hersh, *Edward Kennedy*, 93.

13. John F. Kennedy, "A Democrat."

14. Riggs, "Counter-Insurgency Lessons," 1.

15. Frank Kelley, "Kennedy Talk on Algeria Stirs Protest in France," *New York Herald Tribune*, July 4, 1957, B10; Russell Baker, "Kennedy Urges U.S. Back Independence for Algeria," *New York Times*, July 3, 1957, 1.

16. Judd, "Special Study Mission," 44.

17. Roger Hilsman, letter to Charles U. Daly, John F. Kennedy Presidential Library and Museum, May 5, 2000.

18. Dallek, *An Unfinished Life*, 288.

6. "If It Wasn't for the Russians"

1. Reeves, *President Kennedy*, 100.

2. To a significant extent, JFK's "flexible response" strategy reflected the vision that General Maxwell Taylor, on whom Jack would rely heavily as president, articulated in his book of 1960, *The Uncertain Trumpet* (New York: Harper and Row).

3. Reeves, *President Kennedy*, 41.

4. Jack L. Bell, recorded interview by Joseph E. O'Connor, April 19, 1966, 41–42, John F. Kennedy Library Oral History Program. Jack not only assumed that his aides were smart, but they also told him so. On the day of the invasion, National Security Advisor McGeorge Bundy joked to JFK in the Oval Office that because he and other key aides were former professors, "this was bound to be all right." See McGeorge Bundy, recorded interview by Richard Neustadt, March, 1964, 26, John F. Kennedy Library Oral History Program.

5. Pitts, *Jack and Lem*, 215.

6. Dallek, *An Unfinished Life*, 366.

7. Barry M. Goldwater, recorded interview by Jack Bell, January 24, 1965, 16, John F. Kennedy Library Oral History Program.

8. Dean Acheson, recorded interview by Lucius D. Battle, April 27, 1964, 12–13, John F. Kennedy Library Oral History Program.

9. Sir Howard Beale, recorded interview by Elspeth Davies Rostow, April 16, 1964, 8, John F. Kennedy Library Oral History Program.

10. Henry Brandon, recorded interview by Joseph E. O'Connor, February 7, 1967, 9–10, John F. Kennedy Library Oral History Program.

11. Sidey, *John F. Kennedy*, 11.

12. Sidey, *John F. Kennedy*, 140–41.

13. Charles E. Bohlen, recorded interview by Arthur M. Schlesinger, May 21, 1964, 15–16, John F. Kennedy Library Oral History Program.

14. Sidey, *John F. Kennedy*, 46.

15. Sidey, *John F. Kennedy*, 156–57.

16. Schlesinger, *Robert Kennedy and His Times*, 452.

17. Shesol, *Mutual Contempt*, 71.

18. John F. Kennedy, *Prelude to Leadership*, xliv.

19. "Special Group (Counter-Insurgency)," GlobalSecurity.org, https://www.globalsecurity.org/intell/ops/covert-action-sg-ci.htm.

20. Dallek, *An Unfinished Life*, 439.

21. Shesol, *Mutual Contempt*, 128.

22. Pitts, *Jack and Lem*, 220.

23. John F. Kennedy, *Prelude to Leadership*, xxxi.

24. Reeves, *President Kennedy*, 173.

25. Guthman and Shulman, *Robert Kennedy*, 258.

26. Dallek, *An Unfinished Life*, 426.

27. Edward Kennedy, "Latin America to Go Red? Crisis Is On," *Boston Globe*, September 17, 1961, A7. His next four articles for the *Globe* were "Communists Go All Out to Win Latins," September 18, 1961, 12; "Hunger, Despair Make Politics," September 19, 1961, 16; "Uncle Sam's Vital Task—Providing Bootstraps," September 20, 1961, 12; and "What Must Be Done to Defeat Communism," September 21, 1961, 42.

28. Edward M. Kennedy interview, March 23–24, 2005, Edward M. Kennedy Oral History Project, Miller Center, University of Virginia.

29. Edward M. Kennedy, *True Compass*, 163.

30. Leonard Ingalls, "Democrats Begin Study of Africa," *New York Times*, December 5, 1960, 5.

31. "Ted Goes Over Big in Africa, Flying Home," *Boston Globe*, December 11, 1960, 36.

7. "Whether a Free Society Can Compete"

1. Guthman and Shulman, *Robert Kennedy*, 37.

2. Dudziak, "Desegregation," 83.

3. Muehlenbeck, "John F. Kennedy's Courting," 8.

4. Reeves, *President Kennedy*, 125.

5. McWhorter, "Enduring Courage," 67–69, and Sperber, *Murrow*, 616.

6. "Alabama and the Cold War," *New York Times*, May 23, 1961, 38.

7. James Williams, "49 Miles of Highway and No Place to Stop and Eat," *Baltimore Afro-American*, October 7, 1961, 20.

8. Dudziak, "Birmingham, Addis Ababa," 187.

9. W. H. Lawrence, "Ribicoff is Named to Welfare Post in Next Cabinet," *New York Times*, December 2, 1960, 1.

10. Teodoro Moscoso, recorded interview by Leigh Miller, May 25, 1964, John F. Kennedy Library Oral History Program.

11. Paul B. Fay Jr., recorded interview by James A. Oesterle, November 11, 1970, 237, John F. Kennedy Library Oral History Program.

12. "The Founding Moment," Peace Corps, https://www.peacecorps.gov/about/history /founding-moment/.

13. Thanat Khoman, recorded interview by Ivan Campbell, October 28, 1964, 5–6, John F. Kennedy Library Oral History Program.

14. Shannon, "'One of Our Greatest Psychological Assets,'" 772.

15. Robert F. Kennedy, *Just Friends*, 157.

16. Wernher Von Braun, recorded interview by Walter D. Sohier and Eugene M. Emme, March 31, 1964, 3–4, John F. Kennedy Library Oral History Program.

17. Theodore C. Sorenson, recorded interview by Carl Kaysen, March 26, 1964, 1, John F. Kennedy Library Oral History Program.

18. Hale Boggs, recorded interview by Charles T. Morrissey, May 10, 1964, 14, John F. Kennedy Library Oral History Program.

8. "R. Kennedy Was Very Upset"

1. Paul B. Fay Jr., recorded interview by James A. Oesterle, November 9, 1970, 29, John F. Kennedy Library Oral History Program.

2. George W. Anderson Jr., recorded interview by Joseph E. O'Connor, April 25, 1967, 3–4, John F. Kennedy Library Oral History Program.

3. Dallek, *An Unfinished Life*, 555.

4. Thomas, "Bobby at the Brink."

5. Reeves, *President Kennedy*, 306.

6. Office of the Historian, "Letter from President Kennedy to Chairman Khrushchev," https://history.state.gov/historicaldocuments/frus1961-63v06/d60.

7. Thomas, "Bobby at the Brink."

8. Tom Wicker, "Cuba Emerges as an Issue as Fall Campaign Begins to Roll Throughout U.S.," *New York Times*, October 1, 1962, 12.

9. Thomas, "Bobby at the Brink."

10. Dallek, *An Unfinished Life*, 549.

11. Thomas, "Bobby at the Brink."

12. Robert F. Kennedy, *Thirteen Days*, 69–70.

13. "Cuban Missile Crisis Record of Meeting, Washington, October 19, 1962, 11 a.m.," The Avalon Project, Yale Law School, http://avalon.law.yale.edu/20th_century/msc _cuba031.asp.

14. Divine, *Cuban Missile Crisis*, 43–45.

15. Reeves, *President Kennedy*, 421.

16. Edward M. Kennedy, *True Compass*, 189.

17. Edward M. Kennedy, *True Compass*, 189–90.

18. Stacey Chandler, "A Mother's Day Tale: Rose Kennedy, Nikita Khrushchev, & the Search for a Signature," Archivally Speaking: An Inside Look at the JFK Library Archives, John F. Kennedy President Library and Museum (blog), May 10, 2013, https://archiveblog .jfklibrary.org/2013/05/a-mothers-day-tale-rose-kennedys-signature-collection/.

19. Clymer, *Edward M. Kennedy*, 33.

20. Clymer, *Edward M. Kennedy*, 39.

21. Anthony Lewis, "Edward Kennedy Tours Red Berlin," *New York Times*, February 24, 1962, 2.

22. George Cabot Lodge interview, July 8, 2005, Edward M. Kennedy Oral History Project, Miller Center, University of Virginia.

23. Harold Brown, recorded interview, June 25, 1964, 8, John F. Kennedy Library Oral History Program.

24. John F. Kennedy, *Strategy of Peace*, 51.

25. Schlesinger, *A Thousand Days*, 482–83.

26. Office of the Historian, "Telegram from the Department of State to the Embassy in the Soviet Union," https://history.state.gov/historicaldocuments/frus1961-63v06/d69; Office of the Historian, "Letter from Chairman Khrushchev to President Kennedy," https://history.state.gov/historicaldocuments/frus1961-63v06/d71.

9. "George, You're Just Crazier Than Hell!"

1. Roger Hilsman, letter to Charles U. Daly, John F. Kennedy Presidential Library and Museum, May 5, 2000.

2. Reeves, *President Kennedy*, 30–31; Dallek, *An Unfinished Life*, 304–5.

3. Sorenson, *Kennedy*, 644.

4. Wehrle, "'A Good, Bad Deal,'" 356.

5. George W. Ball, recorded interview by Larry J. Hackman, February 16, 1968, 8, John F. Kennedy Library Oral History Program.

6. Sempa, "A New Take," https://thediplomat.com/2018/10/a-new-take-on-general-macarthurs-warning-to-jfk-to-avoid-a-land-war-in-asia/.

7. Maxwell D. Taylor, recorded interview by Larry Hackman, on November 13, 1969, 47, Robert Kennedy Oral History Program of the John F. Kennedy Library.

8. Guthman and Shulman, *Robert Kennedy*, 394.

9. Schlesinger, *Robert Kennedy and His Times*, 705.

10. Robert F. Kennedy, *Just Friends*, 17–18; Schlesinger, *Robert Kennedy and His Times*, 712–13; and "Robert Kennedy Assures Vietnam," *New York Times*, February 19, 1962, 1.

11. Robert F. Kennedy, *Just Friends*, 18.

12. Reeves, *President Kennedy*, 484.

13. Schlesinger, *Robert Kennedy and His Times*, 711.

14. Reeves, *President Kennedy*, 450.

15. Hilsman, "The Situation."

16. David Halberstam, "Mansfield Is Cool on Vietnam War," *New York Times*, December 3, 1962, 12.

17. Office of the Historian, "Report by the Senate Majority Leader (Mansfield)."

18. Clymer, *Edward M. Kennedy*, 50.

19. Michael V. Forrestal, recorded interview by Joseph Kraft, August 14, 1964, 137, John F. Kennedy Library Oral History Program.

20. "Ms. Nhu Calls Kennedy Appeaser," *New York Times*, September 12, 1963, 1; David Binder, "Ms. Ngo Dinh Nhu Lays a Plot to 6, Including Times Reporter," *New York Times*, September 13, 1963, 3; "Mrs. Nhu Sees Senator Kennedy at Lunch in Belgrade," *New York Times*, September 14, 1963, 1; "Mme Nhu Blames Kennedy," *Boston Globe*, September 18, 1963, 10; Colby Itkowitz, "'The Dragon Lady': How Madame Nhu helped escalate the Vietnam War," *Washington Post*, September 26, 2017, https://www.washingtonpost.com/news/retropolis/wp/2017/09/26/the-dragon-lady-how-madame-nhu-helped-escalate-the-vietnam-war/?utm_term=.0ed38d522142.

21. Office of the Historian, "Memorandum of Conversation."

22. Selverstone, "It's a Date," 485–86.

10. "I Wouldn't Be My Grandfather's Grandson"

1. John Moors Cabot, recorded interview by William W. Moss, January 27, 1971, 22, John F. Kennedy Library Oral History Program.

2. Walter Sheridan, recorded interview by Roberta W. Greene, May 1, 1970, 11, John F. Kennedy Library Oral History Program.

3. Nicholas Katzenbach interview, November 29, 2005, Edward M. Kennedy Oral History Project, Miller Center, University of Virginia.

4. Rafael Steinberg, "Kennedy Is in Tokyo for Sukarno Talks," *Washington Post*, January 17, 1964, A15.

5. Sodhy, "Malaysian-American Relations," 115.

6. Douglass, *JFK and the Unspeakable*, 377.

7. Emerson Chapin, "Robert Kennedy Ends Tokyo Visit," *New York Times*, January 19, 1964, 16.

8. Guthman, *We Band of Brothers*, 249.

9. Kempton, "Pure Irish," 10.

10. Edward M. Kennedy, *True Compass*, 211.

11. "Chant of 'Bobby, Bobby' Greets RFK in Germany," *Boston Globe*, June 26, 1964, 10.

12. "JFK Berlin Plaque Dedicated," *Washington Post*, June 27, 1964, A13.

13. "Soviet Pact on Germany Denounced," *Baltimore Sun*, June 27, 1964, 1.

14. Arthur J. Olsen, "Kennedy's Visit Jolts Regime in Poland," *New York Times*, July 5, 1964, E4.

15. Vincent Buit, "Poles Go Wild over Kennedys," *Boston Globe*, June 28, 1964, 1.

16. "GIs Dying for You: Kennedy to Germany," *Chicago Tribune*, June 28, 1964, 3.

17. Homer Bigart, "Kennedy Offers a Foreign Policy," *New York Times*, September 30, 1964, 32.

18. Ross, *Robert F. Kennedy*, 381.

19. R. W. Apple Jr., "Keating Assails Charge as False," *New York Times*, October 21, 1964, 38.

20. Abram Chayes, "Kennedy Praised," *New York Times*, September 22, 1964, 38.

21. Behr, "A Day of Joy," 36.

22. Clymer, *Edward M. Kennedy*, 76.

23. Clymer, *Edward M. Kennedy*, 61.

11. "Are These People for Real?"

1. Pedro A. Sanjuan, recorded interview by Dennis O'Brien, August 14, 1969, 117, John F. Kennedy Oral History Program; Shesol, *Mutual Contempt*, 279.

2. David Coleman, ed., "National Security Archive Electronic Briefing Book No. 513," National Security Archive, April 28, 2015, http://nsarchive.gwu.edu/NSAEBB /NSAEBB513/.

3. Schlesinger, *Robert Kennedy and His Times*, 691.

4. Robert E. Thompson, "LBJ vs. RFK: Background to the 'Feud,'" *Boston Globe*, May 23, 1965, 71.

5. Rogers, *Twilight Struggle*, 226; quoted in Schlesinger, *Robert Kennedy and His Times*, 689.

6. Rabe, "Johnson Doctrine," 53.

7. Goldman, *Tragedy of Lyndon Johnson*, 382.

8. Rabe, "Johnson Doctrine," 55.

9. John D. Morris, "Kennedy Critical of Johnson Move," *New York Times*, May 8, 1965, 1.

10. Rabe, "Caribbean Triangle," 72.

11. Thomas, *Robert Kennedy*. 139.

12. Chester B. Bowles, recorded interview by Dennis J. O'Brien, July 1, 1970, 47–48, John F. Kennedy Library Oral History Program.

13. Frank Mankiewicz, recorded interview by Larry J. Hackman, June 26, 1969, 7–8, John F. Kennedy Oral History Program.

14. Bohrer, *Revolution of Robert Kennedy*, 228.

15. Schlesinger, *Robert Kennedy and His Times*, 694.

16. Frank Mankiewicz, recorded interview.

17. Pedro A. Sanjuan, recorded interview.

18. Dan Cordtz, "Sen. Kennedy Defends Johnson's Policies on South American Visit," *Wall Street Journal*, November 18, 1965, 1.

19. Martin Arnold, "Robert Kennedy for President, Some Latins Say," New York Times, November 18, 1965, 20.

20. Bohrer, *Revolution of Robert Kennedy*, 237–38.

21. Bohrer, *Revolution of Robert Kennedy*, 241.

22. Martin Arnold, "Kennedy Winning Latins' Acclaim," *New York Times*, November 22, 1965, 14.

12. "Not by Escalation, but by De-escalation"

1. Newfield, *Robert Kennedy*, 128.

2. Schlesinger, *Robert Kennedy and His Times*, 97.

3. Joseph W. Alsop, recorded interview by Roberta W. Greene, June 10, 1971, 1, Robert Kennedy Oral History Program of the John F. Kennedy Library.

4. Guthman and Shulman, *Robert Kennedy*, 326–27.

5. Shesol, *Mutual Contempt*, 3, 183.

6. Guthman and Shulman, *Robert Kennedy*, 407–10, and Shesol, *Mutual Contempt*, 174.

7. Public Broadcasting System, "Primary Sources: President Johnson's 'Peace Without Conquest' Speech," http://www.shoppbs.pbs.org/wgbh/amex/honor/filmmore/ps_peace.html.

8. "Bob Kennedy Urges Share for Reds in Saigon Regime," *Los Angeles Times*, February 20, 1966, 1; E. W. Kenworthy, "Kennedy Bids U.S. Offer Vietcong a Role in Saigon," *New York Times*, February 20, 1966, 1; Murrey Marder, "Viet Coalition Rule Urged by Kennedy," *Washington Post*, February 20, 1966, A1.

9. Schlesinger, *Robert Kennedy and His Times*, 735.

10. "Two Senators Named Kennedy," *Newsweek*, 17.

11. Walter Mondale interview, March 20, 2006, Edward M. Kennedy Oral History Project, Miller Center, University of Virginia.

12. George McGovern interview, March 22, 2006, Edward M. Kennedy Oral History Project, Miller Center, University of Virginia.

13. Schlesinger, *Robert Kennedy and His Times*, 730.

14. Schlesinger, *Robert Kennedy and His Times*, 732–33.

15. Neil Sheehan, "Edward Kennedy Expects Long War," *New York Times*, October 28, 1965, 2.

16. Edward M. Kennedy interview, May 30, 2007, Edward M. Kennedy Oral History Project, Miller Center, University of Virginia.

17. Clymer, *Edward M. Kennedy*, 77.

18. Clymer, *Edward M. Kennedy*, 79.

19. Ruben Salazar, "Viet Camp Holding Out in 5th Day," *Washington Post*, October 25, 1965, A1.

20. Edward M. Kennedy, *True Compass*, 238–39.

21. Edward M. Kennedy interview.

22. Edward M. Kennedy, "Fresh Look," 21.

23. Shesol, *Mutual Contempt*, 285–86.

24. Stone, *Elites for Peace*, 106.

25. Shesol, *Mutual Contempt*, 284–85.

26. Murrey Marder, "Viet Coalition Rule Urged by Kennedy," *Washington Post*, February 20, 1966, A1; Robert Donovan, "Humphrey Raps Viet Coalition Proposal of Robert Kennedy," *Los Angeles Times*, February 21, 1966, 1; John Maffre, "Bundy and Ball Denounce Idea; Some Support It," *Washington Post*, February 21, 1966, A1.

27. David S. Broder, "Kennedy's Vietnam Plea Spurs Popularity on Democratic Left," *New York Times*, February 21, 1966, 1.

13. "We Live in the Same World with China"

1. E. W. Kenworthy, "Kennedy Proposes Treaty to Check Nuclear Spread," *New York Times*, June 24, 1965, 1.

2. John W. Finney, "Kennedy Proposes U.S. Invite Peking to Parlay on Arms," *New York Times*, October 14, 1965, 1.

3. Tom Wicker, "The Peking Enigma," *New York Times*, March 11, 1966, 14.

4. "Fulbright Warns of U.S.-China War as Growing Peril," *New York Times*, March 7, 1966, 1.

5. Murrey Marder, "New Look at China . . . ," *Washington Post*, March 12, 1966, A15.

6. Allard K. Lowenstein, recorded interview by Larry J. Hackman, April 23, 1969, 2, Robert F. Kennedy Oral History Program of the John F. Kennedy Library.

7. Joseph Lelyveld, "Robert Kennedy to Visit South Africa," *New York Times*, October 24, 1965, 1.

8. Nixon, "Asia after Viet Nam."

14. "Not Very Different"

1. Allard K. Lowenstein, recorded interview by Larry J. Hackman, December 2, 1969, 53, Robert F. Kennedy Oral History Program of the John F. Kennedy Library.

2. Allard K. Lowenstein, recorded interview.

3. Frank Mankiewicz, recorded interview by Larry J. Hackman, August 12, 1969, 71–72, John F. Kennedy Library Oral History Program.

4. Fred R. Harris, recorded interview by Roberta W. Greene, July 29, 1970, 7, Robert F. Kennedy Oral History Program of the John F. Kennedy Library.

5. Newfield, *Robert Kennedy*, 140.

6. Clymer, *Edward M. Kennedy*, 95.

7. Edward M. Kennedy, *True Compass*, 257.

8. Edward M. Kennedy, "Kennedy Views War 'With Great Dismay,'" *Boston Globe*, January 26, 1968, 14.

9. Shesol, *Mutual Contempt*, 403.

15. "Dear God, Help Us, This War Must End"

1. Edward M. Kennedy, "Introduction," xviii.

2. Edward M. Kennedy interview, November 29, 2006, Edward M. Kennedy Oral History Project, Miller Center, University of Virginia.

3. "Transcript of Address by Senator Kennedy Denouncing Administration Policy in Vietnam," *New York Times*, August 22, 1968, 22; Walter Pincus, "Bomb Halt Urged by Kennedy," *Washington Post*, August 22, 1968, A1.

4. Interview with Paul Donovan, June 14, 2019.

5. Carey Parker interview, November 17, 2008, Edward M. Kennedy Oral History Project, Miller Center, University of Virginia.

6. Carey Parker interview, October 6, 2008, Edward M. Kennedy Oral History Project, Miller Center, University of Virginia.

7. Nancy Soderberg interview, October 9, 2008, Edward M. Kennedy Oral History Project, Miller Center, University of Virginia.

8. Walter Mondale interview, March 20, 2006, Edward M. Kennedy Oral History Project, Miller Center, University of Virginia.

9. Interview with Nancy Soderberg, May 22, 2019.

10. Edward M. Kennedy, *Decisions for a Decade*, 20–21.

11. Edward M. Kennedy, *Decisions for a Decade*, 19–21.

12. Edward M. Kennedy, *Decisions for a Decade*, 173, 179.

13. Edward M. Kennedy, *Decisions for a Decade*, 132.

14. Nixon, *RN*, 416.

15. Edward M. Kennedy, "Introduction," xiv.

16. Edward M. Kennedy, "Introduction," xvi.

17. "Why the Battle for Hamburger Hill Was so Controversial," *History*, https://www.history.com/news/hamburger-hill-controversy.

18. B. D. Colen, "Memorial Service Held for Kent Four," *Washington Post*, May 9, 1970, A6; Clymer, *Edward M. Kennedy*, 162.

19. Clymer, *Edward M. Kennedy*, 172.

20. Clymer, *Edward M. Kennedy*, 165.

21. M. C. McGinn, "Kennedy on the POWs," *Washington Post*, October 5, 1971, A19.

22. Joseph Alsop, "Attitudes of Young Protesters Recall Federalist Petulance," *Washington Post*, May 13, 1970, A19; Edward M. Kennedy, "Sen. Kennedy Replies to a Letter," *Washington Post*, May 17, 1970, B6.

23. George Lardner Jr., "Kennedy Puts Viet Civilian Toll at 300,000," *Washington Post*, December 3, 1969, A20.

24. Lippman, *Senator Ted Kennedy*, 60–61.

16. "Help Us, Kennedy!"

1. Jake Berry, "Sen. Kennedy: 'A Friend to Chile,'" *Cape Cod Times*, September 24, 2008, https://www.capecodtimes.com/article/20080924/NEWS/809240313.

2. Interview with Mark Schneider, June 18, 2019.

3. Keys, "Congress, Kissinger," 837.

4. Keys, "Congress, Kissinger," 838.

5. Clymer, *Edward M. Kennedy*, 347.

6. Bernard Gwertzman, "A New Policy on Aid for Caribbean Wins Reagan's Approval," *New York Times*, June 4, 1981, A1.

7. Martin Tolchin, "Dodd, in Response by Democrats, Calls Policy 'Formula for Failure,'" *New York Times*, April 28, 1983, A1.

8. Martin Tolchin, "Rebuke to Reagan," *New York Times*, April 11, 1984, A1.

9. Martin Tolchin, "Senators, 88 to 1, Drop Money to Aid Nicaragua Rebels," *New York Times*, June 26, 1984, A1.

10. Juan de Onis, "Kennedy Met with Protest on Chile Visit," *Los Angeles Times*, January 16, 1986, 1; Lydia Chavez, "Protest Hinders Kennedy in Chile," *New York Times*, January 16, 1986, A6; "Chilean Rightists Lay Siege to Sen. Kennedy at Airport," *Washington Post*, January 16, 1986, A25; Douglas Tweedale, "Chilean Officials Snub Kennedy," *Boston Globe*, January 16, 1986, 3; "Chile Protestors Toss Eggs, Rocks at Kennedy's Car," *Los Angeles Times*, January 15, 1986, 1.

11. "Kennedy, 40 Congressmen Call Chile's Vote a Fraud," *Washington Post*, September 11, 1980, A26.

12. Clymer, *Edward M. Kennedy*, 379.

13. "Sen. Kennedy Steals Quayle's Thunder," *Boston Globe*, March 14, 1990, 3.

14. Ann Devroy, "Quayle, Pinochet Meet before Inauguration; Talks Stress Chile's Peaceful Transition," *Washington Post*, March 12, 1990, A12.

17. "Voodoo Arms Control"

1. Edward M. Kennedy and Hatfield, *Freeze!*, 9.

2. Scheer, *With Enough Shovels*, 18.

3. Edward M. Kennedy and Hatfield, *Freeze!*, 1.

4. Clymer, *Edward M. Kennedy*, 335.

5. Edward M. Kennedy, *True Compass*, 339.

6. Hedrick Smith, "Kennedy in Soviet," *New York Times*, April 24, 1974, 2.

7. "A Kennedy Tour," *New York Times*, April 21, 1974, 215.

8. Edward M. Kennedy, *True Compass*, 337.

9. Edward M. Kennedy, "Beyond Détente."

10. Edward M. Kennedy, *True Compass*, 339.

11. Clymer, *Edward M. Kennedy*, 256.

12. "Excerpts from the Address by Kennedy," *New York Times*, March 21, 1969, 3.

13. "Kennedy Blames Nixon for U.N. Attacks," *New York Times*, October 30, 1971, 1.

14. "Kennedy Is Rebuked for Attack on Nixon," *New York Times*, October 31, 1971, 9.

15. Edward M. Kennedy, interviewed in Senate office, October 31, 1997, 9, Edward M. Kennedy, 1997–1999, Adam Clymer Personal Papers. ACLPP-005-008. China, John F. Kennedy Presidential Library and Museum.

16. Carl M. Marcy, Oral History Project, United States Senate, https://www.senate .gov/artandhistory/history/oral_history/Carl_M_Marcy.htm.

17. Pat M. Holt, Oral History Project, United States Senate, https://www.senate.gov /artandhistory/history/oral_history/Pat_M_Holt.htm.

18. Edward M. Kennedy and Hatfield, *Freeze!*, 58.

19. Ralph Keyes, "Ask Now Where This Quote Came From," *Washington Post*, June 4, 2006, https://www.washingtonpost.com/archive/opinions/2006/06/04/ask-not-where -this-quote-came-from/ca3a139f-0060-477e-9693-48b08f6d0e20/.

20. Edward M. Kennedy and Hatfield, *Freeze!*, 140.

21. "Kennedy Denounces Reagan for 'Voodoo Arms Control,'" *New York Times*, June 22, 1982, A6.

22. Lou Cannon, "President Seeks Futuristic Defense against Missiles," *Washington Post*, March 24, 1983, A1.

23. Kampelman, *Entering New Worlds*, 351.

18. "This Year in Be'er Sheva"

1. Boris and Natalya Katz interview, February 15, 2009, Edward M. Kennedy Oral History Project, Miller Center, University of Virginia.

2. Interview with Nancy Soderberg, May 22, 2019.

3. Lee Lescaze, "Kennedy Mobbed by Dacca Students," *Washington Post*, February 15, 1972, A14.

4. "Kennedy, in Gdansk, Declares: 'I Am a Pole,'" *Washington Post*, May 25, 1987, A22.

5. "Open Letter to the United States Congress from Andrei Sakharov," *Congressional Record*, December 13, 1974, http://insidethecoldwar.org/sites/default/files/documents /Jackson-Vanik%20Amendment%20to%20the%20trade%20reform%20act%20of%201972 %2C%20january%204%2C%201975.pdf.

6. Clymer, *Edward M. Kennedy*, 227.

7. Robert Hunter interview, February 11, 2009, Edward M. Kennedy Oral History Project, Miller Center, University of Virginia.

8. Clymer, *Edward M. Kennedy*, 210.

9. Robert Hunter interview.

10. Clymer, *Edward M. Kennedy*, 264.

19. "The Echoes of My Brother Bob's Trip"

1. Edward M. Kennedy interview, January 7, 2008, Edward M. Kennedy Oral History Project, Miller Center, University of Virginia.

2. Culverson, "The Politics," 127.

3. Crocker, "South Africa."

4. Interview with Chris Doherty, September 12, 2019.

5. Gregory Craig interview, July 13, 2010, Edward M. Kennedy Oral History Project, Miller Center, University of Virginia.

6. Edward M. Kennedy interview.

7. Allister Sparks, "Kennedy Describes 'Despairing' Visit in Soweto," *Washington Post*, January 7, 1985, A18.

8. Alan Cowell, "Kennedy Tours Black South Africa Area," *New York Times*, January 7, 1985, A3.

9. Allister Sparks, "Kennedy Describes 'Despairing' Visit."

10. Edward M. Kennedy, "Will Mr. Reagan Denounce Pretoria?" *New York Times*, July 21, 1986, A17.

11. Interview's briefing materials for Gregory Craig interview, July 13, 2010, Edward M. Kennedy Oral History Project, Miller Center, University of Virginia.

20. "He's Not Going to Hug Gerry Adams"

1. Coll, "Northern Ireland."

2. Phil Coulter, "The Town I Loved so Well," https://www.youtube.com/watch?v=2OJSTMC0VjQ.

3. Edward M. Kennedy interview, March 20, 2006, Edward M. Kennedy Oral History Project, Miller Center, University of Virginia.

4. Sanders, "Senator Edward Kennedy," 217.

5. Edward M. Kennedy, "Senator Kennedy on Ulster," *Times of London*, October 25, 1971, 13.

6. Edward M. Kennedy, *True Compass*, 355.

7. John Hume interview, September 29, 2005, Edward M. Kennedy Oral History Project, Miller Center, University of Virginia.

8. Trina Vargo interview, November 7, 2008, Edward M. Kennedy Oral History Project, Miller Center, University of Virginia.

9. Edward M. Kennedy interview.

10. Kevin Cullen, "Kennedy Gets Warm Greeting at N. Ireland Inauguration," *Boston Globe*, May 9, 2007, A3.

11. Bertie Ahern interview, November 8, 2010, Edward M. Kennedy Oral History Project, Miller Center, University of Virginia.

21. "Can't Be a Bully"

1. Sharon Waxman interview, December 19, 2008, Edward M. Kennedy Oral History Project, Miller Center, University of Virginia.

2. Sharon Waxman interview.

3. Interview with Sharon Waxman, October 30, 2019.

4. Dick Cheney, speech to Veterans of Foreign Wars, Nashville TN, August 27, 2002, https://www.theguardian.com/world/2002/aug/27/usa.iraq.

5. Andrew Rosenthal, "Senators Asking President to Call Session over Gulf," *New York Times*, November 14, 1990, A1.

6. Sharon Waxman interview.

7. Edward M. Kennedy interview, December 9, 2007, Edward M. Kennedy Oral History Project, Miller Center, University of Virginia.

8. President George W. Bush, National Security Strategy, September 2002, https://georgewbush-whitehouse.archives.gov/nsc/nss/2002/.

9. Edward M. Kennedy, *True Compass*, 495–96.

10. Edward M. Kennedy, *True Compass*, 496.

11. Joel Roberts, "Kennedy: Case for War a 'Fraud,'" CBS, September 19, 2003, https://www.cbsnews.com/news/kennedy-case-for-war-a-fraud/.

12. David Firestone, "Kennedy, in Sweeping Attack, Faults Bush on Iraq and Taxes," *New York Times*, January 22, 2003, A9.

13. Yvonne Abraham, "Kennedy Attacks Bush on Iraq, Drugs," *Boston Globe*, January 25, 2003, A2.

14. Anne E. Kornblutt, "Bush Calls on UN to Act; He Wants 'Backbone' on Iraq Issue," *Boston Globe*, February 14, 2003, A1.

15. Carl Hulse, "Senate Republicans Back Bush's Iraq Policy, as Democrats Call It Rash and Bullying," *New York Times*, March 8, 2003, A10.

16. Jim VandeHei and Helen Dewar, "Democrats Sharpen Attack on Bush over Iraq," *Washington Post*, July 16, 2003, A17; Susan Milligan, "Kennedy Says Bush Putting Troops in Peril," *Boston Globe*, July 16, 2003, A1.

17. Michael Graczyk, "Bush's Father Honors Kennedy," *Boston Globe*, November 8, 2003, http://archive.boston.com/news/nation/articles/2003/11/08/bushs_father_honors_kennedy/.

Epilogue

1. Fukuyama, "The End of History?"

Bibliography

The Kennedys in the World rests on a vast array of materials by and about Jack, Bobby, and Ted Kennedy.

They include the voluminous collections of speeches, letters, oral histories, and other materials at the John F. Kennedy Presidential Library and Museum; newspaper and magazine coverage, as well as more scholarly treatment, of the global events that occupied the brothers for more than six decades after World War II; White House and executive branch documents from all of the presidencies that stretched across the careers of Jack, Bobby, and Ted; the *Congressional Record* of House and Senate floor speeches, debates, and other proceedings; records of key House and Senate committees; and scores of oral history interviews that the Senate Historical Office has conducted with senators, top staffers, and other leading figures.

Another vital source of information was lengthy oral history interviews that the University of Virginia's Miller Center conducted in conjunction with the Edward M. Kennedy Institute for the United States Senate—more than two dozen with Ted and hundreds more with White House and executive branch officials, Senate and House members, Ted's aides, classmates, friends and family, and others. To supplement these oral history interviews about Ted Kennedy, I conducted fresh interviews with a variety of his former staffers.

The brothers each wrote books and articles about America's global role; delivered hundreds of speeches about it at home and abroad; spoke with journalists about the issue; kept diaries and notes of some of their most important trips; served as foreign correspondents; and wrote letters to one another, to their parents, and to many others. I benefited greatly from compendiums of such materials. *Hostage to Fortune: The Letters of Joseph P. Kennedy*, edited by Amanda Smith (Joe's granddaughter), is an indispensable source of rich and revealing letters among Joe, Rose, and their sons. For Jack, *John F. Kennedy: A Compendium of Speeches, Statements, and Remarks Delivered during His Service in the Congress of the United States*, which Congress commissioned after JFK's assassination, is a vital source on his congressional activities, while Theodore C. Sorenson's *"Let the Word Go Forth": The Speeches, Statements, and Writings of John F. Kennedy, 1947 to 1963* is a useful overview of his career. For Bobby, the Justice Department is home to all of his speeches as attorney general, while useful compendiums include Douglas Ross's *Robert F. Kennedy: Apostle of Change*, Edwin O. Guthman and C. Richard Allen's *RFK: Collected Speeches*, and Edwin O. Guthman and Jeffrey Shulman's *Robert Kennedy in His Own Words: The Unpublished Recollections of the Kennedy Years*. For Ted, the Edward M. Kennedy Institute for the United States Senate is home to many of his most important speeches.

For decades, historians, journalists, and others have dug deeply for information and insights about the brothers, furnishing tens of millions of words that fill thousands of books and articles. The major sources on which I relied, by and about the brothers and about the issues with which they grappled, are listed below.

Abbott, Philip. "The 'Bobby Problem': Intraparty Presidential Rivalry and Factional Challenges." *Journal of Policy History* 25, no. 4 (2013): 489–511.

Ab Ghani, Rohani, and Zulhilmi Paidi. "The Role of the United States and the 'Asian Solution' Approach in the Malaysia-Indonesia Confrontation (1963–1966)." *Journal of International Studies* 9 (2013): 1–16.

Addington, Larry H. *America's War in Vietnam: A Short Narrative History*. Bloomington: Indiana University Press, 2000.

Aldous, Richard. *Schlesinger: The Imperial Historian*. New York: W. W. Norton, 2017.

Allcock, Thomas Tunstall. "The First Alliance for Progress?: Reshaping the Eisenhower Administration's Policy toward Latin America." *Journal of Cold War Studies* 16, no. 1 (Winter 2014): 85–110.

"A Look Behind the Russian Smiles: Interview with Robert F. Kennedy." *U.S. News &
World Report* (October 21, 1955): 62–67, 136–46.

Ambrose, Stephen E., and Douglas G. Brinkley. *Rise to Globalism: American Foreign Policy Since 1938.* New York: Penguin Books, 1997.

Anderson, David L. *The Columbia Guide to the Vietnam War.* New York: Columbia University Press, 2002.

Anderson, David L., and John Ernst, eds. *The War That Never Ends.* Lexington: University Press of Kentucky, 2007.

Aremu, Johnson Olaosebikan, and Stephen Olayiwola Soetan. "Fidel Castro and the Consol-
idation of the Cuban Revolution, 1959–1963." *World Scientific News* 87 (2017): 60–76.

Barkaoui, Miloud. "Kennedy and the Cold War Imbroglio: The Case of Algeria's Independence." *Arab Studies Quarterly* 21, no. 2 (Spring 1999): 31–45.

Bawden, John R. "Cutting Off the Dictator: The United States Arms Embargo of the Pinochet Regime, 1974–1988." *Journal of Latin American Studies* 45, no. 3 (2013): 513–43.

Beauchamp, Cari. "Two Sons, One Destiny." *Vanity Fair,* December 2004, https://www
.vanityfair.com/news/2004/12/kennedy-200412.

Beckerman, Gal. "How a Quest to Save Soviet Jews Changed the World." NPR. October 30, 2010. https://www.npr.org/templates/story/story.php?storyId=130936993.

———. "The Soviet Jewry Movement in America." My Jewish Learning. https://www
.myjewishlearning.com/article/the-soviet-jewry-movement-in-america/.

———. *When They Come for Us, We'll Be Gone: The Epic Struggle to Save Soviet Jewry.*
Boston: Houghton Mifflin Harcourt, 2010.

Behr, Edward. "A Day of Joy and Sadness." *Saturday Evening Post,* 237 (July 11, 1964): 36–37.

Berg, Dorothy. "Notes on Roosevelt's 'Quarantine' Speech." *Political Science Quarterly*
72, no. 3 (September 1957): 405–33.

Billington, Ray Allen. "Anti-Catholic Propaganda and the Home Missionary Movement,
1800–1860." *Mississippi Valley Historical Review* 22, no. 3 (December 1935): 361–84.

———. *The Protestant Crusade: 1800–1860.* Chicago: Quadrangle Books, 1938.

Bohrer, John R. *The Revolution of Robert Kennedy: From Power to Protest after JFK.* New
York: Bloomsbury Press, 2017.

Boline, Nicholas V. "Fidel Castro's Grand Strategy in the Cuban Revolution: 1959–1968."
Interdisciplinary Journal of Undergraduate Research 4, article 14 (2015): http://
digitalcommons.northgeorgia.edu/cgi/viewcontent.cgi?article=1115&context=
papersandpubs.

Borg, Dorothy. "Notes on Roosevelt's 'Quarantine' Speech." *Political Science Quarterly*
72, no. 3 (September 1957): 405–33.

Bostdorff, Denise, and Steven Goldzwig. "Idealism and Pragmatism in American Foreign
Policy Rhetoric: The Case of John F. Kennedy and Vietnam." *Presidential Studies
Quarterly* 24, no. 3 (Summer 1994): 515–30.

Boyle, Ryan. "A Red Moon over the Mall: The *Sputnik* Panic and Domestic America."
Journal of American Culture 31, no. 4 (December 2008): 373–82.

Brands, H. W., Jr. "The Age of Vulnerability: Eisenhower and the National Insecurity
State." *The American Historical Review* 94, no. 4 (October 1989): 963–89.

———. "Decisions on American Armed Intervention: Lebanon, Dominican Republic, and Grenada." *Political Science Quarterly* 102, no. 4 (Winter 1987–88): 607–24.

Brighton, Stephen A. "Degrees of Alienation: The Material Evidence of the Irish and Irish American Experience, 1850–1910." *Historical Archaeology* 42, no. 4 (2008): 132–53.

Brinkley, Alan. *John F. Kennedy.* New York: Times Books, 2012.

———. "The Legacy of John F. Kennedy." *The Atlantic*, September 18, 2013, https://www .theatlantic.com/magazine/archive/2013/08/the-legacy-of-john-f-kennedy/309499/.

Bruno, Andorra. "Iraqi and Afghan Special Immigrant Visa Programs." Congressional Research Service. (March 29, 2019): 1–22.

Bryan, Ferald J. "Joseph McCarthy, Robert Kennedy, and the Greek Shipping Crisis: A Study of Foreign Policy Rhetoric." *Presidential Studies Quarterly* 24, no. 1 (Winter 1994): 93–104.

Bzdek, Vincent. *The Kennedy Legacy: Jack, Bobby and Ted and a Family Dream Fulfilled.* New York: St. Martin's Griffin, 2009.

Carter, Donald Alan. "Eisenhower Versus the Generals." *Journal of Military History* 71, no. 4 (October 2007): 1169–99.

Casey, Francis M. "Soviet Strategy for the Third World: Wars of National Liberation." *Journal of East Asian Affairs* 2, no. 1 (Spring/Summer 1982): 152–69.

Castor, Suzy, and Lynn Garafola. "The American Occupation of Haiti (1915–34) and the Dominican Republic (1916–24)." *The Massachusetts Review* 15, no. ½, Caliban (Winter–Spring 1974): 253–75.

Chang, Gordon H. "JFK, China, and the Bomb." *Journal of American History* 74, no. 4 (March 1988): 1287–310.

Clark, Victor Figueroa. "The Forgotten History of the Chilean Transition: Armed Resistance against Pinochet and US Policy towards Chile in the 1980s." *Journal of Latin American Studies* 47, no. 3 (August 2015): 491–520.

Clymer, Adam. *Edward M. Kennedy: A Biography.* New York: Harper Perennial, 2009.

Cochrane, Feargal. "Irish-America, the End of the IRA's Armed Struggle and the Utility of 'Soft Power.'" *Journal of Peace Research* 44, no. 2 (March 2007): 215–31.

Coffey, J. I. "The Anti-ballistic Missile Debate." *Foreign Affairs*, April 1967, https://www .foreignaffairs.com/articles/1967-04-01/anti-ballistic-missile-debate.

Cohen, Barbara. "Integrating Human Rights in U.S. Foreign Policy: The History, the Challenges, and the Criteria for an Effective Policy." Foreign Service Institute (2008). https://www.brookings.edu/wp-content/uploads/2016/06/04_human_rights _cohen.pdf.

Cohen, Jerome A. "Ted Kennedy's Role in Restoring Diplomatic Relations with China." *New York University Journal of Legislation and Public Policy* 14, no. 2 (May 2011): 347–55.

Cohen, William B. "The Algerian War, the French State, and Official Memory." *Historical Reflections/Reflexions Historiques* 28, no. 2 (Summer 2002): 219–39.

Cohn, Raymond L. "Nativism and the End of the Mass Migration in the 1840s and 1850s." *Journal of Economic History* 60, no. 2 (June 2000): 361–83.

Colhoun, Jack. *Gangsterismo: The United States, Cuba and the Mafia, 1933 to 1966.* New York: OR Books, 2013.

Coll, Bryan. "Northern Ireland Remembers Ted Kennedy, the Peacemaker." *Time*, August 28, 2009, http://content.time.com/time/world/article/0,8599,1919293,00.html.

Connelly, Matthew. "Rethinking the Cold War and Decolonization: The Grand Strategy of the Algerian War for Independence." *International Journal of Middle East Studies* 33, no. 2 (May 2001): 221–45.

Cox, Jeff. "'They Aren't Friendly, Mr. Vice President': The Eisenhower Administration's Response to Communist-Inspired Attacks during Vice President Nixon's 1958 Tour of Latin America." *American Diplomacy*, Dec. 19, 2012, https://go.gale.com /ps/anonymous?id=GALE%7CA315921747&sid=googleScholar&v=2.1&it=r &linkaccess=abs&issn=10948120&p=AONE&sw=w.

Cox, Michael. "The War That Came in from the Cold: Clinton and the Irish Question." *World Policy Journal* 16, no. 1 (Spring 1999): 59–67.

Crocker, Chester A. "South Africa: Strategy for Change." *Foreign Affairs*, Winter 1980–81, https://www.foreignaffairs.com/articles/south-africa/1980-12-01/south-africa -strategy-change.

Culverson, Donald R. "The Politics of the Anti-apartheid Movement in the United States, 1969–1986." *Political Science Quarterly* 111, no. 1 (1986): 127–49.

Dallek, Robert. *An Unfinished Life: John F. Kennedy: 1917–1963*. New York: Bay Back Books, 2003.

———. "Franklin Roosevelt as World Leader." *American Historical Review* 76, no. 5 (December 1971): 1503–13.

Dean, Richard N. "Contacts with the West: The Dissidents' View of Western Support for the Human Rights Movement in the Soviet Union." *Universal Human Rights* 2, no. 1 (January–March 1980): 47–65.

Deignan, Tom. *Irish Americans*. Hauppauge NY: Barron's Educational Services, 2002.

Deutsch, Richard. "The Good Friday Agreement: Assessing Its Implementation 1998–2001." *Nordic Irish Studies* 1 (2002): 95–109.

Dickson, David A. "U.S. Foreign Policy toward Southern and Central Africa: The Kennedy and Johnson Years." *Presidential Studies Quarterly* 23, no. 2 (Spring 1993): 301–15.

Divine, Robert, ed. *The Cuban Missile Crisis*. Chicago: Quadrangle Books, 1971.

Dixon, Paul. "Performing the Northern Ireland Peace Process on the World Stage." *Political Science Quarterly* 121, no. 1 (Spring 2006): 61–91.

Dolan, Jay P. *The Irish Americans: A History*. New York: Bloomsbury Press, 2008.

Dorsey, Bruce. "Freedom of Religion: Bibles, Public Schools, and Philadelphia's Bloody Riots of 1844." *Pennsylvania Legacies* 8, no. 1 (May 2008): 12–17.

Douglass, James W. *JFK and the Unspeakable: Why He Died and Why It Matters*. New York: Touchstone, 2008.

"Dragon Lady, Dragonfly." *Time* (September 20, 1963): 33–34.

Dudziak, Mary L. "Birmingham, Addis Ababa, and the Image of America." In *Window on Freedom: Race, Civil Rights and Foreign Affairs, 1945–1988*, edited by Brenda Gayle Plummer, 181–99. Chapel Hill: University of North Carolina Press, 2003.

———. "Birmingham, Addis Ababa, and the Image of America: Managing the Impact of Foreign Affairs on Civil Rights in the Kennedy Administration." Emory Legal

Studies Research Paper, April 23, 1998. https://papers.ssrn.com/sol3/papers.cfm ?abstract_id=79048.

———. "Brown as a Cold War Case." *Journal of American History* 91, no. 1 (June 2004): 32–42.

———. "Desegregation as a Cold War Imperative." *Stanford Law Review* 41, no. 1 (1988): 61–120.

———. "The Little Rock Crisis and Foreign Affairs: Race, Resistance, and the Image of American Democracy." *Southern California Law Review* 70, no. 6 (September 1997): 1641–716.

Dulles, John Foster. "The Evolution of Foreign Policy." Text of speech before the Council on Foreign Relations, New York, January 12, 1954. Vol. 2. Washington DC: Department of State, 1954.

Dunne, Michael. "Kennedy's Alliance for Progress: Countering Revolution in Latin America, Part 1: From the White House to the Charter of Punta del Este." *International Affairs* 89, no. 6 (2013): 1389–409.

Erikson, Robert S., and Laura Stoker. "Caught in the Draft: The Effects of Vietnam Draft Lottery Status on Political Attitudes." *American Political Science Review* 105, no. 2 (May 2011): 221–37.

Falcoff, Mark. "Chile: Pinochet, the Opposition, and the United States." *World Affairs* 149, no. 4 (Spring 1987): 183–94.

Farber, Samuel. "The Cuban Communists in the Early Stages of the Cuban Revolution: Revolutionaries or Reformists?" *Latin American Research Review* 18, no. 1 (1983): 59–83.

Fatalski, Marcin. "The United States and the Fall of the Trujillo Regime." *Ad Americam* 14 (2013): 7–18.

Fatton, Robert. "The Reagan Foreign Policy toward South Africa: The Ideology of the New Cold War." *African Studies Review* 27, no. 1 (March 1984): 57–82.

Fay, Paul B., Jr. *The Pleasure of His Company.* New York: Harper & Row, 1966.

Felten, Peter G. "The Path to Dissent: Johnson, Fulbright, and the 1965 Intervention in the Dominican Republic." *Presidential Studies Quarterly* 26, no. 4 (Fall 1996): 1009–18.

Fisher, James T. "The Second Catholic President: Ngo Dinh Diem, John F. Kennedy, and the Vietnam Lobby, 1954–1963." *U.S. Catholic Historian* 15, no. 3 (Summer 1997): 119–37.

Fry, Joseph A. "To Negotiate or Bomb: Congressional Prescriptions for Withdrawing U.S. Troops from Vietnam." *Diplomatic History* 34, no. 3 (June 2010): 517–28.

Fukuyama, Francis. "The End of History?" *The National Interest*, no. 16 (Summer 1989): 3–18.

Gaskin, Thomas M. "Senator Lyndon B. Johnson, the Eisenhower Administration and U.S. Foreign Policy, 1957–60." *Presidential Studies Quarterly* 24, no. 2 (Spring 1994): 341–61.

Geelhoed, E. Bruce. "Dwight D. Eisenhower, the Spy Plane, and the Summit: A Quarter-Century Retrospective." *Presidential Studies Quarterly* 17, no. 1 (Winter 1987): 95–106.

Gibbs, David N. "Political Parties and International Relations: The United States and the Decolonization of Sub-Saharan Africa." *International History Review* 17, no. 2 (May 1995): 306–27.

Gleijeses, Piero. "Moscow's Proxy? Cuba and Africa 1975–1988." *Journal of Cold War Studies* 8, no. 4 (Fall 2006): 98–146.

Bibliography

Goldman, Eric F. *The Tragedy of Lyndon Johnson.* New York: Alfred A. Knopf, 1969.

Goodby, James E. "The Limited Test Ban Negotiations, 1954–63: How a Negotiator Viewed the Proceedings." *International Negotiation* 10 (2005): 381–404.

Goodwin, Doris Kearns. *The Fitzgeralds and the Kennedys.* New York: St Martin's, 1987.

Greene, Graham. *The Quiet American.* New York: Viking, 1956.

Guelke, Adrian. "The United States, Irish Americans and the Northern Ireland Peace Process." *International Affairs (Royal Institute of International Affairs 1944–)*72, no. 3 (July 1996): 521–36.

Guthman, Edwin O. *We Band of Brothers.* New York: Harper & Row, 1971.

Guthman, Edwin O., and C. Richard Allen, eds. *RFK: Collected Speeches.* New York: Viking, 1993.

Guthman, Edwin O., and Jeffrey Shulman, eds. *Robert Kennedy in His Own Words: The Unpublished Recollections of the Kennedy Years.* New York: Bantam Books, 1988.

Haight, John McVickar, Jr. "France and the Aftermath of Roosevelt's 'Quarantine' Speech." *World Politics* 14, no. 2 (January 1962): 283–306.

———. "Roosevelt and the Aftermath of the Quarantine Speech." *Review of Politics* 24, no. 2 (April 1962): 233–59.

Hamilton, Nigel. "The Influence of Europe on the Young JFK." *New England Journal of Public Policy* 9, no. 1 (June 21, 1993): 5–17.

Handlin, Oscar. *Boston's Immigrants: A Study in Acculturation.* Revised and enlarged edition. New York: Atheneum, 1969.

Haynes, George H. "The Causes of Know-Nothing Success in Massachusetts." *American Historical Review* 3, no. 1 (October 1897): 67–82.

Hersh, Burton. *Edward Kennedy: An Intimate Biography.* Berkeley: Counterpoint, 2010.

Hertzberg, Hendrik. "Ted and Harvard, 1962." *The New Yorker*, August 27, 2009, https://www.newyorker.com/news/hendrik-hertzberg/ted-and-harvard-1962.

Hill, Kenneth L. "President Kennedy and the Neutralization of Laos." *Review of Politics* 31, no. 3 (July 1969): 353–69.

Hilsman, Roger. "The Situation and Short-Term Prospects in South Vietnam." Department of State, Bureau of Intelligence and Research, research memorandum, RFE-59, December 3, 1962. https://www.mtholyoke.edu/acad/intrel/pentagon2/doc119.htm.

Hiroshi, Matsuoka. "We Shall Keep on Asking, 'What If': The Assassination of John F. Kennedy and the Quagmire of Vietnam." *Nanzan Review of American Studies* 36, (2014): 63–80.

Humphrey, Hubert H. "U.S. Policy in Latin America." *Foreign Affairs* 42, no. 4 (July 1964): 585–601.

Huntington, Samuel P. *The Third Wave: Democratization in the Late 20th Century.* Norman: University of Oklahoma Press, 1991.

Hyman, Zoe. "'To Have Its Cake and Eat It Too': U.S. Policy toward South Africa during the Kennedy Administration." *The Sixties* 8, no. 2 (2015): 138–55.

Jarman, Baird. "The Graphic Art of Thomas Nast: Politics and Propriety in Postbellum Publishing." *American Periodicals* 20, no. 2 (2010): 156–89.

John F. Kennedy Library Foundation. *Rose Kennedy's Family Album*. New York: Grand Central Publishing, 2013.

Judd, Walter H. "Special Study Mission to Southeast Asia and the Pacific." Washington DC: United States Government Printing Office, 1954.

Justice, Benjamin. "Thomas Nast and the Public School of the 1870s." *History of Education Quarterly* 45, no. 2 (Summer 2005): 171–206.

Kalb, Marvin. *The Road to War: Presidential Commitments Honored and Betrayed*. Washington DC: Brookings Institution Press, 2013.

Kampelman, Ambassador Max M. *Entering New Worlds: The Memoirs of a Private Man in Public Life*. New York: HarperCollins, 1991.

Kanet, Roger E. "The Superpower Quest for Empire: The Cold War and Soviet Support for 'Wars of National Liberation.'" *Cold War History* 6, no. 3 (August 2006): 331–52.

Kay, W. D. "John F. Kennedy and the Two Faces of the U.S. Space Program, 1961–63." *Presidential Studies Quarterly* 28, no. 3 (Summer 1998): 573–86.

Kempton, Murray. "Pure Irish: Robert R. Kennedy." *New Republic* (February 1964): 9–11.

Kennedy, Edward M. "Beyond Détente." *Foreign Policy*, no. 16 (Autumn 1974): 3–29.

——— . *Decisions for a Decade*. Garden City: Doubleday, 1968.

——— . "The First Steps." *New Leader* (March 3, 1969): 12–14.

——— . "A Fresh Look at Vietnam." *Look*, February 8, 1966, 21–23.

——— . "Introduction." In *ABM: An Evaluation of the Decision to Deploy an Antiballistic Missile System*, edited by Abram Chayes and Jerome B. Wiesner, xiii–xxii. New York: Signet Books, 1969.

——— . "My Boston." *Esquire*, December 1965, https://classic.esquire.com/article/1965/12/1/my-boston.

——— . "Normal Relations with China: Good Law, Good Policy." *American Bar Association Journal* 65, no. 2 (February 1979): 194–97.

——— . *True Compass: A Memoir*. New York: Twelve, 2009.

——— . "Ulster Is an International Issue." *Foreign Policy* 11 (Summer 1973): 57–71.

——— . "What Path Offers More Security? Star Wars vs. the ABM Treaty." *Arms Control Today* 14, no. 6 (July/August 1984): 1, 18–19, 24.

Kennedy, Edward M., and Mark O. Hatfield. *Freeze!: How You Can Help Prevent Nuclear War*. New York: Bantam Books, 1982.

Kennedy, John F. *A Compendium of Speeches, Statements, and Remarks Delivered during His Service in the Congress of the United States*. Washington DC: United States Government Printing Office, 1964.

——— . "A Democrat Looks at Foreign Policy." *Foreign Affairs*, October 1957, https://www.foreignaffairs.com/articles/united-states/1957-10-01/democrat-looks-foreign-policy.

——— . *Prelude to Leadership: The European Diary of John F. Kennedy: Summer 1945*. Washington DC: Regnery, 1995.

——— . *Profiles in Courage: Memorial Edition*. New York: Harper & Row, 1964.

——— . "Report on Communist-Controlled Poland." Office of Senator John F. Kennedy, October 10, 1955.

——— . *The Strategy of Peace*. New York: Popular Library, 1960.

————. *Why England Slept.* Garden City NY: Dolphin Books, 1961.

Kennedy, Robert F. *Just Friends and Brave Enemies.* New York: Popular Library, 1963.

————. *Thirteen Days: A Memoir of the Cuban Missile Crisis.* New York: W. W. Norton, 1969.

————. *To Seek a Newer World.* New York: Ishi Press, 2017.

————. "What We Can Do to End the Agony of Vietnam." *Look* 31, no. 24 (November 28, 1967): 34–46.

Kennedy, Rose. *Times to Remember: An Autobiography.* London: Pan Books, 1974.

Keys, Barbara. "Congress, Kissinger, and the Origins of Human Rights Diplomacy." *Diplomatic History* 34, no. 5 (November 2010): 823–51.

Kirkendall, Andrew J. "Kennedy Men and the Fate of the Alliance for Progress in LBJ Era Brazil and Chile." *Diplomacy & Statecraft* 18, no. 4 (2007): 745–72.

Krock, Arthur. *Memoirs: Sixty Years on the Firing Line.* Funk & Wagnalls, 1968.

Krueger, Kimbra. "Internal Struggle over U.S. Foreign Policy toward Central America: An Analysis of the Reagan Era." *Presidential Studies Quarterly* 26, no. 4 (Fall 1996): 1034–46.

Landers, Robert K. "Statecraft as Stagecraft: How JFK Managed the Cuban Missile Crisis." *Commonweal* (October 26, 2012): 20–23.

Langland, Stanley G. "The Laos Factor in a Vietnam Equation." *International Affairs (Royal Institute of International Affairs 1944–)* 45, no. 4 (October 1969): 631–47.

Leamer, Laurence. *The Kennedy Men, 1901–1963: The Laws of the Father.* New York: Perennial, 2001.

Lederer, William J., and Eugene Burdick. *The Ugly American.* New York: W. W. Norton, 1958.

LeMoyne, James. "El Salvador's Forgotten War." *Foreign Affairs* 68, no. 3 (Summer 1989): 105–25.

Le Sueur, James D. "Beyond Colonialization? The Legacy of the Algerian Conflict and the Transformation of Identity in Contemporary France." *Historical Reflections/Réflexions Historiques* 28, no. 2 (Summer 2002): 277–91.

Library of Congress. "Khrushchev's Speech of January 6, 1961: A Summary and Interpretive Analysis." Washington DC: United States Government Printing Office, 1961.

Lincoln, Evelyn. *My Twelve Years with John F. Kennedy.* New York: David MacKay, 1965.

Lippman, Theo, Jr. *Senator Ted Kennedy: The Career Behind the Image.* New York: W. W. Norton, 1976.

Lowenthal, Abraham F. "The United States and the Dominican Republic to 1965: Background to Intervention." *Caribbean Studies* 10, no. 2 (July 1970): 30–55.

Lugar, Richard. *Letters to the Next President.* Bloomington: AuthorHouse, 2004.

Maechling, Charles Jr. "Camelot, Robert Kennedy, and Counter-Insurgency: A Memoir." *Virginia Quarterly Review* 75 no. 3 (Summer 1999): 438–58.

Mahajani, Usha. "President Kennedy and United States Policy in Laos, 1961–1963." *Journal of Southeast Asian Studies* 2, no. 2 (September 1971): 87–99.

Maher, Theodore James. "The Kennedy and Johnson Responses to Latin American Coups D'Etat." *World Affairs* 131, no. 3 (October, November, December 1968): 184–98.

Mahoney, Richard D. *Sons & Brothers: The Days of Jack and Bobby Kennedy*. New York: Arcade, 1999.

Maier, Thomas. *The Kennedys: America's Emerald Kings*. New York: Basic Books, 2003.

Mark, Hans. "War and Peace in Space." *Journal of International Affairs* 39, no. 1 (1985): 1–21.

Mastny, Vojtech. "The 1963 Nuclear Test Ban Treaty: A Missed Opportunity for Détente?" *Journal of Cold War Studies* 10, no. 1 (Winter 2008): 3–25.

Matthews, Chris. *Bobby Kennedy: A Raging Spirit*. New York: Simon & Schuster, 2017.

———. *Jack Kennedy: Elusive Hero*. New York: Simon & Schuster, 2011.

———. *Kennedy and Nixon: The Rivalry that Shaped Postwar America*. New York: Touchstone, 1996.

Matusevich, Maxim. "Revisiting the Soviet Moment in Sub-Saharan Africa." *History Compass* 7, no. 5 (July 2009): 1259–68.

———. "Russia in Africa: A Search for Continuity in a Post-Cold War Era." *Insight Turkey* 21, no. 1 (Winter 2019): 25–39.

McCaffrey, Lawrence J. "Ireland and Irish America: Connections and Disconnections." *U.S. Catholic Historian* 22, no. 3 (Summer 2004): 1–18.

———. "Irish America." *Wilson Quarterly* 9, no. 2 (Spring 1985): 78–93.

McClintock, Michael. *Instruments of Statecraft: U.S. Guerilla Warfare, Counterinsurgency, and Counterterrorism, 1940–1990*. New York: Pantheon Books, 1992.

McDonagh, Emmet. "Political Naïvete and Despair." *Fortnight* 463 (December 2008/January 2009): 10.

McDonagh, Philip. "The Good Friday Agreement: 1998." *India International Centre Quarterly* 31, no. 1 (Summer 2004): 12–22.

McIntyre, Anthony. "Chuckle Ar La, 8 May 2007." *Irish Review* 38 (Spring 2008): 65–68.

McPherson, Alan. "Misled by Himself: What the Johnson Tapes Reveal About the Dominican Intervention of 1965." *Latin American Research Review* 38, no. 2 (2003): 127–46.

McWhorter, Diane. "The Enduring Courage of the Freedom Riders." *Journal of Blacks in Higher Education* 61 (Autumn, 2008): 66–73.

Meagher, Michael E. "'In an Atmosphere of National Peril': The Development of John F. Kennedy's World View." *Presidential Studies Quarterly* 27, no. 3 (Summer 1997): 467–79.

Medhurst, Martin J. "Atoms for Peace and Nuclear Hegemony: The Rhetorical Structure of a Cold War Campaign." *Armed Forces and Society* 23, no. 4 (Summer 1997): 571–93.

Merom, Gil. "A 'Grand Design'? Charles de Gaulle and the End of the Algerian War." *Armed Forces & Society* 25, no. 2 (January 1999): 267–87.

Millen, Raymond. "Eisenhower and U.S. Grand Strategy." *Parameters* 44, no. 2 (June 22, 2014): 35–47.

Millsap, Chase. "America's Ronin Refugees: Forgotten Allies of the Wars in Iraq and Afghanistan." *Journal of International Affairs* 69, no. 2 (Spring/Summer 2016): https://jia.sipa.columbia.edu/americas-ronin-refugees-forgotten-allies-wars-iraq-afghanistan.

Morley, Morris, and Chris McGillion. "Soldiering On: The Reagan Administration and Redemocratisation in Chile, 1983–1986." *Bulletin of Latin American Research* 25, no. 1 (2006): 1–22.

Muehlenbeck, Philip E. "John F. Kennedy's Courting of African Nationalism." *Madison Historical Review* II, September 2004, https://commons.lib.jmu.edu/cgi/viewcontent.cgi?article=1036&context=mhr.

Muravchik, Joshua. "Kennedy's Foreign Policy: What the Record Shows." *Commentary*, December 1979. https://www.commentarymagazine.com/articles/kennedys-foreign-policy-what-the-record-shows/.

———. "The Nicaragua Debate." *Foreign Affairs* 65 no. 2 (Winter 1986): 366–82.

Nagle, John. "Between Conflict and Peace: An Analysis of the Complex Consequences of the Good Friday Agreement." *Parliamentary Affairs* 71 (2018): 395–416.

National Security Archive. George Washington University. https://nsarchive.gwu.edu/.

Nelson, Bryce. "The Senate Revolt: Protesting U.S. Overcommitment Abroad." *Science* 154, no. 3750 (Nov. 11, 1966): 751–53.

Newfield, Jack. *Robert Kennedy: A Memoir*. New York: E. P. Dutton, 1969.

Nixon, Richard M. "Asia after Viet Nam." *Foreign Affairs*, October 1967, https://www.foreignaffairs.com/articles/asia/1967-10-01/asia-after-viet-nam.

———. *RN: The Memoirs of Richard Nixon*. New York: Grosset & Dunlap, 1978.

Office of the Attorney General. "Speeches of Attorney General Robert F. Kennedy." Department of Justice, https://www.justice.gov/ag/speeches-25.

Office of the Historian. "Foreign Relations of the United States, 1961–1963." Vol. VI, Kennedy-Khrushchev Exchanges, Department of State, https://history.state.gov/historicaldocuments/frus1961-63v06/comp1/.

Office of the Historian. "John F. Kennedy Administration (1961–1963)." Historical Documents, Department of State, https://history.state.gov/historicaldocuments/kennedy.

Office of the Historian. "Memorandum of Conversation." September 10, 1963, Foreign Relations of the United States, 1961–1963, Vol. IV, Vietnam, August–December 1963, https://history.state.gov/historicaldocuments/frus1961-63v04/d83.

Office of the Historian. "Report by the Senate Majority Leader (Mansfield)." Foreign Relations of the United States, 1961–1963, Vol. II, 1962, Department of State, https://history.state.gov/historicaldocuments/frus1961-63v02/d330.

Oral History Project. Senate Historical Office, U.S. Senate, https://www.senate.gov/history/oralhistory.htm.

Pastor, Robert. "Continuity and Change in U.S. Foreign Policy: Carter and Reagan on El Salvador." *Journal of Policy Analysis and Management* 3, no. 2 (Winter 1984): 175–90.

Patrick, Richard. "President Leadership in Foreign Affairs Reexamined: Kennedy and Laos without Radical Revisionism." *World Affairs* 140, no. 3 (Winter 1978): 245–58.

Perkovich, George. "Soviet Jewry and American Foreign Policy." *World Policy Journal* 5, no. 3 (Summer 1988): 435–67.

Pfeiffer, Jack B. "Adlai Stevenson and the Bay of Pigs." *Studies in Intelligence* 27 (Fall 1983): 37–47.

Pious, Richard M. "The Cuban Missile Crisis and the Limits of Crisis Management." *Political Science Quarterly* 116, no. 1 (Spring 2001): 81–105.

Pitts, David. *Jack and Lem: John F. Kennedy and Lem Billings: The Untold Story of an Extraordinary Friendship*. New York: Da Capo Press, 2007.

Power, Margaret. "The U.S. Movement in Solidarity with Chile in the 1970s." *Latin American Perspectives* 36, no. 6 (November 2009): 46–66.

Pregelj, Vladimir N. "The Jackson-Vanik Amendment: A Survey." Congressional Research Service (August 1, 2005), https://fas.org/sgp/crs/row/98-545.pdf.

Rabe, Stephen G. "The Caribbean Triangle: Betancourt, Castro, and Trujillo and U.S. Foreign Policy, 1958–1963." *Diplomatic History* 20, no. 1 (Winter 1996): 55–78.

———. "The Johnson Doctrine." *Presidential Studies Quarterly* 36, no. 1 (March 2006): 48–58.

Rafter, Kevin. "George Mitchell and the Role of the Peace Talks Chairman." *Irish Review*, no. 38, (Spring 2008): 13–21.

Reeves, Richard. *President Kennedy: Profile of Power*. New York: Touchstone, 1994.

Renehan, Edward J., Jr. *The Kennedys at War: 1937–1945*. New York: Doubleday, 2002.

Rich, Paul. "United States Containment Policy, South Africa and the Apartheid Dilemma." *Review of International Studies* 14, no. 3 (July 1988): 179–94.

Riggs, Robert M. "Counter-Insurgency Lessons from the French-Algerian War." Naval War College, February 9, 2004, https://apps.dtic.mil/dtic/tr/fulltext/u2/a422755.pdf.

Rogers, William D. *The Twilight Struggle: The Alliance for Progress and the Politics of Development in Latin America*. New York: Random House, 1967.

Ross, Douglas. *Robert F. Kennedy: Apostle of Change*. New York: Pocket Books, 1968.

Sabato, Larry J. *The Kennedy Half-Century: The Presidency, Assassination, and Lasting Legacy of John F. Kennedy*. New York: Bloomsbury Press, 2013.

Sanders, Andrew. "Congressional Hearings on Northern Ireland and the 'Special Relationship,' 1971–1981." *Diplomacy & Statecraft* 27, nos. 1 and 2 (2011): 121–41.

———. "Senator Edward Kennedy and the 'Ulster Troubles': Irish and Irish-American Politics, 1965–2009." *Historical Journal of Massachusetts* 39, nos. 1 and 2 (Summer 2011): 206–40.

Sarantakes, Nicholas Evan. "Lyndon Johnson, Foreign Policy, and the Election of 1960." *Southwestern Historical Quarterly* 103, no. 2 (October 1999): 147–72.

Scheer, Robert. *With Enough Shovels: Reagan, Bush and Nuclear War*. New York: Random House, 1982.

Schlesinger, Arthur M., Jr. "The Lowering Hemisphere." *The Atlantic* 225, no. 1 (January 1970): 79–88.

———. *Robert Kennedy and His Times*. Boston: Houghton Mifflin, 1978.

———. *A Thousand Days: John F. Kennedy in the White House*. Boston: Houghton Mifflin, 1965.

Schmitz, David F., and Natalie Fousekis. "Frank Church, the Senate, and the Emergence of Dissent on the Vietnam War." *Pacific Historical Review* 63, no. 4 (November 1994): 561–81.

Schriftgiesser, Karl. "Mr. Ambassador Kennedy." *North American Review* 246, no. 2 (Winter, 1938/1939): 267–76.

Schuyler, Michael W. "Ghosts in the White House: LBJ, RFK and the Assassination of JFK." *Presidential Studies Quarterly* 17, no. 3 (Summer 1987): 503–18.

Scott, James M. "Interbranch Rivalry and the Reagan Doctrine in Nicaragua." *Political Science Quarterly* 112, no. 2 (Summer 1997): 237–60.

Security Resources Panel. "Deterrence & Survival in the Nuclear Age." Science Advisory Committee, Washington D C: November 7, 1957. https://nsarchive2.gwu.edu //NSAEBB/NSAEBB139/nitze02.pdf.

Selverstone, Marc J. "It's a Date: Kennedy and the Timetable for a Vietnam Troop Withdrawal." *Diplomatic History* 34, no. 3, (June 2010): 485–95.

Sempa, Francis P. "A New Take on General MacArthur's Warning to JFK to Avoid a Land War in Asia." *The Diplomat*, September 5, 2018. https://thediplomat.com/2018/10 /a-new-take-on-general-macarthurs-warning-to-jfk-to-avoid-a-land-war-in-asia/.

Senate Permanent Subcommittee on Investigations, Committee on Government Operations, "Control of Trade with the Soviet Bloc: Interim Report." July 21, 1953.

Serhan, Yasmeen. "The Good Friday Agreement in the Age of Brexit." *The Atlantic*, April 10, 2018, https://www.theatlantic.com/international/archive/2018/04/good-friday -agreement-20th-anniversary/557393/.

Sestanovich, Stephen. *Maximalist: America in the World from Truman to Obama*. New York: Vintage Books, 2014.

Shannon, Michael K. "'One of Our Greatest Psychological Assets': The New Frontier, Cold-War Public Diplomacy, and Robert Kennedy's 1962 Goodwill Tour." *International History Review* 36, no. 4 (2014): 767–90.

Shaw, John T. *JFK in the Senate: Pathway to the Presidency*. New York: Palgrave MacMillan, 2013.

Shesol, Jeff. *Mutual Contempt: Lyndon Johnson, Robert Kennedy, and the Feud That Defined a Decade*. New York: W. W. Norton, 1997.

Sidey, Hugh. *John F. Kennedy, President*. New York: Atheneum, 1963.

Smith, Amanda, ed. *Hostage to Fortune: The Letters of Joseph P. Kennedy*. New York: Viking, 2001.

Smith, Jean Kennedy. *The Nine of Us: Growing Up Kennedy*. New York: HarperCollins, 2016.

Sodhy, Pamela. "Malaysian-American Relations during Indonesia's Confrontation against Malaysia, 1963–66." *Journal of Southeast Asian Studies* 19, no. 1 (March 1988): 111–36.

Soper, Kerry. "From Swarthy Ape to Sympathetic Everyman and Subversive Trickster: The Development of Irish Caricature in American Comic Strips between 1890 and 1920." *Journal of American Studies* 39, no. 2 (August 2005): 257–96.

Sorenson, Theodore C. *Kennedy*. New York: Harper & Row, 1965.

Sorenson, Theodore C., ed. *"Let the Word Go Forth": The Speeches, Statements, and Writings of John F. Kennedy, 1947 to 1963*. New York: Delacorte Press, 1988.

Sperber, A. M. *Murrow: His Life and Times*. New York: Freundlich Books, 1986.

Stevenson, Richard W. *The Rise and Fall of Détente: Relaxation of Tension in U.S.-Soviet Relations, 1953–1984*. Houndmills: MacMillan Press, 1985.

Stone, Gary. *Elites for Peace: The Senate and the Vietnam War, 1964–1968*. Knoxville: University of Tennessee Press, 2007.

Streeter, Stephen M. "Nation-Building in the Land of Eternal Counter-Insurgency: Guatemala and the Contradictions of the Alliance for Progress." *Third World Quarterly* 27, no. 1 (2006): 57–68.

Swift, Will. *The Kennedys Amidst the Gathering Storm: A Thousand Days in London, 1938–1940.* New York: HarperCollins, 2008.

Talbot, David. *Brothers: The Hidden History of the Kennedy Years.* New York: Free Press, 2007.

The Avalon Project: Documents in Law, History and Diplomacy, Yale Law School. https://avalon.law.yale.edu/.

"The History Place Presents The Vietnam War." http://www.historyplace.com/unitedstates/vietnam/index.html.

The Vietnam Hearings. New York: Vintage Books, 1966.

Thomas, Evan. "Bobby at the Brink." *Newsweek*, August 13, 2000, https://www.newsweek.com/bobby-brink-159013.

———. *Robert Kennedy: His Life.* New York: Simon & Schuster, 2000.

Thomson, Alex. *U.S. Foreign Policy Towards Apartheid South Africa, 1948–1994: Conflicts of Interest.* New York: Palgrave MacMillan, 2008.

"Two Senators Named Kennedy." *Newsweek*, January 17, 1966, 17–25.

Tye, Larry. *Bobby Kennedy: The Making of a Liberal Icon.* New York: Random House, 2016.

Ungar, Sanford J., and Peter Vale. "South Africa: Why Constructive Engagement Failed." *Foreign Affairs*, Winter 1985, https://www.foreignaffairs.com/articles/south-africa/1985-12-01/south-africa-why-constructive-engagement-failed.

Vargo, Trina. *Shenanigans: The U.S.-Ireland Relationship in Uncertain Times.* New York: Cavan Bridge Press, 2019.

Walker, Vanessa. "At the End of Influence: The Letelier Assassination, Human Rights, and Rethinking Intervention in U.S.-Latin Relations." *Journal of Contemporary History* 46, no. 1 (January 2011): 109–35.

Warner, Geoffrey. "Review: Eisenhower and Castro: U.S.-Cuban Relations 1958–60." *International Affairs (Royal Institute of International Affairs 1944–)* 75, no. 4 (October 1999): 803–17.

Wehrle, Edmund F. "'A Good, Bad Deal': John F. Kennedy, W. Averell Harriman, and the Neutralization of Laos, 1961–1962." *Pacific Historical Review* 67, no. 3 (August 1998): 349–77.

Welch, David A., and James G. Blight. "An Introduction to the EXCOMM Transcripts." *International Security* 12, no. 3 (Winter 1987–88): 5–29.

Wenger, Andreas, and Marcel Gerber. "John F. Kennedy and the Limited Test Ban Treaty: A Case Study of Presidential Leadership." *Presidential Studies Quarterly* 29, no. 2 (June 1999): 460–87.

West, Stephen. "Nikita Khrushchev's Support for Developing Regimes in Sub-Saharan Africa from 1955 to 1964." *Colgate Academic Review* 3, article 15 (Spring 2008): 224–41.

Whalen, Richard J. "Joseph P. Kennedy: A Portrait of the Founder." *Fortune*, April 10, 2011, https://fortune.com/2011/04/10/joseph-p-kennedy-a-portrait-of-the-founder-fortune-classics-1963/.

White, Mark. "Robert Kennedy and the Cuban Missile Crisis: A Reinterpretation." *American Diplomacy*, September 2007, http://americandiplomacy.web.unc.edu/2007/09/robert-kennedy-and-the-cuban-missile-crisis-a-reinterpretation/.

Wildavsky, Aaron. "The Politics of ABM." *Commentary* 48, no. 5 (November 1969): 55–63. https://www.commentarymagazine.com/articles/the-politics-of-abm/.

Wilkins, Robert P. "The Nonpartisan League and Upper Midwest Isolationism." *Agricultural History* 39, no. 2 (April 1965): 102–9.

Williams, Michael Vinson. *Medgar Evers: Mississippi Martyr*. Fayetteville: University of Arkansas Press, 2011.

Wills, Garry. "America's Nastiest Blood Feud." *New York Review of Books*, May 24, 2012, http://www.nybooks.com/articles/2012/05/24/americas-nastiest-blood-feud/.

Worsthorne, Peregrine. "And Ulster Will Be Right." *National Interest* 44 (Summer 1996): 16–23.

Zelikow, Philip. "The Dangers of Back Channels." *American Interest*, June 7, 2017, https://www.the-american-interest.com/2017/06/07/the-dangers-of-back-channels/.

INDEX

Bay of Pigs invasion, xx–xxi; factors leading to, 77, 78–79, 293n4; goals of, 78; lessons learned from, 75, 79–82, 121–22, 154, 155, 218; results of, 85–86

Beaverbrook, Lord, 35

Be'er Sheva, Israel, 248

Berlin, Germany, 31, 32, 88, 106, 113–14, 117

Berlin Wall, 117, 247

Bernstein, Leonard, 246

Billings, Lem, 6, 25, 32, 79

Birmingham AL, 95

Bissell, Richard, 82, 84

Blair, Tony, 277

Bloody Sunday, 266

Boesak, Allan, 252–53

Boggs, Hale, 103

Bohlen, Charles, 50, 81

Bolshakov, Georgi, 108

Bonner, Yelena, 249

Borba (Yugoslav newspaper), 229

Borneo, 138

Bosch, Juan, 148, 149–50

Boston Daily Globe, 9, 55

Boston Globe, 87–88, 89, 225, 271

Boston Post, 35, 38

Botha, "Pik," 257

Botha, P. W., 253

Bowles, Chester, 84, 85, 155, 179

Brandt, Willy, 229

Brazil, 157, 158, 222

Brezhnev, Leonid, 228–30, 236–37, 241, 246, 248–49

Britain: Germany and, 14–15, 26, 27–29, 31, 141; Iraqi situation and, 277; Irish situation and, 263–67, 271–72; Jews in Palestine and, 39; Malaysia and, 138; in test-ban treaty, 117–18; in Trieste, Italy, 61

Brown, Gordon, 272, 277

Buddhists and Buddhism, 128–29, 130

Bulganin, Nikolai, 53

Bundy, McGeorge, 107, 108, 139, 150, 163, 176–77, 293n4

Burke, Arleigh, 77, 82

Burma, 179

Bush, George H. W., 274–76, 280, 283–84, 286–87

Bush, George W.: Iraq and, 273–74, 276–77, 278, 279, 280–82, 283–84, 287; Ireland and, 271, 272

Bush Presidential Library Foundation, 283–84

Cabot, John Moors, 143

Cambodia, 71, 121, 215, 221

Cape Cod Standard-Times, 5

Carey, Hugh, 264, 266

Carolina Political Union, 17

Carter, Jimmy, 179, 224–25, 227, 232–33, 234, 237, 253, 254, 266–67

Castro, Fidel, 37, 75, 77–78, 84–85, 104, 107

Catholics: bigotry against, 10–11, 58; Buddhism and, 129, 130; in Northern Ireland, 263, 264, 266, 268, 269; in Poland, 58, 144; Rose Kennedy and, 8

Catton, Bruce: *Never Call Retreat*, 174

Chamberlain, Neville, 4, 14, 29

Chappaquiddick incident, 210, 212, 224, 257, 265

Chayes, Abram, 145; *ABM: An Evaluation of the Decision to Deploy an Antiballistic Missile System*, 210–11

Cheney, Dick, 274, 276–77

Chiang (Taiwanese head of state), 41, 178

Chile, 160–61, 216, 219–20, 221, 222–26

China: changing policy for, 178–79, 181–84, 187–88, 227, 234; Jack Kennedy and, 40–41, 73; Malaysia and, 138; nuclear power and, 179–81, 183; speculation about, 286; Taiwan and, 231–34; Ted Kennedy and, 231–34, 241–42, 243; as threat, 170–71; trading partners of, 49–51

Christian Science Monitor, 154

Church, Frank, 94

Churchill, Winston, 4, 14, 28–29; *While England Slept*, 29

CIA, 77, 78–79, 80, 83, 106, 127, 219

Clifford, Clark, 163

Clinton, Bill, 267–69, 273, 277

Cohen, Jerome, 181

Cold War, xx–xxii, xxiii, xxv; Alliance for Progress and, 218; diminishing influence of, 185, 187, 189–90, 199; escalation of, 88; Jack Kennedy and, 75, 116, 285; Lyndon Johnson and, 151, 177; Ronald Reagan and, 216–17, 222, 253; South Africa and, 184; Southeast Asia and, 47, 71, 138; Soviet Union and, 230;

Index

space race and, 103; Ted Kennedy and, 207, 208; Vietnam and, 120, 131, 175, 177

Cold War consensus, xx, xxiii; attempted rebuilding of, 222; China and, 182; end of, 199; Kennedy brothers and, 131; purpose of, 49, 72–73; South Africa and, 184; Vietnam and, 175, 178, 188

Collins, James Lawton, 45

colonialism, 55, 56, 69–71, 77, 128

communism, xx, xxi; American attitudes toward, 116, 189–90; Bobby Kennedy and, 37, 136; causes of, 46–47, 89–91; in Chile, 219; in China, 40–41, 49, 178–79, 181, 183–84, 187; as choice, 93; counterinsurgency and, 84; in Cuba, 78, 104; Dominican Republic in path of, 148, 150–51; Europe in path of, 16, 17, 18; as foreign policy concern, 52, 54, 153; Greek shipping crisis and, 49–51; in Italy, 61; Joe Kennedy on, 40; Joe McCarthy and, 49, 50–51; Kennedy brothers and, 245, 285–86; in Latin America, 149, 158–61, 208; Nikita Khrushchev and, 76; in Poland, 57–58, 143, 243; Portugal in path of, 242; South Africa and, 185, 186, 253–54; in Southeast Asia, 100–101, 119–21, 138; in Soviet Union, 56; Vietminh and, 71–72; in Vietnam, 124, 126, 195, 212; West Berlin and, 86–87, 101, 117

Congressional Record, 154

Connor, Eugene "Bull," 95

constructive engagement, 254, 258, 259, 260, 261

Contras, 222, 223

Coogan, Tim Pat, 269

Coulter, Phil, 262

Crocker, Chester, 254

Crocker, Ryan, 283

Cronkite, Walter, 119, 130, 199

"Crush Malaysia" campaign, 138, 139–40

Cuba, 75–78, 84–85, 110, 114, 218, 222–23, 253–54

Cuban Missile Crisis, xx, xxii; Bobby Kennedy and, 82, 153–54; comparisons with, 192, 281; as dangerous situation, 109–10; as example of success, 144; initial reaction to, 107–8; Jack Kennedy and, 105–7, 153–54; Lyndon Johnson referring to, 174; military and, 104–

5, 108–9; negotiations during, 110–11; results of, 114, 116

Cuba Study Group, 82

Cultural Revolution, 187

Czechoslovakia, 57, 208

Decisions for a Decade (Ted Kennedy), 207–8

Defense Department, 48, 50, 83–84, 210

De Gaulle, Charles, 85

Democrats: Cold War outlook of, 49; Cuba and, 81, 107, 113; Iraq and, 280; National Conventions of, 59, 65; Nicaragua and, 223; South Africa and, 251–52, 261; Taiwan and, 234; Ted Kennedy and, 214, 228; Vietnam and, 174, 176–77

demonstrations. *See* protests and demonstrations

Deng, Xiaoping, 231, 232, 233, 234

Derry, Northern Ireland, 262

détente, 228–29, 229–30, 231, 244, 245

Diem, Ngo Dinh, 72, 119, 123–24, 126, 127, 128–29, 130

Diplomatic Corridor (Route 40), 96, 97

Dirksen, Everett, 212

disarmament, 115, 178, 181

Dobrynin, Anatoly, 109, 111, 238

Dominican Republic, 148–51, 152, 153–56, 159, 184

domino theory, 120–21, 172

Douglas, William, xxi, 53, 55

draft, military, 169, 192–94

Dulles, Allen, 77, 82

Dulles, John Foster, 48–49, 70, 71

Dutton, Fred, 156

Eagleton, Tom, 228

East Berlin, Germany, 113–14, 140

East Germany, 85, 86, 101, 107, 141, 143, 208, 249

Eastland, James, 96

East Pakistan, 242

East Timor, 221

Eden, Anthony, 53

Eisenhower, Dwight David: ABM (antiballistic missile) system and, 209; Africa policy of, 97; autograph of, 112; China and, 179; Cuba and, 78; Dominican Republic and, 149; at Geneva summit, 53; Jack Kennedy on, 67,

Protestantism, 11, 263, 271
protests and demonstrations, 98, 129, 165, 169, 194, 209, 213–14, 224, 252, 255
PT-109 incident, 24, 29–30
Putin, Vladimir, 247, 288

Quayle, Dan, 225–26

race relations: in Africa, 94–95; in America, 55, 93–94, 95–96, 97–98, 101, 128; in South Africa, 97, 184–85, 187, 253–55, 255–56, 257–61; in United Nations member countries, 93
Rayburn, Sam, 81
Reagan, Ronald: Cold War outlook of, 216–17, 222, 253–54; Iraq and, 275; Ireland and, 267; Mstislav Rostropovich and, 247; nuclear arms policy of, 237–39; prisoner release and, 249–50; right-wing alliances of, 216–17, 222–23; South Africa policy of, 252, 253, 254, 258, 259–60; veto of, overridden, 251, 261
Reedy, George, 181
refugees, 172, 173, 196, 197, 214, 282–83
refuseniks, 240–41, 244–46, 248–49
Reid Cabral, J. Donald, 148, 150
Reischauer, Edwin, 100
Republicans, 49, 107, 212, 223, 234, 251–52, 258–60, 261, 280
Reynolds, Albert, 268
Ribicoff, Abe, 266
Rice, Condoleezza, 283
Robert F. Kennedy Human Rights Award, 243
Robertson, Ian, 185, 186–87
Rogers, William, 152
Roitburg, Lev David, 249
Roosevelt, Franklin Delano, xv, xvi, 9–10, 13–15, 28, 37–38, 66, 153–54
Rostow, Walt, 124
Rostropovich, Mstislav, 246–47
Route 40 (Diplomatic Corridor), 96, 97
Rumsfeld, Donald, 276–77
Rusk, Dean, 98, 110, 155, 174, 175, 176, 182–83
Russell, Richard, 54, 165, 193
Russia, 16, 31–32, 37–38, 40, 102–3, 288. *See also* Soviet Union

Sakharov, Andrei, 245, 249
SALT treaties, 230, 236–37
Sandinistas, 222, 223
Scheer, Robert, 228

Schlesinger, Arthur, Jr., 19, 82, 124, 150, 217
Schulz, Charles: *Happiness Is a Warm Puppy*, 144
Schwartz, Harry, 54
Scott, Hugh, 212
SDI (Strategic Defense Initiative), 237–38, 239
Selective Service System, 193
Senate Armed Services Committee, 211, 228, 236, 277–78, 279
Senate Arms Control Observers Group, 238
Senate Banking Committee, 258, 259
Senate Foreign Relations Committee, 68, 88, 174, 183–84, 235–36, 258–59, 260, 261, 275
Senate Judiciary Subcommittee on Refugees and Escapees, 172, 214, 282–83
Senate Permanent Subcommittee on Investigations, 49
Sharansky, Avital, 249
Sharansky, Natan, 239, 246, 249–50
Shepard, Alan, 102
Sheridan, Walter, 136
Shriver, Eunice Kennedy, xviii, 5, 50
Shriver, Mark, 273
Shriver, Sargent, 99
Shultz, George, 238
Singapore, 138
Sinn Fein, 267, 269
Smith, Jean Kennedy, xviii, 6, 27, 54, 267–68
Soderberg, Nancy, 268
Solidarity movement, 243
Solzhenitsyn, Aleksandr, 246
Sorenson, Ted, 102, 122, 210, 217
South Africa: American policy in, 97, 251–55, 257–61; Bobby Kennedy and, 184–88; Ted Kennedy and, 251–53, 254–61
South Korea, 40
South Vietnam: counterinsurgency strategy and, 125–26; discord over, 149, 177; formation of, 72; pre-war policy for, 119–20, 122–25, 126–28, 130–31; religious conflict in, 129
Soviet Union, xx–xxi, xxv; America negotiating with, 37, 85–86; America threatened by, 17, 67–68, 72–74; arms control and, 117–18, 203, 209, 227, 236–39; Berlin situation and, 86–87; changing perceptions of, 189–90; China and, 178, 183, 188; Cuban Missile Crisis and, 104, 106–11, 114; developing world and, 90–91; Europe threatened by, 33, 41, 43;

insurgency strategy and, 169–70; doubts about, 163–64, 189–92, 194–95, 197–99, 203–4; draft and, 193–94; human costs of, 171–73, 196–97, 198, 214, 221; Iraq War compared to, 274, 275–76; Irish situation compared to, 264–65, 272; justification for, 175; medical care during, 195–96; optimism expressed about, 170–71; plans for ending, 165–67, 174, 175–76, 212–15; in retrospect, 285–87

violence: in Algeria, 69; in Chile, 218–19, 224–25; in Iraq, 282; in Italy, 18; in Latin America, 98, 208; in Northern Ireland, 263–64, 266, 268; opposition to, 265–67; in South Africa, 252, 255–56, 257, 260; in Southern states, 93–94, 95–96, 97; in Vietnam, 195

visas, 55, 185, 232, 243, 246, 247, 267, 268–69

Voice of America, 47

Vorster, Balthazar, 185

Vostok I, 102

Walesa, Lech, 243

Wallace, George, 97

Wall Street Journal, 222

Warner, John, 237

Washington Post, 70, 166, 233, 283

Watergate scandal, 228–29

Waxman, Sharon, 273–74

West Berlin, Germany, 85, 86–87, 101, 107, 113–14, 117, 135, 140–42, 249

West Germany, 140–42, 229, 242

Westmoreland, William, 194

While England Slept (Churchill), 29

Why England Slept (Jack Kennedy), 3, 23, 26–29, 42, 74, 208

Wiesner, Jerome, 209, 210, 211

Wiley, Alexander, 43

Williams, "Soapy," 96–97

Wilson, Woodrow, 149

Winiewicz, Jozef, 135

Wofford, Harris, 95

Wolfowitz, Paul, 276–77

World War I, 105

World War II, 16, 24, 29–32, 37–38, 71, 77

Wyszynski, Stefan Cardinal, 144

Yalta Conference, 37–38

Yugoslavia, 61, 229